DERBY PORCELAIN

Derby Porcelain

JOHN TWITCHETT, FRSA

Foreword by Anthony Hoyte

DJC BOOKS

Barrie & Jenkins Ltd

An imprint of the Hutchinson Publishing Group

3 Fitzroy Square, London W1P 6JD

Hutchinson Group (Australia) Pty Ltd
30–32 Cremorne Street, Richmond South, Victoria 3121
PO Box 151, Broadway, New South Wales 2007

Hutchinson Group (NZ) Ltd
32–34 View Road, PO Box 40–086, Glenfield, Auckland 10

Hutchinson Group (SA) (Pty) Ltd
PO Box 337, Bergvlei 2012, South Africa

First published 1980

Designed by John Leath MSTD

Set in Monophoto Bembo Series 270 & 428

Printed and bound in Great Britain
by Balding & Mansell, Wisbech, Cambridgeshire

Distributed in USA and Canada by DJC Books,
164 Ronald Drive, Montreal West, Quebec H4X 1M8

British Library Cataloguing in Publication Data
Twitchett, John
    Derby porcelain
    1. Derby porcelain
    I. Title
738.2'7   NK4399.D4
ISBN 021420507X

This book is dedicated
TO THE MEN AND WOMEN
too numerous to mention individually
who worked
AT THE NOTTINGHAM ROAD FACTORY
during its long existence

Contents

List of Illustrations

MONOCHROME

Foreword

Derby, more than any other English porcelain factory, lends itself to research of a highly specialized nature. Its output was vast in terms of variety of decoration and styles, its lifespan was long, and more is known about the lives of its artist decorators and modellers than about those from most other factories. This is largely the result of the work of a one-time painter at the Derby Factory, John Haslem, whose book *The Old Derby China Factory: The Workmen and Their Productions*, published in 1876, is still one of the cornerstones of ceramic literature. Many dedicated writers have followed Haslem, adding their contributions to the fabric of factory knowledge, and we are indebted to them all.

There are, however, still many areas where our knowledge is slight. The author of this book, John Twitchett, is in a unique position, combining vast experience as a dealer in fine porcelain with his curatorship of the Royal Crown Derby Museum, and above all with his twenty years of specialized research into the subject. He is thus supremely fitted to lead us into new areas, widen our horizons and open up new vistas.

To succeed, a comprehensive work should provide the amateur, the advanced student, and the general reader with something for each of their respective stages of development and requirements, and John Twitchett's book achieves this with great clarity.

The Vatican Museums, the Hermitage in Leningrad, museums and other collections in the United States from New York through the Middle West to California, as well as British private collections, public museums and leading auction houses have been assiduously combed in order to find subjects for the illustrations, which represent a veritable galaxy of some of the finest pieces produced by the factory, and whose study will immeasurably enlarge our knowledge.

As a work of reference *Derby Porcelain* will provide unrivalled information for all sections of the ceramic field. Long-standing collectors will delight in the historical detail, the first complete description of the pattern books, the paste analysis, and the biographies, while the novice will without doubt have his appetite whetted and be induced perhaps to take his first tentative steps into the world of Derby porcelain.

ANTHONY HOYTE

Nottingham, 1979

Acknowledgements

The author wishes to express his thanks to Mr John Bellak, Chairman of Royal Crown Derby and Managing Director of Royal Doulton Tableware Limited, to Mr W. H. Fisher and Miss Ann Linscott, also of Royal Doulton Tableware Limited, to Mr Arthur Rigby, Chief Executive of Royal Crown Derby, to Miss Betty Bailey, Assistant Curator of the Royal Crown Derby Museum, and to Secretary, Miss Ellen Gore, for their continued support during the years of research necessary to write this book.

Thanks are also due to the many British and foreign museum curators, collectors, auctioneers and dealers, and to members of the public, who have so kindly provided information and illustrations. In particular the author would like to express his gratitude to the Vice-Director of the Hermitage Museum, Leningrad, USSR, for providing for the very first time illustrations of the Derby collection housed there; to Catherine Lippert, Associate Curator of Decorative Arts at the Indianapolis Museum of Art; to the Director and Keeper of Ceramics at the Victoria and Albert Museum, London; to Ms Rosemary Bower, Keeper of Ceramics at the Derby Museum and Art Gallery; to my friends Bill Saks of Montreal, Bill Dickenson of Ironbridge and Pierre Jeannerat; to Anton Gabszewicz of Christie's; to Paul Mack and Jo Whitely of Sotheby's for supplying photographs and relevant information; and finally to Miss Gaye Blake Roberts, Curator of the Wedgwood Museum and formerly in the Department of Ceramics at the Victoria and Albert Museum, for her patience in the face of so many enquiries.

Geoffrey Godden's dedicated enthusiasm, which has done so much for British ceramics, has been of immense assistance. David Levin was responsible for most of the colour photography as well as a great deal of the black-and-white. Hubert King, of W. W. Winter of Derby, has taken other photographs sometimes at extremely short notice. Roy Beeston, David Holborough, Brian Quinn and Bill Mordecai read manuscripts for me. Lindsay Leech typed some of the copy. Major Guy Dawnay threw his home open as a studio for all the pieces from the Welsh collectors.

The Foreword is written by Anthony Hoyte, a third-generation Derby collector, researcher and writer whose knowledge and enthusiasm are comparable with that of Major Tapp, who did so much valuable work in the 1930s.

Finally, thanks are due to all the people concerned in the production of this book, on both the editorial and design side, and especially to Michael Hodson, Senior Editor at Barrie & Jenkins, with whom the author has worked over a period of five years.

Introduction

During the last twenty years my interest in the history of the products of the three china works in Derby has completely dominated my life style, though I am the first to admit to being a very willing victim!

It must be said that I have been fortunate to have been curator of the Royal Crown Derby Museum since 1972 and to have enjoyed the two-way flow of information and exchanges of knowledge which have come from the Open Days at Derby.

During my lecture programmes I am often asked about relevant literature regarding the Old Derby Porcelain works on the Nottingham Road in Derby. Whilst this work is intended to be the most comprehensive and profusely illustrated volume published to date, we must not neglect the other earlier works produced on this most fascinating factory and indeed all of these should form part of any library. Details of these will be found listed in the bibliography. Care should of course be taken to check any undocumented statements taken from these in the light of modern researches and findings.

It will be noticed that in the absence of documentation, subjects illustrated are attributed on stylistic grounds to the various modellers or painters and where documentation exists it will be stated.

There has been considerable interest in the Derby Porcelain works not only from the English-speaking peoples but world wide, and particularly from the continent of Europe. There were many distinguished visitors to the factory and many of their visits are described in this book. An extract from the Journal of François de la Rochefoucauld is given in French as well as with an English translation.

The majority of the colour and black-and-white plates were reproduced from the photography of David Levin, with whom I have enjoyed some very long sessions. It may not be generally known how much time is involved in taking an individual shot. Several Polaroids have to be used to check lighting and shape details before actually taking the final approved shot; some pieces taking more than an hour to shoot.

The Old Derby Pattern books, so well described here by Betty Clark, are given together with various figure and shape lists; when one realizes the importance of shapes and patterns, the basic need for ceramic manufacture, we rejoice at the survival of the Osmaston Road factory shapes and patterns published in *Royal Crown Derby* in 1976. Whilst doing this we must regret the passing of those relevant to the Nottingham Road works during the respective ownerships of the Duesburys and Robert Bloor.

The major discovery of the 'Quaker' Pegg sketch book, signed and dated 1813, has proved to be one of the most important finds of this century. The sketches show the variety of Pegg's work and underline the dangers of being too dogmatic about his work. They have vindicated my many statements regarding this fine natural painter. I used to be told in spite of the fact that he was a gardener's son that he always used English names to describe his botanical subjects and that there could be no work by Pegg with the puce or blue mark, in spite of the fact that his other contemporaries were thus marking. This is shown by his name appearing on patterns, at this period, in the Old Derby Pattern books. Also stated, by other authorities, that Pegg would only paint single plant services and these only with simple coloured borders or that if a root was drawn it must be the work of another painter. The reality was that most botanical services were copied or in the case of Pegg freely adapted from the Curtis Botanical Journals that were available to the Derby painters from about 1792. Remarkable! but one can understand how people can become over romantic when the painting of china is discussed, forgetting that the employer would direct the painters to do the work he required. Thank goodness for my connection with a live ceramic industry!

JOHN TWITCHETT

A Century of Derby Porcelain

The Planché period	*c.* 1748–56
William Duesbury I	1756–86
William Duesbury II	1786–95
Duesbury and Kean	1795–1811
Robert Bloor	1811–48

1

History from 1748 to 1848

The date when porcelain manufacture in Derby actually began remains uncertain. The author, however, holds the view that it was in about 1748, when Andrew Planché, the son of a Huguenot immigrant moved to Derby. It can here be noted that Planché, who had been living in Soho, where his father worked as a coffee-man, would surely have been aware of the Chelsea China works, as well as the works at Bow and Greenwich. Nicholas Sprimont was also living in the St Anne's parish of Soho, having registered himself as a silversmith in 1742, when aged twenty-six, and it seems most likely that he was acquainted with Planché. Again, with regard to the Chelsea works it may well be that he knew Thomas Briand,* who according to the Royal Society's Journal Book of 10 February 1742–3 had 'shew'd the Society several Specimens of a sort of fine White Ware made here by himself from native materials of our own Country'. The author further believes that either Sprimont or Briand may have given Andrew Planché the secret of making and firing china, and that further research may well yield this as an alternative to Jewitt's suggestion, mentioned below, that Planché had been into Saxony. When discussing the subject one must of course realize the close community of the Huguenot craftsmen. Indeed, according to Llewellyn Jewitt, the ceramic historian, it is to Planché that the honour of starting porcelain manufacture in Derby belongs. Andrew Planché was christened at the Ryder's Court Chapel, St Anne's, Westminster, and in 1740 was apprenticed to Edward Mounteney, a goldsmith. Their entries in the Apprenticeship Book 6 are reproduced on page 24 by courtesy of the Worshipful Company of Goldsmiths.

Since the records are missing, we do not know whether Andrew Planché completed his apprenticeship. It would have been quite possible for him to have completed his full term and to have visited the Continent during 1747–8, where he may have visited the Meissen factory, before returning to England and going to Derby.

A *Derby Mercury* report of a drowned workman who had gone missing from the china works, which appeared on Friday 26 January 1753, gives us our first references to the site of the original works:

We hear that yesterday morning the body of a man who appeared to have lain a considerable time in the Water, was taken out of the River near Borrowash. 'Tis said he was one of the Workmen belonging to the China Works near Mary Bridge, and that he had been missing since Christmas Eve, at which time the Waters being much out 'tis thought he fell in accidentally near the said bridge and was drowned.

An important piece of evidence concerning the start of Planché at Derby is a

---

* *E.C.C. Transactions*, Vol. 7, Part 2, pp. 87–99.

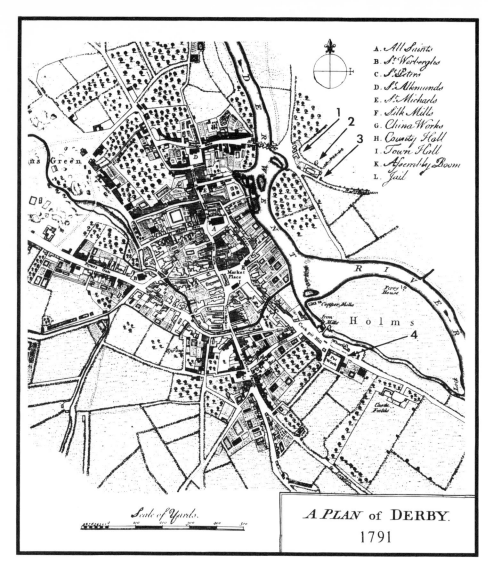

1
Plan of Derby, dating from 1791, showing the China Works, close to St Mary's Bridge, and the position of the Pot Works at Cockpit Hill.
1 Suggested site *c.* 1748.
2 1756 Nottingham Road factory. Heath, Duesbury, Planché.
3 Calver Close ('New China Works'). Duesbury and Kean.
4 Cockpit Hill.
(Burdett's *Map of Derbyshire*, London, 1791, engraved by Thomas Kitchin, hydrographer to His Majesty. Improvements by George Snowden.)

letter from Josiah Wedgwood written on New Year's day, 1775, to Bentley. Wedgwood tells how he was interrupted, whilst writing,

> *by a Man from the Derby China works who wants to be hired – He is a Derby Man, has a Wife & Family there & has work'd at the Factory 28 Years. His name is Holmes – I rather suspect he is sent to learn something from us – However I have learnt from him that they have been making h*[ds] *for Smith,*[1] *& have many more to make, I must break off here to save the post – Shall finish my L*[r] *tomorrow & am ever yours*

    J WEDGWOOD

Many happy returns of the Seasons attend you

This indicates, if one relies on Holmes's statement, that the start of Planché in Derby was in 1747 or 1748. The letter, now in the Wedgwood Archives at Keele University, was incorrectly ascribed by Major Tapp in his paper to the English Ceramic Circle (Vol. 2, 1939, No. 6, p. 60) to two Derby men, Holmes and Smith, seeking work. In fact the letter was from Josiah Wedgwood, who had been interrupted by one man from Derby.

For reasons of clarity individuals will be dealt with first, followed by a discussion of the site of the factory at Derby.

Andrew Planché

Jewitt tells us that Planché was in Derby for eight years but gives us no insight into this statement. The following extracts from the St Alkmund's[2] parish registers tell us that he married and had children:

22

2
Impression of the old Nottingham Road factory drawn from memory by Moses Webster in 1870, and approved, according to Bemrose, by several of the old china painters, who recollected the Old Works.

1751	Sept 21	Baptized Paul Edmund, the son of Andrew Planché and Sarah his wife.
1754	12 Oct	Bap. James, the son of Andrew Planché and Sarah his wife.
1754	Dec 10	Buried James, the son of Andrew Planché and Sarah his wife.
1756	March 4	Bap. James, the bastard son of Andrew Planché and Margaret Burroughs.
1756	July 3	Bap. William, the son of Andrew Planché and Sarah his wife.

We also know from an unsigned partnership agreement, formerly in Jewitt's possession, which is quoted in full on page 25, that 'China Maker' is how Planché was described. In the London account books of William Duesbury I, who was described in the above-mentioned agreement as 'Enamellor', we read of 'Darbeyshire sesons'; '2 pr. of Dansers Darby figars'; '1 pr. Large Darbey Figars'; 'Staggs'; a pair of 'Boors'; and '7 pr. of Small Single figars'.

In June 1837 Samuel Keys wrote his account of the history of the Derby china manufactory which is given in full at the end of this chapter. He refers to a 'Man in a very humble way (but his name I cannot recollect)'. It would certainly seem that the majority of items produced were figures and animals, since very little, if any, domestic ware remains that could be attributed to Planché. The three white cream jugs, one in the Victoria and Albert Museum, which have been much discussed, may indeed have been experimental pieces. One jug bears the incised date 1750, with a script 'D', another a 'D' without a date, and the third has 'Derby' incised in script.

Another interesting record is that of the marriage of James Marchand, of the parish of St Anne's, Westminster, who married Mary Oldfield at St Alkmund's in June 1752. He is described as a potter, and the obvious conclusion is that he was helping Planché to set up the 'China Works near Mary Bridge'.

William Duesbury I's grand-daughter, Sarah Duesbury, wrote after reading Wallis and Bemrose's *The Pottery and Porcelain of Derbyshire*, 'Messrs. Wallis & Bemrose have done my grandfather justice – while this fellow Jewitt tries to take the credit out of his hands and give it to the man Planché, "Master Planchey", as Betty Shipley called him.' By this remark she unwittingly corroborated Planché's existence. William Duesbury did not, in fact, start making china until 1756. Before that time he had been an enameller and quite obviously would have found Planché's knowledge of china- or porcelain-making invaluable.

The third party mentioned in the unsigned partnership agreement was John Heath, 'Gentleman', the Derby banker who was concerned in the partnership owning Cockpit Hill, where creamware and other pottery was made. Claims have been made that Planché's wares were made at this pottery. The author refutes this claim on the grounds that the 1753 *Derby Mercury* report talks of 'the China Works near Mary Bridge', and no local reporter would have referred in those words to Cockpit Hill, which lies a considerable distance down river from St Mary's Bridge.

[Manuscript facsimile — Apprenticeship Book entries:]

14th Memorandum That I Edward Mounteney — Son of Nathaniel Mounteney late of the parish of St Vedast als Foster's London Gent Decd — Do put my self Apprentice to William Richards Citizen & Goldsmith of London for the Terme of Seven years from this Day (there being paid to my sd mar the Sum of Thirty pounds—

Edward Mounteney

£30 Be it Remembred that I Andrew Planche son of Paul Planche of the parish of St Anns Westmr in the County of Midd Coffeeman — Do put my self Apprentice to Edward Mounteney Citizen & Goldsmith of London for the Term of Seven years from this day there being paid to my said Master the Sum of Twenty pounds/

Andrew Planché

John Haslem cites the factory tradition, that, 'the site first occupied by William Duesbury when he commenced . . . in 1750 . . . was near to the foot of St. Mary's Bridge'. We know, of course, that it was not Duesbury who started china-making in Derby, but the quotation gives traditional siting to the factory. The plan of Derby reproduced in this chapter is useful evidence concerning suggested early sites for the factory.

It should also be pointed out that porcelain could not be fired along with pottery without the obvious risk of damage by impurities from the coarser ware. Secondly, there is not a shred of evidence to suggest that china or porcelain was ever manufactured on a commercial basis at Cockpit Hill. There is, though, evidence in an advertisement in the *Derby Mercury* of 30 July 1756 of 'Mr. Heath and Company' being tenants of a site near St Mary's Bridge:

> TO BE SOLD, a freehold estate consisting of seven houses and a barn, situate all together near St Mary's Bridge, which are now occupied by Mr Heath and Company in the China Manufactory and let at £10 per annum exclusive of all taxes. For further particulars enquire of Charles Shepherdson at Kings Newton, five miles from Derby, or of Mr Mills at the Green Dragon, Derby.

Franklin Barrett, in his excellent paper[3] given at the Victoria and Albert Museum on 15 February 1958, gives a detailed history of the sites. The author is in full agreement with his statements; indeed, even as late as January 1978, when giving a lecture to the Shropshire Antique Society in Shrewsbury, at which Mr Barrett was present, it was refreshing to see that two Derby fanatics of different generations were so much in agreement on this matter.

It has not, as yet, been possible to ascertain exactly when a lease was first granted, but it seems certain that the 'China Works' was on this site or adjacent to it. It is known that Heath had later acquired five of the properties; after his bank's failure in

3
Entries in Apprenticeship Book 6 of the Worshipful Company of Goldsmiths for Edward Mounteney and Andrew Planché.

1779 the properties were acquired by William Duesbury who added two more to complete the site of the Old China Manufactory, which is bounded on the west by Wood Street and on the east by the Liversage Arms.

The agreement between Heath, Planché and Duesbury is reproduced below. Although this copy is unsigned, it is possible that there was a further copy held by the Heath brothers.

Articles of agreement between John Heath of Derby in the County of Derby Gentleman, Andrew Planché of ye same Place China Maker & Wm Duesberry of Longton in ye County of Stafford Enamellor. Made and enter'd into the 1st of Jany 1756.

FIRST IT IS AGREED *by ye said John Heath Andrew Planché & Wm Duesberry to be Copartners together as well in ye Art of making English China as also in buying and selling of all sorts of Wares belonging to ye Art of making China Wch said Copartnership is to continue between them from the Date of these Presents for & during ye Term of Ten years from thence & then fully to be compleated & ended And to that end He ye said John Heath hath ye day of ye date of these Presents deliver'd in as a Stock ye sum of one Thousand pounds to be used & employed in Common between them for ye carrying on ye sd Art of making China Wares And that one third share of Profits arising therefrom It is mutually agreed between all ye sd parties shall be receiv'd by & paid to ye said John Heath till ye said Prin^l Sum of £1000 be paid in Also it is agreed between ye said Parties to these Presents that ye sd Copartners shall not at any time hereafter use or Follow ye Trade aforesaid or any other Trade whatsoever during ye sd Term to their private Benefit and advantage. And also that ye sd Copartners shall during ye said Term pay and discharge equally and proportionably between them all expenses they shall be at in managing ye Art and Trade aforesaid And also that all gain or profit that shall arise from ye Art and Trade aforesaid during ye said Term shall be divided between them ye sd Copartners Share and Share alike And likewise that all such Losses as shall happen by bad Debts Ill Commodities or otherwise shall be borne equally between them And it is further agreed by ye sd Parties that there shall be kept during ye sd Term Just and True Books of Accounts to Wch sd Books any of ye sd Copartners shall have free access without Interruption of ye other And it is further agreed that at any time hereafter at ye request of ye said John Heath New Articles shall be made and an additional Term of years not less than Ten shall be added with such alterations as may be found necessary And that ye said Copartners shall from time to time communicate to each other every Secret of ye said Art And that ye said John Heath shall have it in his power to appoint any other Person to Act for him if he should chuse so to do Wch Person shall be as fully impowered to Act with regard to all Covenants herein contained as ye sd John Heath himself.*

WITNESS OUR HANDS *the day & Year above written.*

4
Derby figure of a street-seller, which has had the base ground down to make it stand evenly, believed by the author to have been possibly decorated at the Planché Works. Note the glassy glaze beneath her left foot and lack of 'dry-edge' band on the base. The decoration is simple. A similar figure is in the Wernher Collection where, with its pair, it is dated 1751. These appear to have decoration associated with Duesbury's London decorating studio. No mark. Andrew Planché, 'dry-edge' period. 1750. 12.9 cm. *Ronald W. Raven Collection.*

We know that Andrew Planché was present in Derby from the previously quoted remarks of Sarah Duesbury, but it is likely that Duesbury gained all the information from him and was able to increase the output of the manufactory, bringing it to international level. Planché was in Bath and it seems likely that he was the Andrew Planché Floor (*sic*) listed in the Bath directory of 1800, as carrying on the trade of dyer at 25 Stall Street. He died and was buried in St James's church, Bath, in January 1805. In 1809 a certain Catherine Floor was registered at the same address, pursuing the same trade. She died in 1813, aged seventy-four, and was buried at St Michael's church, Bath. She may well have been his widow and, therefore, his second wife, but it is of course possible that she was an unmarried sister some eleven years his junior. It is interesting to note that Andrew Planché's nephew was J. R. Planché, the Somerset Herald. He was also a well-known playwright in his day and was responsible for pantomime in its present form.

William Duesbury I

Now that we have established that Duesbury was not the original founder of the 'China Works' in Derby, we can place the Duesbury ownership in its proper perspective. William Duesbury I was in fact the son of another William, a carrier of Cannock, Staffordshire. He was born on 7 September 1725 and later married Sarah James of Shrewsbury. In his early days he lived at Longton Hall, and it is possible that he learned the art of porcelain-decorating or enamelling at the Longton Hall Factory. We know from his London account book that he was in London from

5

A pair of goats on floral-painted oval bases. Andrew Planché, 'dry-edge' period. *c.* 1755. 16.5 cm. and 11 cm. *Victoria & Albert Museum, 414/207 and 414/207A – 1885.*

1751 until 1753. We also know that he not only decorated china but had a workshop for repairs of all kinds, including metalwork and woodwork. It was in London that his first son, William, was born, and died in infancy in 1752. Eleven years later he named another son William – born in Derby in 1763 – and it was this William who was to succeed him as William Duesbury II. Another important date is the birth of a daughter, Anne, at Longton on 3 October 1754; it is likely, though not yet documented, that he returned there to work for the firm of Littler & Co. which features in the account book already mentioned. In the unsigned agreement Duesbury was described as 'of Longton in ye County of Stafford Enamellor'. Anne Duesbury married Richard Egan of London, who afterwards became a dealer in china, earthenware and glass in Bath. Another daughter, Mary, had been born in London in 1753, and was christened at St Alkmund's after the Duesburys' arrival in Derby, but died young. A second Mary was born in Derby in 1756 and died in 1783; Sarah was born in 1758, but died in infancy; another Sarah was born in 1759 and buried in 1767; Dorothea was born in 1761 and later married the Revd John Chawner, of Church Broughton, in 1786; William II was born in 1763; James Henry was born in 1765 and is mentioned in connection with Bernice Banford in the biographies (see page 197). He was said to have been much misunderstood and a wayward member of the family!

William Duesbury I was quite obviously an astute and very successful business-man, and it was he who brought the manufactory international recognition and fame. According to Jewitt, he purchased not only the Chelsea and Bow Works but also Vauxhall and Kentish town. Of these, the Chelsea Works were continued until 1784. This expansion enabled dinner, dessert and tea services to be made in large quantities and figure production was increased, as will be seen in later chapters. On his death on 30 October 1786[4] William Duesbury I left his son a sound business which had survived the bankruptcy of the Heath brothers in 1779. The factory site was conveyed to Duesbury II on 1 August 1780 'to the use of the said William Duesbury, his heirs and assigns for ever'. As mentioned earlier, Duesbury II added two more properties and became owner of what was called The Old China Manufactory, to distinguish it from the New Works, built on leased land

26

6
Figure of a dancer, quite possibly enamelled by William Duesbury in his London studio. Andrew Planché, 'dry-edge' period. *c.* 1751–3. 19 cm. *David J. Thorn Antiques.*

7 ■
Seated figure on mound base with applied flowers. This figure was not only for table decoration, as carrying the basket made her useful. Andrew Planché, 'dry-edge' period. *c.* 1753–5. Approx. 18.5 cm. *Mr & Mrs J. Bottom Collection.*

by Michael Kean at the end of the eighteenth century, and known as Calver Close.

Originally, wares were sold by auction, but in 1773 Duesbury I had taken the lease of premises in Bedford Street, Covent Garden, London, with William Wood as his agent.

It would appear that less Derby china was decorated by James Giles, the outside decorator, than say that of the Worcester and other factories.

Duesbury did however assist Giles financially, as one can see from Jewitt's papers.

Paid Mr. Heath a Bill on Mr. Giles, dated Feb. 20. at two months, value £120
April I, James Giles's note due 4th June 1777, £50

Jewitt lists an account '£25 2s. 10d. for enamelling sundries to complete stock . . . work done for Duesbury August 28th. 1776, by Js. Giles.'

The list is mainly simple and mentions 'blue edge', 'green edge' and 'brown edge' which would indicate cheaper than gold decoration!

18 Desert Plates in Large birds £3   0   0

On the failure of Giles, Duesbury took over his stock and entire concern in December 1779.

William Duesbury II

After his father's death William Duesbury II married Elizabeth Edwards, the daughter of a Derby solicitor, on 4 January 1787. They had three sons: William, later known as William Duesbury III; Nathaniel, who died in 1809 aged nineteen; and Frederick, who became an eminent physician in London. Of their two daughters, Sarah never married and died in 1875 at 151 Edgware Road, London, in her eighty-seventh year; while Anne Elizabeth married Francis Jessop, a Derby solicitor. The following letter (in the author's possession) was written by Sarah Duesbury on 25 August 1870 to Alfred Wallis:

151. Edg. road. W (not far
below Oxford &
Cambridge
Terrace.
Thursday Aug. 25/70

My dear Sir,

 I cannot write, I cannot see – nor can I sit up writing. I have no
'Documents' – whi you speak of – <u>none</u> – I could give anyone by my side –
<u>facts</u> from recollection – but if there <u>shd</u> be anyone in London with time to take
these down they must bring another <u>Book</u> – as I have sent mine to Mr Jessopp.
I wish I could do more for you – again I repeat 'the spirit is willing'.

 I remain your

 Sincere well wisher.

 S. Duesbury.

After six in the Even'g I am most likely to be found <u>up</u>.

William Duesbury II had perhaps more artistic flair than his father and was able
to surround himself with the finest modellers, painters and other workers in
ceramic history. (Chapter 2 provides an appraisal of the craftsmanship of these
times.) He was also a man of discipline, as we can see from the notices to which
Jewitt first drew attention. (Note: the columns of names should be read
downwards, from left to right.)

Derby China Manufactory, 23rd Nov., 1787. If any person in Future, either within the
working Hours or at any other time, is seen or discover'd in the Rooms, Kilns,
Apartments, or other Premises of the other (not having any proper Business relative to his
particular Occupation there) he will positively be fined the sum of five Shillings. The
fines (if any are incur'd) to be put into the Box of Donations at pay time, on the
Saturday after the detection.

J. Duesbury	Kay	Porter	Robins	Wathews
Boreman	Fogg	T. Moore	Horsley	Ball
Smith	Webster	Shipley	Green	Thos. Soare[6]
Billingsley	Clarke	B. Orme	Lovegrove	Jos. Stables
Stables	Barton	———[5]	Whitiall	Wm. Cooper
Jno. Yates	Mason	Wells	G. Holmes	Jno. Yates
Wm. do.	M. do.	Keen	Hill	Wm. Billingsley
Longdon	Atkins	Parish	Farnsworth	Jno. Blood
Tayler	Wedgwood	Spooner	Whitaker	Wm. Yates
Blood	Ash	Son	Laurance	Wm. Longdon
Cooper	Morledge	Wardle	Atkins	Wm. Taylor
Butler	Watthews	Rogers	Morledge	Jno. Buttler
Soar	Lawrence	Musgrove	Wedgwood	Wm. Smith
Dickinson	Whitaker	Morrell	Ash	Z. Boreman

Again, in 1788:

In November last notice was given that persons of one branch of the manufactory were not
to go into the premises of the other, unless they had real business there relative to theire
particular occupation, notwithstanding which the practice is still by some Individuals
continued. Notice is therefore hereby finally given, that if any person in future (having
received this Notice) shall intrude themselves to this injunction they will positively be
fined 3 shillings.

         Sept. 24th, 88.

Boreman	Jno. Yates	Taylor	Borton	T. Simes
Billingsley	Wm. do.	Smith	T. Rogers	Webster
Soare	Josph. Doe	Buttler	Clarke	M. Mason
Stables	Longdon	Key	Dickinson	Shirley, Arthr.
Cooper	Blood	Fogg		

8
Chinoiserie group showing a high standard of modelling and freedom of movement. Andrew Planché, 'dry-edge' period. *c.* 1750–55. Approx. 19 cm. *Sotheby's, New Bond Street.*

9
Group of musician and lady, the former seated on a tree-stump support and the lady on the mound base. This appears to be decorated in London and the model is previously unrecorded. Andrew Planché, 'dry-edge' period. *c.* 1750–55. Approx. 16 cm. *Christie, Manson & Woods.*

10
A fine pair of figures from the 'Seasons', he representing 'Winter' and she 'Spring' (she is sometimes known as the gardener's companion). Andrew Planché, 'dry-edge' period. *c.* 1750–55. 20 cm. and 19.5 cm. *Christie, Manson & Woods.*

11
Figure of Venus and Cupid. The figure of a dancer is of a later period. Andrew Planché, 'dry-edge' period. *c.* 1750–55. Approx. 19 cm. *Sotheby's, New Bond Street.*

12
A small charging bull. Andrew Planché, 'dry-edge' period. *c.* 1750–55. 6 cm. *Royal Crown Derby Museum.*

13
Pair of sheep. Andrew Planché, 'dry-edge' period. *c.* 1750–55. Approx. 12 cm. *Sotheby's, New Bond Street.*

This document, signed by Billingsley along with other artists, is also of interest:

From the many injuries done to the trade by employing Women in Painting of China, &c., Particularly not being employ'd in London in any Painting or Gilding Shop whatsoever, we hope you will not withstand granting us the favour of their not being employ'd here.

Edwd. Withers	*Wm. Cooper*	*Thos. Rogers*	*Billingsley*	*Jno. Yates*
Samuel Keys	*Wm. Longdon*	*Benj. Brocklesby*	*Soare*	*Wm. Taylor*
Jno. Brown	*Wm. Yates*	*Jos. Stables*		

In this matter of opposition to the employment of women Billingsley seems, later on, to have relented, as can be seen by a letter from Bernice Banford, given in full in James Banford's biography in chapter 11.

'The curious draft of an order to the painters employed at the Derby China Works' (in the author's possession) is how Jewitt described the following list:[7]

Every Painter to mark underneath each Article he may finish, the number corresponding to his name, and any other mark which may be required, in such manner as he may be directed (viz.):

Thos. Soar	*1*	*Wm. Longdon*	*8*
Jos. Stables	*2*	*Wm. Smith*	*9*
Wm. Cooper	*3*	*Jno. Blood*	*10*
Wm. Yates	*4*	*Wm. Taylor (except on blue*	
Jno. Yates	*5*	*and white)*	*11*
		Jno. Duesbury	*12*
William Billingsley	*7*	*Jos. Dodd*	*13*

The painter in fine blue, and inlaying grounds to use for his mark the like colours.

Ditto, in other colours .... *Orange-red.*
Ditto, in Gold .... *Purple.*

On omission of the above Injunctions, for the first Offence (after this public notice), the person so offending shall forfeit to the Box which contains donations for the Manufactory at large, one-fourth of the value of the Article or Articles found to be deficient in marking; for the second, one-half of its value; and for the third, the whole of the value, and discharged the Manufactory. And if any Painter is found working at any hour contrary to those already appointed for Business, without Permission or Orders, such person shall, for the first offence forfeit to the Box 6d.; for the second, 1s.; for the third, 2s., and so on, doubling each time.

In 1777 the London agent had been succeeded by Joseph Lygo (whose letters to his employer are given in the Appendix), from whom we have it that 'Duesbury had the Royal Appointments first in 1775'.

In 1971 the author published in a small limited edition *The Old Derby Pattern Books* (described by Betty Clark in chapter 4). These books were started about 1780 and completed very early in the nineteenth century.

14
A pair of boars, modelled from the antique. Animals such as these are mentioned in Duesbury's London account books in 1752, costing 5s. 0d. Andrew Planché, 'dry-edge' period. c. 1750–55. 10.1 cm. *Christie, Manson & Woods.*

15
Chinoiserie group from the 'Senses' representing 'Sight'. Again this is a fine example of sophisticated modelling of very high standards. Andrew Planché, 'dry-edge' period. c. 1750–55. 18.4 cm. *Christie, Manson & Woods.*

Michael Kean

In 1795 Duesbury II took Michael Kean, an Irish miniature painter, into partnership. After Duesbury's death in 1797 Kean married his widow, Elizabeth, and the relationship was to cause long legal battles.

In February 1797 Kean acquired a portion of Calver Close, east of the Old Works, on lease at a rent of £16 per annum. Heath had leased the same site as early as 1764 but it had remained undeveloped during the Duesburys' lease. The site was never owned by any of the successive partnerships as it had been leased from the Liversage Trust, Kean continuing to pay the rent during the Bloor period until his death in 1823. A memorandum of March 1814, taken from the Duesbury papers in the British Museum, states:

A plot of ground adjoining the porcelain manufactory which had been rented by Duesbury during his life and previously by his father and which continued to be used in the partnership concern was taken on a lease of 91 years by Mr Kean in his own name and on a part of which he in his own name erected an earthenware manufactory and then discontinued the same and occupied the buildings . . . for the purpose of the porcelain manufactory as part of the partnership concern.

On 5 July 1798 the following notice appeared in the *Derby Mercury*:

To Dealers in Earthenware

The Proprietors of the Derby Porcelain manufactory having erected works for the manufacture of Earthen Ware acquaint dealers that a Wharehouse is opened for Orders and Sale.

On 15 June 1809 and for four successive weeks the following advertisement appeared in the *Derby Mercury*:

A Manufactory

To be sold, a Manufactory in Derby, and a Wharehouse, conducted at present by an agent, in London. The whole concern has been long established, and is the first in quality of the kind in the kingdom. The Manufactory is correct in its plan, with ground capable of any necessary extension, and the Warehouse is the completest and best situated in London. The Works are in the fullest employment and have the best hands. This concern is well worth the attention of people of capital. (For particulars, enquire of Messrs. Ward, Lockett, and Balguy, of Derby.)

This veiled announcement hailed the beginning of the end of Duesbury and Kean. In 1811 Robert Bloor, who had been clerk to the partnership, leased the factory and so the Bloor period began.

William Duesbury III

After his father's untimely death, William Duesbury III's mother had married Michael Kean. Young Duesbury was only ten in 1797 and was sent to boarding school when his mother remarried. In 1815, at the age of twenty-eight, he was made an Overseer of the Poor in the parish of St Alkmund's. He did not play an active part in the running of the porcelain works but set up with William Chawner, his cousin, a colour works at Bonsal, Derbyshire, with eventual disastrous results as described in this report from the *Derby Mercury* of 20 September 1826:

Whereas a Commission of Bankrupt is awarded and issued forth against William Chawner and William Duesbury, of Bonsal, in the county of Derby, Color Manufacturers and Co-partners ——
—— All persons indebted to the said bankrupts, or that have any of their effects, are not to pay or deliver the same but to whom the commissioners shall appoint, but to give notice to Messieurs Philpot and Stone, 3 Southampton Street, Bloomsbury Square, London: or to Messieurs Balguy, Porter & Barber, Solicitors, Derby.

Soon afterwards Duesbury left for America, where he eventually died. In 1834 his sister served notice on him to sell the Old China Works property, and it was sold

16
A white glazed lion attributed to Derby. Note the benign look on Leo's face. Andrew Planché, 'dry-edge' period. *c.* 1750–55. Approx. 8.9 cm. *Schreiber Collection. Victoria & Albert Museum, I 1–18.*

17
A white glazed set of 'Seasons';
'Winter', 'Spring', 'Autumn', and
'Summer'. Andrew Planché, 'dry-edge'
period. *c.* 1750–55. Average height
approx. 11 cm. *Victoria & Albert
Museum: C531 – 1909 left; C1 – 1917
centre left; C532 – 1909 centre right; C2
– 1917 right.*

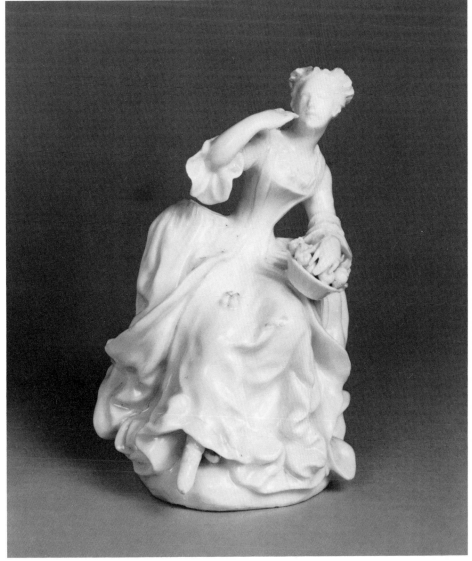

18
Lady representing 'Taste' from the
European sets of 'Senses'. Andrew
Planché, 'dry-edge' period. *c.* 1750–55.
15.3 cm. *Schreiber Collection. Victoria &
Albert Museum.*

19
Chinoiserie group representing 'Touch' from the set of Chinese 'Senses'. Andrew Planché, 'dry-edge' period. *c.* 1750–55. 23.9 cm. *Schreiber Collection. Victoria & Albert Museum, 414/140 – 1885.*

20
A coloured version of the chinoiserie 'Sight'. Andrew Planché, 'dry-edge' period. *c.* 1750–55. 18.4 cm. *Christie, Manson & Woods.*

in November 1840 to Francis Wright, William Jessop and James Oakes. Finally, in March 1847, the property was conveyed to two Roman Catholic priests for £1,960. A nunnery, designed by Pugin, was erected on the site and was said to have cost £10,000, but because it was so near the river Derwent it was considered unhealthy and was pulled down about 1863 (see plate 399).

Before the author discovered Lockyer's indenture[8] of 1809 the earliest reference to Robert Bloor was made by Michael Kean, about November 1811, in an application to William Duesbury III and his sisters for their agreement of the lease of the New Works (Calver Close) 'to a Mr. Bloor [a person employed as a servant in the Manufactory at the time the partnership was discontinued] of the stock in trade and utensils at Derby together with the New Works, being those erected on the ground taken on lease by Mr. Kean'. The Old Works were closed in 1835, but Haslem tells us that two buildings were used, and he himself had worked all his time at the factory in one of them. From 1835 until its close in 1848 the Bloor Manufactory conducted its business at the leased site (Calver Close).

The years of trouble that Michael Kean endured after leaving Derby obviously had an adverse effect upon him, and in his obituary on Wednesday 19 November 1823 the *Derby Mercury* dismissed him thus: 'A few days since in London, after a short illness, Michael Kean Esq., formerly Proprietor of the Porcelain Manufactory in this Town.' The disputes had continued, Duesbury versus Kean, for many years, but Elizabeth survived her second husband and by her will, proved in 1840,

21
'Winter' from the European set of
'Seasons'. Andrew Planché, 'dry-edge'
period. 1750–55. 16.5 cm. *Royal Crown
Derby Museum.*

22
An interesting pair of figures, she
representing 'Touch' and he possibly
'Air' from the 'Senses' and 'Elements'
respectively, but here they seem to be
matched as 'Liberty' and 'Matrimony'.
Andrew Planché, 'dry-edge' period.
c. 1750–55. Approx. 15 cm. *Sotheby's,
New Bond Street.*

23
Male figure (snuff-taker), representing 'Smell' from the European set of 'Senses'. Andrew Planché, 'dry-edge' period. *c.* 1750–55. Approx. 16.4 cm. *J. S. Buxton Collection.*

appointed her daughter Sarah as sole executrix. The following extract from the *Derby Mercury* of 31 May 1798 is, however, fairer to Michael Kean:

TO MICHAEL KEAN ESQ.

From a large majority of the Citizens and other persons employed in the Derby Porcelain and Earthenware Manufactories:

Sir,

We should esteem ourselves remiss in our duty did we not return to you our sincere thanks for the immediate communication of the answer of the court of Lieutenancy to our offer of service which you did us the honour and favour of presenting to the Government.

By that rational and flattering answer we are given to understand that the respectable Corps of Infantry already established in the Borough of Derby, and the strength it may gain from additional single names, is so fully adequate to the purpose of supporting the Civil power withen any stage thereof, for which we offered our assistance, that Government deems it unnecessary for any additional Company to be formed, however creditable the persons may be.

We likewise consider it would be want of respect in us if we did not take this method of publickly acknowledging the gratitude we owe to you, for the activity and politeness you have manifested in presenting our service to the King, and the happiness we feel that the zeal of the country has given sufficient strength to the Government whereby all men are released from the anxious solicitude attendant on a stage of danger to their families and themselves and those not already enrolled, from defending in their own persons (however glorious) the rights and constitution of their country.

And we beg leave to assure you, that should circumstances unfortunately change and such service be called for by His Majesty, we will be happy to renew our confidence in your loyal zeal at our head, and in the attention we are persuaded you are willing to shew to our characters as men and honour as soldiers.

> *We are, Sir,*
>
> *Your most humble servants,*
>
> *&c &c &c*

Porcelain Manufactory
May 21st. 1798.

Robert Bloor

As already stated, Bloor leased the New Works in 1811 and in 1815 leased the Old Works site from Duesbury III, the rent being £110 per annum. He was unable to discharge his original agreement, and so it was agreed between the parties that the amounts should be paid in instalments. The capital sum for the business and utensils, stock in trade, etc, was to be £5,000. However, it is recorded that the amount was not settled until 30 December 1822, when Bloor in fact paid the sum of £3,544 12s 8d. He did not start paying the lease rent for the New Works until after Kean's death in 1823.

The following piece from the *Derby Mercury* of 19 May 1814 shows Bloor's efforts to raise money:

VALUABLE CHINA

TO BE SOLD AT AUCTION

By Mr. Cross.

In the large warehouse at the Porcelain Manufactory, Derby, on Monday May 23rd 1814 and Thirty following days (Sundays excepted)

THE FIRST PART

of the extensive Stock of Messrs Robert Bloor and Co. of the above Manufactory

Consisting of Dinner, Dessert, Breakfast, Tea and Coffee Services, Cabinet and Chimney Ornaments &c. &c. superbly decorated in flowers, figures, landscapes &c. Groups and Single Figures in biscuit, together with five thousand sets of white china in useful and ornamental Articles, some large plaster figures and casts &c. &c. which will be positively sold without the least reserve.[9]

At Phillips' London sale on 26 September 1979 a service consisting of 41 pieces was sold with its original invoice, signed and dated by Robert Bloor, 1813. 'A complete Tea Serv (the teapot and cream ewer excepted) wreath of roses and gold – £12'.

The factory continued under Bloor's control until his mental health deteriorated in 1828, and from that date John Haslem's uncle, James Thomason, managed the firm with declining success until 1844. In that year Bloor's surviving descendant married Thomas Clarke, a corn factor and maltster. She took out a statute of lunacy on Bloor, and carried on the works until the end of 1848, when much of the equipment was sold to Boyle whose works at Fenton were formerly owned by Mason's of ironstone fame. James Hancock, together with several other old hands, joined Boyle, but his success was short-lived and some of his moulds were eventually sold to Copeland. Bloor had died on 11 March 1846 at Hathern in Leicestershire.

Included here for the benefit of the reader is the following personal history of the factory by one of its most respected workmen, although – particularly concerning the small pipe kiln – it cannot be entirely trusted.

Samuel Keys' History, 1837

The History and Origin of the Derby China Manufactory being very little known, I shall endeavour to give a few of my own recollections.[10]

China was first made in Derby I believe by a man in a very humble way (but his name I cannot recollect). He resided in Lodge-lane in some old premises up a yard by the

1 ▷
Seated figure of 'Music' from the European set of 'Senses'; 'Hearing' clearly indicates the 'dry-edge' period to which she belongs. No mark. Andrew Planché. 1752–5. 13.9 cm. *Royal Crown Derby Museum.*

2 ▷▷
Seated figure of a gallant holding a shell, showing typical 'dry-edge' characteristics. No mark. Andrew Planché. 1753–5. 15.8 cm. *Ronald W. Raven Collection.*

3 ▷▷▷
Boy flower-seller: earlier versions of this figure have been noted. No mark. William Duesbury & Co. 1756. 12 cm. *Ronald W. Raven Collection.*

4
A fine pair of dancers produced by William Duesbury & Co. at the Nottingham Road Works. It may well be that these originated in the Planché era, because although Duesbury added many figures to the production lists, some were undoubtedly carried on from the earlier period. No mark. 1758. 12 cm. and 11.2 cm. *George Woods Collection.*

5
'Harlequin & Columbine', taken from the 'Commedia dell' Arte' series. Note the strong Meissen influence. Patch marks, from standing on balls or pads of clay in the kilns, no factory mark. William Duesbury & Co. 1758–60. 16.8 cm. *Private collection.*

6
Coffee pot and cover showing bird decoration so typical of its period. It is usual to find the Derby forms of this decoration in subdued palette. No mark. William Duesbury & Co. *c.* 1760. 23.5 cm. *Brayshaw Gilhespy Collection. Royal Crown Derby Museum.*

7
A large and forceful figure of Jupiter,
showing signs of fire-cracking. No
mark. William Duesbury & Co. 1760.
45 cm. *Royal Crown Derby Museum.*

8
Figure of vintner with similar base to
black and white plate 45. Patch marks,
no factory mark. William Duesbury &
Co. 1760. 13.5 cm. *Ronald W. Raven
Collection.*

9 ◁◁
Blue and white coffee pot and cover, painted in underglaze blue with Chinese figures. It is interesting to note that, although it is a different pot, it has almost identical decoration to the one illustrated by Gilhespy in *Crown Derby Porcelain* (plate 118). Patch marks, no factory mark. William Duesbury & Co. 1760. 20.5 cm. *The property of a sporting gentleman, on loan to the Royal Crown Derby Museum.*

10
Blue and white chestnut bowl and pierced cover with a rope-twist finial. A similar example, dated 1762, is in the possession of Geoffrey Godden. No mark. William Duesbury & Co. 1760–65. 16.5 cm. *Venners Antiques, London.*

11
Shell salt consisting of three deep scallop shells on a coral and shell encrusted base, with a conch shell finial. Painted in underglaze blue with flowers and insects. No mark. William Duesbury & Co. 1760–65. 10.5 cm. *Gilbert Bradley Collection.*

(now Brown Bear) public-house. When he first began, he fired his articles in a small pipe kiln very near, till he had constructed a small kiln in a fireplace in the old premises he lived in. He had only small animals and birds, laying-down lambs etc. Mr William Duesbury the first, got his knowledge firstly from that man and improved on it. I never knew much of Mr Duesbury's origin, but believe he came from Walsall, or the neighbourhood.

Mr Duesbury was on friendly terms with Mr Heath, the banker and the proprietor of Pot Works on Cockpit-hill, and which I well remember.

Mr Duesbury had improved in his small experience with small China Toy making, and Mr Heath assisted him in the most liberal and friendly manner, with money and other means to carry on, which he did with credit to himself and benefit to others.

Mr Heath became a bankrupt, the Pot Works were broke up, and Mr Duesbury was a debtor to a considerable amount. Mr Duesbury had a stock of goods by him, and if I recollect right, was entrusted with a large cargo of ware from the Pot Works as they were called. He undertook what at that time was considered a serious undertaking: a journey and voyage to Ireland on speculation with the goods. The result was favourable. He parted with all his goods to great advantage, returned and paid all with satisfaction to the bankrupt, and opened a connection which enabled him to go on with spirit, and as a respectable manufacturer.

Mr Duesbury was a very old man when I first met, and the manufactory had been established several years.

Several painters having served their apprenticeships, and were working as journeymen, I will try to recollect their names – Thomas Soar and Joseph Stables, the only men who used gold, and that genuine brown gold, William Cooper, William Yates, John Yates, Edward Withers, William Billingsley, Joseph Dutton, John Blood, William Smith, William Longden, William Taylor, then a biscuit blue painter, John Butler, colour grinder, and three women burnishers, all in the two old painting rooms in the old works. John Duesbury overlooker.

T. Soar did the principal part of the useful and rich gilding and painting. J. Stables was chiefly employed in gilding figures and slight tea ware. The others were employed at figures, and slight flowers on tea ware. Painters were then alarmed at a useful Kiln of ware being drawn, being mostly employed in the ornamental branch. I was the last that was bound apprentice to the first William Duesbury. In a short time after he was affected with a stroke, which deprived him of his speech, and use of his limbs. He lived several months in that state.

The China Manufactory at Chelsea had failed while Mr Duesbury was going on in a very prosperous way, and he established his manufactory on the most respectable style with models, moulds etc, from there, and numbers of them are now in use (or might be) to good advantage. He had likewise opened a warehouse in Henrietta Street, Covent Garden.

In a few years after I went, the figure trade was on the decline, and was thought owing to Mr Duesbury introducing Mr Browns Spar Ornaments in his show rooms.

Very soon after his death, flower painting was at a very low ebb. Withers was then looked upon as the best flower painter on China in England. But they could not find employ for him, and drove him for refuge to Staffordshire, by giving him a quantity of basket boys, or 'buggards' as they were then called.

Several painters and gilders were put down, and Derby was beginning to rank as the first Manufactory in the Kingdom. All were then put to gilding, and superior kind of painting. Zachariah Boreman, a Chelsea painter, came from London, and may justly be called the father of China Painting. He excelled in landscape painting, and was on intimate terms with Mr Wright, the celebrated artist [Wright of Derby].

When Mr Duesbury had been here a short time, an order came for some plates, to match a Chelsea plate with a single plant in a curious style from nature. Withers was gone (no one knew where at the time) and Billingsley made the attempt with the instructions of Mr Boreman. He copied any garden or wild flowers that suited, and when the order was sent off it gave great satisfaction. This order was followed by others, and flower painting was raising in very high estimation. Single plants were then most fashionable, and Billingsley persevered in flower painting under the instructions of Mr Boreman, who first taught him the modern method of grouping, and with what success every China painter knows without any further comment from me.

Derby, about this time (1790), and a many years after, was the first for ware and workmanship in the Kingdom.

I have no wish to go on with the history of the next Mr Duesbury, he brought it to the highest pitch of excellence, and how it has since been conducted, and by who, with the

history of them, would be distressing to my own feelings and unpleasant to others.

There are a few, perhaps who may now recollect part of the remarks I have here given entirely from memory on my part and what I believe correct. My statements are very brief, and I have given it merely for information to the rising generation, and for them to make their own remarks from what they see and hear.

When I first went to work, Mr Taylor painted only blue under the glaze on biscuit. That failed, and he asked permission to paint on the glaze, and paid his foot-ale for it. He was set to matching India patterns, and became very clever and useful.

Very few then knew how to use the wheel, and only water colour lines were made. All circles, lines, and edges were done by hand. Painters resisted the wheel being used in any other way. Taylor had some ware to 'match', with red lines in the pattern. He attempted to do them on the wheel, but they were rubbed out, and the head of the wheel taken out and hid. In the end he was allowed to do them, by proving how much better and more true the lines were. Privately after that, some time gold circles, etc were done, and the use of the wheel became more general and useful. Withers after being harassed-about in the potteries very much, went to Birmingham, and was employed at the Japan trade. He then went to London, and was very much distressed among the Japan painters. Flower painters were wanted, and he was found out and sent for. But was a considerable time before he could be made useful, and was almost despairing. He at last managed pretty well, and became a respectable flower painter again, but very inferior to Billingsley.

He died in Bridge-gate in great distress, chiefly owing to misconduct, and was buried by his shopmates.

An interesting account of the origin of the manufactory is given in the different histories of Derby.

Who ever may be at the trouble of persuing this, let them bear in mind I have no motive but giving information. It is wrote without the least study, but merely from recollection as I went on. No pains is taken in the writing, and of course I hope there may be no criticism made, but take the act and deed together, being merely a trifling respect towards the trade I class myself a humble member.

S. KEYS

21st June, 1837.

24

Important chinoiserie pair of musicians, the woman playing a double drum and the man a lute. Andrew Planché, 'dry-edge' period. *c.* 1750–55. 15.2 cm. and 12.8 cm. *Indianapolis Museum of Art. The gift of Mrs Herbert R. Duckwall in memory of her husband.*

The continuing story of Derby may be found in *Royal Crown Derby.*

2

The Old Derby Works:
Visitors' Accounts

This chapter contains reports by important and influential visitors to the Old Works, taken from their various writings and contemporary press cuttings. These reports can of course offer only a small insight into the history of the Old Derby China Works, since although a large number of distinguished people from all over the world visited the Derby factory, many of the records have unfortunately been lost. The author has gathered here an interesting collection of mostly unpublished material in an attempt to show why Derby porcelain so fascinated Europe and indeed much of the world. It should be pointed out that in some cases the accuracy of the reports cannot be guaranteed, and a certain bias will also be noted. The reports are given in chronological order.

Foreign nobility found the factory worth a visit on their travels in England; from the *Derby Mercury* of 11 October 1770:

On Saturday last dined at the George Inn, the Chevalier D'Eon; and on Monday breakfasted at the said Inn, the Prince of Hesse Darmstadt with his retinue. After seeing the Silk Mills and China Manufactory they went to Lord Scarsdale where they partook of an elegant entertainment, thence they proceeded to Matlock Bath to view the wonders of the Peak.

The unknown author of *A Short Tour in the Midland Counties of England Performed in the Summer of 1772*, published in London in 1775, speaks thus of the Derby Works:

The manufacture of porcelain employs in all, near a hundred men and boys, several of the painters earn a guinea and a half per week: W. Duesbury (who has also bought the manufactory at Chelsea) is every day bringing the art nearer to that perfection at which it has arrived in other Countries: Derby Porcelain is at present by no means contemptible; figures and other ornaments are among their most capital articles.

Here is also a pottery [the pot works on Cockpit Hill], and I was shown one imitation of the Queens ware, but it does not come up to the original, the produce of Staffordshire.

Visitors also went to the London show-rooms. The *Derby Mercury* of 5 July 1775 contained this report of a visit made by Queen Charlotte:

On Friday last, her Majesty accompanied with the Duchess of Ancaster, was pleased to honour with her presence, W. Duesbury's ware Rooms in Bedford St, Covent Garden; and condescended to express great approbation at those beautiful articles of Derby Porcelain, and patronise the same by making some purchases.

The last few words seem to confirm Lygo's statement about the royal appointment being made in 1775.

Dr Johnson visited the Derby China Works in 1777; here is Boswell's note about it:

When we arrived at Derby Dr Butter accompanied us to see the manufactory of China

48

25
An extremely rare pair of candlestick figures, modelled as 'Seasons'. William Duesbury & Co. *c.* 1758–60. Approx. 24 cm. *Christie, Manson & Woods.*

there. I admired the ingenuity and delicate art which a man fashioned clay into a cup, a saucer, or a teapot, while a boy turned round a wheel to give the mass rotundity. I thought this as excellent in its species of power as making good verses in its species. Yet I had no respect for this potter. Neither, indeed, has a man of any extent of thinking for a mere verse-maker, in whose numbers, however perfect, there is no poetry to mind. The China was beautiful; but Dr Johnson justly observed it was too dear; for that he could have vessels in silver of the same size, as cheap as what were here made of porcelain.

In spite of his comment about the price Dr Johnson still bought some!

W. Bray, in his *Tour into Derbyshire and Yorkshire*, the first edition of which was published in 1777 and the second (from which this excerpt is taken) in 1783, says:

The China manufactory is worthy of notice. Under the care of Mr Duesbery [sic] it does honour to this country. More indefatigable in his attention; he has brought the gold and the blue to a degree of beauty never before obtained in England, and the drawing and colouring of the flowers are truly elegant. About 70 hands are employed in it, and happily many very young are enabled to earn a livelihood in the business.

Again we have a reference to the number of employees.

Comte François de la Rochefoucauld, a French nobleman, visited Derby as a young man in 1785. The author is grateful to Monsieur Jean Marchand and Miss Marian Bell for making available material on this visit. Miss Bell's notes, followed by La Rochefoucauld's original journal entry and its English translation, appear below.

The Comte François de la Rochefoucauld (1765–1848) was the eldest son of the Duc de Liancourt, Grand Master of the Wardrobe to Louis XVI of France. In January 1784 he was sent to England to learn the language, observe the English way of life, and make a special study of agriculture. He was accompanied by his younger brother Alexandre, and by Maximilien de Lazowski, his father's secretary.

They spent a year at Bury St Edmunds in Suffolk, where they became the friends of Arthur Young, the eminent agriculturist, who supervised their studies and tours in East Anglia. In 1785 Young planned a grand tour of England for them.

All three travellers kept journals for submission to the Duc de Liancourt. The present whereabouts of Alexandre's and Lazowski's manuscripts is not certain, but I have copies of parts of them.

About thirty years ago François' manuscript was found in the Library of the National Assembly in Paris by Monsieur Jean Marchand, then Librarian and Archivist, and the author of many works on the La Rochefoucauld family. Realizing its significance, M. Marchand made a transcription of the journal, and began preparing it for publication. For various reasons he abandoned the project; but in 1974, knowing about my work on the travels of members of the La Rochefoucauld family and Arthur Young in the British Isles and France, he sent me a copy of part of his transcription.

26
Transitional period figure of Cybele. William Duesbury & Co. *c.* 1756. 21.5 cm. *Royal Crown Derby Museum.*

Derby. 25 février 1785.

La place y est très bien bâtie et carrée. La salle d'assemblée est dans le fond; elle est grande et ornée de colonnes à l'extérieur; les autres maisons qui donnent sur la place sont aussi bien bâties; le reste de la ville est fort médiocre, excepté une rue de faubourg qu'ils appellent High Row Green, où il y a un grand nombre de jolies maisons.

La ville est partout bien éclairée, et il y a partout des trottoirs pour les gens de pied; la grande quantité de maisons pour les manufactures ne font pas partie de la ville; elles sont répandues à quelque distance sur la rivière, qui ne passe que par les faubourgs.

La lettre que nous avions de M. Bakewell n'était que pour un manufacturier dont nous avions peu de besoin, puisqu'en arrivant, les gens de notre auberge nous dirent que nous pourrions voir toutes les manufactures sans aucune recommandation. Cependant, nous allâmes le soir voir sa manufacture, et j'en parlerai dans son temps. Cependant, comme nous n'avions à dîner aucune bonne connaissance, nous ne pûmes nous instruire de la messe du commerce. Je ne parlerai que des détails que j'ai vus.

La manufacture de porcelaine est un objet assez important pour la ville. Elle entretient environ trois cents personnes. La terre est tirée des environs; la pâte est légère et le vernis pas bien bon. Le défaut que j'y ai trouvé est d'être un peu trop vitrifié; les qualités, d'être fort légère et à bon marché.

Elle est peinte et dorée, mais sans grande perfection. Leurs ouvriers ne sont pas très bons. Communément ils envoient tout ce qu'ils font chez leur correspondant à Londres, qui le débite abondamment. J'ai vu un service de table en entier doré et peint agréablement

27
A garniture of three vases and covers, with panels of figures reserved in gilt panels on blue ground, the reverse panels depicting birds in branches. It has been suggested that these might have been decorated at the studio of Thomas Hughes of London but the author believes them to be factory productions. William Duesbury & Co. *c.* 1758–60. Side vases 26 cm. *Christie, Manson & Woods.*

28
Pair of ribbed sauce-boats showing
oriental influence, decorated in colours.
William Duesbury & Co. *c*. 1758.
Length 17.8 cm. *Brayshaw Gilhespy
Collection. Royal Crown Derby Museum.*

29
Sauce-boat of moulded shape with
polychrome decoration. The reserves
are painted in the manner of the
'cotton-stalk' painter, whose name is
not known. William Duesbury & Co.
c. 1758. Length 19.5 cm. *Mendl &
Barbara Jacobs Collection.*

30
Group known as 'Isabella, Gallant and
Jester', adapted from the 'Commedia
dell'Arte'. This was probably modelled
originally in the Planché period.
William Duesbury & Co. *c*. 1758.
Approx. 13.5 cm. *Winifred Williams,
London.*

31
Pair of leaf-shaped dishes with moulded basket borders, decorated in polychrome. William Duesbury & Co. *c.* 1758–60. Approx. 16.5 cm. *Delomosne & Son, London.*

32
Writing set decorated in colours with European landscapes and random insects. William Duesbury & Co. 1758–60. Length 19 cm. *Christie, Manson & Woods.*

pour dix-huit guinées. La tasse que j'ai achetée, que je trouve très jolie, ne m'a coûté que 8 shillings.

Les procédés de cette manufacture sont entièrement semblables à ceux de toutes celles de cette même espèce. J'observerais seulement qu'ils cuisent trois fois; une fois pendant douze heures avec du charbon de terre, puis on met les couleurs et on les recuit avec du charbon de bois dans un grand four à réverbère, et après avoir passé le vernis on recuit encore la porcelaine avec le charbon de terre et à petit feu dans un très petit fourneau.

La position de la manufacture de porcelaine est heureuse près de la rivière, au bout de pont, de manière à jouir de la vue de l'eau et de toute la ville.

Derby, 25 February 1785

The square here is well built and regular. The assembly room is at the bottom; it is large and is adorned with columns outside; the other houses round the square are also well built; the rest of the town is very ordinary, with the exception of one suburban street which is called High Row Green, where there are a large number of pretty houses.

The whole town is well lit, and there are footpaths for pedestrians everywhere; most of the factory houses are just outside the town; they are spread out at some distance from the river, which only passes through the suburbs.

The letter which we had from M. Bakewell[1] was for a manufacturer whose help we needed very little, since on arrival the people at our inn told us that we could see any of the factories without recommendation. However we went to his factory this evening, and I will talk about it in its place. However as we did not dine with any well-informed person, we could not get any information about the ways of the trade. I will only talk of things I have seen.

The manufacture of porcelain has quite an important place in the town. It employs in the region of three hundred people. The clay is found locally; the paste is light and the glaze not very good. The fault that I have found is that it is a little too vitrified; the merits that it is very light and cheap. It is painted and gilt, but not well. Their workmen are not very good. Normally they send all that they make to their London agent, who sells it in quantities. I have seen a complete table service attractively painted for eighteen guineas. The cup which I bought, which I find very pretty, only cost me eight shillings.

The procedure at this factory is exactly similar to that elsewhere. I would observe only that they fire three times; firstly for twelve hours with coal, then after enamelling they refire with charcoal in a large reverberating kiln,[2] and after glazing they refire the porcelain at a lesser heat, with coal, in a very small kiln.

The position of the porcelain manufactory is happily near the river [the Derwent], at the foot of the [St Mary's] bridge, in such manner as to afford a good view of the water and the whole town.

Sawrey Gilpin, RA, a painter of sporting subjects who exhibited from 1762 to 1808 and was in Derby about 1786, wrote:

The object of the China-works there is merely ornament; which is particularly unhappy, as they were at the time we saw them, under no legislation of taste. A very free hand we found employed in painting the vases: and the first colours were laid in *with spirit; but in the finishing, they were richly daubed, that all freedom was lost in finery. – It may now be otherwise.*

The author believes that the wares refute Gilpin's criticisms.

Alfred Wallis wrote:

It is very probable that the famous Rodney Jug, which celebrates Admiral Rodney's victory over the French fleet on 12 April 1782, was potted and decorated at a later date – say five years later – for we find Lord Rodney at Kedleston in Derbyshire in 1787. The Derby Mercury of 12 July says: 'We are happy to inform the Public that Lord Rodney has already received great Benefit from Bathing and drinking the water of Kedleston.' The date upon the jug is, of course, that on which the victory was won, but it is more than likely that the piece commemorates a personal visit of the admiral to the China Works.

Wallis's statement in the first line is, however, unlikely to be true.

Royalty were sufficiently impressed by the quality of the ware produced at Derby to order it for their private use, as the *Derby Mercury* of 14 May 1788 reports:

The Prince of Wales from a wish to patronise the Derbyshire China Manufactory, lately gave orders for a complete dessert set to be prepared for his Highness's table, and we are

33
Frill vase and cover, lacking the bird finial on the domed cover, heavily applied with flowers and decorated in many colours with flowers, moths and other insects. Patch marks. William Duesbury & Co. *c.* 1760. 24.5 cm. *The Hermitage, Leningrad, USSR, no. 19866.*

34 ▷ ▷
Tankard decorated with a full-length portrait of Shakespeare, reserved within a scrolled panel, and flanked by two large floral sprays in colour. William Duesbury & Co. *c.* 1760. Approx. 16 cm. *Sotheby's, New Bond Street.*

35
Fine punch pot decorated with naturalistic birds, including swans, in colours. William Duesbury & Co. *c.* 1760. 20.3 cm. *Sotheby's, New Bond Street.*

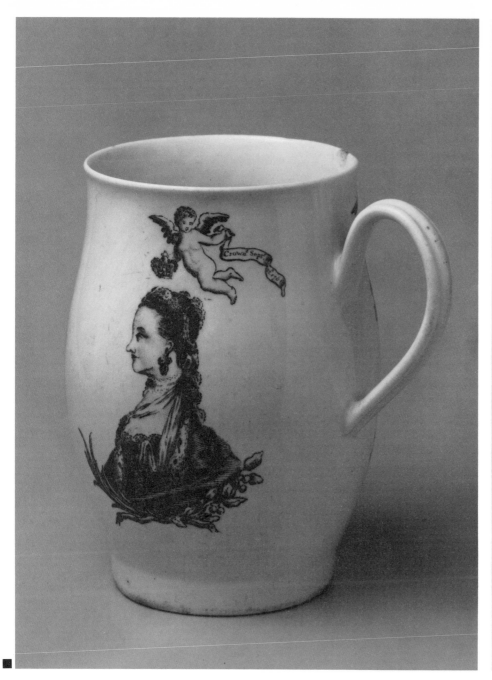

36 ■
Rare coronation mug made to celebrate the crowning of George III and Queen Charlotte in 1761. The cupid above Queen Charlotte's head drapes a banner on which is written 'Crown'd Sept. 22nd 1761'.

happy to add for the honour of England, that the order has been executed highly to the satisfaction of the Prince. The different articles are in the centre decorated with the Prince's Crest beautifully painted, and around the edges is a rich border of a Garter-blue colour intersected with burnished gold.

This dessert set should not be confused with the service mentioned on page 169, which was pattern 65. Plate 230 illustrates a shell-shaped dish.

Pilkington, in his *View of the Present State of Derbyshire*, published in 1789, mentions this magnificent service:

About forty years ago the manufacture of porcelain was begun by the late Mr Duesbury. This ingenious artist brought it to such perfection as, in some respects, to equal the best foreign china. The ornamental part of the business was at first almost solely attended to. But the foreign demand being much interrupted by the last war, the proprietor turned his thoughts to the manufacture of useful porcelain. At this work a very rich and elegant dessert service, consisting of one hundred and twenty pieces, was lately made for His Royal Highness the Prince of Wales [see plate 230]. The number of hands at present employed by Mr Duesbury is seventy-two, and the manufacture is in a flourishing state.

A piece in the *Derby Mercury* on 2 April 1789 describes some lavish illuminations which Duesbury had put up at his house:

We should think ourselves remiss if we did not notice the particularly splendid and elegant

37
The same mug showing Britannia with outstretched hand to Hibernia or Minerva, below which is the rebus for Holdship.

38 ●
The same mug showing an angel crowning George III. All three views are transfer-printed in black. William Duesbury & Co. 1761. 13 cm. *Royal Crown Derby Museum.*

manner in which Mr Duesbury Porcelain Manufacturer had illuminated his house [rejoicing for the so called recovery of George 3rd] Mr Duesbury displayed the words of the coronation Anthem 'God Save the King' 'Long Live the King' 'May the King Live forever,' with the Kings crest in elegant transparency's encircled with rays. The house was alluminated with nearly 500 glass lamps which he had provided for the occasion and disposed so as to form the letter G.R. And above them on a crown with several Festoons. The novelty of illuminating with lamps (as they were the first we ever recollect to have been made use of in this Town) drew together an immense concourse of people.

William Hutton, the historian of his native town (Derby) and of Birmingham, wrote about the factory in his *History of Derby*, published in 1791. Again he mentions the service made for the Prince of Wales, and refers specifically to the number of employees.

Porcelain began about the year 1750. There is only one manufactory, which employs about seventy people. The clay is not of equal fineness with the foreign, but the workmanship exceeds it. The arts of drawing and engraving have much improved within these last thirty years. The improvements of the porcelain have kept pace with these. They adhere to nature in their designs, to which the Chinese have not attained. A dessert service of one hundred and twenty pieces was recently fabricated here for the Prince of Wales. The spot upon which this elegant building stands, which is internally replete with taste and utility, was once the freehold of my family. It cost £35, but the purchaser, my

39 ◁ ◁
Frill vase and cover showing variation of shape and piercing (cf. black and white plate 38). Patch marks. William Duesbury & Co. *c.* 1760. 21.6 cm. *Royal Crown Derby Museum.*

40 ◁
Group possibly representing 'Autumn', illustrating the high standard of figure production under William Duesbury I. Patch marks, no factory mark. William Duesbury & Co. 1765. 16.1 cm. *Royal Crown Derby Museum.*

42
A pair of figures modelled as Turks in dancing position and enamelled in colours. Patch marks. William Duesbury & Co. *c.* 1760. 21.1 cm. *Royal Crown Derby Museum.*

41 ◁
Pair of dancers copied from a painting by Antoine Watteau in the National Gallery of Scotland, Edinburgh. An engraving by Laurent Cars entitled 'Fêtes Vénitiennes' is with the collection and was taken from Watteau's original. Patch marks. William Duesbury & Co. *c.* 1760. Male 28.1 cm., female 27.4 cm. *Schreiber Collection. Victoria & Albert Museum, 414/177 and 414/177A – 1885.*

43
Fluted coffee pot and cover with good floral decoration. No mark. William Duesbury & Co. *c.* 1760. 23 cm. *Brayshaw Gilhespy Collection. Royal Crown Derby Museum.*

44
Pair of pedlars supported by tree-
stumps on round bases. The man carries
a basket of bottles slung in front of him
and the woman carries a box of trinkets
fastened round her waist. Patch marks.
William Duesbury & Co. *c.* 1760.
25·4 cm and 26·2 cm. *Schreiber
Collection. Victoria & Albert Museum,
Sch I 294.*

46
A pair of figures in the form of a negro
and negress holding shells for
sweetmeats. Patch marks. William
Duesbury & Co. *c.* 1760. 19.6 cm.
*Schreiber Collection. Victoria & Albert
Museum, 414/187 and 414/187A – 1885.*

45
Figure of a piper taken from an earlier
model. Note the use of a rectangular
base with tree-stump support to assist
in firing. Patch marks, no factory
mark. William Duesbury & Co. 1760.
15.6 cm. *Ronald W. Raven Collection.*

grandfather's brother, being unable to raise more than £28, mortgaged it for £7.
Infirmity, age, and poverty obliged him to neglect the interest, when, in 1743, it fell into
the hands of my father as heir-at-law, who, being neither able nor anxious to redeem it,
conveyed away his right to the mortgages for a guinea.

And again, in his manuscript, *History of the Hutton Family*, written in 1799, he writes
of John Hutton:

*He was the man who purchased the house east of St Mary's Bridge, now the China
works, for £35, but being master of only £28, mortgaged the premises to Mr Crompton,
a banker, for the other seven. He becoming old and poor, and inheriting the supineness of
the Hutton family, suffered the trifling interest to remain unpaid till the mortgagee seized
the premises. The freehold in 1743 fell into the hands of my father, as heir-at-law, who
assigned over his interest to Mr Crompton for a guinea.*

G. M. Woodward, the caricaturist, was a Derbyshire man born at Stanton-in-
Peak. In 1796 he published his *Eccentric Excursions*, in which he mentions the Derby
Factory and the quality of its ware:

*After passing the Turnpike (on the Nottingham Road) about a mile brings the traveller to
the foot of the bridge leading to the entrance of the town of Derby, near which is the
porcelain manufactory, where the different articles are brought to the highest perfection,
equal if not superior to the foreign china, in a variety of patterns.*

Another contemporary description of the factory by a local historian comes from
John Mawe, who wrote in his *The Mineralogy of Derbyshire*, published in 1802:

The porcelain manufactory belonging to Messrs Duesbury and Kean *is worthy of the
illustrious family who have honoured it with their approbation. Here the whole process of
making what we call China may be seen; and the beautiful painting and gilding have
conferred on this manufacture a great reputation.*

This is an extract concerning a visit to Derby, from *Travels in England and
Scotland*, by a foreign visitor, Johanna Schopenhauer.[3]

From Birmingham we travelled via Burton to Derby. Burton is a pleasant little town,

47
Mrs Cibber in the part of Vivandière.
Patch marks. William Duesbury & Co.
c. 1760. 20.5 cm. *Victoria & Albert
Museum, 301A – 1885.*

48 ▷ ▷
David Garrick in the role of Tancred,
in Thomson's 'Tancred & Sigismunda'.
Patch marks. William Duesbury & Co.
c. 1760. 22.6 cm. *Schreiber Collection.
Victoria & Albert Museum, 414/185 –
1885.*

49
A pair of figures, the male with a lamb and a basket of fruit, the girl with a basket of eggs and her apron full of fruit. Possibly intended to be street-sellers. Patch marks. William Duesbury & Co. *c.* 1760. 24.6 cm. *Herbert Allen Collection. Victoria & Albert Museum. C196 – 1935 man; C196A – 1935 woman.*

50
Sweetmeat stand decorated in blue and white. Patch marks. William Duesbury & Co. *c.* 1765. Approx. 23.5 cm. *Sotheby's, New Bond Street.*

52
A pair of figures taken from the Meissen originals. Both hold chickens, the cockerel in the man's arms and the hen in the woman's. The central figure of the drummer is unusual. Patch marks. William Duesbury & Co. *c.* 1765. Man with cockerel 20.4 cm. *Sotheby's, New Bond Street.*

51
A kingfisher-mounted shell sweetmeat
stand decorated in colours. Patch
marks. William Duesbury & Co.
c. 1765. Approx. 15.3 cm. *Sotheby's,
New Bond Street.*

world-famous for its ale, which nowhere is brewed as tasty as here. In peace time a lot is exported all over Europe but especially to Russia. Large quantities are also sent to America. In England the middle classes drink it after their meals, but then it must have been stored for some years. It has then reached such a strength that it can be compared with any wine and has completely lost its taste of beer.

Derby is a rather big, but not very attractive town. There are many factories, among them one for silk. The most important factory is the porcelain factory. Only judging by the quality of the clay, this porcelain is not as good as the porcelain from Saxony and Sèvres, but when it comes to colours, gilding and beautiful design it cannot be matched. The figures are bisquit and not as nice as the ones from Saxony neither in design nor in finish. Here again it is clearly illustrated that the English sense of design can only produce the useful and practical but that they can do with perfection.

In 1803 the Revd E. Butcher of Sidmouth went on a journey to Chester, taking in Derby on the way. In 1805 he published his ideas and impressions in two volumes. In Vol. 2 he writes:

We past on to the porcelain manufactory – it lies a little beyond the bridge and furnishes a vast variety of excellently finished articles . . . the clay is not equally fine with the foreign, but the workmanship is greatly superior. Drawing and engraving have amazingly improved within the last 40 years; and with these arts the improvement of the porcelain keeps pace. Many exquisitely beautiful figures, both single and in groups were shown to us which seems to rival some of the finest efforts of statuary. A head of the Duke of York was fired and taken out of the mould in little more than a minute . . . we observed with pain that the finer, most ornamental parts of the business seemed very hurtful to the eyes of those who were employed in it – all of them wore green eye shades but these did not seem to entirely remedy the evil. A few years ago a very rich and elegant dessert service was made for the Prince of Wales.

The *Derby Mercury* was always proud to report the visits to the factory of royalty and nobility, both English and foreign. A tour of the factory was clearly an essential part of the traveller's itinerary. On 16 December 1816 the paper proclaimed:

The Grand Duke Nicholas of Russia with his suite . . . accompanied by Sir William Congreve arrived at Hore's (the New Kings Head in this place), late on Thursday evening. On the following morning his Imperial Highness, joined by the Duke of Devonshire proceeded to inspect the Infirmary, messrs Cox and Poyser's patent shot works. The Grand Duke, with his grace etc ascended to the top of the shot tower and visited the Porcelain Manufactory and messrs Brown & Spar Marble works at both places his Imperial Highness purchased specimens of the manufacture and highly admired their beauty and elegance.

A few weeks earlier it had noted the arrival of more foreign royalty:

On Thursday November 9th 1816 the Archduke John Louis of Austria, with their suite arrived at the George Inn.

The following year it noted in its issue of 26 November:

The Duke and Duchess of Argyle and suite slept at the George Inn last night, and after visiting the extensive Porcelain Manufactory of Messrs. Blore & Co. this morning, proceeded on their route from Scotland.

It was possibly at this time that the Duke and Duchess ordered their service (see plate 356).

Although the plan of Derby in the antiquarian Lysons' *Derbyshire* of 1817 localizes the 'Pot-work', there is no mention of an earthenware factory there. The china works is described thus:

The Porcelain manufacture was established at Derby about the year 1750 by W. Duesbury. The Derby porcelain has long been held in esteem and has of late years been much improved in its own position and ornaments. The clay and granite used in this manufacture are brought from Cornwall. This manufactory now belongs to Mr Bloor who lately employed about 200 workmen.

The Manchester *Commercial Directory* for 1818, 1819 and 1820 contains the following reference to the factory:

The manufacture of porcelain was originally established here about the year 1750 by the

53
Figure of Diana the huntress. William
Duesbury & Co. *c.* 1765. 31.1 cm.
Royal Crown Derby Museum.

ingenious W. Duesbury [not accurate – see chapter 1], *but the most considerable
improvements have been effected since his decease by the judicious method of preparing the
paste, and increasing the beauty of the decorations. The ware itself is not of equal fineness
with the French and Saxon, but its workmanship and ornaments are far superior.*

This entry appears in the Directory:

> *China Manufacturer*
> BLOOR, ROBERT (porcelain) Nottingham-Road.

In about 1818, or perhaps a year or so earlier, Ebeneezer Rhodes of Sheffield was collecting material for his *Peak Scenery*. He describes a visit he made to the porcelain works at Derby:

They were established about seventy-five years since [the usual error – see chapter 1] by a gentleman of the name Duesbury and the wares they now produce are unrivalled in richness and elegance. There is a classical taste and beauty in the forms of their wares, urns, vases and ure's: and some excelent artists are employed to adorn them with landscapes, portraits, groups and figures. Mineral colours only, are used in painting porcelain, and it is finished with a rich enamel. The gold with which it is splendidly ornamented is reduced to a liquid previously to its being placed upon the different articles to which it is applied; they are then committed to the fire when the gold reasumes a solid form and is afterwards brilliantly burnished.

In 1825 the *Derby Mercury* wrote in glowing terms of a service which had been commissioned from the factory. The issue of 3 August contained the following:

The admirers of the fine arts and the public in general will be highly gratified with the inspection of a most magnificent Service of China which has been completed at the porcelain manufactory of Mr Bloor, for the express use of a Nobleman in a distant part of England. – The China is of the whitest and most beautiful composition, superior in every respect to any ever before got up in this town. Each plate presents a different view, which are of the most picturesque description, both by sea and land, intermixed with juvenile figures, &c. &c. finished in the most exquisite manner, and the border of each plate is ornamented with emboss'd & painted birds, fruit, landscapes, flowers, animals, figures, &c. &c. so that the border of every plate presents a different appearance. The dishes are ornamented with groups of roses, &c. corresponding with the borders of the plates, and the remainder of the service are ornamented in unison. – The plates alone comprise a cabinet of paintings finely executed after the manner of the best masters, and would be valuable to encircle with splendid frames, (but they are intended for use,) and the best judges that have seen them are of opinion the whole are a collection of the most superior specimens of china ever produced in this Kingdom.

This was probably Lord Ongley's service. The children were painted on Nantgarw by Plant, who was a London decorator. William Corden, who had recently left the factory, was employed to paint the figure subjects. Again we have proof of the ability of the factory under Robert Bloor. The author once possessed a plate from this service, painted by Corden with a portrait of the Duchess of Leinster. The plate bore a blue mark, which was out of period.

Another local historian, Glover, described the factory in his *History of Derbyshire* of 1833. It is unusual to find a good report of Robert Bloor.

The Porcelain Manufactory occupies an area equal to 6000 square yards, and affords sufficient room for the employment of 400 workmen. The front extends 170 feet. This Business was established in Derby, by Mr Duesbury. Since his decease considerable improvements have been effected through the judicious method employed in preparing the paste, and in increasing the beauty of the decorations. The Porcelain manufactured here, being superior to any other for the finish and taste of the execution, has obtained great celebrity. The Works have long been carried on by Mr Robert Bloor with much spirit and credit. This gentleman has erected a steam engine, added new biscuit and glaze Kilns, and made other improvements to accelerate the production, and increase the durability and beauty of the ware.

The last piece of interest from the *Derby Mercury* in the period under consideration in this book was published on 7 December 1842, and concerns a magnificent service (see plate 396) which had been made for the young Queen Victoria:

DERBY CHINA MANUFACTORY. – *A few days since, we had the gratification of seeing at this celebrated manufactory, a splendid Dessert Service, ordered for Her Majesty, and which is about to be forwarded. In a few days, we understand, the set may be seen at Mr Bloor's warehouse, 34 Old Bond Street, London, where it will remain until the 21st. instant. The number of pieces contained in the service are 96 plates – 16 dessert plates, varying in height from 16 to 24 inches – 16 fruit dishes, mounted upon cornucopias – and two pair of ice pails, the shapes of which are perfectly new, having been modelled from designs prepared for the purpose. The whole are painted in equal portions of fruit, flowers, birds, and insects, and are enriched with embossed, chased, and burnished gold borders upon a green ground. Altogether it is one of the most beautiful sets of porcelain we ever saw, and does infinite credit to the manufactory from whence it proceeds.*

3

Figure Productions: the Haslem and Bemrose Lists

This chapter deals with the list of figures produced by John Haslem in The Old Derby China Factory (London, 1876), the source of which he did not give, and with William Bemrose's list of moulds and models.

The Haslem list would, in its earliest stages, appear to date from the Chelsea merger of 1770, since before this date it was not the normal procedure to incise numbers on the bases of figures. Haslem numbers up to 390 in his list, and Bemrose to 397, but the numbers in the two lists do not always agree. If both lists were compiled from the incised numbers mentioned above, one would have expected them to tally exactly. A word of warning must be given here, since some figures reissued after 1770 would carry an incised number. Careful study of the two lists will give great insight into the productions of the factory. In addition, the Bemrose list was produced by four workmen for use in the lawsuits of Duesbury versus Kean in 1819.

As can be seen from the colour plates, the earlier productions were more restrained in colouring, but those of the later Bloor period have heavier colours, in particular cobalt blue and burgundy, and their bases are washed with a strong green. Marks, apart from the incised crown, crossed batons, six dots, and 'D' on the later biscuit pieces produced *c.* 1790, denote Bloor production from 1811 to 1825, and later printed Bloor marks are self-explanatory. (See chapter 14 for further discussion of marks.)

It is indicative of the very high quality of the biscuit figures that, as can be seen from the following list, they were considerably more expensive than the enamelled and gilt ones. The obvious conclusion is that imperfect pieces were disguised under enamel.

PRICE LIST OF
GROUPS AND SINGLE FIGURES

ENAMELLED AND GILT, AND IN BISCUIT

———

No	Names of Figures and Groups	Size	Height inches	Enamelled and Gilt (£ s. d.)			Biscuit (£ s. d.)		
1	Group of the Virtues	1st	11½	2	2	0			
	,, ,,	2nd							
3	The Elements, Stephan	1st		3	3	0	3	13	6
	,,	2nd		2	12	6	3	3	0
	,,	3rd	7⅛	1	16	0	2	2	0
4	Pastoral Group			2	12	6	3	3	0
5	Four Antique Seasons, in a Set	1st	8	1	4	0	1	8	0
	,, ,,	2nd	6½	0	16	0			
	,, ,,	3rd	4⅛	0	12	0			
6	Four Seasons, in a Set		4	0	10	6			
7	Gardening	1st	6¾	0	15	0	0	16	0
	,,	2nd	5	0	8	0	0	9	0
8	Fruit and Flowers		5⅜	0	10	6	0	12	0
9	Music	1st	6¼	0	14	0	0	16	0
	,,	2nd	6	0	10	6	0	12	0
	,,	3rd	4⅝	0	6	0	0	7	0
10	Flute and Cymbal	1st	6¼	0	14	0	0	16	0
	,, ,,	2nd	5⅝	0	10	6	0	12	0
	,, ,,	3rd	4¾	0	6	0	0	7	0
11	Flute and Guitar		6⅞	1	10	0	1	11	6
12	Pastoral Group		12¼	2	12	6			
13	Cupid and Bacchus riding		7	1	1	0			
14	Sacrifice Figures, Pair			1	0	0	1	4	0
15	Small Prudence and Discretion, with Urns		9¼	1	8	0			
16	Dancing Group		6⅝	0	16	0			
17	,, ,,		6⅝	0	16	0			
18 & 19	Names of Figures not given								
20	Fruit and Flowers, Pair	1st	6¼	0	14	0	0	16	0
	,, ,, ,,	2nd	5¾	0	10	6	0	12	0
	,, ,, ,,	3rd	4⅝	0	6	0	0	7	0
21	Garrick as Richard III, Bacon		9¾	1	5	0	1	5	0
22 & 23	Names not given								
25 to 34	Ten Figures of Apollo and Muses, 5 in in height, 5/3 each								
35	Four Seasons		6	1	1	0	1	4	0
36	Sitting Fruit		5	0	10	6	0	12	0
37	Jason and Medea	1st		3	3	0	3	13	6
	,, ,,	2nd	12¾	2	2	0	3	3	0
	,, ,,	3rd		1	11	6	2	12	6
38	Prudence and Discretion		5½	0	7	0	0	8	0
39 to 45	Seven Groups of Arts and Sciences, various, at 16/– each, with Pedestals – 14/– without								
46	Dancing Figures and Group		5½	0	9	0			
47	Grotesque Seasons		5¼	0	16	0			
48	Elements in two Groups		8¾	2	12	6	3	4	0
49	Cat and Dog Figures		5¾	0	13	0			
50	Sporting and Companion		5⅝	0	12	0	0	14	0
51	Cat and Dog Figures		5	0	10	6	0	14	0
52	Dragon Candlesticks								
53	Griffin ,,								

No	Names of Figures and Groups	Size	Height inches	Enamelled and Gilt (£ s. d.)			Biscuit (£ s. d.)		
54	Justice		9½	0	15	0			
55	Dresden Shepherd	1st	9¼	1	6	0			
	,, ,,	2nd	8¾	1	2	0			
56	Garland ,,	1st	9¾	1	6	0			
	,, ,,	2nd	9	1	2	0			
	,, ,,	3rd	7⅝	0	18	0			
	,, ,,	4th	6¾	0	15	0			
57	French Shepherds, Pair	1st		1	8	0			
	,, ,,	2nd		1	2	0			
	,, ,,	3rd		0	18	0			
	,, ,,	4th		0	14	0			
	,, ,,	5th		0	10	6	0	12	0
	,, ,,	6th		0	7	0	0	8	0
58	Piping Shepherd			0	15	0			
59	Set of Five Senses		7½	2	12	6			
60	Singers	1st		1	0	0			
	,,	2nd	7	0	16	0			
	,,	3rd	5⅜	0	9	0			
61	Four Sitting Seasons	1st		1	1	0			
62	Welch Taylor and Family, large size			2	12	6			
	,, ,, small		5½	1	1	0			
63	Small Turks		3½	0	5	0	0	6	0
64	Four Standing Seasons		5½	0	18	0			
65	Diana	1st		1	1	0	1	4	0
	,,	2nd	8½	0	14	0			
66	Venus and Cupid		6½	0	10	6	0	12	0
67	Venus, Chelsea Model								
68	Group of Four Seasons		9¼	1	10	0	1	18	0
69	Sitting Flute Figures			0	6	0			
70	Figure of Christie		12⅛	1	5	0			
71	Pair Sitting Figures, with Cat and Dog		5½	0	16	0	1	5	0
72	Pastoral Group, with Goat		5⅜	0	12	0			
73	,, ,, with Dog		5⅜	0	12	0			
74	Dancing Group of two Figures		6½	0	12	0			
75	Group of Cephălus and Procris		8½	1	1	0			
76	,, of Renaldo and Armida		8½	1	1	0			
77	Stocking Mending			0	12	0	0	18	0
78	Shoemaker, Group of two Figures		5⅞	0	12	0	0	18	0
79	Complimenting Group of two ,,		6¾	0	13	0			
80	Spinning, Group of two ,,			0	12	0			
81	Shoeblack, Group of two ,,			0	12	0	0	18	0
82	Fury Group, Broken Fiddle								
83	,, Broken Chair								
84	,, Hairdresser, two Figures			0	12	0	0	18	0
85	Macaroni			0	14	0			
86	Set of Elements, in Groups of two Figures each			2	2	0			
87	Pair of Salutation Figures		4¾	0	7	0			
88	Mrs Macaulay								
89	Fury group, Family								
90	Cook and Companion								
91	Female Macaroni			0	14	0			

No	Names of Figures and Groups	Size	Height inches	Enamelled and Gilt £ s. d.	Biscuit £ s. d.
92	Three Figures learning Music				
93	Group of three Figures playing at Hazard		6	1 1 0	
94	Group of three Figures at a Raree Show		6	1 1 0	
95	Sphinx Candlestick				
96	,, of a Vase				
97	Griffin ,,				
98	Group of Prudence and Discretion		11½	2 2 0	
99	Pair of Figures, Æsculapius and Hygeia		7½	0 16 0	0 18 0
100	Andromache weeping over the ashes of Hector	1st		1 10 0	1 11 6
101	Pair, Grotesque Boy and Girl		4½	0 5 0	
102 to 113	Twelve Figures of Nuns & Monks				
114	Pair of Figures, Mars and Venus		6¼	0 16 0	0 18 0
115	,, ,,			0 16 0	
116	Apollo		6¾	0 8 0	0 9 0
117 & 119	Pair of Figures, Jupiter & Juno		6½	0 16 0	0 18 0
118	Neptune		6¾	0 8 0	0 10 6
120	Diana		6½	0 9 0	0 10 6
121	Minerva		6½	0 8 0	0 9 0
122	Hercules		6¼	0 8 0	0 9 0
123	Set of Seasons, from French	1st		4 4 0	
	,, ,,	2nd		3 13 6	4 4 0
	,, ,,	3rd		3 3 0	3 13 6
	,, ,,	4th	7½	1 16 0	2 2 0
124	Time and Cupid	1st		2 12 6	
	,, ,,	2nd		1 11 6	
	,, ,,	3rd	7¾	1 1 0	
125	Set of four Chelsea standing Seasons	1st	6⅜	1 8 0	
	,, ,, ,,	2nd	6¼	1 4 0	
	,, ,, ,,	3rd	5⅛	0 14 0	0 16 0
126	Wilkes			1 5 0	
127	Small Figures				
128 to 136	Nine Figures, names not given				
137	Madonna, a Group		8¼	0 18 0	1 1 0
138	Prudent Mother, a Group		8¼	0 18 0	1 1 0
139	Music Group of two Figures		6½	0 12 0	
140	,, ,, ,,		6½	0 12 0	
141	Pair of Fighting Boys		3½	0 4 0	0 5 0
142 & 143	Pair of small Boys riding on Dolphin and Swan	1st	5 to 5¼	0 12 0	
	,, ,, ,,	2nd		0 10 0	
	,, ,, ,,	3rd		0 7 6	
144 to 158	Fifteen Figures, names not given				
159 & 160	Pair, Laughing and Crying Philosophers		5¾	0 10 6	
161	Antique Figure of Wisdom	1st	8½	0 12 0	0 18 0
	,, ,,	2nd			
162	,, of Justice	1st	8½	0 12 0	0 18 0
	,, ,,	2nd			
163	Antique Figure of Plenty	1st	8½	0 12 0	0 18 0
	,, ,,	2nd			
164	,, of Peace	1st	8½	0 12 0	0 18 0
	,, ,,	2nd			
165 to 174	Ten Figures, names not given				
175	Pair of Boy and Girl Figures		4	0 4 0	
176 to 178	Three Figures, names not given		13¼	2 12 6	
179	Music Group of four Figures		13¼	2 12 6	
180	Pair of Boys, Autumn and Spring			0 3 0	
181	Name not given				
182	Pair of Cupids riding on Bucks			0 10 6	
183	,, Prudence and Discretion			0 4 0	
184	,, Boy and Girl Figures			0 4 0	0 5 0
185	,, Cupids riding on Swan and Dolphin			0 7 0	
186 to 188	Three Figures, names not given				
189	Boy riding on Sea-horse		4½	0 4 6	
190	Triton		2¾	0 3 0	
191 & 192	Names not given				
193 & 194	Pair, large Bacchus & Ariadne	1st	9	1 8 0	1 11 6
	,, ,, ,,	2nd	8¼	1 1 0	1 4 0
	,, ,, ,,	3rd	7½	0 16 0	0 18 0
195	Group of two Virgins awaking Cupid		12½	2 2 0	3 3 6
196	,, of two Bacchantes adorning Pan		12½	2 2 0	3 3 0
197	Cupid riding on Sea-lion		2¾	0 4 0	
198	Pair of Haymakers		6½	0 15 0	0 16 0
199	,, Harlequin and Columbine		5½	0 10 6	0 12 0
200	Set of four Quarters of the Globe	1st	6	1 12 0	1 12 0
	,, ,, ,,	2nd	5¼	1 4 0	1 4 0
201 & 202	Pair of Cupids		4	0 5 0	0 7 0
203	Pair of Cupids, with Dog and Falcon				0 10 6
204	,, of Gardeners		5	0 8 0	0 12 0
205 & 206	Pair of Cupids		4½	0 5 0	0 7 0
207	Sea Nymph riding on a Dolphin		4⅛	0 4 6	
208	,, playing the Tabor		3	0 2 6	
209	Syren with a Shell		2½	0 2 6	
210	Triton		3	0 2 6	
211 & 212	Names not given				
213 & 214	Pair of Cupids, with Dog & Falcon		4⅜	0 10 0	0 10 6
215	Name not given				
216 & 217	Pair, Groups, Music & Poetry	1st	9¾	3 3 0	3 15 0
	,, ,, ,,	2nd		2 16 0	3 3 0
	,, ,, ,,	3rd		2 10 0	2 16 0
218 & 219	Names not given				
220	Pair Basket Figures	1st	6½	0 15 0	
221	,, ,,	2nd	5¼	0 10 6	
222	Figure of Time		6½	0 9 0	0 10 6
223 to 226	Four Figures, names not given				
227	Pair Grotesque Punches		7	0 18 0	
228 to 230	Three Figures, names not given				
231	Large Falstaff				
232 & 233	Names not given				
234	Group of four Cupids		10	1 1 0	1 11 6
235	Group of Three Graces distressing Cupid	1st	14¾	3 13 6	4 4 0
	,, ,, ,,	2nd		2 12 6	3 3 0
236 & 237	Pair of Cupids		4	0 5 0	0 7 0
238	Name not given				
239	The Virgin Mary		10½	1 1 0	
240	Pastoral group of two Figures		7¾	0 8 0	
241 & 242	Names not given				
243	Apollo		9½	1 1 0	
244	Plenty		9⅜	1 4 0	
245	Peace		9¼	1 4 0	1 11 6
246	Name not given				
247	Pastoral Group of two Figures		12¼	2 5 0	
248	Group of four Seasons, Antique		11⅛	1 11 6	2 2 0
249 & 250	Names not given				
251	Group of four Cupids		9	0 18 0	1 5 0
252	,, of three ,,			1 1 0	1 11 6
253	Pair of Cupids, with Dog & Birdcage		3¾	0 4 0	0 7 0
254	Pastoral group of two Figures		13¼	2 10 0	
255	,, ,,		12	2 0 0	
256	,, ,,		12¼	2 0 0	
257	Group of four Cupids		9¾	1 1 0	1 11 6
258	Pair Sitting Boy Candlesticks		6½	0 16 0	
259	Britannia	1st		2 2 0	
	,,	2nd		1 11 6	
	,,	3rd		1 1 0	
260	Crying Boy and Laughing Girl	1st			
	,, ,,	2nd	7⅝	0 14 0	
261	No name				
262 to 278	Seventeen Figures of Cupid in Disguise			0 2 6	
279	No name				
280	Pair Pipe and Guitar Candlesticks,				
	with Ornamental Branches		8½	1 10 0	
	,, with Chandelier Branches		8½	1 16 0	

No	Names of Figures and Groups	Size	Height inches	Enamelled and Gilt £ s. d.	Biscuit £ s. d.
281	Pair Spring Candlesticks		6¼	0 16 0	
282	,, Small Fame and Mercury		8½	0 18 0	
283	,, Gardener Candlesticks		6⅞	0 16 0	
284	,, Pipe and Guitar ,,		9½	1 10 0	
285	,, ,, ,,		8	1 6 0	
286	No Name				
287	Pair Garland Shepherd Candlesticks		9½	1 10 0	
288	,, Mars and Venus ,,		8	1 6 0	
289 & 290	Names not given				
291	Falstaff	1st		2 12 6	
	,,	2nd		1 11 6	
	,,	3rd		1 5 0	
	,,	4th		0 15 0	
	,,	5th		0 12 0	
292	Pair of Dessert Gardeners	1st		0 7 0	
	,, ,,	2nd	4¾	0 6 0	
293	Tythe Pig Group, three Figures		7	0 15 0	
294	Group of the four Seasons, with an Obelisk		8	1 11 6	2 2 0
295	,, of the four Quarters of the Globe		10⅛	2 2 0	2 12 6
296	Pair of Haymakers		9¼	1 11 6	
297	Milton		10⅝	1 5 0	1 11 6
298	Minerva	1st		2 2 0	2 12 6
	,,	2nd		1 11 6	2 2 0
	,,	3rd		1 1 0	1 10 0
299	Neptune on Rock Pedestal	1st	9¼	1 1 0	1 4 0
	,, ,,	2nd		0 16 0	0 18 0
300	,, without ,,		5⅜	0 9 0	0 10 6
301	Pair, Sitting Pipe and Guitar	1st		1 0 0	
	,, ,,	2nd	6¼	0 16 0	
	,, ,,	3rd	5⅜	0 12 0	0 18 0
302	,, of Fame and Mercury			1 1 0	1 11 6
303	,, of Pipe and Tabor	1st		0 17 0	
	,, ,,	2nd	6⅜	0 14 0	
304	No name				
305	Shakespeare		10½	1 5 0	1 11 6
306	No name				
307	Set of four Seasons, sitting		4⅝	1 0 0	
308	No name				
309	Music Group of four Figures, with an Obelisk		10	1 11 6	
310	No name				
311	Pair, Pipe and Tabor Figures		8¼	1 0 0	
312	No name				
313	Pair of Sitting Figures		5¾	2 2 0	3 3 0
314	,, ,,				
315	Set of four Seasons, Sitting		7		
316	Pair, Sailor and his Lass	1st		1 16 0	
	,, ,,	2nd			
	,, ,,	3rd			
317	,, Dancing Figures			0 18 0	
318	,, ,, ,,			0 14 0	
319 to 321	Three Figures, names not given				
322	Pair, Hen and Chicken Candlesticks		6¼	1 1 0	
323	,, Cupid and Flora ,,		8¾	2 2 0	
324	No name				
325	Set of four Elements		8¾	2 2 0	
326	Pair of Singers	1st			
	,, ,,	2nd			
	,, ,,	3rd			
	,, ,,	4th	5¾		
327 to 330	Four Figures, names not given				
331	Pair of Candlesticks with Bird and Dog		11¼	3 3 0	
332	Set of the four Quarters of the Globe	1st			
	,, ,,	2nd			
	,, ,,	3rd		1 16 0	
333	Group of four Boys			1 11 6	2 2 0
334	,, ,,			1 11 6	2 2 0
335 to 359	Twenty-five – Described as "Spangler's and Coffee's Figures and Groups," with no further particulars				

No	Names of Figures and Groups	Size	Height inches	Enamelled and Gilt £ s. d.	Biscuit £ s. d.
360	Johnny Wapstraw and Companion			1 16 0	
361	Pair, Gardener and Companion			1 16 0	2 2 0
362	,, Sitting Cat and Dog, William and Mary			1 10 0	
363	,, Figures, with dead Bird		8	1 5 0	
364	Group of Figures Waltzing		6½	1 1 0	
365	Pair of Dancing Figures			0 18 0	
366	Spanish Group			1 16 0	
367	No name				
368	Pair Dancing Figures			0 18 0	1 1 0
369	Shepherd and Shepherdess			1 16 0	2 2 0
370	Belisarius and Daughter, Spangler			1 16 0	
371	No name				
372	Sailor and Lass		7½	0 18 0	
373 to 377	Five Figures, names not given				
378	Pair, Scotchman and Lass, Coffee			1 16 0	
379 to 389	Eleven Figures, names not given. No. 384 is on a Statuette, probably of Lord Howe or Lord Hood, 12 inches in height; and 385 is on a Figure, probably of Hygeia, 10 inches				
390	Group of Gaultherus and Griselda			1 11 6	

The following are also in the List but are not numbered

	Enamelled and Gilt £ s. d.	Biscuit £ s. d.
Pointer and Setter, per pair, Coffee	0 7 0	
Large Pug Dogs ,, ,,	0 4 0	
Less ,, ,, ,,	0 3 0	
Small ,, ,, ,,	0 2 0	
Begging Pugs ,, Chelsea	0 2 0	
,, French Dogs ,, ,,	0 2 0	
Large Sheep and Lambs, per pair, Holmes	0 7 0	
Sheep lying down ,, ,,	0 4 0	
Standing Sheep ,, ,,	0 4 0	
,, ,, two smaller sizes ,,		
Lambs with Sprigs, per pair, Chelsea	0 2 0	
,, without ,, each ,,	0 0 10	
Canary Birds, each ,,	0 1 0	
Tomtit ,, ,,	0 1 0	
Linnet ,, ,,	0 1 0	
Birds on Branches, two sizes ,,		

THE FOLLOWING ARE FROM BOW AND CHELSEA MODELS

	Enamelled and Gilt £ s. d.	Biscuit £ s. d.
Large Stags, per pair	0 15 0	
,, two smaller sizes		
Large Sitting Cat		
Cat lying down	0 0 6	
,, with gold collar	0 1 0	
Cow and Calf, per pair	0 6 6	0 9 0
,, ,, lying down		
Large Swan	0 1 3	
Two smaller sizes of same, 1/- & /10 each		
Large Squirrel	0 1 3	
Two smaller sizes of same, 1/- & /10 each		
Large Boy – Four other sizes of the same were made, prices respectively 1/9, 1/6, 1/3, 1/-, & /10 each. This is a naked boy, standing with basket of flowers, usually white and gold		
Satyrs' Heads, each	0 7 0	
Small Neptune's Heads	0 6 0	
Large Duck Boats, gold dontil edges	0 3 0	
Small ,, ,,	0 2 0	
Trouts' Heads, with mottoes – "Angler's Delight," &c.	0 6 0	
,, two smaller sizes, 5/- & 3/6 each		

12
A pair of fruit- and flower-seller
candlesticks. Note the increasing use of
bocage or flower bush backgrounds for
figures destined for mantlepiece use.
Patch marks, no factory mark. William
Duesbury & Co. 1765. 29.5 cm. *Royal
Crown Derby Museum.*

13
Group known as 'Isabella, Gallant &
Jester', taken from the 'Commedia
dell'Arte' series. An earlier version of
this figure appears in black and white
plate 30. This figure was loaned to the
Nottingham Castle 'Clowning'
exhibition and was featured number 77
in the catalogue (1977). Patch marks.
William Duesbury & Co. 1765. 30 cm.
Royal Crown Derby Museum.

14

Butter tub of cylindrical shape, with upright handles and cover with foliate finial, all decorated with strong underglaze blue cornflowers and flies, with a cobweb-style border; the stand en suite. No mark. William Duesbury & Co. c. 1765–70. Tub 10.7 cm., stand diameter 15.5 cm. *Gilbert Bradley Collection.*

Names of Figures and Groups	Size	Height inches	Enamelled and Gilt			Biscuit		
			£	s.	d.	£	s.	d.
Hares' Heads, each			0	7	0			
Foxes' ,, ,,			0	4	6			
,, two other sizes 4/– & 3/6 each								
Mice, each			0	1	6	0	1	6
Poodle Dogs and Fleecy Sheep, each						0	5	0
Lowing Cow, each			0	5	0			
Sitting Foxes, per pair			0	7	0			
Pointers' Heads, each			0	7	0			
Tulip Egg Cups, each			0	4	0			
Inkstands, on Cats, &c., each			0	18	0			
Large Panthers								
Small ,, per pair			0	3	0			
Large Duck Boats, & several smaller ,,								
Pigeon Boats			0	12	0			
Set of five Senses			2	12	6			
Foxes, per pair			0	10	6			
Small Turks, each			0	2	6			
Basket Boys, enamelled and gilt, pair			0	5	0			
Set of Season Busts			0	14	0			
Cupids grinding, from the Element group			0	5	3			
Dogs from the Dresden Shepherd, each			0	1	0			
London Pointer and Greyhound, each			0	1	6			
Season Vases, each						0	7	0
Vases, Common Festoons						0	12	0
Vases, Best Festoons						1	11	6
Fountain Vase, on Pedestal						5	5	0
Cupid Sleeping, on Pedestal, from Spangler's Group						0	10	6

THE FOLLOWING MODELLED BY EDWARD KEYS

Names of Figures and Groups	Size	Height inches	Enamelled and Gilt			Biscuit		
Paris Cries, Set of six Figures			1	4	0	1	16	0
Archers, per pair			1	16	0			
Large Elephant, with Driver			0	10	6			
,, ,, with cloths, no Driver			0	9	0			
Peacock			0	2	0	0	3	6
Large Napoleon								
Small Napoleon			0	3	0			
Lean Cows, per pair			0	3	6			
Small Elephant			0	1	6			
Key's Fancy Figures, per pair			0	9	0			

15

Pair of Chelsea-Derby card bottles and covers, the central panels depicting the King and Queen of Clubs filled in with gold. The colourings are typical of this period. No mark. William Duesbury & Co. c. 1775. 24.2 cm. *Mary Field Collection.*

Names of Figures and Groups	Size	Height inches	Enamelled and Gilt			Biscuit		
			£	s.	d.	£	s.	d.
New Sitting Pugs, on Cushions			0	1	6			
Small Sitting Foxes			0	1	6			
Tragedy and Comedy			1	4	0			
Bust of Nelson			0	5	0			
Vicars, Curates and Wardens, each			0	6	0			
Large Monkey Musicians, each			0	7	6			
Small ,, ,,			0	5	0			
Dusty Bob and African Sall, each			0	4	0			
Doctor Syntax Walking	5		0	7	6			
,, in Green Room			0	7	6			
,, at York			0	7	6			
,, at Booksellers			0	7	6			
,, Drawing			0	5	0			
,, Going to Bed			0	5	0			
,, Tied to a Tree			0	5	0			
,, Scolding the Landlady			0	5	0			
,, Playing the Violin			0	4	0			
,, Attacked by a Bull			0	9	0			
,, Crossing the Lake			0	7	6			
,, Mounted on Horseback			0	12	6			
,, Landing at Calais			0	7	6			
Doctor Syntax's Landlady, No. 8			0	3	6			
Grimaldi as Clown, Thomas Griffin			0	7	6			
Liston as Paul Pry, S. Keys			0	8	0			
,, as Mawworm, S. Keys			0	7	0			
Vestris in Buy a Broom			0	6	0			
Bucks and Does			0	4	0	0	7	0
Small Standing Sheep						0	7	0
Rabbits on Plinths			0	2	0			
,, without Plinths			0	1	6			
Large Horses			0	2	0			
Pony			0	1	6			
Set of Tyrolese Minstrels, each			0	7	0			
Canton Girls			0	7	6			
Liston as Domine Sampson, S. Keys			0	8	0			
Industrious Boy & Girl ,, per pair			0	15	0			
Cats on Cushions, large E. Keys each			0	2	0			
,, ,, small ,, ,,			0	1	6			
Lion and Lioness ,, ,,			0	2	0			
Worcester Mice ,, ,,			0	2	0			
New Poodle Dogs ,, ,,			0	2	0			
New Cats with prey ,, ,,			0	1	6			
Billy Waters, the Black Fiddler ,, ,,			0	4	0			
Small Fruit Basket ,,			0	2	0			
Sheep in Fold ,,			0	4	0			
Pair of Topers Douglas Fox ,,			0	5	0			

A number of other Figures were published which are not entered in this list, the keeping of the list probably having ceased at the time they were modelled. Thus Louis Bradley modelled two Dancing Figures, and John Whitaker, between 1830 and 1847, among others modelled the following:

An Eastern Lady	Boy with Greyhound
Guitar Player	Girl with Falcon
Child in Arm Chair	Bust of Queen Victoria
Virgin Mary	,, of Duke of Wellington
An Angel	Group of Stags
Boy and Dog	,, of Dogs
Girl and Dog	Leaping Stag
Sleeping Nymph	Peacock among Flowers
Mazeppa on Wild Horse	Parrot

54

A pair of negro figures, the male holding a sheath of arrows and the female an apple. Patch marks. William Duesbury & Co. *c.* 1765. Approx. 30.5 cm. *Herbert Allen Collection. Victoria & Albert Museum: C193 – 1935; C193A – 1935.*

55 ▷

A fine jug painted with birds in the typically sombre naturalistic colourings of birds of the period. William Duesbury & Co. *c.* 1765. 19 cm. *Victoria & Albert Museum.*

57 ▷ ▷

A finely modelled taper-stick with loop handle, the figure supporting the candle sconce above his head. Patch marks. William Duesbury & Co. *c.* 1765. Approx. 15 cm. *Formerly in the John Twitchett Collection.*

58 ▷

A figure of Harlequin. Patch marks. William Duesbury & Co. *c.* 1765. Approx. 15.2 cm. *Ashworth Collection.*

59 ▷ ▷

Figure representing Britannia which has no marks but has been ground down to stand freely. The national flag is not visible at this angle, but is in fact on the opposite side to the lion. No marks. William Duesbury & Co. 1760. 35.4 cm. *Victoria & Albert Museum, C766 – 1926.*

60 ▷

Pair of figures modelled as shepherd and shepherdess. It is interesting to note that the gold anchor Chelsea period was influencing Derby before the merger, with more colourful decoration being added to the figures. Patch marks. William Duesbury & Co. 1765–70. Approx. 14 cm. *David John Ceramics, Woodstock.*

56

A fine set of 'Seasons' taken from the original Meissen set modelled by Eberlein. Patch marks. William Duesbury & Co. *c.* 1765. Approx. 26.7 cm. *Sotheby's, New Bond Street.*

61
Pair of figures representing a sailor and lass; he carries a stick and three gold coins in the palm of his left hand, whilst she coyly beckons him. Both stand on scrolling pierced bases, picked out with pink enamel and gilding. No marks. Later versions, i.e. after 1770, may bear a number 316 listed in the Haslem list as 'Pair, Sailor and his Lass' (see black and white plate 69). William Duesbury & Co. 1765. 24.6 cm and 24.1 cm. *Formerly in the possession of the late Sir Terence Rattigan. Photograph by courtesy of Sotheby's, New Bond Street.*

62
A pair of children representing 'Liberty' and 'Matrimony' with their double sconces and robust scrolling bases. Patch marks, no factory mark. William Duesbury & Co. 1765–70. 28 cm. *Royal Crown Derby Museum.*

A LIST OF MOULDS AND MODELS

1	A boy, 2 sizes
3	Elements, 3 sizes
3	Tryangular trypod
5	Set of Antique Seasons
7	Gardeners, 2 sizes
7	A vase, antique
8	Pair siting fruit and flower figures
8, 9	Pair Laying Goats
9	French horn and cymbal, 3 sizes, single figures
10	,, ,, 2 ,, ,,
11	Pair of new lace figures – Spangler
11	Cupid Candlesticks
12	Fountain group
13	Pair of boys, each on a goat
14	Two sacrafice figures, 3 sizes
15	Small dancing figures, group
16	Large old Jupiter and Juno
17	A group, two figures
17	A vase
19	Large fountain vase
20	Fruit and flower figures, 4 sizes
20	Vase – octagon
21	David Garrick, Esqre., 2 sizes
23	Fragments of the Royal family
32	Fisherman and woman
35	Four Seasons
37	Large group, Jason and Midia
38	Pair, Prudence and discression
39	Two Figures
39	Group, Arts and Scyances
40	,,
41	,,
42	Group, Arts and Scyances
43	,,
44	,,
45	,,
46	Small groups, 2 figs. dancing
47	Group, 4 Seasons
48	Four antique seasons, group
49	Pair grotesque cat and dog figures
50	Pair small figures, Sportsman and companion
51	Small cat and dog figures
54	New Justice
55	Dresden shepherd, 1st size, 2 figures, 3 sizes
56	Pair of Garland shepherds, 4 sizes
56	Eight small vases
57	French shepherds, 6 sizes
58	Two pair piping shepherd and companion
59	Five sences, small
60	Singers, 3 sizes
61	Pair Spring figures, 2 sizes
61	Group, Arts and Scyances
62	Welch taylors, 2 sizes
63	Turks, 3 sizes
64	Set of small seasons, 3 sizes
65	Dyanna, 2 sizes
66	Venus
66	A Trypod Vase
67	Small ewer
67	Small Term Vase
68	Group of 4 musical figures
69	Grotesque seasons, small
71	Boy and girl sitting in chair
71	A vase
73	Small group, boy and girl
74	Dancing group
76	French flower pots, 2 sizes
76	Large Group
77	Stocking mender
78	Shoemaker
80	Large oval vases, 2 sizes
81	Shoeblack
82	Fury group, 2 figures
84	Hairdresser

85	Macaroni
86	Pair boy and girl siting on basket
86	Four element groups, 2 figures each
86	Large Term vase
90	Cook and companion
91	Macaroni
92	Fencer
92	Small ewer, 2 sizes
93	Children group
95	Sphinks and griffin candlesticks, 3 sizes
97	Vase, supported by 3 griffins
98	Hydra
98	Small ewer
99	Esculapius and companion
99	Small ewer
100	Large figure of Andromache weeping over the ashes of Hector, 2 sizes
101	Pair small figures
104	Six small vases
109	Dominican
111	A Father Confessor
114	Mars
114	Season vases
114	Group of 4 small musical figures
115	Venus
116	Apollo
117	Jupiter
118	Neptune
119	Juno
120	Dianna
121	Minerva
122	Time
123	Four French Seasons, 4 sizes
123	Vase by Spangler
124	Vase by Spangler
125	Large Chelsea Seasons, 4 sizes
126	John Wilkes, Esqre
126	Vase by Spangler
128	Oval Vase
129	Vase
130	Vase by Spangler, 3 sizes
131	,, ,, large
137	Pair figures, Madonna and prudent mother.
138	,,
139	Two groups, boy and girl, two in each
141	Pair small seasons, boy and girl
141	Fencing boy
142	Swan and dolphin, 4 sizes
143	,, ,,
161	Four figures, Wisdome, Justice, Peace, and Plenty
162	Wisdome and Justice, 2 sizes
176	Hydra
177	Ditto
178	Macaroni
179	Four small musical figures
182	Four boys riding on goat and panther
183	Boy and girl, Cupid and Discression
184	Small boy and girl
185	Swan and dolphin
192	Neptune
193	Baccus and Areadney, 2 sizes
194	,, large
195	A group Virgins awaking Cupid
196	Two Virgins adorning Pan
198	Haymaker and companion
199	Harlequin and Colombine
200	Four quarters, 2 sizes
201	2 pair small Cupids
202	,,
204	Pair small gardeners
205	Pair small Cupids
206	Pair small Cupids
211	Fame and Mercury standing on a globe

63
A pair of birds in branches adapted as candlesticks, which indicate the useful adaptation of figure subjects which were originally intended for ornamental purposes only. Patch marks, no factory mark. William Duesbury & Co. 1765. 23.9 cm. *Royal Crown Derby Museum.*

65 ▷
A pair of figures, known as 'Ranelagh Dancers', the young man holding a letter in his left hand and the lady flowers in her hand. The name is taken from the Ranelagh Gardens in Vauxhall. William Duesbury & Co. *c.* 1765. Approx. 20 cm. *Christie, Manson & Woods.*

67 ▷ ▷
An early figure of Shakespeare after the Scheemaker figure in Poets' Corner in Westminster Abbey. William Duesbury & Co. *c.* 1760. Approx. 23 cm. *Christie, Manson & Woods.*

64
Group depicting a youth playing a hurdy-gurdy, whilst the girl teaches a dog, dressed as Harlequin, to dance on a pedestal. Taken from a composition by Carlo Vanloo. Patch marks. William Duesbury & Co. 1765–70. 28 cm. *Schreiber Collection. Victoria & Albert Museum, 414/178 – 1885.*

66
A fine figure of James Quinn in the role of Falstaff. Patch marks. William Duesbury & Co. 1765–70. 13.4 cm. *Royal Crown Derby Museum.*

68 ▷ ▷
A pair of birds modelled on tree-stump supports. Patch marks. William Duesbury & Co. 1765. Approx. 12 cm. *Victoria & Albert Museum, 414/229 and 414/229A – 1885.*

69
A pair of pug dogs. William Duesbury & Co. 1765–70. Approx. 6.5 cm. *Sotheby's, New Bond Street.*

70
Pair of classical figures on chariots raised above simulated waves, representing Juno and Jupiter. William Duesbury & Co. *c.* 1765. Approx. 26.7 cm and 28 cm. *Sotheby's, New Bond Street.*

71
Fine pair of stag and doe with bocage. Patch marks. William Duesbury & Co. 1765–70. Approx. 14 cm. *Sotheby's, New Bond Street.*

213 Pair of small figures, Dog and Falcon
214 ,, ,,
215 Four small seasons
216 Music and Poetry
217 Music and Poetry, 3 sizes
219 Pair basket figures
220 ,,
222 Hercules
227 Pair Grotesque punches
231 Figure of a nun, large
234 Group of 4 Cupids
235 Three virgins distressing Cupid, 3 sizes
240 Group, two figures
241 Large fountain group, 4 quarters, 3 sizes
244 Figure of Plenty
245 ,,
246 Pair small figures
248 A group of antique seasons
250 Two small Elements
251 Group of 4 Cupids
252 Group of 3 Cupids
253 Pair small Cupids, dog and birdcage
254 Large group
255 Pastoral group
256 ,,
257 Group of four boys
257 Group of 4 Cupids
259 A large Britannia, 2 sizes
259 Five Small elements
260 Crying boy and laughing girl, 2 sizes
261 Peace and Plenty, 2 sizes
261 Pair large Cupids, Dove and Key
280 Two chandileer figures
281 Two Spring candlesticks, boy and girl
283 Gardener candlesticks
284 Pair Bagpiper candlesticks
288 Pair Mars and Venus
289 Large old Dianna
291 Falstaff, 5 sizes
293 Tyth pig group
294 Two seasons group
295 Group, 4 quarters, large
296 Pair of haymakers
297 Shakespeare and Milton
298 Large figure of Minerva
299 Small Neptune without rock
299 Large Neptunes, 2 sizes
301 Pair single Bagpipers, 3 sizes
302 Fame and Mercury, 2 sizes
303 Old pipe and tabor, 3 sizes
304 Pair pheasant figures
305 Milton
306 Large sitting Cupid
310 Old justices, 4 sizes
311 Pair pipe and triangle figures, 2 sizes
314 Two pair of Dresden figures
316 Saylor and lass
320 Four coronation figures
333 Group, 4 musical boys
334 Pastoral Group, 4 boys
335 Group, 4 boys
351 Four quarters of the day
352 ,,
353 ,,
354 Pair figures
358 Large Venus and Cupid
359 Gardener and companion
360 Shepherd and shepherdess
361 Pair figures Fruit and flowers
362 Boy and companion with birds' nest
363 Two pair female figures with dead bird (Spangler)
364 Small group, two figures
365 Pair small figs. Symbols and pipe
366 Paliman and Lavinia
366 Large Venus and Cupid
367 Bugbear and companion
368 Pair Tryangle and tamborene figures
369 Pair Shepherd and shepherdess playing on fluit
370 2 figs. Group, blind beggar and daughter
371 Pair small figures, Spangler
372 Saylor and lass
373 Figure of Spangler
374 Large Britannia
375 Pompey's poems
375 Group 3 Virgins distressing Cupid
376 Large fountain group
381 Pair figures, Spangler
382 Pair of figures
383 Farming figures
384 Lord Howe
385 Farmer figure
387 Large group, 4 figures, Russian shepherd
389 Pair of figures
390 Pair of single figures
391 Duke of York
392 Pair of large figures
392 A figure
393 Russian shepherd and shepherdess
395 Shepherd and shepherdess
396 ,,
397 Venus and boy, large

Five figures of Time
The Hunting group
Jason and Midia, 2 sizes
Group, boy and girl peep show
,, 4 figures, musical
Group, 4 quarters, with obalisk, 2 sizes
Two groups, 2 elements
Fluting shepherd with shepherdess
Large chandelier figures, etc
,, different figures
Group, Seasons, broken
Pair small figures (wax) damaged
Small Fame and Mercury, square plinth
Hydra group, obalisk
,, ,,
Group, French horn and Cymbal
Small pastoral group, 3 sizes
Standing Chelsea seasons, 3 sizes
French shepherdess, 6 sizes
Pair figures, Tragedy – Comedy
Four grotesque seasons
Pair Spanish dancers
,, cat and dog figures, siting
,, fruit and flower figures, siting
,, grotesque cat and dog
,, Spanish dancers
Odments of Neptune figure
Cow cream ewer
Our Saviour on the cross, 4 sizes
Old pheasant and companion, 3 sizes
Two pair swan and dolphin figures
Crying boy and laughing girl, 2 sizes
Old sporting figures, 3 sizes
A Garrick, 2nd size
Pipe and tabor figures, 2 sizes
Cupids, with dove and key, 6 sizes
Pair dessert gardeners
Pair small sacrifice figures
Cook and companion
Pair old Chelsea basket figures, 2 sizes
Pair cat and dog figures
Spring candlesticks
Four siting boy seasons
Two boy candlesticks
Old singers, 4 sizes
Piping shepherd
Four siting boy seasons, as above
Bag Piper candlesticks
Four siting seasons
Dianna, 2 sizes
New ,,
Pair pheasant figure candlesticks
Dianna, largest size
Pair grotesque boy and girl
Four large siting french seasons
Four smaller french seasons (different)
Spanish shepherds, 4 sizes (1st size 2 figures)
Britania and Minerva, 3 sizes
Europa and Lydia, 4 sizes
One pair Cupids and Discression
Farmer and companion
Pair fox candlesticks
Pheasant ,,
Two shepherd chandeleirs

72
Pair of squirrels in colour. Patch marks.
William Duesbury & Co. 1765–70.
Approx. 9 cm. *Victoria & Albert
Museum, C371 and C371A – 1902.*

73
'Europa and the Bull' decorated in
colours. Patch marks. William
Duesbury & Co. 1765. 27.9 cm. *Victoria
& Albert Museum, C306 – 1940.*

Pair Cupid candlesticks
Cock candlestick
Pair piping shepherd candlesticks
Pair dessert gardener   ,,
A fox and hern   ,,
Pair large pipe and tabor figures
Pair large sporting figures, with branch behind
Mars and Venus candlesticks, 1 pair
Pair large siting bagpipes, round pedestals
Pair dancing baboons
Pair small harlequin and colombine
Figure of Christ
Pair old shepherds
Pair old singer candlesticks
Set large seasons, old
Pair Spanish shepherd candlesticks
Pair Spanish shepherds, 4 sizes
Pair pipe and guitar, large
Pair piping shepherds and companion
Pair bagpipers and companion
Large haymaker and companion
Pair singer candlesticks
Pair siting figures, with basket
Oval inkstand, embossed roses
Two ditto, plain
Five heads – Bacus, Satyr
Two foxes heads, 2 sizes
Three pillar candlesticks
One small trouts drinking cup
One large sized pidgeon
One small   ,,
Duck boats, four pairs
Four quarters of the day
Piping shepherd and companion
Cupid and Venus, wants the plinth
Small gardener and companion
Saylor and lass, 2 sizes
Old justices, 4 sizes
Redstart candlesticks
Five sences
Old gardener candlestick
Six old Chelsea figures, not complete
Old Spanish dancers, large size
Pair Spanish figures
Birdcatcher boy and girl
Pair large pipe and guitar
Pair siting figure candlesticks, old
Pair Spanish shepherds, small
Small boy and girl
Two old figures, with a shield
Pair old shepherd figures – man without a head
Pair grotesque boy and girl (Chelsea)
Pair Spanish candlesticks
Pair standing sheep, with sprigs
Pair laying sheep, with sprigs
Pair laying cats, 2 sizes
Pair large siting cats
Pair laying sheep, without sprigs, 2 sizes
Pair standing sheep and lambs, 2 sizes
Six small Cupids riding triumphant
Pair large pug dogs, 3 sizes
Pair lambs, with sprigs
Pair lambs, without sprigs
Pair standing cows, with calf
Pair canaries
Pair large tygers, 2 sizes
Pair bucks and does, 2 sizes
Pair greyhounds, with ground pedestal
Pair laying cows, small
            ,,   larger
Pair large stags
Pair large tomtits
Pair smaller   ,,
Pair redstarts
Redstart candlestick, small
Pair thrushes
        ,,   smaller
Pair woodpeckers
Pair large woodpeckers
Rose soap boxes, 2 sizes
Squirrels, 3 sizes
Swans, 3 sizes
Seventeen loves, disguised (Chelsea)
Fifty smelling bottle figures (Chelsea)

Five small busts from Chelsea, 2 inches high
Boy, 3 sizes
Two pair basket boys
Eight thimbles
One hundred seal trinkets
Thirteen heads for noding figures
Two egg bell pulls
Four rouge pots
Six small-sized loves, disguised
Four tobacco stopers
Two pair small figures, 2 inches high
Ten partridges, for sauce boats
Cock grouse
Nineteen middle-sized busts
Two busts, laughing and crying philosopher
Two duck vases
Fourteen Chelsea wax casts
Admiral Rodney
Shakspeare
Milton
A Turk and companion
Four seasons, large, by Bacon
Group, two figures, pastoral
A nun
Cupid and Flora
Four large quarters
Four less   ,,
        ,,   ,,
        ,,   ,,
        ,,   ,,
        ,,   ,,
        ,,   ,,
        ,,   ,,
A girl crying over a dead bird
Pair small groups
Five smelling bottles
Figure of King Charles, and pedestal
Trypod vase, goat's legs
Five paper weights, sphinxs, etc
Nine small vases
A vase, small
The Margravin of Heanspoch, vase, 4 sizes
Large term vase, in wood
Middle-size vase
Small save-shaped (Sèvres-shaped) vase
Tall save (Sèvres) vase
Fisherman, figure
Pair figures, with branch
Female figure, with casket
Three figures, various
Two small ,,
Nine figures, various
Pair figures, fiddlers
Figure, with a dish
Pair small figures
Tinker and companion
Small figure, in lead
        ,,   in wax
Female figure, on earth pedestal
Two figures
Thirty-four figures, various
Two figures, terra-cotta. Inosence and Hebe
One pair cows and calves, standing
Bucks and does, 2 sizes
Large stags
    ,,   laying cats, 2 sizes
Dancing french dogs
Laying cows
Small woodpeckers
Canary birds
Proud taylors
Thrushes
Small foxes
Large swans, 3 sizes
Standing sheep, with lambs
Lambs, with sprigs
    ,,   without sprigs
Laying sheep
A Minerva and Britannia
Six tobacco stopples
Innosence and Hebe, very large
Two Saters heads
Two Neptunes
Two foxes

74
'The Tithe Pig' group represents a farmer's wife offering her child to the clergyman in lieu of the pig which her husband holds. This group provides a glimpse of the social history of the period. William Duesbury & Co. *c.* 1765–70. 16.5 cm. *Victoria & Albert Museum.*

75
Figure of a fisher boy, and a larger figure of a seated piper with an incised number 301, which in Haslem's list is called 'Pair Sitting, Pipe and Guitar'. This figure also has the incised mark said to be that of Isaac Farnsworth. In chapter 12 this piece was part of the report made by Dr Hedges of Oxford University. William Duesbury & Co. 1770–75. Piper 17.5 cm, fisher boy 12.7 cm. *Joan Neat Collection.*

76
A fine figure of Milton decorated in colours. William Duesbury & Co. 1765–70. Approx. 23 cm. *Sotheby's, New Bond Street.*

77
A pair of Derby blue-tits flanking a bust of George IV supported on a pedestal. Birds: patch marks. William Duesbury & Co. *c.* 1765. Approx. 12 cm. Bust (formerly in the possession of Princess Marie-Louise): marks and size not known, possibly modelled by Edward Keys. Bloor Derby. *c.* 1830 *Sotheby's, New Bond Street.*

Two trouts
Thirty different pedestals
Eighteen squirrels, 3 sizes
Some Catarine (made for a man named Catharine)
    moulds
Pair dancing figures
Pair Spanish dancers
Large figure of Time
Figure of Time, 2 sizes
Six small tritons
Cupid asleep
A Carmalite
Old basket boy
Pair boy candlesticks
Pair Cupid candlesticks
Cupid shuteing at a heart
Nine small muses and Apollo
Thirty confectioner Cupids
Small loves, disguised
Seventeen loves, disguised
Bybles and condr
Lot oddments
Four Chelsea boys
Thirteen small dessert figures
Spining-wheel figures
Complimenting figures
Fury figures
       ,,
Magic lanthorn figures
French group
A group, two figures
Seven old religious figures
Two busts, Voltaire and another
Crying and laughing philosopher
Four season busts, large
      ,,   smaller
Our Saviour on the cross, 3 sizes
Standing figure of our Saviour
Pair small harlequins and colombine
Europa and Lydia, large
Figure, Piolla
French seasons
Europa and Lydia
Four large siting seasons
Pair Dresden figures
Tragidy and Comedy
A boy coming down a tree to crown
    a figure with a garland, and small bust,
    with pedestal
Boy and girl
Pair fox candlesticks
Large chandilier candlesticks, pair
Large Bagpiper   ,,

Shepherd and shepherdess candlesticks, pair
New candlesticks, pair
Redstart   ,,
New shepherd candlesticks, pair
Pair religious figures
Pair draggon candlesticks
Ten old ducks and swans for confectoners
Small dessert figures
Dessert gardeners figures
Three ditto smaller
Pair twilight candlesticks
Four seasons
Figure of Pitt
Venus and Adonis
Two river gods
Set old quarters, 2 sizes
Six small sheep
French siting seasons
Bacchus in a car
Fox and hearn candlesticks
Pair old singers
Pair Dresden cat and dog figures
Siting boy and cage, incomplete
Four shells
Baccus bung for punch barrel
Pair laying goats
Old term vase
Tryangular trypod
Six pillar candlesticks
A trypod
Lot smelling bottles (twenty)
Large trout
Two oval Chelsea baskets
Eight small vases
Four sphinx paper weights
Dresden shepherds, pair
Redstart candlesticks
Four quarters
Pair Dresden shepherds
Set new standing french seasons
Spoartsmen, one pair
Four small gardeners
Cock candlestick
Pheasant figures
Spanish candlesticks
Spanish shepherds
Pipe and tabor
Large haymakers
Old lamb inkstand
Pair sporting candlesticks
Old beker
Thirty vases, different one with another
Three hundred trinkets and seals

4

The Old Derby
Pattern Books

Note by J. Twitchett

Betty Clark's magnificent achievement in describing the patterns has performed a great service to all students of Derby porcelain, for until now no one has had the courage to tackle this subject as a whole. Haslem discussed the books but commented on only a small proportion of the patterns; Bemrose, Hurlbutit, and Barrett and Thorpe largely ignored them; Gilhespy discussed a good deal more; but this is the first time that they have been described in full. Pattern books and shapes are essential in any china works, and in the study of its products.

The point made by Barrett and Thorpe in their two-page commentary on the pattern books, that the remarks written against the patterns are merely opinions, must be taken up, since it is quite without foundation. Their other comment about it possibly having been a later effort to bring together a mass of scattered drawings is equally groundless. In fact a group of patterns existed which were numbered and were obviously remnants of an earlier pattern book. The reader may study Lygo's letters which form an Appendix to this book, where reference is often made to the pattern books of 1786: for example, 'Mr Elliot, tea-pattern 69'.

It seems certain that pattern books were prepared not only so that the painters could have access to them and be given instructions, but so that visitors to the London showrooms might see the full range of wares and decoration. There are obvious dangers in accepting all named patterns as being by a single named painter, for in a large service other painters would quite possibly assist. Indeed, the author has noticed that pattern 178, which is ascribed 'Landskip near Critch by Boreman', was painted in a composite service by several hands, including John Brewer, Jockey Hill and George Robertson. It is therefore important to check the dates of the painter's period at the factory, and in this particular case Boreman's stay was from 1779 to 1795. Certainly, these documented patterns must not be ignored, as they provide a fine guide for attribution, but actual attributions should be made upon stylistic grounds only. In conclusion one should mention Complin, whose name first appears in the Plate Book (pattern 136). Since it was in 1789 that Complin came to Derby, it may reasonably be assumed that pattern 136 dates from about then.

These surviving patterns would appear to date from the early 1780s and would have been completed by about 1805. Their origins and interpretations were discussed by the author and Henry Sandon in *The Collector's Guide*, September 1971, and yield further information on the pattern books.

The Pattern Books, by Betty Clark

In my attempt to describe the designs in the pattern books of the Derby Factory in the late eighteenth century I have, wherever possible, made use of the text and of the descriptive terms which were in current use in the Duesbury period. Where no text was available to me, I have deliberately avoided an esoteric approach and the use of saleroom terminology, and have instead tried to provide an instant visual picture of the design in the belief that no reference material should require the aid of a dictionary to elucidate its meaning and intent. The reader will, however, find on page 311 a short Glossary of ceramic terminology to assist with identification, and this includes many of the descriptive terms used in the pattern books.

It should be mentioned that the patterns do not always appear in chronological order, and in their numerical sequence produce anomalies and anachronisms which can be confusing, in that no pattern number was inserted before 1782 when the crossed batons were added to the crown and 'D' mark – usually in puce.[1] Pattern no. 1 in the Tea Book always appears to be marked and numbered in this way, but much later patterns, for example no. 29 in the Tea Book, may be found with the crown and 'D' in puce without a number. Other early patterns may carry the Chelsea Derby mark in gold or the blue mark crown and 'D', in which case no pattern number is likely to be found. In the case of the higher numbers in the Tea Book (700 series), the mark may be found in red, usually carefully drawn with the crown surmounted by jewels and the pattern number immediately beneath. In order to concentrate on the design I have omitted from the description of patterns the frequent reference to the rate of payments for gilders given in the pattern books themselves.

Where it is found that two 'Landskips' and/or classical subjects are mentioned against one pattern, it is safe to assume that the article is one of a pair and one subject would appear on each item, not two on the one item as appears at first glance.

Each piece of hollow-ware has been described as it appears in the sketch, but as the patterns will be found on items of varying shapes and sizes, this sometimes produces slight variations. Designs can also vary when painted by different hands, but seldom enough to cast doubt on their authenticity.

It will be seen that although some of the patterns are missing from the books, examples have been located and described. It is hoped that over the years other 'missing' patterns will come to light, but as it is not unheard of for a workman to have appended the wrong number to a design, this particular treasure hunt can hold many pitfalls for the unwary.

The Plate Book records nearly four hundred patterns and has presented almost as many problems. The sketches represent only a section of the plate – rather like a slice of cake – and it has not always been easy to assess the size of the slice or in fact whether the rest of the cake carried the same design. Ground colours, unless written into the text, are somewhat doubtfully described, for most of them have faded to a pale khaki colour and distinguishing 'fawn' from 'bloom' has been virtually impossible. The Plate Book is, however, helpful in that it provides some clues about probable dates when patterns were put into production: for example, work by Hill is unlikely to appear before 1794, and there is mention of 'Peg' which brings us to 1796 or slightly later, when this artist replaced Billingsley as the principal flower painter. Once again, missing patterns have been filled in from examples in private collections, and now that it has been established that a pattern need not necessarily be marked in puce to be 'right', it is hoped that many gaps in the pattern books and in our knowledge of the factory's production may be filled.

I end on a note of apology to the artist-workmen of Duesbury's china factory. My descriptions fail abysmally to give any real visual concept of the beauty of their creations. I hope – for their sakes – that the many illustrations will compensate for my inadequacy in this respect. I have deliberately retained the original quaintnesses of spelling.

These plates illustrate two typical sheets from the Old Derby Pattern Books, showing plate pattern numbers 138–142, and tea pattern (cups) numbers 207–214. *The Worcester Royal Porcelain Co. Ltd.*

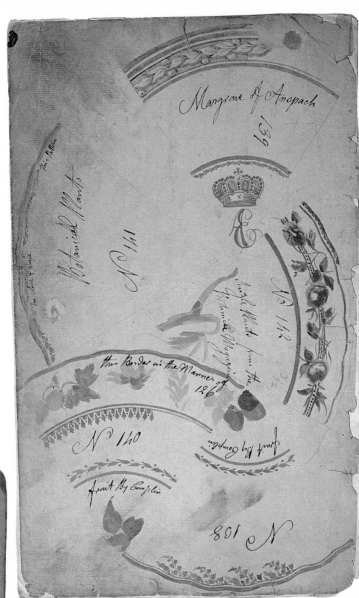

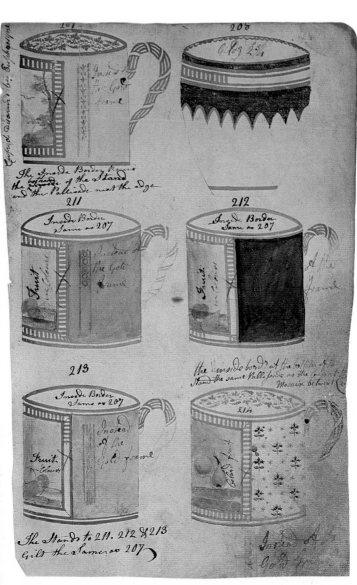

16
A fine biscuit group of two lovers. This group is called 'La Bergère des Alpes' and is inspired by the Sèvres model by Etienne Falconet. This figure is analysed by Dr Robert Hedges in chapter 12. Patch marks, no factory mark, incised number 256. William Duesbury & Co. 1775. 27 cm. *Royal Crown Derby Museum.*

Tea Book I

1 Shown as tall tea bowl. Dentil edge in gilt to inner and outer rims.
2 Tall tea bowl. Gilt dentil rims. Slight gilt sprays over remainder of body. (No sketch in pattern book – described from marked and numbered item in Betty Clark's collection.)
3 Shown as tall tea bowl. Gilt dentil rims. No pattern inserted.
4 As 3.
5 Tall tea bowl. Gilt dentil rim. Borders of flowers in natural colours beneath.
6 Tall tea bowl. Gilt dentil rims. No pattern inserted.
7 Shown as shallow tea bowl. Gilt dentil rims. Pendant swags of flower sprays in natural colours suspended from gilt rings.
8 Similar to 7, but flowers in turquoise.
9 Shallow tea bowl. Gilt dentil rims. Below, a gilt line from which hang pendant swags of grey husks outlined in pink, between which are sprigs of small flowers painted in natural colours.
10 No sketch in pattern book. A creamer of sparrow-beak form in a private collection is marked in puce with a crown, 'D' and crossed batons with an 'X' inserted where one would normally expect to find the pattern number. It is possible that this is representative of the pattern, as it is painted very much in the Bristol manner with pendant swags of flowers including roses, tulips and daffodils in natural colours.
11 Shallow tea bowl. Illustrated in Haslem and usually follows the moulding of the cup shape. The Smith's blue border is overlaid with gilt, below which are wreaths of flowers between swags of pendant husks. A further, narrow blue border surmounts the sunflower moulding at the base of the cup or bowl, which is outlined in Smith's blue and gilt.
12 Shallow tea bowl. Gilt dentil inner rim. outer rim scalloped and decorated with plain green border with gilt edge to lower scallops. Plain green border at base from which sunburst gilding follows the line of each flute.
13 Shallow tea bowl. Gilt dentil edge to inner rim. Smith's blue border, decorated with gilt, has scalloped underside. Body decorated with sprays of flowers in natural colours.
14 Shallow tea bowl. Gilt dentil edges to inner and outer rims. Pink flower sprigs over body of cup. Pink line above foot rim.
15 Shallow tea bowl. Smith's blue border decorated with gilt. Blue line above foot rim with gilt enrichment.
16 Shallow tea bowl. Mid-blue line round outer rim of cup. Scattered sprays of flowers in monochrome blue over body.
17 Shallow tea bowl. Gilt rims. Single line of gilt beneath rim and above foot rim.
18 Shallow tea bowl. Mid-blue border, decorated with darker blue, from which are suspended pendant swags in same colour blue.
19 Shallow tea bowl. Dark blue border to rim with added gilt decoration. Blue enriched with gilt above foot rim.
20 Shallow tea bowl. Gilt dentil edge to outer rim, below which is a narrow dark blue border between two gilt lines, with continuous line of gilt dots beneath. Pattern usually found on acanthus-moulded flute shape, the leaf fronds being overpainted in dark blue and decorated in gilt.
21 Missing.
22 Missing.
23 Shallow cup with handle. Narrow border in rich blue decorated with gilt at rim and repeated half-way down cup. Moulded sunburst base overpainted in blue and gilt.
24 As 23, but with addition of pendant swags of grey husks between borders.
25 Missing.
26 Missing.
27 Shallow tea bowl. Gilt rims. Border of Chantilly sprigs between two gilt lines. Scattered sprigs over body. Gilt line to foot rim.
28 Shallow tea bowl. Gilt dentil edges to inner and outer rims. Simple arched border in green and black(?) with small pink flower in each arch.
29 Shallow tea bowl. Gilt dentil edge to inner rim. Border of blue scallops outlined in gilt and with tiny gilt tassels. Scattered sprays of flowers in natural colours on body of cup and a rose inside. Blue line with gilt enrichment above foot rim.
30 Shallow tea bowl. Narrow blue border with gilt dentil edge overlaid and gilt line beneath.
31 Shallow tea bowl. Smith's blue border to rim with slight gilt decoration below. Narrow gilt border on inner rim.
32 Shallow tea bowl. Dark blue croquet-hoop design extending from base to rim of cup following fluted moulding, with gilt spots forming background.
33 Shallow tea bowl. Narrow blue border with slight gilt leaf decoration to rim, below which are pendant gilt swags of husks suspended from gilt loops.
34 Shallow tea bowl. Deep border of Smith's blue decorated with gilt leaves and tiny white flowers. Gilt feathers beneath, extending to line above foot rim.
35 Tall tea cup. Narrow border of dark blue, below which is a deep border of dark blue finished with Vandyke edging and decorated with gilt. Gilt border on inner rim.
36 Tall tea bowl. Gilt dentil edge to outer rim. Dark blue border below with arched underside, each arch containing tiny gilt flower and added gilt enrichment. Design repeated above foot rim with arches inverted, but without gilt flower.
37 Shallow tea bowl. Gilt dentil edge to inner rim, gilt line on outer. Lilac border with darker-toned leaf motif to outer rim, below which are pendant swags in green suspended from gilt loops. Scattered single roses in natural colours over body of bowl.
38 Shallow tea bowl. Gilt dentil edge to inner rim. Narrow lilac-pink border, gilt line beneath with pendant swags of grey husks suspended from gilt loops.
39 Shallow tea bowl. Narrow band of lilac-pink and gilt band of equal width to inner and outer rims, below which are swags and roses as in 37.
40 Shallow tea bowl. Green and gilt bands to inner and outer rims with pendant swags of grey husks outlined in pink below outer borders.
41 Shown as fluted tea bowl with green borders to inner and outer rims and swags of husks in pink.
42 Tall tea bowl. Green border to outer rim with scalloped underside. Green border inside cup with gilt border below. Scattered sprays of roses in natural colours over body. Green border at base with scallops inverted.
43 Tall tea bowl. Gilt border to inside rim. Narrow blue border overlaid with gilt dentil edge to outer rim. Below, a deeper border of dark blue in Vandyke design overlaid by smaller gilt Vandyke border with four gilt dots placed vertically between each motif.
44 Shallow fluted tea bowl. Narrow gilt border to inside rim. Narrow blue border to outer rim decorated in gilt and overlaid with white dots, with continuous line of gilt dots beneath this border.
45 Shallow tea bowl. Gilt border to inside rim of *chat langue* form interspersed with gilt dots. Narrow dark blue border to outer rim overlaid with white dots between two gilt lines.
46 Shallow fluted tea bowl. Gilt border to inside rim. Narrow blue border to outer rim overlaid with gilt leaves and white dots. Continuous line of gilt dots beneath this border.
47 Shallow fluted tea bowl. Gilt border to inside rim. Narrow blue border on outer rim overlaid with gilt leaf decoration.
48 Shallow fluted tea bowl. Gilt border to inside rim. Simple gilt border of cinquefoil leaf motif to outer rim between two rows of gilt dots.
49 Shallow tea bowl. Gilt dentil edge. Narrow gilt borders to inner and outer rims.
50 Shallow tea bowl. Gilt border to inside rim. Gilt line to outer rim with lovers' knots at intervals from which are suspended swags of husks graduated in size.
51 Tall tea bowl. Gilt border to inside rim. Band of gilt to outer rim below which is a deep border of vertical ovals in a continuous line, each containing an eight-petalled flower contained within another oval, and with additional gilt decoration at the narrow ends of each oval.
52 Shallow tea bowl. Narrow gilt border to inside rim. Deep border of dark blue finished with Vandyke edge on outer rim with continuous line of gilt ovals overlaying each other, each oval containing three gilt dots. Beneath this border are gilt feathers to a line above the foot rim.
53 Shallow fluted tea bowl. Narrow border to inside rim. Gilt dentil edge on outer rim; below, a border of gilt ovals overlaying each other and each containing three gilt dots. This border is contained within two narrow and two broader gilt lines. A further gilt line round the middle of the cup is intertwined by simple leaf sprays.

54 Shallow fluted tea bowl. Very narrow Smith's blue border to outer rim with gold line beneath. Scattered sprigs in gilt over body of oval.

55 Shallow tea bowl. In all respects similar to 53, but ovals are placed horizontally, do not overlay each other, and each contains one gilt spot.

56 Tea cup with handle. Band of blue round outer rim. Sprays of blue flowers over body of cup. Handle outlined in blue.

57 Shallow tea bowl. Band of blue to outer rim. Below, a line of blue decorated with intertwining leaf sprays. Sprig pattern on body – all in blue.

58 Shallow fluted tea bowl. Narrow gilt border to inner rim. Gilt dentil edge to outer rim, below which is a gilt line with intertwining leaf motif. Gilt line beneath this border.

59 Shallow tea bowl. Gilt border to inner rim. Narrow border of dark blue between two gilt lines on outer rim, overlaid with ovals placed horizontally in a continuous line, each containing gilt spot in centre. Further border below of single gold line with intertwining leaf motif.

60 Tall tea bowl. Gilt rim with blue line immediately beneath. Deep border of fawn/bloom ground with bends overlaying in (indecipherable) between two gilt lines.

61 Shallow tea bowl. Gilt dentil edge over narrow dark blue border at rims. Below, a wider border of dark blue decorated with gilt leaves from which gilt swags are suspended.

62 Shallow tea cup. Gilt border to inside rim. Narrow dark blue border to outer rim decorated with vertical lines in gilt and having a continuous row of gilt dots beneath. This border is repeated above sunburst moulding on base of cup, which is overpainted in Smith's blue and gilt.

63 Tea cup with handle. Gilt rims. Deep border of gilt dots and leaf sprays intertwining a gilt line inside cup. Body of cup decorated with six rows of gilt spots graduating in size from rim to line above foot rim.

64 Shallow fluted foot rim. Narrow gilt border to inside rim. Narrow border of dark blue with gilt dentil edge to outer rim, with scalloped edge to underside of border. Slight gilt border beneath.

65 Shallow tea bowl. Gilt rims with slight additional gilding to inside rim. Narrow dark blue border overlaid with cinquefoil leaf motif alternating with two white dots at outer rim.

66 Shallow fluted tea bowl. Gilt rim with additional gilding to inside of bowl. Very narrow dark blue border with gilt dentil edge to outer rim. Below, a further and slightly wider border in dark blue overlaid with gilt flower heads and, underneath, embossed fronds painted in dark blue and gilt.

67 Tea cup with handle. Inside border in gilt as described in 63. Gilt dentil edge to outer rim, below which is an inverted scallop border containing a linked chain motif, from which hang pendant swags of leaves. Sunburst embossing at base of cup outlined in gilt, above which is a single line of small gilt dots.

68 Shallow tea bowl. Gilt rims with additional gilding to inside rim. Single gilt line approximately three-tenths of an inch below rim.

69 Fluted tea cup with handle. Border to inside rim as 63. Narrow dark blue border with gilt dentil edge to outer rim. Below, a slightly wider dark blue border decorated with gilt floret heads and white dots. Single line of continuous gilt dots round middle of cup.

70 Tea cup with handle. Gilt line with intertwining leaf motif inside cup. Gilt dentil rims. Body of cup entirely covered with tiny gilt floret heads with five festoons of blue roses pendant in reserves. (This pattern is very rare – illustrated in Gilhespy's *Derby Porcelain*, col. plate 11.)

71 Shallow fluted tea bowl. Gilt dentil rims. Foliate border in gilt inside cup. Deep border of gilt floret heads and intertwining leaf decoration.

72 Tall tea cup. Gilt dentil rims. Inside border of foliate design in gilt. Scattered cornflower sprigs in pink and blue with leaves in natural colours over body of cup.

73 Shallow tea bowl. Narrow foliate border inside cup. Gilt dentil edge under which is a narrow border of ovals overlaying each other and each containing two gilt dots. Feather decoration below Vandyke edging.

74 Shallow fluted tea bowl. Gilt rims. Gilt border of overlaying ovals, each containing two gilt dots to inside of bowl. Body covered with gilt spots of graduated size with large spray of blue roses overlaying.

75 Fluted tea cup. Narrow gilt border to inside rim. Gilt dentil edge on outer rim, below which is a narrow border of dark blue with gilt foliate decoration overlaying.

76 Shallow tea bowl. Gilt border of foliate design intertwining single gilt line to inner rim. Narrow border of Smith's blue with gilt line beneath at outer rim. Body of bowl decorated with scattered sprigs in gilt.

77 Tall tea cup. Gilt dentil edges. Gilt foliate border to inside rim. Deep border of chintz pattern with open reserves at intervals.

78 Shallow tea bowl. Gilt rims. No other decoration shown in sketch.

79 Exactly as 77, but reserves containing a gilt motif.

80 Shallow tea bowl. (NB this is an example which quotes rates for painting with or without feathers – see page 311.) Gilt dentil rims. Deep border finished with Vandyke edge and decorated with gilt overlaid ovals broken at regular intervals by small oval reserves, each containing gilt flower heads surrounded by white dots, the border being contained within two gilt lines. Feather decoration beneath Vandyke edge to line above foot rim.

81 Fluted tea cup with handle. Dentil edge to inside rim. Narrow dark blue border to outer rim decorated with gilt leaves and finished with continuous line of gilt dots. The moulded leaf decoration on the body of the cup is painted in dark blue and outlined in gilt.

82 Tall tea bowl. Gilt dentil edge to inside rim, under which is a narrow border of leaves and ferns. Border of gilt laurels to outer rim, below which is a deeper border containing blue and pink cornflowers with leaves in natural colours. Border of gilt laurels repeated beneath. Scattered sprigs of cornflowers over body of bowl.

83 Similar to 18, but in purple.

84 Tall tea cup. Gilt dentil edge to inside rim with further border of gilt leaves and ferns. Narrow border in fawn ground colour to outer rim, contained within two gilt lines with additional gilt decoration beneath.

85 Tea cup with handle. Gilt band to inner rim, under which is a border of finely drawn and closely spaced vertical lines in red with additional decoration in gilt. Oval reserve on side opposite handle painted with a landscape and surrounded by a border of cornflowers and leaves in natural colours and framed by a gilt line and a continuous line of gilt spots.

86 Tall tea cup. Gilt dentil rims. Deep border of gilt through which is drawn a single dark blue line. Landscape in bottom of cup (usually by Boreman in examples which author has seen).

87 Shallow tea bowl. Gilt rims. Deep border of leaf garlands in undulating form, each undulation decorated with a single flower sprig in natural colours.

88 Tall tea cup with handle. Gilt rims. Deep border of gilt inside cup. Bloom body colour decorated with nine rows of gilt circles, each containing a pearl graduating in size from rim to foot rim.

89 Fluted shallow tea bowl. Gilt rims. Narrow border of fawn ground colour between two gilt lines with continuous line of gilt dots below.

90 Fluted shallow tea bowl. Gilt dentil edge. Narrow border of fawn ground colour between two gilt lines with added gilt decoration beneath.

91 Fluted tea bowl. Gilt line to inner rim, dentil edge on outer rim. Bloom body colour with croquet-hoop designs from rim to foot rim, each 'hoop' having a gilt chain running through it with gilt dots round outer edge.

92 Fluted tea bowl. Gilt rims. Slight gilt border below inner rim. Narrow border of bloom/fawn to outer rim.

93 Fluted tea cup. Gilt rims. Narrow border of bloom ground to outer rim. Further border of bloom having arched under-edge, each arch being outlined in gilt and having pendant spray of leaves suspended from top of arch.

94 Tall tea cup. Gilt rims. Deep border of bloom finished with Vandyke edge, below which are four rows of feathers in gilt.

95 Fluted tea bowl. Gilt rims. Narrow dark blue border to outer rim decorated with cinquefoil leaf motif with two vertically placed white dots between each leaf.

96 Fluted tea cup. One wide and two narrow gilt lines to inside rim. Fawn border to outer rim between two gilt lines with two further gilt lines on underside of border.

97 Shallow fluted tea bowl. Three gilt lines to inside rim. Narrow border of dark blue decorated with gilt cinquefoil leaf motif with white dot between each. Marked with '4 gold sprigs on saucer and one in bottom of cup'.

98 Shallow tea bowl. Gilt rims. Border of cornflower sprigs and leaves in natural colours between two gilt lines, each line decorated with continuous line of gilt dots. A further single gilt line below this border and small sprigs of cornflowers just above foot rim.

99 Shallow tea bowl. Gilt dentil rims. A continuous line of gilt flower heads intertwined with leaf garlands form deep border below outer rim.

100 Tall tea cup with handle. Gilt dentil rims. Four rows of single upright cornflower sprigs, alternating with two gilt stars, decorate the cup from rim to foot rim.

101 Tall fluted tea cup. No discernible difference between this and 96. Ground colour possibly bloom instead of fawn.

102 Tall tea cup. Gilt rims. Fawn or bloom border to inner rim between gilt lines with continuous line of gilt dots to underside of border.

103 Missing.

104 Shallow fluted tea bowl. Gilt line to inner rim with additional gilding beneath. Gilt dentil edge to outer rim, below which are two gilt lines.

105 Tall tea cup. Exactly as 100 but with addition of foliate gilt border to inside rim.

106 Tall tea cup. Gilt dentil rims. Vandyke border outlined in dark blue and 'shaddowed' with lighter blue with intertwining gilt garlands. This border is repeated at base of cup just above foot rim.

107 Tall tea cup. Gilt line to inner rim. Dentil edge to outer rim. Simple border in gilt immediately below.

108 Shallow tea bowl. Gilt dentil rims. Deep border comprising single gilt line intertwined with garlands of cornflowers in blue and pink with gilt leaves and stalks.

109 Tall tea cup. Gilt rims. Gilt border of chain pattern with lovers' knots in gilt, from which are suspended swags and sprays of cornflowers in pink and blue with leaves in natural colours.

110 Shallow tea bowl. Gilt dentil rims. Border of blue line intertwined with sprays of gilt leaves and berries. (Very popular pattern which was reproduced by the factory in the late nineteenth century.)

111 Shallow tea bowl. Gilt dentil rims. Border of single gilt lines intertwined by cornflowers in pink and blue with gilt leaves and stalks. Scattered sprigs of cornflowers and harebells over body of bowl.

112 Tall tea cup. Gilt dentil rims. Swags of leaves and ferns in gilt suspended from gilt loops at outer rim.

113 Shallow tea bowl. Gilt dentil rims. Swags and festoons of cornflowers in pink and blue with leaves in natural colours pendant from gilt loops at rim.

114 Tall tea cup. Gilt dentil rims. Border of blue grapes with vine leaves and tendrils in gilt.

115 Shallow tea bowl. Gilt dentil rims. Border of scrolls decorated with blue leaves and brown leaves with small floret head at the centre of each scroll.

116 Shallow tea bowl. Gilt dentil rims. Deep border between two gilt lines of scallop-shell motif in blue and gilt with added gilt scrolling.

117 Tall tea cup. Simple gilt border of dentil form to inner rim, below which there appears to be a landscape painting which covers the whole of the inside of the cup. Narrow border of fawn ground to outer rim. Below, a gilt border of ovals overlaying each other and each containing three gilt dots. Below a deeper border of fawn ground with Vandyke edge. Gilt feathers to line above foot rim.

118 As 117, but with the addition of a narrow gilt border to the gilt line surrounding the landscape.

119 Outside of tea cup as 117 but marked inside 'Fawn Colour Peacock'.

120 Tall fluted tea cup. Gilt dentil rims. Border has gilt line intertwined with undulating leaf sprays and an undulating line of gilt dots.

121 As 120, but with addition of single dark blue line immediately below gilt dentil edge on outer rim.

122 Tall tea cup. Gilt rims. Narrow border of pearls beneath band of gilt to outer rim with further band of gilt below. Yellow ground colour with landscape in oval reserve surrounded by frame of tiny pearls on a dark background. The border of pearls is repeated at foot rim.

123 Fluted tall tea cup. Gilt rims with added gilt decoration following the line of flutes to inside rim. Narrow border of bloom ground colour decorated on underside with large gilt leaf motif – one leaf to each flute.

124 No appreciable difference between this and 122, but the pearls in the border are slightly smaller in size.

125 Tall tea cup. Gilt rims. Narrow border of Vandyke form in dark blue outlined in lighter blue with intertwining garlands of tiny leaves in gilt. Yellow ground colour and Vandyke border repeated at line above foot rim.

126 Tall fluted tea bowl. Gilt rims. Border of dark blue ovals alternating with gilt diamond shapes in continuous line.

127 Tall tea cup. Gilt dentil edge to inner rim. Narrow dark blue border to outer rim decorated with (indistinguishable). Additional slight gilt decoration beneath this border.

128 Tall tea cup. Gilt rims. Deep border of bloom ground colour with bends in dark blue.

129 Shallow tea bowl. Gilt rims. Scattered Chantilly sprigs over body of bowl.

130 Shallow tea bowl. Gilt dentil rims. Single narrow line of dark blue immediately below dentil edge. Scattered flower sprigs in gilt over body of bowl.

131 Tall fluted tea cup. Gilt dentil edge to inside rim. Narrow dark blue border to outer rim between two gilt lines. Below, a gilt border of overlaying ovals broken at intervals by tiny oval reserves, each containing a gilt flower head framed by band of gilt. Immediately below, a wider dark blue border with Vandyke edging to underside. Gilt feathers to line above foot rim.

132 Tall tea cup. Gilt bands to rims. Bloom ground colour over body of cup with gilt bands below narrow gilt lines at foot rim.

133 Tall fluted tea cup. Gilt rims. Border of diamond shapes in black and gilt, each containing 'pearl'. Plain bloom ground colour beneath, extending to foot rim.

132 As 131, but fawn ground instead of dark blue.

135 Tall fluted tea cup. Gilt rims, outer rim gilding shadowed in pale blue. Border of black diamond shapes, outlined in gilt, each containing a pearl. Beneath this border is a further gilt line with blue shadow.

136 Shallow fluted tea bowl. Very narrow dark blue border to outer rim with gilt line below. Scattered sprigs of gilt flowers and leaves over body of bowl.

137 Tall tea cup with handle. Gilt rims. Outer border of large leaves in pendant habit. Oval landscape on side opposite handle surrounded by single gilt line.

138 Tall tea cup with handle. Gilt dentil edge to inner rim. Border of roses in natural colours between two gilt lines. Yellow body colour over remainder of cup.

139 Tall tea cup. Gilt rims. Border of cornflower sprigs in natural colours. Single cornflower sprigs in formal rows over remainder of cup.

140 Tall fluted tea cup. Gilt line to inner rim, below which is a single gilt line border with leaf sprays and continuous line of intertwining gilt dots. Narrow dark blue border to rim overlaid with gilt dentil edge and gilt line beneath. Further border of single dark blue line with intertwining leaf and berry garlands in gilt. Gilt line beneath this border, below which fawn body colour to gilt line above foot rim, decorated with single cornflower sprigs in formal line.

141 Shallow fluted tea bowl. Gilt dentil rims. Deep border of single gilt line

with cornflower sprays and intertwining leaves in natural colours. Small scattered Chantilly sprigs over body of bowl.

142 Shallow tea bowl. Three lines of gilt to inside rim. Gilt dentil edge to outer rim. Two vertical gilt lines spiral from rim to foot rim with intertwining dark blue leaves – this is repeated round the bowl (possibly six in all).

143 Shallow tea bowl. Gilt rims. Lovers' knots in gilt immediately below rim, from which hang pendant festoons of dark blue flowers and leaves.

144 Tall tea cup. Gilt rims. Intricate border to inner rim carried out entirely in gilt dots. Deep border of 'open fan' motifs in green, red and gilt, and between each 'fan' is a 'Catherine wheel' in the same colours. Beneath this is a further border of green and red ribands, overlaid to form horizontal ovals through the middle of which runs a gilt line decorated with tiny green leaves.

145 Tall tea cup. Gilt rims. Simple intertwined leaf border in gilt to inside rim. Slight gilt border below outer rim. (Indecipherable) ground colour two-thirds of the depth of cup, with ornate scale pattern in dark and light blue with added gilt to foot rim.

146 Tall tea bowl. Gilt rims. Added border of gilt leaves to inside rim. Deep border of dark blue with streaks of gilt to outer rim, this border finished with continuous line of gilt dots.

147 Tall tea bowl. Gilt rims with addition of gilt leaf border to inside rim. Deep border of dark blue with undulating white bends between two black lines, through which runs a continuous line of tiny gilt dots. Gilt tassel edge to underside of this border.

148 Tall tea bowl. Gilt dentil edge to inside rim. Deep border of dark blue between two gilt lines to outer rim, decorated with gilt leaves and white bends with continuous line of gilt dots running through each bend. Border finished with continuous line of gilt dots below.

149 Tall tea bowl. Gilt dentil edge to inside rim. Dark blue 'curtain drape' border to outer rim with gilt tasselled edging and two long dark blue tassels between each drape.

150 Tall tea bowl. Gilt rims. Slight border of gilt leaves alternating with ferns to inside rim. Narrow border of alternating light and dark blue lines to outer rim finished with gilt line. This border is repeated above foot rim with bloom ground colour between the two borders.

151 Tall tea bowl. Gilt dentil edges. Additional border of leaves intertwining single gilt line inside bowl. Oval reserve painted with a landscape surrounded by single gilt band. Remainder of bowl is decorated with formal rows of single cornflower sprigs alternating with two gilt stars.

152 Tall tea bowl. Gilt dentil edge to inner rim. Narrow border of dark blue between two gilt lines to outer rim. Below, a gilt border of closely spaced vertical lines between two horizontal gilt lines. Further border of dark blue with Vandyke edge to underside. Feathers to line above foot rim.

153 Tall tea bowl. Border of gilt half-moons between which are fern sprays to inside rim. Outer border of pink and blue cornflower heads connected by gilt scrolls between two gilt lines. Scattered cornflower sprigs in pink and blue with gilt leaves over remainder of bowl.

154 Tall tea cup. Gilt dentil edge to inside rim. Two narrow borders of fawn ground between gilt lines separated by a narrow gilt border of scrolls overlaying a continuous gilt line.

155 Tall tea bowl. Gilt rims, with added gilt to inside rim. Deep border of dark blue with scalloped edges, each scallop containing large single leaf in gilt with single white spots between each motif and additional gilt decoration to scallops on underside of border.

156 Tall tea bowl. Gilt rims. Simple gilt border of linked chains to inside rim. Narrow dark blue border to outer rim decorated with white flower heads, each connected by gilt scrolls.

157 Tall tea bowl. Gilt rims. Delicate leaf border to inner rim. Border of harebells in natural colours with gilt leaves and stems and a narrow border of gilt leaves below.

158 Tall tea bowl. Narrow border of gilt dots between gilt lines to inside rim. Outer border of blue and red flowers with gilt leaves and stems, below which the inside border is repeated.

159 Tall tea cup. Gilt rims. Additional leaf and fern gilt border to inside rim. Border of gilt vertical lines below outer rim, and, below, large formal sprays of leaves in red and blue.

160 Tall tea bowl. Gilt rims. Simple gilt border of alternating diamond shapes and ovals in gilt in continuous line. Gilt line below.

161 Similar to 153, but scroll appears to go underneath rather than to connect the flower heads.

162 Tall tea cup. Gilt dentil rims. Narrow border of dark blue below outer rim with gilt scrolls and floret heads.

163 Tall tea bowl. Gilt dentil edges and gilt festoons as 112, but with addition of Chantilly sprigs scattered over body of bowl.

164 Tall tea bowl. Gilt dentil rims. Undulating line, with long strands of gilt dots at intervals, decorates inside of bowl. Body decorated in vertical wavy lines of gilt from just below rim to line above foot rim with swags of blue roses in swag-shaped reserves.

165 Tall tea cup with handle. Gilt rims. Landscape in oval reserve on side opposite handle with ornate gilt cornucopias on each side. Additional gilt decoration to rim.

166 Tall tea bowl. Gilt dentil edges to rims. Narrow dark blue border below

outer rim with simple decoration in gilt and contained within two gilt lines.

167   Saucer. Kakiemon pattern in dark blue, red and gilt. Gilt line to fluted rim.

168   Tall tea cup with handle. Gilt dentil edge to inner rim. Deep border of yellow ground finished with Vandyke edge and gilt feathers to line above foot rim.

169   Tall tea bowl. Gilt rims. Deep border of roses in natural colours. Gilt line beneath this border.

170   Tall tea bowl. Gilt rims. Deep border of blue gingham effect overlaid with a red scroll motif. One band of gilt and one narrow gilt line beneath this border. Scattered cornflower sprigs over body of bowl.

171   Tall tea cup with handle. Gilt rims. Narrow border of gilt laurel leaves below outer rim. Oval reserve on opposite side to handle painted with landscape and surrounded by single gilt line. (Pencilled in the sketch is the outline of an emblematic star, but no clue given as to colour or whether this was in fact part of the decoration.)

172   Tall tea bowl. In all respects as 171, but without addition of pencilled emblematic star.

173   Tall tea cup with handle. Gilt rims. Gilt border to inside rim and tiny laurel leaf border below outer rim, under which is a deep border of blue and red flowers with gilt leaves and stems in undulating form. Gilt line beneath this border.

174   Tall tea cup with handle. Gilt rims with added gilt border to inside rim. Outer border of blue and red flowers with gilt leaves and stems in undulating form and, below, a narrow border of two gilt lines with a continuous line of gilt dots running through.

175   Tall tea cup with handle. Gilt rims. Oval reserve on side opposite handle framed by three gilt lines. Narrow gilt border to outer rim. Remainder of cup in bloom ground colour.

176   Tall tea cup with handle. Gilt rims. Additional border to inner rim in the form of linked chains. Narrow dark blue border to outer rim with overlaid decoration in gilt with white dots added.

177   Shallow tea bowl. Gilt dentil edges with added border of leaves intertwining single gilt line to inner rim. Sprays of single roses in natural colours and gilt leaf sprays scattered over body of bowl.

178   Tall tea bowl. Gilt rims. Narrow dark blue border with gilt enrichment to outer rim and just above foot rim. Between these borders ornate scrolls in blue, purple and gilt with swags of tiny flowers below and a bell-shaped motif between the scrolls.

179   Tall tea cup with handle. Gilt dentil edges. Landscape in oval reserve surrounded by gold band and a row of continuous gilt dots. Body of cup decorated with single cornflower sprigs alternating with two gilt stars.

180   Tall fluted tea cup with handle. Very narrow blue border to rims with gilt line immediately beneath. Scattered Chantilly sprigs over body of cup.

181   Tall tea bowl. Gilt rims. Border, extending over two-thirds of cup, of scrolls in blue and red with pendant swags in gilt connecting each scroll.

182   Tall tea bowl. Gilt dentil edge to inside rim. Deep border of mid-blue finished with Vandyke edging below and gilt feathers to line above foot rim.

183   Tall tea cup with handle. Gilt dentil edge to inside rim. Border, of cornflower heads and leaves in natural colours, to outer rim contained within two gilt lines, below which is a very deep border of pale blue ground colour overlaid with three rows of dark blue 'arrows' with vertical zigzags in gilt and spiralling vertical lines giving fluted effect.

184   Tall tea bowl. Gilt dentil rims with additional gilt border to inner rim. Single cornflower sprigs in natural colours alternate with gilt stars over body of bowl.

185   Tall tea bowl. Gilt dentil rims. Large flower spray with central rose on body of bowl.

186   Tea cup with handle. Gilt dentil rims. Landscape in oval reserve. Remainder decorated with single cornflower sprigs alternating with gilt stars in formal rows.

187   Tall tea bowl. Gilt rims. Border of black diamond shapes outlined in gilt and each containing a pearl. Yellow ground colour over remainder.

188   Similar to 34, but border in lilac(?) or peach bloom(?).

189   Shallow fluted tea bowl. Gilt rims with narrow gilt border below inside rim. Single gilt line below outer rim. Scattered sprigs in gilt.

191   Tall tea bowl. Gilt rims. Narrow gilt border with pearls, below which is a further gilt line. Remainder of bowl in green ground colour with border of pearls above foot rim.

192   Similar to 191, but ground colour is yellow.

190   (Out of sequence.) Shallow tea bowl. Dark blue border to inner and outer rims. Large sprays of leaves and ferns in two shades of blue and gilt.

193   Tall fluted tea bowl. Gilt dentil rims. Fawn (or bloom) ground colour with croquet-hoop forms from foot rim to rim in dark blue decorated with white enamel dots and framed by border of simple gilt chain design with added gilt dots to outer edge of this border.

194   Tall tea cup with handle. Gilt rims. Narrow gilt border with pearls. Landscape in oval reserve framed by black border with pearls. Bloom ground colour over remainder of body with gilt border and pearls to foot rim.

195   Tall tea bowl. Gilt rims with slight foliate border to inside rim. Narrow

dark blue border to outer rim overlaid with gilt flower heads and scrolls. Scattered gilt sprigs over remainder.

196   Tall tea bowl with handle. Similar to 192, but there appear to be fewer pearls to each border and the yellow is of a much paler hue.

197   As 196, but ground colour dark blue.

198   Tall tea bowl. Gilt rims. Scattered sprigs over body in gilt.

199   Shallow tea bowl. Gilt rims. Chantilly sprigs in pink, blue and gilt over body of bowl.

200   Tall fluted tea cup with handle. Gilt rims. Fawn ground colour with croquet-hoop shapes as described in 193, but these are outlined in dark blue with white enamel dots. Pattern marked with '9 blue fuits in the cup' (sic).

206   Shown as coffee can. Very ornate inner rim border in gilt. Fawn ground colour with painting in square reserve described as 'fruit upon shaded brown ground' (sic). (NB this also carries a notation 'instead of the gold border', but it is not at all certain to what this refers.) The handle is of the rope type.

201   Shown as double-handled beaker. Jewelled gilt borders to outer rim and foot rim, yellow ground colour with oval landscape in reserve with jewelled border.

202   Simple gilt inner rim border. Gilt dentil edge to outer rim with narrow dark blue border, below which is a gilt border with florets in oval reserves, and immediately below this border is a plain dark blue Vandyke border.

203   As 202, in green.

204   As 202, in claret.

205   As 202, in black(?).

206   Shown as coffee can with rope handle. Ornate gilt foliate border to inner rim. Bloom ground colour with 'colord fruit' in square reserve on side opposite handle.

209   Shown as two-handled beaker. Gilt line on outer rim with delicate foliate border in gilt directly below. Landscape in oval reserve on one side and 'figures on the other side'.

210   Gilt lines to inner and outer rims with simple but attractive borders below.

207   (Out of sequence.) Shown as coffee can with rope handle. Gilt lines to inner and outer rims. Deep inner border of foliate design. Bloom ground colour with 'Cupid [rest indecipherable]' in square reserve on side opposite handle. Gilt border round reserve.

208   (Out of sequence.) Gilt dentil edge to inner rim. Deep border in claret in Vandyke pattern with additional gilt border just below outer rim.

211   Shown as coffee can with rope handle. Green ground colour with fruit in reserve, gilt frame around painting. (See Thorpe and Barrett, Plate 144.)

212   Again shown as coffee can with rope handle. Inside border as 207. Dark blue ground colour with 'fruit in colour'.

213   Shown as coffee can. Similar in most respects to 212 but with yellow ground colour. (NB the pattern books add a note: 'The stands to 211, 212 and 213 Gilt the same as 207.') And in each case there is a note to the effect that 'Inside border same as 207'. Also in each case the border surrounding the reserve is marked with a cross and a different gilt border has been painted over the ground colour with the note 'instead of the gold frame'.

214   As previous cans, but instead of ground colour the body has scattered sprigs interspersed with two-star design previously mentioned. (NB all notation described above applies in this case.)

215   Gilt lines to inner and outer rims. Narrow gilt border beneath outer rim. Reserve side opposite handle with 'Dancing girl with tinkling cymbal'. (Note on cup states: 'this border round the top of the stand likewise round outside of the circle'; it is then illustrated, showing the circle in the centre of the stand.)

216   Very ornate gilt borders to inner and outer rims under plain gilt line. Repeated at base of can. Sprig and two-star decoration over body of can. Oval reserve 'Painted with beggar Girl and Boy before a distant Landscip' (sic). Reserve has square border of dark blue with jewelled border.

217   This has been cut or torn out of pattern book.

218   Very similar to 170, but overlaying scrolls on border are in yellow.

219   Shown as coffee can with rope handle. Gilt lines to inner and outer rims. Inside border of ornate foliate design. Sprigs outlined with stars over body of cup. Landscape in square reserve with 'frame' crossed out and more attractive gilt border substituted. Note in reserve: 'fruit before shaded Olive ground upon Dark Colord Pedistall' (sic) and 'Just ½ size of the Compartment'.

221   Coffee can with rope handle. Ornate inner border under gilt rim. Square reserve with 'Groop off fruit a Gold finch before an olive shaded ground upon Dark Pedistall as 219 – this 1 size of compartment' (sic).

222   (Marked 221 in pattern book.) Coffee can with fawn ground overlaid with gilt stars and showing roses in alternating oblong and oval reserves. Gilt lines to inner and outer rims and usual rope handle.

223   (Marked 222 in pattern book.) Delicate wheatsheaf inner gilt border under gilt line to inner rim. Bloom ground colour with square reserve opposite rope handle. Painted with 'A Groop of fruit with tom tit before an Olive ground upon Dark Pedestall as 219' (sic). Again the frame is crossed out, and a note appears on the ground colour: 'this border on the Stand instead of the Gold frame'.

Side 1   Side 2

T. H. Clark

14

J. L.

1, vertically fluted coffee cup (rare shape). 2, embossed acanthus fluted coffee cup. 3, plain coffee cup. 4, Hamilton fluted coffee cup (concave). 5, ribbed coffee (convex). 6, ogee scalloped coffee. 7, embossed teacup. 8, ogee scalloped teacup. 9, large plain cup. 10, tall teabowl. 11, embossed pine cone moulded low teabowl. 12, incised twist low teabowl. 13, embossed sunflower (so called because the circular saucer looks like a sunflower) moulded coffee cup. 14, rare embossed design with gold dentils and base band on low teabowl. 15, caudle cup. 16, cylindrical coffee cup with rope twist handle. 17, chocolate cup and cover with ring knop.

224 The error in numbering is discovered here, and 223 has been altered to 224. This is shown as a tea bowl similar to the 203/5 series, but it has a dark blue border immediately beneath the gilt dentil edge and the Vandyke border appears in fawn with feathers to foot rim.

220 (Out of sequence.) Gilt line rims with narrow foliate border on inside rim. Sprig and two-star pattern on body of cup with square reserve opposite rope handle painted with 'Landskip a . . . Drawing by Banford'. Note appended to frame of reserve: 'this border at the top of the stand'; and to inside border: 'this border at the bottom of the stand'.

225 This pattern is similar in most respects to 216 but without ornate gilt border to base of can and painting depicting 'Happy and Tender Mother [indecipherable]'.

226 Cup and saucer with ornate gilt border on outer rim and landscape in reserve on side opposite handle surrounded by a border of pearls. Note in pattern book states 'pearls done with pale blue'. Landscape in middle of saucer also framed by border of blue pearls.

223 (Out of sequence.) Shown as two-handled beaker with œil-de-perdrix decoration on a yellow ground. Oval reserve bearing inscription: 'One cup two virgins awaking cupid the other Two baccante ador(n)ing Pan and on the other sides coloured Landskips'. Underneath the sketch of the cup is the note 'London 223 highish'.

Here follows a note: 'No. 224/5/6 are taken up on the proceeding page' and this is immediately contradicted by number 226.

226 (Second version.) Gilt lines to inner and outer rims. Gilt foliate inner border. Outer border of gilt scroll pattern between two narrow borders of fawn.

227 Gilt lines to inner and outer rims. Chantilly sprig decoration in pink, blue and gilt over body of cup.

228 Gilt lines to inner and outer rims. Outer border of narrow foliate design in gilt. (There is a suggestion of a sunburst design on the inside of this cup, which may have been pencilled in and not used as no note appears against this addition.)

241 Shown as coffee can (out of sequence). The ground colour appears to be fawn, and a note is appended stating 'Ground same manner as 221'. Square reserve opposite handle with 'Cupid Disarmed by Euphrosyne by Banford'.

230 As 228 but with landscape in oval reserve on side opposite handle.

231 Shown as two-handled beaker. Gilt borders to outer rim and foot rim. Ground colour (indistinguishable) with central oval reserve bearing inscription 'The First [indecipherable] Second Lessons of Love On the One sides And Landskips on the other Both in black on moon Light ground'. Additional note underneath sketch: 'The handle same as No. 223'.

232 Shown as coffee can with elaborate inner border with jewels. 'Ground in same Manner as 221'. Oval reserve with jewelled border 'Venus Chiding Cupid' by Banford.

233 Shown as coffee can, 'Ground same manner as 221'. Very attractive border inside rim comprising alternating dots and florets and marked 'this inside border done bottom of the Stand'. Painting in square reserve of 'the Genius of Modesty preventing Love unveiling Beauty by Banford'. Square gilt frame surrounding reserve from rim to foot rim.

234 Unfinished sketch showing coffee can with yellow ground and jewelled borders to rim and foot rim.

235 Gilt lines to inner and outer rims with simple border in gilt on inside of can. Deep Vandyke border in bloom overlaid with gilt and split by 'fence' border. Feathers to foot rim.

236 Coffee can. Gilt lines to inner and outer rims. Ornate gilt inner border. Yellow ground with red roses in reserves. 'Fruit with birds by Complin' in square reserve on side opposite handle. Gilt frame to reserve.

237 Coffee can. Gilt lines to inner and outer rims. Inner gilt border of two continuous bands of leaves. Fawn ground with red roses in small circular reserves, between which are gold stars and blue stars in very tiny circular reserves. 'Fruit and birds by Complin' in square reserve opposite handle.

238 Tea bowl. Gilt lines to inner and outer rims. Outer border of single continuous gilt line interwind with floret and leaf design in gilt.

239 Coffee can. Gilt lines to inner and outer rims. Formal inner border in gilt marked 'this border at the edge of the saucer'. Gilt stars over body of can with oval reserve with square blue frame surrounded by a square jewelled border. Painting in reserve 'Hope in Colore by Banford' (sic).

240 Tea bowl. Gilt lines to inner and outer rims. Outer border of pale blue with 'Pale Gold beads and dots'.

242 Coffee can. Very ornate inner border showing three lines of gilt with continuous line of closely spaced gilt dots between with added gilt decoration below third gilt line. Star and sprig decoration in blue and gilt over body of can. Oval reserve delicately painted by Banford from 'Lady's' Paper flower jars. Ornate gilt frame to oval reserve.

243 'The same in every respect as 216 Except Brown Landskip instead of the begger Girl'.

244 Shown as coffee can with inside border as 242. Green ground with oval reserve in square dark blue frame surrounded by a border of pearls. Painting in reserve of 'Brown Landskip by Boreman'.

245 Coffee can with gilt lines to inner and outer rims. Attractive wheat-ear

inner border in gilt. Green ground colour with square reserve on side opposite handle of 'fruit by Complin with tom tit and Bull finch before Dark Landskip'.

246 Shown as tea cup. Gilt line to inner and outer rims. Outer border fawn with scalloped edge outlined in gilt with added gilt decoration below. Body of cup painted with 'Blue-leaved Coronilla Plant by Billingsley'. (This is helpful in dating the first pattern book of tea ware, as Billingsley left the factory in 1796.)

247 Shown as tea cup. Gilt line to inner and outer rims. Gilt foliate border below outside rim. Ground colour yellow with oval reserve painted with flowers and surrounded by oval frame of delicate leaf design in gilt.

248 Shown as tea cup with flutes (Hamilton shape). Very simple gilt inner border. Deep outer border of green terminating in Vandyke pattern. This border is split by gilt border of ovals overlaying each other and each containing three gilt dots. Feather to foot rim.

249 Gilt dentil edge to inner rim. Outer border of 'green 176' between two gilt lines and additional decorative gilt border immediately beneath.

250 Gilt lines to inner and outer rims. Inner border of alternating stars and dots in gilt. On three sides of the cup is an ornate scroll design in red, blue and gilt which extends half-way down the cup. These scrolls are joined by a narrow border of sloping conjoined ovals in green, each decorated within by polychrome florets and above and below by tiny gilt arrows.

251 Shown as tea cup. Gilt lines to inner and outer rims. Outer border of continuous scroll design in blue and gilt between two gilt lines. Chantilly sprigs in pink, blue and gilt over body of cup.

252 Shown as tea cup. This is similar to 250 but has two gilt lines on inside of cup, and there would appear to be some slight difference on the decoration of the handle. However, it is noted in the pattern book that there are 'Ten of these (green ovals) in the cup and twelve in the saucer'. Also it is mentioned that there are '3 Compartments in the Cup and 4 in the saucer'.

253 Shown as coffee can. Gilt lines to inner and outer rims with delicate foliate gilt border inside can. ground colour yellow with rectangular and oval reserves painted with roses. Oval reserve on side opposite handle with square frame in dark blue surrounded by a square border of pearls. Reserve contains 'A figure of Hope painted in different colours'.

254 Shown as coffee can. Inner border as 242. Formal sprigs and stars over body of cup with square reserve opposite handle painted with 'Fruit and Birds by Complin'. Square gilt frame to reserve from rim to bottom of can.

255 Coffee can. Gilt lines to inner and outer rims. Simple gilt border to inside of can. Body overlaid with gilt stars alternating with two gold dots placed vertically. Oval and rectangular reserves alternate round the top and base of the can, each one containing pink roses and leaves on a black background. Each reserve framed with tiny gold dots.

256 Coffee can. Gilt line to inner rim with simple gilt border below. Gilt dentil edge to outer rim, below which is a formal sprig in blue and green alternating with two gilt stars. Oval reserve on side opposite handle with square dark blue frame decorated with gilt. The reserve contains 'Romeo & Juliet by Banford in Colore'.

257 'In every respect finished the same as 256 – Except this border at the bottom of the Stand'. The border in question appears to be the typical harebell border of the time, executed in gilt.

258 Gilt lines to inner and outer rims of this can. Very simple inner border immediately beneath this line. Introduction of leaf sprig (which actually looks like a bunch of three crocuses!) alternating with stars and green dots over body of can. Oval reserve surrounded by border of pearls and square frame in fawn with additional gilt decoration. Reserve contains 'Cupid Disarm'd and . . . by Banford'.[2]

259 Gilt lines to inner and outer rim of can. Simple gilt inner border of alternating stars and florets. Gilt stars and gilt and blue dots alternate over body of can. Square reserve on side opposite handle painted with 'fruit & birds by Complin'. Simple gilt frame to reserve.

260 'Ground the same as 237' on this can, as is the inner border. Square reserve on side opposite handle of 'View from Cheltenham by Boreman'. Very simple gilt frame to reserve, flanked on each side by festoon of pink roses and green leaves.

261 Coffee can. Gilt lines to inner and outer rims with ornate foliate border in gilt on inside of can. Ground colour (undistinguishable) with square reserve on side opposite handle of 'Fruit and Birds by Complin'. Square frame in 'fence pattern' which appears to have been deleted and a very slight sketch inserted of different design.

262 Shown as tall tea bowl. Gilt lines to inner and outer rims. Narrow gilt border of foliate design below outer rim with scattered Chantilly sprigs over body of bowl – all in gilt. An additional sprig is shown, and it is assumed this will be found in the bottom of the bowl.

263 'In Every respect same as 150 Except the Ground to be White instead of Bloom'. (It is assumed that this also is a tea bowl.)

264 Coffee can with yellow ground and the alternating oval and rectangular reserves with roses previously described. Square reserve with 'Coloured Landskip by Boreman'. Ornate gilt frame to reserve.

265 Shown as tea cup of Hamilton shape. Two gilt lines on inner rim. Outer border claret(?) or puce(?) overlaid with gilt.

266 Shown as tea cup. Gilt line to inner rim. Outer border of pearls between

80
Well modelled figure of a seated boy decorated largely in three dominant colours, yellow, puce and lettuce green. This figure is attributed to the 'pale period' but in the author's opinion this is incorrect, as the colourings are by no means pale. Patch marks. William Duesbury & Co. 1758–60. Approx. 14 cm. *Victoria & Albert Museum.*

81 ▷ ▷
Female companion to the figure in black and white plate 80: the colourings are identical. Patch marks. William Duesbury & Co. 1758–60. 12.5 cm. *The Litchfield Collection.*

82
Fine pair of candlestick figures indicating why William Duesbury was so successful in the expansion of his figure market. Predominant colours are yellow, puce and lettuce green. Patch marks. William Duesbury & Co. *c.* 1758–60. Approx. 24 cm. *Sotheby's, New Bond Street.*

83
Figure of Shakespeare, taken from the statue by Scheemaker which is in Poets' Corner in Westminster Abbey. Patch marks. William Duesbury & Co. *c*. 1765. Approx. 31 cm. *Royal Crown Derby Museum.*

84 ◁ ◁
Seated figure of an elegant shepherd with an oval basket on his knees. Note the movement towards the rococo base. Patch marks. William Duesbury & Co. *c*. 1758–60. 22.7 cm. *Royal Crown Derby Museum.*

85
Pair of figures known as 'The Mapseller and Companion'. These were copied from the red anchor Chelsea versions. Patch marks. William Duesbury & Co. *c*. 1765. Approx. 16 cm. *Christie, Manson & Woods.*

88
A figure of St Philip, companion figure to St Thomas, otherwise called King Lear or Roman soldier (see black and white plate 78). Patch marks. William Duesbury & Co. 1758–60. 24.1 cm. *Victoria & Albert Museum, C299 – 1940.*

89
A rare figure of a boy holding a pot of flowers, perhaps representing 'Spring' from a set of 'Seasons'. William Duesbury & Co. 1758–60. Approx. 12 cm. *Private European collection.*

86 ▷
Rare figure of a boy, an early version of the hundreds of Derby putti that were later to come from the Nottingham Road Works. Patch marks. William Duesbury & Co. *c.* 1756–8. Approx. 12.7 cm. *David J. Thorn Antiques.*

87 ▷ ▷
Figure of a piper which is a faithful copy of the Meissen figure by J. J. Kandler. An example of the Meissen figure is in the Ashmolean Museum, Oxford. Patch marks. William Duesbury & Co. *c.* 1760. 17 cm. *Barry Waiting Collection.*

90
Fine figure of an elegant shepherd on
an open scrolled base. Patch marks.
William Duesbury & Co. *c.* 1760.
Approx. 23 cm. *Victoria & Albert
Museum, C303 – 1940.*

91
A leopard, glancing behind him. Patch
marks. William Duesbury & Co.
c. 1760. Approx. 8.9 cm. *City Museum
& Art Gallery, Derby.*

two gilt lines. Oval reserve with landscape opposite handle – also surrounded by a frame of pearls within two gilt lines.

267   As 267, but ground colour of cup is dark blue.

268   Shown as tea cup. Gilt line to inner rim. Chain border between two gilt lines on outer rim and above foot rim. Ground colour (indecipherable) with single sprig each side of oval reserve painted with landscape and framed by border as already described.

269   Shown as tea cup. Yellow ground with gilt stars and rectangular and oval reserves in which are naturalistic roses and leaves. Very ornate gilt frond border on inside rim below plain gilt line.

270   Gilt dentil edge to inner rim. Two gilt lines on outer rim with scroll decoration in gilt between. The body of the cup has formal pattern of alternating leaf sprigs, dots and stars.

271   Shown as coffee can. Gilt lines to inner and outer rims. Inner border of wheat-ear pattern in gilt. Blue spots and gilt stars alternate in formal lines over body of cup. Oval reserve on side opposite handle in square dark blue frame with added gilt decoration. Painting in reserve of '2 Virgins with flowers from Complin Print by Banford'. Rope handle.

272   (Indistinguishable colour) line to outer rim. Leaf and flower sprays over body of cup (or bowl) in (indecipherable colour).

273   Described: 'In every respect same as 200 Except bloom ground instead of fawn'.

274   (Out of sequence.) Gilt rims to inner and outer rims. Narrow dark blue border overlaid with gilt fence pattern with line of small gilt dots under the blue border.

275   Shown as coffee can. Very ornate scroll and floret border inside can. Gilt

line to outer rim with gilt stars and dots in formal lines over body of can. Oval reserve on side opposite handle with square surround in fawn overlaid with gilt decoration. Painting of 'Sheltered Lamb by Banford'.

276   Shown as tall tea bowl. Gilt lines to inner and outer rims. Scattered Chantilly sprigs over body of cup in pink, blue and green.

277   Shown as shallow tea bowl. Gilt lines to inner and outer rims. Outer border of simple green (blue?) foliate design between two gilt lines.

278   Gilt lines to inner and outer rims. Simple gilt sprig border inside cup. Leaf sprig pattern in formal design over body of cup. Note is given in pattern book: 'ground colour same as 270 (only to go up to the edge of cup and saucer) & the Leaf Done this Manner [sketch omitted] not this [sketch omitted]. Border in the saucer.'

279   Shown as coffee can with rope handle. Gilt lines to inner and outer rims. Deep gilt border consisting of large and smaller gilt dots between three gilt lines and additional gilt decoration under third line to outer rim and foot rim. Square reserve on side opposite handle of 'Scofton Hall near Worksop, Nottinghamshire'. Plain gilt frame round reserve.

280   Shown as coffee can. Gilt lines to inner and outer rims. Outer border of sprig and leaf decoration in natural colours. 'Green to ground and border No. 1'. Two gilt lines round base of can.

281   Shown as tall tea cup. Two gilt lines on inside of cup. Gilt dentil edge to outer rim. Leaf sprig decoration interspersed with dots and gilt stars in formal rows round body of cup.

282   Gilt lines to inner and outer rims. Outer border under dentil edge of (indistinguishable colour) in Vandyke pattern overlaid with gilt foliate border between two gold lines.

Tea Book II

283   Gilt outer border of gilt dots between three gilt lines. Pendant fronds of leaves and red berries. Note to artist: 'In Gilding the same as 67 Except the Green swag and inside border'. (No inside border shown in pattern book.)

284   Shown as tea cup with handle. Dentil edges in gilt to inner and outer rims. Deep scroll-type border in green on outer rim with added gilt decoration between each scroll. A narrow gilt border immediately below this and finally a green foliate border with red berries half-way down the cup. Note on pattern: 'Green 847 finished with Black'.

285   Shown as tea cup with handle. Gilt lines to inner and outer rims. Inner border comprising two rows of tiny gilt circles in continuous line between continuous line of gilt dots and plain gilt line, under which is a further line of dots. Outer border consists of two pink borders decorated with deeper pink fronds. Between these two borders is a leaf and berry design in natural colours. Finally, a narrow gilt border immediately underneath the pink border, in scroll and leaf design.

286   Dentil edge in gilt to outer rim and ornate foliate gilt border inside cup. Deep border below dentil edge in dark blue ground colour with red berries and green stalks painted in lozenge-shaped reserves, each one outlined in gilt. Gilt leaf swags and festoons under this border.

287   Gilt dentil edge to inner rim and plain gilt line to outer rim. Deep border containing five roses within octagonal medallions. Scroll design in red and gilt between each rose. (NB '7 [roses] in saucer.)

288   Gilt dentil edge to inner rim and plain gilt line to outer rim. Deep border of gilt dots with fourteen palms in green. Leaf and berry border immediately below. (NB '20 palms in saucer'.)

289   Gilt dentil edge to inner rim. Outer rim has continuous line of gilt dots between two gilt lines, below which is a deep border of 'vases' in two different designs separated by ornate scroll design. Additional border immediately below comprising gilt swags and festoons pendant from gilt loops.

290   Shown as tall plain cup with handle. Design shown in monochrome, and this appears to be exactly similar to 203, 204 and 205, but without inside gilt border.

291   No pattern filled in. The sketch merely shows outline of tall tea cup.

292   Very slight sketch of pattern in the form of swathes with some floral decoration in each. Alternating stars and dots to outer rim. Rope-type handle.

293   As above, but stars and dots alternate over the whole of the cup between the swathing, and flower spray can be seen quite clearly as roses.

294   Gilt dentil edges to inner and outer rims. Slight outer border of leaf and berry design.

295   No pattern filled in.

296   Gilt lines to inner and outer rims. On outer rim, deep border of sprig and foliate design in blue and gilt between two lines of gilt leaves. Grey(?) ground colour to gilt line above foot rim.

297   Gilt lines to inner and outer rims. Outer border of sprigs and leaves in natural colours. Two gilt lines above foot rim.

298   Design shown in monochrome but consisting of deep border with medallions of formal design (possibly four on cup), each connected by broad swags laid over a deep ground colour.

299   The plainest pattern in the book, consisting of gilt lines to inner and outer rims. A very narrow gilt line underneath line on outer rim.

300   Gilt lines to inner and outer rims. A continuous border of sloping ovals in green, each containing a small floret in blue with added gilt decoration, forms the outer border.

301   Missing.

302   Shown as coffee can with rope handle. Gilt lines to inner and outer rims with ornate gilt frond decoration inside can. Claret ground colour with square reserve on side opposite handle containing 'Lord Winchelsea View'. Gilt frame surrounding reserve repeated below outer rim and at foot rim.

303   Shown as coffee can with rope handle. Gilt dentil edge to inner rim with additional decorative gilt border. Gilt line to outer rim with jewelled border below, repeated at base of can. Alternating stars and dots over body of can with square reserve also marked 'Lord Winchelsea'.

304   Shown as coffee can. Plain gilt lines to inner and outer rims with most unusual striped design over body of can in light and dark blue. Oval reserve on side opposite handle, again marked 'Lord Winchelsea'. Border round reserve in dark blue overlaid with white dots between two gilt lines.

305   Shown as coffee can with rope handle. Gilt lines to inner and outer rims with additional inside borders in gilt. Ornate gilt border to outer rim. Green ground colour with square reserve on side opposite handle with jewelled frame. Again, reserve marked 'Lord Winchelsea'.

306   Shown as coffee can with rope handle. Ornate border to inner rim. Deep outer border showing gilt foliate design, which is repeated at base of can. A striped effect is shown in the sketch between the two gilt borders, and the square reserve on the side opposite the handle is marked 'Lord Winchelsea'.

307   Missing.

308   Shown as coffee can with rope handle. Ornate gilt frond border inside can. Claret ground colour with square reserve. Frame round reserve is repeated as border at rim and base of can.

309   Shown as coffee can with rope handle. Gilt lines to inner and outer rims with additional inner border of gilt dots between two narrow lines. Formal leaf sprigs interspersed with stars and blue dots over body of can with square reserve opposite handle marked 'Lord Winchelsea'.

310   Coffee can with rope handle. Gilt lines to inner and outer rims. Border of wheat-ear pattern inside can. Gilt stars and blue and gilt dots over body of can. Square reserve with jewelled border marked 'Lord Winchelsea'.

311   Shown as tea cup. Gilt dentil edge to inner rim. Outer rim has narrow blue line between two gilt lines and a further blue border immediately below, overlaid with gilt and white florets. Oval reserve painted with landscape on side opposite handle is framed by a jewelled border.

312   Gilt lines to inner and outer rims. Inside cup, gilt border of circles and dots with wavy line between two gilt lines. Deep outer border of arches containing gilt 'rose' alternating with fan design, the widest part of the fan opening at the rim. Below, a narrow polychrome border of leaves and berries, and towards the base of the cup swags of roses in natural colours.

313 Shown as coffee can with rope handle. Inside border as 309. Narrow blue border to outer rim between two gilt lines. Light and dark blue stripes over body of can with square reserve on side opposite handle, marked 'Lord Winchelsea'.

314–9 Missing.

320 Shown as tea cup with handle. Narrow gilt border of dots between two gilt lines to outer rim. Seaweed pattern over body of cup, with landscape in reserve.

321 Gilt dentil edges to inner and outer rims. Very simple swags of husks, each swag overlaid with single leaf spray in pink(?) and separated by slight gilt motif.

322 Gilt line to inner rim and gilt dentil edge to outer rim. Simple inside border and deep outer border in Vandyke pattern (indecipherable colour); this border is separated by gilt border of overlaid ovals, each containing three gilt dots. It is difficult to be certain, but it would appear that the inside of this cup has a painted landscape.

323 This would appear to be exactly the same as 192 but it is shown with a handle.

324 Gilt lines to inner and outer rims. A further very narrow gilt line on outer rim, under which is shown a deep border of a geometrical variation of the *oeil-de-perdrix* pattern. (NB it may be that this pattern covers the whole of the body of the cup, but this cannot be stated with any degree of certainty; however, the pattern does have a certain unfinished look.)

325 Shown as coffee can with rope handle. Gilt Greek key border inside can. No sketch of actual pattern but marked in three sections: (1) 'fruit and birds & flower by Complin'; (2) three festoons in the cup; (3) five in the saucer. Inside border of the cup. Bottom of the Saucer.

326 Shown as coffee can with rope handle. Gilt lines to inner and outer rims. Ornate gilt border inside can. Broken gilt lines (ie similar to Morse Code without dots) over body of can with square reserve on side opposite handle, marked 'Basket of flowers upon pedestal before olive ground by Billensley'. Ornate gilt frame surrounding reserve extending from rim to base of can.

327 Shown as coffee can with rope handle. Gilt lines to inner and outer rims. Gilt border below inner rim. Narrow blue border on outer rim between two gilt lines and overlaid with continuous line of white dots. Below, a deep border comprising spaced vertical lines in red with reserves in which are medallions in floreate form. The narrow blue border at the rim is repeated immediately below, and this is followed by a further design in the form of large overlaid ovoid shapes decorated with gilt dots and marked 'not this work in saucer' (for which small mercy one feels the decorator must have been truly thankful since, there are thirteen medallions to each saucer!).

328 Gilt lines to inner and outer rims. Coffee can with rope handle. Light and dark blue alternating stripes over body of can with square reserve on side opposite handle, marked 'Plain ring centre of saucer'.

329 Coffee can with rope handle shown to be taller than previous cans. Gilt rims and deep gilt border inside can. Dark blue stripes over body of can, each stripe overlaid with gilt decoration.

330 Shown as tall tea cup with handle. Gilt lines to inner and outer rims with very slight additional gilt border inside cup. Leaf and berry decoration over body of cup from rim to foot rim with oval reserve on front of cup marked 'Landskip by Boreman – 3 in saucer and Lie[?] contrary to the cup'. (It may perhaps be assumed that there are three landscapes in the cup also.)

331 Shown as tall tea bowl. Gilt lines to inner and outer rims. Yellow ground colour very slightly decorated with gilt borders at rims and above foot rim.

332 Shown as coffee can with rope handle. Gilt dentil edges to rims. Ornate gilt border inside can. Gilt border below outer rim and above base of foliate design intertwining with two gilt lines. Sprigs and stars over body of can with oval reserve marked 'Landskip by Banford' with jewelled frame of pearls.

333 Shown as tea cup with handle. Gilt line to inner rim, dentil edge to outer rim. Outer border of gilt key design interspersed with leaf and berry sprigs. Slight scattered sprig design on body of cup.

334 Shown as tea cup with handle. Gilt lines to inner and outer rims. Inside border as 309 and 313. Deep outer border of ovals overlaying each other with large oval reserve of Landskip in colours by Boreman – 3 in cup 3 in saucer.

335 Shown as tea cup with handle. Gilt dentil edge to inner rim. Gilt edge to outer rim under which are three borders, two of cobalt blue separated by a plain border comprising gilt line ornamented by gilt scroll design.

337 Shown as tea cup with handle. Narrow gilt border at inner rim under which is a deeper gilt border and 'Bottom of ye Cup a Landskip'. Deep Vandyke border in fawn from outer rim to base of handle. Gilt feathers to gilt line above foot rim.

338 Shown as tea cup with rope handle. Gilt dentil edge to inner rim, under which is a further border consisting of scroll design intertwining with a plain gilt line. Blue dots and gilt stars alternate over body of cup. Fruit and birds in oval reserve on side opposite handle, framed by a border of gilt dots between two gilt lines.

339 Outline sketch of cup with handle, but no pattern inserted.

340 Gilt lines to inner and outer rims. Further gilt line below outer rim with scattered Chantilly sprigs over body. Gilt line at foot rim.

341 Gilt line to inner rim. Gilt dentil edge to outer rim. The alternating oval and rectangular reserves (see 236 and 264) have been outlined, but no pattern design inserted. It is fairly safe to assume that these would have been roses. No ground colour given, but a design of alternating large and small dots has been indicated in monochrome.

342 Shown as tea cup with handle. Two narrow gilt borders to outer rim. Alternating stars, circles and dots over body of cup. Oval reserve on side opposite handle with borders identical to those at rim, forming frame. These borders are repeated above foot rim. (Pattern filled in sketchily in monochrome.)

343 Shown as tea cup with rope handle. Single narrow gilt border to outer rim, as frame of reserve and above foot rim. No ground colour given.

344 Tea cup with handle. Gilt(?) lines to inner and outer rims. Slight gilt foliate border below rim. Gilt(?) line above foot rim.

345 Shown as tea cup with handle. Gilt(?) lines to inner and outer rims with additional gilt decoration below inner rim. Deep border of small dots interspersed with florets. Very narrow foliate border immediately below. (This has been sketched in monochrome and gives no indication of colour.)

346 Tea cup with handle. Gilt(?) lines to inner and outer rims. A geometrical version of *oeil-de-perdrix* is indicated, but it is uncertain whether this covers the whole of the body of the cup or is merely intended to form a deep border. Shown in monochrome.

347 Shown as tea cup with handle. Narrow border of dots within circles between two lines to inner rim. Outer border of pearls within lozenge shapes between two gilt(?) lines – a line of continuous (gilt) dots immediately below second line, under which is a further border consisting of an undulating continuous line.

348 Shown as tea cup with handle. Gilt lines to inner and outer rims. Narrow border of circles between two lines below outer rim.

349/50 No sketch bearing these numbers. However, there are three sketches inserted on this page which do not bear numbers. Two of these appear to follow designs for 345 and 347, but the third has a 'Blue Celeste' deep Vandyke border and feathers to foot rim.

351 Shown as coffee can with rope handle. Gilt inner and outer rims with added gilt border inside can. Ground of coloured flowers by Billingsley filled in with gold. Oval reserve on side opposite handle, of 'Cupid Disarmed by Banford'.

352 Shown as double-handled beaker and marked 'Ground same as 271'. There are four reserves, two of which are by Banford – 'Love Sleeps' and 'Maid of Corinth'. On the reverse are 'Two Dove Dale Landskips'. ('All in colours'.)

353 Missing.

354 Shown as fluted cup with handle – Hamilton shape. Gilt dentil edge to inside rim. Plain gilt line on outer rim. Narrow blue border below between two gilt lines.

355 Shown as tea bowl. Gilt dentil edge to inner rim. Narrow blue border between two gilt lines on outer rim.

356 Missing.

337 Shown as fluted tea bowl. Gilt rims. Narrow gilt border below outer rim, under which is an alternating pattern of pendant fronds and leaves in natural colours.

358 Shown as coffee can with rope handle. Gilt rims with additional inner rim decoration of alternating florets and stars. Circles and gilt stars alternate over the body of the can. Reserve on side opposite handle painted with 'Young girl feeding a Rabet' and surrounded by dark blue border.

359 Marked 'Same is Pattern No. 129 with the addition of this blue line'. (Blue line just below outer rim of cup.)

360 Shown as coffee can with rope handle. Gilt rims. Blue ground colour overlaid with alternating circles and stars in gilt. Oval reserve on side opposite handle in narrow gilt frame, with similar design for borders at the top and bottom of can.

361 Coffee can with rope handle. Gilt rims with very attractive inner gilt border of heart-shaped motifs in a continuous line. Broken gilt lines over body of cup with oval reserve 'Love Sleeps by Askew', surrounded by heavily gilded frame.

362 Missing.

363 Coffee can. Narrow blue border with gilt enrichment to outer rim and foot rim. Oval reserve of 'Figures in Colors by Askew', surrounded by simple frame of gilt line with added decoration in gilt.

364 Marked 'Exact the same as 269 Except the blue Ground under the roses and two Gold lines at the foot'.

364 Marked 'Exact the same as 269 Except the blue Ground under the roses and two Gold lines at the foot'.

365 Marked 'The same as 364 but [indecipherable] in these pannels'. (NB there appears to be no ground colour to the oval reserves; the roses are applied to the body and framed by gilt lines. In addition there is only one line at the foot rim.)

366 Shown as tea cup with handle. Gilt dentil edges to inner and outer rims. There is a gilt line intertwined with leaf and berry design round the middle of the cup, but with the addition of an oval reserve on side opposite handle, marked 'Landskips in Colors'.

92
A fine pair of dancers on scrolled mound bases. Patch marks. William Duesbury & Co. *c.* 1760. Approx. 18 cm. *Christie, Manson & Woods.*

94 ▷ ▷
Centrepiece modelled as two tiers of three scallop shells, decorated with butterflies and insects and gilt rims, resting upon a rocky base applied with coloured shells, seaweed and other marine life. The whole is surmounted by a gallant dressed in fine clothes and holding another shell on his head. William Duesbury & Co. 1765. 24.8 cm. *Christie, Manson & Woods.*

93
A pair of partridge tureens and covers painted in enamel colours. William Duesbury & Co. 1760–65. Approx. 11.9 cm. *Sotheby's, New Bond Street.*

95 ▷
Figure of a dancing girl adapted from the 'dry-edge' version. The companion figure is that of a Scotsman playing bagpipes. William Duesbury & Co. 1758–60. 15.5 cm. *Barry Waiting Collection.*

96 ▷ ▷
Group known as 'The Three Maries'. The Virgin Mary stands with clasped hands. William Duesbury & Co. 1765. 26.7 cm. *Schreiber Collection. Victoria & Albert Museum, 414/170 – 1885.*

97 ◁ ◁
A fine cruet set with polychrome
decoration. William Duesbury & Co.
c. 1765. Size not known. *Christie,
Manson & Woods.*

98 ◁
A jug painted in enamel colours, with a
Grenadier of the 1st Foot Guards on
one side, and on the reverse with
military trophies. It is interesting to
note that the jug must date before 1768
which is when bear-busbies were
introduced. William Duesbury & Co.
1760–65. Approx. 17.9 cm. *Winifred
Williams, London.*

100
An oval, open-work pierced basket
with rope-twist handles, painted with
figures in a landscape. Patch marks.
William Duesbury & Co. c. 1760.
Length approx. 8.8 cm. *Christie,
Manson & Woods.*

101
Important bowl which bears, in the
interior, the inscription 'Success to
Mine Innocent' in the form of words
issuing from a smoker's mouth. This
mine was a Derbyshire lead mine
which also yielded white clay. It has
not proved possible to ascertain
whether Duesbury owned or had any
interest in this mine. He did, however,
own another lead mine known as
Sucstone mine. William Duesbury &
Co. c. 1770. Diameter 25.4 cm.
Sotheby's, New Bond Street.

99 ◁
Two figures representing Kuan-Yin.
The left-hand example is from the
Derby works, and dates from 1756–60;
the other is a raised anchor-marked
Chelsea example dating from 1750.
The Derby example has patch marks. It
is interesting to note that the Victoria &
Albert Museum possesses a Chinese
example from Fukien province in
'blanc de Chine'. Derby example no
factory mark. William Duesbury &
Co. c. 1756–60. 11.4 cm. *Geoffrey
Godden.*

367 Gilt dentil edges to inner and outer rims. The same gilt line with intertwined berry and leaf design (as 366) form a border underneath outer rim. Gilt line above foot rim.

368 Gilt line to outer rim, below which is an undulating gilt line with leaves and berries attached to it. Gilt line above foot rim.

369 Coffee can with rope handle. Deep ornate inner border in gilt. Two gilt lines to outer rims. Ground the same as 365. Square reserve on side opposite handle marked 'Painting and the frame from 326'.

370 Shown as coffee can with rope handle. Two gilt lines to inner rim with additional heart shapes in continuous line immediately below. Broken line decoration on body of can with oval reserve on side opposite handle marked '[indecipherable] Colors by Askew'. Ornate gilt border framing reserve.

371 Shown as fluted tea cup with (double?) handle. Gilt lines to inner and outer rims. Simple gilt scroll design below outer rim appears to be the only decoration. No ground colour given.

372 Shown as coffee can. Gilt lines to inner and outer rims. Green no. 2 ground colour with deep border of pearls, each within a lozenge shape.

373 Tea cup with handle. Gilt lines to rims. Border in no. 2 green, decorated with roses in natural colours. Marked '6 roses in Cup 8 in Saucer 5 in Coffeas'.

374 Coffee can with rope handle. Gilt rims. Slight scroll decoration below outer rim. Oval reserve painted with 'Boy on A Board by Askew Colors'. Ornate sunburst frame to reserve in gilt, marked 'This border top of the stand'.

375 Shown as fluted cup. Gilt rims. Border of single blue line with gilt leaves and berries intertwining. Slight scroll border beneath blue line with added gilt decoration above foot rim.

376 Marked 'Ornament done same as 317 but continued round. 3 Vases in Can 3 in Saucer'.

377 Coffee can with rope handle. Gilt rims with narrow foliate border inside can. Square reserve with 'Landskips & Ships by Brewer'. No ground colour given, but there is an ornate gilt border which appears to go 'betwixt' whatever ground colour is laid on the can.

378 Presumably a coffee can, 'finished same as 377' with 'Moonlight Landskip by Brewer' in reserve. Another note states 'this border betwixt frame on the border of the stand'.

379 Shown as tea cup. Gilt rims. Narrow border of green no. 2 to outside rim overlaid with two lines of dark blue (black?) (dark green?).

380 Missing.

381 Tea cup with handle. Gilt rims. Outer border of blue with scalloped under-edge. Heavily gilded and a small white dot added to the upper part of the design.

382 Shown as coffee can. Gilded rims. Narrow border of greens to outer rim with large green sprigs on outside of can and in bottom.

383 Coffee can. Gilt rims. Two very narrow gilt borders to outer rim and at base of can. Green ground colour.

384 Shown as very splendid pair of beakers with twist handles. Pink body colour with large swags in ornate floral and leaf design. Oval reserves painted by Brewer 'in collors', 'Lesson in Love' and 'Landskip on the other'.

385 Missing.

386 Marked '386 is 382 without the sprigs'.

387 Shown as coffee can with rope handle. Gilt rims and slight gilt border inside can. Painted with 'Colord Groop by Banford'.

388 Gilt line to inside rim. Gilt dentil edge on outside rim, under which is a deep border in 'fawn' heavily decorated in gilt.

389 Coffee can with gilt rims. An overall design on body of floret heads on a blue spotted background. Oval reserve of 'Venus and Cupid in Colors by Askew'.

390 Coffee can with rope handle. Gilt dentil edges to inner and outer rims. Additional gilt border inside and deep borders in gilt to outer rim and base of can. Alternating star and spot design over body with painting in square reserve with jewelled frame. Painting of reserve probably flowers.

391 Coffee can. Gilded rims with additional narrow borders inside can. Yellow ground with square reserve painted with 'Basket of flowers Brewer in colors'. Ornate gilt frame to reserve.

392 Tea cup with handle. Gilt line to inner rim – dentil edge to outer rim. Narrow border below dentil edge of alternating leaf and star design in green and red.

393 Double-handled beakers with double twist handles. Fawn ground colour with reserves in the form of swags, each containing sprays of flowers in natural colours. One reserve 'Flora' by Brewer, and the other 'A Muse'. The body is overlaid with alternating gilt stars and black spots.

At this point the pattern books revert to 391 showing a tea cup with a rope handle in the exact manner of the coffee can already described. Pattern 392 is as described, but the border has a yellow ground. Pattern 393 is again as described, but shown as a tea cup with a handle.

394 Gilt dentil edge to inner rim, gilt line to outer rim, below which is a deep border of oak leaves and acorns.

395 As 392, but with addition of sprigs below border and to inside of cup.

397 (Out of sequence.) Gilt lines to inner and outer rims. Narrow border of

17

Finely modelled group, known as 'Pensent-ils au raisin?', based on an engraving by Jacques-Phillipe Le Bas after a Boucher painting dated 1747. Patch marks, no factory mark, incised number 20. William Duesbury & Co. 1775. 22 cm. *Ronald W. Raven Collection. Other examples in the Victoria & Albert Museum and Royal Crown Derby Museum.*

---

two fine lines (gilt?) between two thicker lines. No ground colour or design shown.

399 (Out of sequence.) Shown as cup with handle. Gilt dentil edges. Outer border of single blue line with intertwining gilt foliate decoration. Similar though slighter border at foot rim.

398 (Out of sequence.) No sketch added to outline cup shape.

396 (Out of sequence.) Gilt lines to inner and outer rims. Border on outer rim (pen and pencil only) suggests single line with added floral sprays at intervals, suggesting there are perhaps six sprays in all.

400 Gilt lines to inner and outer rims with scattered sprays over body of cup. In pen/pencil, giving no clue to colour.)

401 Cup with handle outlined – no pattern inserted.

402 As 400, but with slight alteration in design of sprigs.

403 Gilt line to inner rim, dentil edge to outer rim. Very slight leaf-type border in blue with added gilt. Single blue line at foot rim.

404 Dentil inner rim, gilt line to outer rim. Shown as cup with handle which has an oval reserve in outline. No other details.

405 Fawn inner border between two gilt lines with gilt foliate border below. No decoration on outside of cup.

406 Cup with handle – no pattern inserted.

407 Ditto.

408 Gilt lines to inner and outer rims. Slight foliate border between two gilt lines. (In pen/pencil, offering no clue to colour). Border repeated at foot rim.

409 Marked '409 same as 408 except Yellow Ground' (*sic*).

NB inserted in pencil between 409 and 410 '[indeciperable] 1790'.

410 Tea bowl shape with outlined oval reserve marked 'Landskip done with Olive 1331 finished by a little Black 693 and tinted with soft flesh'. It is also noted: 'Oval nearly $2\frac{1}{2}$ by $1\frac{3}{4}$'.

Not numbered: at this point there is a pattern without a number, but given in great detail and shown as a jug, with the following notes: '6 of Each sort of Pattern in this and the Pint Jug and Straight Pint. The Pint Jugs and the Quart Jugs done the same as this.' The border comprises lozenge-shaped reserves with blue centre and gilt sunburst design to outer edges. There is an additional border of gilt foliate design intertwined with a blue ribbon.

Not numbered: the next design, again un-numbered, shows a saucer with a border of pearls set in black and gold with gilt stars between each pearl and marked 'Pearls Common Pearl Color' (*sic*). Deep border marked 'Bloom very faint' with the additional note 'this pair of [indecipherable] Markt No. 2' (*sic*).

411 Narrow yellow border between two gilt lines to outer rim and narrow gilt foliate border below. Gilt line on inner rim.

412 Shown as coffee can with rope handle. Gilt(?) foliate borders to outer rim and foot rim. Oval reserve with 'Colord Groop of flowers on faint Olive ground' (*sic*). Also marked 'No flowers on the stand to this can'.

413 Shown as coffee can with rope handle. Gilt borders to inner and outer rims. Yellow ground colour overlaid with ornate scrolls and alternating vase and bell motifs in blue, olive, green and purple. Also shown is a star motif which occurs in the bottom of the (indistinguishable).

Coffee can with rope handle. Gilt borders at rim and foot rim. Yellow ground with oval reserve painted with 'Colord Landskips by Hill'. Marked (a) 'not numbered'; (b) 'No Landskip on the stand of this can'.

'Not numbered'. Coffee can with rope handle. Narrow blue and gilt border on outer rim. Gilt foliate border above foot rim. Marked in oval reserve 'Landskip painted with 1365 by Hill'. Also marked 'Landskip on the Stand – this in the hollow of the stand'.

Very ornate design on what appears to be a *sucrier* or bowl. Bloom or fawn ground colour with '2 Vases in bottom same in top'. Foliate gilt border to rim marked 'this border edge of the top'. Similar border with additional gilding at base marked 'this inside [indecipherable] Line Circle on the top'. Colours overlaying ground colour are noted as 'purple, olive, green, blue'.

414 Coffee can with rope handle. Ornate border to inside rim in gilt marked 'this border bottom of the stand'. Ground colour possibly pink. Square reserve marked 'A Bachante in Colors by Brewer. Adelaid in colors on other can by D°'.

415 Coffee can with rope handle. Gilt lines to inner and outer rim. Body colour green no. 2. Oval reserve painted with 'Love Sleeps in Colors by Brewer. Maid of Corinth on the other Can'.

18
A seated musician well modelled and decorated and coming from the Chelsea–Derby era, showing a more sophisticated approach to modelling in the chair and base, with his hat nonchalantly hanging on the corner of the chair. Note that at around this time the figures began to be incised with a number and sometimes an indication of size. No factory mark, number 69. William Duesbury & Co. 1775. 15.5 cm. *Ronald W. Raven Collection.*

19
An interesting tankard of normal shape and decoration, with the exception of the portrait medallion pendant from a pink ribbon. The initials are not identified: this prompts the author to stress the foolishness of removing labels and/or any information that may be present when a piece is discovered. Crown over 'D' in blue. William Duesbury & Co. 1780–85. 17.6 cm. *Private collection.*

416 Coffee can with rope handle. Narrow gilt foliate borders to outer rim and foot. Green no. 2 body colour. Square reserve painted with 'Landskips in Colors by Robertson'.

417 Marked 'In Every Respect same as 416 Except Yellow Instead of Green'.

418 Marked 'Same as 416 Except Bloom Instead of Green'.

419 Marked 'Autumnal border repeated twice in cups 3 times in saucer'. 'Middle of the Circle in Saucer $2\frac{1}{2}$ Inches and $\frac{1}{8}$'.

420 'Same as 411 Except Green No. 5 Instead of Yellow'.

421 Shown as tea cup with handle. Gilt inner and outer rimes. Marked 'Colord flies 3 to each Peice. Circle in suacer'.

422 Tea cup with handle. Marked 'Colord feathers to Each Peice. Circle in Saucer'.

423 Blank.

424 Coffee can. Ornate gilt border comprising semicircles pendant from top and upright from base of border, touching in middle, with added star decoration. Bloom ground. Square reserve of 'Groop of fruit before a Ground [indecipherable]'. Small foliate gilt border at base.

425 Missing.

426 Shown as tea cup with handle. Gilt lines to inner and outer rims. Marked '4 Colord feathers Outside 1 in Bottom'.

427 Tea cup with handle. Narrow gilt foliate border. 'Grey ground Distance for Hills'. Oval reserve painted with 'Colord Landskip $2\frac{1}{2}$ inches by 2 inches within' (*sic*). 'Painting in saucer $2\frac{3}{8}$'.

430 (Out of sequence.) Coffee can with rope handle. Ornate foliate border to inner rim. Yellow ground colour. Square reserve of 'Colord Ships $3\frac{1}{2}$ by $2\frac{1}{2}$'.

428 Coffee can with rope handle. Slight gilt border to inner rim. Bloom ground. Oval reserve of 'Camp Scene by Brewer in Colors $3\frac{1}{4}$ by $2\frac{1}{4}$'.

429 Coffee can with rope handle. Marked 'Same in every Respect as 428 Grey Ground instead of Bloom'.

431 Coffee can with plain handle. Deep borders to rim and foot rim with trellis design in gilt over light fawn ground with additional decoration of blue spots. Between these borders is a gilt border of leaves and sprays.

432 Coffee can with rope handle. Narrow yellow borders between gilt lines to rim and foot rim. Trellis design in gilt over body of can with oval reserve of 'Colord figures by Brewer allmost 3 inches by $2\frac{1}{4}$'.

432 (Additional.) Coffee can with rope handle. Marked 'Ships in Colors all round'.

433 Deep borders of intersecting ovals with added decoration between two narrow borders. The sketch is in monochrome, and no written information is available concerning colour and/or gilding.

434 Shown as tea cup with handle. Slight gilt border to inner rim. Two 'Soft yellow' borders intersected by gilt foliate and spray border marked 'Gilt same as 431'.

435 Marked '435 same as 187 Except Grey Ground Instead of Yellow'.

436 Marked 'Yellow Dejeune with Shipping'.

437 Missing.

438 Marked '438 same as 411 Except Purple Instead of Yellow'.

439 Tea bowl with fluted rim. Scattered sprigs of blue flowers with gilt stems and leaves.

440 Tea cup with handle. Gilt rims. Outer border of two narrow yellow borders intersected by florets of red between two gilt lines, with additional decoration overlaying the whole in the form of sixteen black 'fish-hooks'.

441 As above, but the two narrow borders are green instead of yellow.

442 Tea bowl with fluted rim. Narrow yellow border between two gilt lines with six small oval reserves outlined in blue with gilt floret in centre of each.

443 Tall tea bowl with fluted rim. Gilt line to inner and outer rims. Border in fawn overlaid with classical border in black(?). A note appended to this pattern states 'Strong hard Roseburst blue Kiln'.

444 'Large breakfast cup and stand finished same as 445 painting etc'. Monochrome drawing of can showing gilt lines to inner and outer rims. Border below rim contains twenty-eight circles at regular intervals. Forty-seven of these on stand.

445 Large breakfast cup and stand (can shape) with ornate rope handle. Gilt rims. Blue border with thirty-nine pearls and gilt enrichment. Fifty pearls round edge of stand. Gilt line to bottom of can.

446 Narrow blue border to inside of tea bowl between two gilt lines. Gilt line to outer rim with scattered sprigs in gilt over body of bowl. Marked '3 sprigs outside [indecipherable] in bottom. sprigs Different in the [indecipherable] saucer'.

447 Probably a coffee can, but shape is difficult to determine. Ground colour faded but possibly green. Square reserve painted with 'Colord Shipping very near $3\frac{1}{4}$ inches square in centre of saucer $2\frac{1}{2}$'. There is a sprig border about three-quarters of an inch below rim with a star motif between each sprig. The colour has faded, but it seems probable that it is in the typical pink and blue Chantilly sprig colours.

448 Coffee can with serpentine handle. Gilt rims. Border of light blue overlaid with classical border in black, the motif of which appears ten times on the can and sixteen times on the stand. The recipe for an 'Orange mix' is given against this pattern, ie 'Soft Orange 1 part and red 2 parts', but this seems to have no connection with the pattern as shown and described above.

449 This is similar to 448, but the classical motif varies slightly and it also gives a new recipe for an orange mix, viz. 'Orange made of soft Orange and red Equall' (*sic*). In addition, it bears the further instruction 'Green No. 2 laid inside bottom of the Can and Green brick bottom of the Stand Incompas'd with black lines'.

450 As 448 and 9 but with leaf motif (14) on the border. A further recipe for orange is included: 'Orange made of 3 red 2 soft Orange Black 666 all one fire [indecipherable] to London April 28th'.

451 Shown as coffee can with rope handle. Celeste blue ground with formal design of alternating sprigs and stars. Very ornate gilt border to inner rim. Gilt dentil edge to outer rim. Oval reserve painted with 'Basket of flowers by Withers as G... Distance for Hill. 3 inches; this W[indecipherable]' (*sic*).

452 Tea bowl showing fluted rim. Narrow blue border to outer rim with slight gilt enrichment.

Not numbered: pattern marked 'Not numbered' but following after 452 and shown before 454. Coffee can with rope handle. Gilt rims. Inner gilt border about a quarter of an inch deep. Body of can shows two rows of medallions of ovoid form. The medallions intersect each other in each row and are interspersed with gilt stars and dots. The oval reserve is painted with 'Basket of flowers before a grey ground and on an Olive Pedestall by Withers 3 inches thick'.

Not numbered: pattern 453? Marked 'New Chocolate'. Outline only showing gilt outer rim and deep border marked 'This border from Dessert pattern 122'. 'Handles rich'. There are two narrow gilt borders shown – one at base of can, and the other immediately below the deep outer border.

454 Again marked 'New Chocolate'. Gilt outer rim below which is narrow border of black overlaid with pearls. 'Ground dark blue'. 'Dots and flowers white' (these appear to cover the whole of the body of the can in formal rows).

Pattern marked 'Large New Chocolate Not Numbered'. Gilt rim below which is a deep border of flowers in natural colours between two gilt lines, with additional gilt decoration below. New angular handle.

Pattern marked 'Large New Chocolate'. Deep border painted with 'Roses and blue [indecipherable] by Withers Esq.'. Additional note: 'This Pattn. whould be much better with this Laid a Ground of Yellow or Darker Color to relieve the roses and blue'.

456 Marked 'Grey border. Gilt. Exact same as 411'.

456 Marked 'New Chocolate same as 372 Except bloom instead of Green Ground'.

457 Marked 'New Chocolate same as 372 Except Yellow Ground marbled, Instead of Green'.

458 Shown as tea cup with handle. Very attractive 'draped' border with tassels to inside rim. Very narrow gilt border to outer rim. Yellow ground with square reserve which has unusual triangular additions to frame at each side. Reserve painted with '3 inch Camp View by Brewer in colors'.

459 Tea cup with handle. Deep gilt border to inside rim. Narrow gilt border of foliate design below outer rim. Yellow ground colour. Oval reserve painted with 'Landskip in Colors by Hill rather better than $2\frac{1}{2}$ by rather better than $1\frac{3}{4}$. Saucer $2\frac{1}{4}$ and this plain line [gilt] round the Landskip' (*sic*).

460 Tea cup with handle. Gilt rims. Deep border in brown 325 in classical design of swags pendant from half-moon shapes between scroll motifs with scattered sprigs above each pendant swag.

461 Tea cup with handle. Gilt rims. Deep border in brown 325 in classical scroll pattern.

462 Tea cup with handle. Gilt rims. Deep border of yellow overlaid by border in black exactly as described in 460. '5 stars' (over body of cup). Very interesting note: 'Border of Mr. Kean's to be Done same Black. $2\frac{1}{4}$ each Gilding'. (This probably referred to the payment the gilder was to receive for each item executed.)

463 Border exactly as 462 but on bloom ground. No stars on body of cup but marked '4 Moons in Cups'. 'Gilding same as 462'.

464 Tea cup with handle. Gilt rims. Pink ground colour with additional border about three-eighths of an inch from rim of triangles, each containing three dots (possibly in gilt). Square reserve with very narrow

20

Pair of chamber pots and covers, originally made for the daughter of Johann Zacharias Beck of Saxe-Gotha in Germany, Mararetta Henrietta, who married Sir George Buchan-Hepburn in 1781. The decoration on the covers is in blue monochrome by William Billingsley and the rose, thistle and pendant blue monochrome chains are also painted by him. This is one of the very few pairs of chamber pots to have survived. Crown, crossed batons, dots in puce. William Duesbury & Co. 1781–5. 17.5 cm. *The Marquis of Bute. David Graham Collection.*

102 ◁ ◁
A punch or harvest jug with a mask lip in the form of a man wearing a tricorn hat. The body is finely painted with flowers, used in such a manner as to hide blemishes and fine-cracks. The flower at the top of the large tulip has a thick ball of pooled glaze as its centre. Edges gilt. William Duesbury & Co. *c.* 1770–75. 24 cm. *D. Sulley Collection.*

103 ◁
'A large group of Jason and Medea, vowing before the altar of Diana, enamelled and richly finished with gold' is how such a figure group was listed in 1773 catalogue (Nightingale). Incised number 37 and a 2 for second size. William Duesbury & Co. *c.* 1773. 32 cm. *Marian Jenkinson, Christchurch. C. B. Shephard & Sons.*

105
A pair of figures in the role of 'Sportsman and Lady', taken from the gold anchor Chelsea models. Patch marks. William Duesbury & Co. *c.* 1765–70. Approx. 19 cm. *Victoria & Albert Museum: C152 – 1931; C165 – 1931.*

106
A fine pair of Kedleston-shaped ewers, richly decorated with gold stripes, upon which are panels of figure subjects, possibly the work of Richard Askew. On the reverse side are landscape panels which might reasonably be attributed to Zachariah Boreman. Ewers, together with a pair of therm vases and a centre vase, form a complete garniture of five vases. A complete set is in the Herbert Allen Collection in the Victoria & Albert Museum. Crown over 'D' in gold on the top side of the plinth. The pair of therms decorated by James Rouse Senior and produced by Derby Crown Porcelain Company were so marked (see *Royal Crown Derby* p. 48 for colour illustration). William Duesbury & Co. *c.* 1780. 27.7 cm. *Private collection. Delomosne & Son, London.*

104 ◁
A set of the 'Four Quarters' on flat bases, appearing at this period without being named. Patch marks. William Duesbury & Co. *c.* 1765. Approx. 20.3 cm. *Christie, Manson & Woods.*

109 ▷
Fine portrait figure of John Wilkes which might with good reason be attributed to Pierre Stephan. Wilkes became Lord Mayor of London in 1775 after overcoming earlier setbacks, which included a term in prison. It is reasonable to attribute most of the national heroes series to Stephan, as some original models in clay have survived and are signed. William Duesbury & Co. 1772–5. 30.5 cm. *Victoria & Albert Museum, 414/201 – 1885.*

107
Small cabaret teapot and cover with rose painting strongly attributed to Edward Withers. Crown over 'D' in blue. William Duesbury & Co. *c.* 1780. Approx. 12 cm. *Private collection.*

108
Pair of claret-ground vases and covers in neo-classical style on plinths. Vases: incised 'B' and small gold anchor; one plinth marked with a red anchor, the other marked with gold anchor. William Duesbury & Co. *c.* 1780. Vases 18.9 cm, bases 9.1 cm. *Victoria & Albert Museum: C211 and A – 1935; 485 and A – 1875.*

110
Finely modelled set of 'Seasons' attributed to Pierre Stephan. It is interesting to note that this set was re-issued later on round bases and traditionally these have always been known as 'Coffee Seasons' (see colour plate 32 for such a set in the Indianapolis Museum of Art). William Duesbury & Co. *c.* 1775. Approx. 25 cm. *Christie, Manson & Woods.*

111
Two groups of cupids representing 'Commerce' (1773) and 'Astronomy and Geometry' (1773). The third group represents 'Arithmetic', copied from Michel Victor Acier's Meissen group of 1770. This Derby version is dated on one of the books 'Apr. 6th. 1773'. William Duesbury & Co. Average height 17.8 cm. *Schreiber Collection. Victoria & Albert Museum: 414/427 – 1885 left; 414/411 – 1885 centre; 414/427A – 1885 right.*

112
Biscuit figure of a child. William Duesbury & Co. 1790. Approx. 13 cm. *Victoria & Albert Museum, C1308 – 1919.*

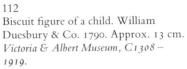

113
Pair of figures known as the 'French Shepherd and Shepherdess'. William Duesbury & Co. 1775. 18 cm. *Victoria & Albert Museum: C256 – 1935 boy; C256 A – 1935 girl.*

114
A rare and elegant French-shaped chocolate cup and stand, with borders of elaborate tooled gilding, reserved upon which are three panels in Watteau style, which the author attributes to the hand of Fidelle Duvivier. Note particularly the hair of the male lover holding the sundial in the top panel of the stand. Christie's catalogue of 1782 states: 'Superbly elegant French-shape cup and saucer enamelled in compartments with figures, fine ultramarine blue ground.' Gold anchor and an incised script 'N' near foot rim. William Duesbury & Co. 1770–75. Cup 10 cm. *Mary Field Collection.*

frame painted with 'Shipping...inches on the bottom Line of the border'. Also marked 'Saucer square [reserve?] 2½ inches'.

465 Tea cup with handle. Gilt rims. Deep yellow border overlaid with flowers and fern motifs in black. Marked '9 black flowers in Cup 13 in saucer 8 in coffee 16 in bowl 16 In Plates 10 Ewer'. Gilt stars and small fern motifs alternate round the body of the cup.

466 Tea cup with handle. Inside border as 458. Gilt line to outer rim with additional decoration of stars inside and outside cup.

467 Tea cup with handle. Border to inner rim as 458. Deep border of roses with buds painted in natural colours between two gilt lines from outer rim to base of handle, with additional gilt decoration below. A further border of thirteen stars above foot rim.

469 (Out of sequence.) Tea cup with handle. Gilt rims with added border below inside rim. No other decoration illustrated.

468 Tea cup with handle. Ornate gilt border inside cup. Very deep border from outer rim to base of handle painted with '8 roses with buds' in natural colours. Small additional gilt border.

470 Pencil outline of tea cup with handle. Fluted rim with deep border below marked 'Same as 465 Except bloom Instead of Yellow'.

471 No sketch but marked 'brown border from 465' and a recipe: 'Brown mixt with 2 parts Brown 325 1 Black 693'.

472 Shown as large breakfast cup with handle. Deep inside border of yellow between two gold lines with narrow gilt line under the border. Narrow gilt foliate border about a quarter of an inch below outer rim, marked 'this border in the stand betwixt the Lines and the Circle'.

473 No sketch, but marked 'same as 472 Except the Gold [indecipherable]'.

474 Tea cup with handle. Three narrow gilt lines to inner rim. Single gilt line on outer rim. Very ornate trellis pattern in diamond form, each diamond extending from rim to foot rim. Eighteen diamonds in cup and thirteen in saucer, each having embellishments of leaves and stars. Design in monochrome, but black 666 is mentioned.

475 Tea cup with handle. Three narrow gilt lines to inner rim. Narrow blue border between two gilt lines to outer rim. Very wide diamond-shaped trellis over body of cup with added leaf decoration and intersected by diagonal foliate festoons which stretch from rim border to foot rim border. Oval reserve painted with 'flowers on Warm Olive Ground in oval 2¼ by 1¾ Peg' (sic).

476 Tea cup with handle, marked 'Just the same as 475 but no painting'.

477 Tea cup with handle. Gilt rims. Narrow dark blue border to outer rim and foot rim between two gilt lines. Yellow ground lavishly gilded in ornate design repeated sixteen times round cup, twenty-two times round saucer.

478 'Exact same as 477 with the addition of a Landskip'. The painting in an oval reserve marked with 'Landskip rather better than 2¼ × 1¾'.

479 Tea cup with handle. Gilt rims. Deep border of dark blue overpainted with oval medallions, each with border of tiny white dots and gilded in sunburst manner. The medallions are separated by gilt stars and scattered white dots. Eight medallions on cup, eleven in saucer.

480 Tea cup with handle. Gilt rims. Deep border of dark blue overlaid with undulating foliate festoon in gilt. Additional decoration of gilt stars and scattered white dots.

481 Tea cup with handle. Shown in chestnut-brown monochrome. Deep border entirely covered with tiny dots over which are laid festoons of leaves, interspersed with small butterflies – six in cup, eight in saucer.

482 Marked only 'Fawn border exact same as 411'.

483 Marked 'Dark blue border exact same as 411'.

484 Marked 'Same as 474 Except black Lines'.

485 Tea cup with handle. Gilt rims. Deep border in celeste blue with trellis design in gilt. Each diamond shape formed by trellis contains two gilt dots and tiny leaf at each 'point'.

486 Tea cup with handle. Gilt rims. Narrow border in yellow between two gilt lines below outer rim.

487 Exactly as above but border in bloom, and gilt decoration on handle comprises line of dots interspersed with leaf motif.

488 Marked 'Yellow Instead of Bloom 487'.

489 'Same as [indecipherable] except fawn instead of Blue' (sic).

490 Marked 'Same as 331. With the addition of In Side Border to 333 but rather bolder' (sic). There is an additional note: 'flat pieces 2¾d. each' and 'upright pieces 3¼d. each' (presumably the price paid to the artist-workmen).

491 No sketch. Marked 'Same as 488 Except Green Ground instead of Yellow' (sic).

492 No sketch. Marked 'Same as 471 except sprigs under Line' (sic). Additional note tells us '7d. per dozen gilding. Painting 3d. ea.'.

493 No sketch. Marked 'same as 452 fawn Instead of Blue Border' (sic).

494 No sketch. 'Same as 492 with Bloom ground' (sic).

495 No sketch. 'Same as 492 with A strong yellow ground below Border. The border contracted by having the gold lines broader'.

496 No sketch. 'Same as 188 except yellow instead of bloom'.

497 No sketch. 'Same as 55 with the Inside border of 157 done bold'.

498 Shown as tea cup with handle. Gilt rims with additional gilding to inside rim. Outer border below rim appears to consist of a monochrome orange leaf design of formal habit, two small ovoid leaves alternating with two much larger spatular leaves decorating a single orange line.

499 No sketch. 'Same as 498 except no inside border. Each handle the same' (sic).

500 Tea cup with handle. Gilt rims. Deep border below outer rim showing broad red ribands 'Done common orange red' with tiny gilt dots added to the broad bands of riband. Heavily gilded with foliate design between the undulating ribands. '10 ribbands in cup. 14 Ribbands in Saucer'.

501 Gilt rims to tea cup with handle. Ornate gilt inner border. Two broad borders of yellow at outer rim and foot rim, leaving a band of similar width round middle of cup undecorated except for gilt decoration of leaves and fronds in continuous line.

502 Shown as tea cup with handle. Slight border to inner rim. Deep border of dark blue between two gilt lines and overlaid to top and bottom of border with a row of black spots at intervals, between which is a gilt border of leaves in a formal design.

503 Gilt rims to tea cup with handle. Slight additional gilt border to inner rim. A narrow border in bloom to outer rim. Below this is a narrow undecorated border, and the remainder of the cup has a bloom ground.

504 Tea cup with handle. 'Same as 131 Except Yellow instead of blue and the top blue rather broader'. Dentil edge to inner rim.

505 Cup with handle. Gilt rims. Attractive border of gilt scallops to inside of cup (twenty-two in all). An undulating border (described as a bend) of yellow, blue and purple finished with tiny gilt dots one-third of the way down the cup with additional sprays of leaves in gilt. Described as having '4 Bends in Cup 6 in Saucer' and 'Bottom Color Velvet Purple, middle Dark Blue, top Yellow' (sic).

506 No sketch. 'Same as 503 Except Yellow Instead of Bloom' (sic).

507 'Same as 35 with the Addition of 3 heights of Feathers'. Another difference is that the outer rim has a plain line instead of a 'Dontell'.

508 Yellow border, same gilt as number 90.

509 No sketch. 'As 411 Except the Laurells' (sic).

510 No sketch. Possibly the note 'Same as 504 except feathers' refers to this pattern.

511 No sketch. 'Gold Ornament as 463 and yel[indecipherable] Laurel below' (sic).

512 Marked 'Pearls after 135'. The border design is sketched in, showing pearls contained within lozenge shapes, each one being separated by a gilded leaf motif of formal design. There is no clue to colouring as the sketch is carried out in brown monochrome.

513 Gilt rims. Border as 498. Yellow ground over remainder of cup.

514 'Same as 508 Bloom Instead of Yellow' (sic).

515 No sketch. 'Same as 500 Except Orange Instead of Red. Gilding same'.

516 Sketch shows tea cup with handle. Gilt rims and border to outer rim in yellow. Sketch marked '[indecipherable] outside the cup very narrow [indecipherable] of the Saucer broad as Inside the Cup'.

517 No sketch. 'Same as 512 with the addition of Yellow Ground' (sic).

518 Tea cup with handle. Gilt rims. Identical blue borders inside and outside cup with overlaid leaf sprays in gilt, each separated by two vertical gilt bars which appear to be 'shaded' with black.

519 Tea cup with handle. Gilt rims. Deep border containing pearls in lozenge shapes, each separated by a single large gilt dot. Remainder of cup has yellow ground without decoration.

520 Cup shape and handle very carelessly drawn but marked 'Same as 411 Except Brown 325 Instead of Yellow'.

521 Again very carelessly drawn sketch and writing almost obliterated by repair tape, but believed to read '½ Pearls and Bloom Ground'.

522 Similar careless sketch marked 'Broad Yellow same as 473 Gilt with one Line Leaving Out the small Line' (sic).

523 Shown as tall tea bowl without handle. Gilt rims. Border of red ribands, each connected to the other by a line of graduated gilt dots leaning in opposite direction to ribands and with small leaf motif in centre. Marked 'Plain shank^d tea[?]'.

524 Carelessly drawn outline of tea bowl (no handle) and marked '½ Pearls same as 519 Omitting the Yellow' (sic).

525 No sketch. 'Same as 463 Except Yellow Instead of Bloom. Gilt same as 462' (sic).

526 No sketch. 'Same as 473 Except Green Instead of Yellow' (sic).

527 No sketch. 'Blue instead of Black to pearls and bloom Ground' (sic). (Possibly a variation on 519 already described.)

528 No sketch. 'Same as 411 Except Red instead of Yellow'.

529 Shown as tall tea bowl. Handle illustrated separately. Gilt rims. Two similar borders in trellis design, one to rim and the other at foot rim with a border of roses in natural colours round the middle of the cup. 'Same as 431 Except roses instead of gold Laurell'.

530 Tall tea bowl. Handle shown separately. Gilt rims. Simple gilt border of foliate design below outer rim. Gilt line above foot rim.

531 Tall tea bowl. Handle design shown separately. Gilt rims. Scalloped border to inner rim. Narrow gilt foliate border to outer rim. Yellow ground with landscape in reserve. Simple gilt line framing reserve.

532 Tea bowl. Gilt rims. Deep outer border of alternating ribands and leaf sprays to form pyramids – ribands in red, leaves in gilt. Gilt line beneath this border and above foot rim.

533 Tea cup with handle. Sketch outline very carelessly drawn and marked 'Same as 520 Except no Laurrell and plain line down the handle edge each side the handle' (sic).

116
Pastoral group. Patch marks, incised number 12. William Duesbury & Co. *c.* 1772. 29.5 cm. Group of Bacchantes adorning Pan. Incised number 196. *c.* 1775. 27.9 cm. *Christie, Manson & Woods.*

115 ■
Pair of figures, boy with a dog and girl with a cat. In the Derby and Chelsea sale catalogue for 29 March 1773, one lot reads, 'A pair of laughing figures enamelled white and gold, dressing a macarony dog and cat 17s.' (see Nightingale, p. 45). The figures were bought in Paris on 18 April 1873 by Lady Schreiber from a dealer called Mme Flaudin. In her journals she writes, 'They were very dear, but quite irresistable at £14'. Incised number 49. William Duesbury & Co. 1770–75. 14.5 cm. *Schreiber Collection. Victoria & Albert Museum: 414/416 – 1885 man; 414/416A – 1885 woman.*

119
Group of boy and girl dancing, taken from the Etienne Falconet model called 'La Danse Allemande' and produced by the Sèvres factory in 1765. William Duesbury & Co. *c.* 1775. 16 cm. *Schreiber Collection. Victoria & Albert Museum, 414/415 – 1885.*

117
Lord Chatham (1708–78); at his side an
Indian woman representing America.
Pitt was raised to the peerage and
became Lord Keeper in 1776, and in
the same year declared himself in
favour of a conciliatory policy towards
the American Colonies. Gold anchor
mark. William Duesbury & Co.
c. 1775. 41.9 cm. *Schreiber Collection.*
Victoria & Albert Museum, 414/202 –
1885.

118 ●
A pair of singers. William Duesbury &
Co. c. 1775. Male 24.1 cm, female
20.6 cm. *Sotheby's, New Bond Street.*

120
Portrait figure of General Conway.
The shield carries his family crest, a
Moor's head. William Duesbury & Co.
c. 1772–5. 30.5 cm. *Victoria & Albert*
Museum, 414/200 – 1885.

121

A figure of a boy, probably representing 'Spring', and an interesting figure of a dog which is probably taken from Bewick and might well have been modelled by William Coffee. In the 1976 Morley College Exhibition there was a signed dog by this modeller. See *Ceramics of Derbyshire* plate 42 depicting setter. William Duesbury & Co. Figure *c.* 1775, dog *c.* 1795. Figure 12.5 cm, dog 12.2 cm. Figure: *Mrs L. Horwood Collection.* Dog: *David John Ceramics, Woodstock. Mr & Mrs T. Casey Collection.*

124

Bust of Jean-Jacques Rousseau (1712–78), adapted from a portrait painted by Taraval, which was in turn based on a bronze medal dated 1761 by Frans Gabriel Leclerc, and engraved in 1766 by C. H. Watelat. The philosopher wears his Armenian costume. William Duesbury & Co. *c.* 1770. 16 cm. *Schreiber Collection. Victoria & Albert Museum, 414/432 – 1885.*

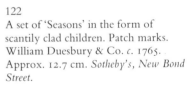

122

A set of 'Seasons' in the form of scantily clad children. Patch marks. William Duesbury & Co. *c.* 1765. Approx. 12.7 cm. *Sotheby's, New Bond Street.*

123

'Prudence' and 'Discretion', thought quite likely to have been modelled by Pierre Stephan. William Duesbury & Co. *c.* 1770–75. 'Discretion' 20.3 cm, 'Prudence' 21.3 cm. *Schreiber Collection. Victoria & Albert Museum, 414/410 and 414/410A – 1885.*

534 Tall tea bowl. Handle illustrated separately. Gilt rims. Pearls within lozenge shapes form continuous border below outer rim. Colour difficult to determine.

535 Cup with handle outlined. Marked 'Blue instead of Black to Pearls and yellow ground'. (Probably variation on 534.)

536 'Same as 188 Except Strong Rose Collor' (sic).

537 Tea cup with handle. Gilt rims. Narrow border of outlined ovoid shapes overlaying each other between two narrow gilt lines. Narrow gilt line round centre of cup with very slight foliate garland intertwined through this. Gilt line above foot rim.

538 Tea cup with handle. Gilt rims. Outer border of harebell design. Colours difficult to determine as sketch is shown in monochrome. Gilt line above foot rim.

539 Outline of cup only.

540 Cup with handle. Gilt rims. Outer border comprising ribands arranged to form oval lozenge shapes, each containing a tiny red floret and decorated above and below with tiny gilt leaves.

541 Tea cup with handle. Gilt rims. Outer border of ivy leaves and tiny flowers. Sketch in monochrome brown.

542 Tea cup with handle. Deep outer border of large corn stalks with leaves on a coloured ground between two gilt lines. Gilt line to inner rim.

543 Tea cup with handle. Gilt rims. Border of scallops bisected with inverted border of scallops forming an attractive chain effect. Single gilt line above foot rim.

544 Tea cup with handle. Gilt rims. Simple undulating foliate border to outer rim. Gilt line below border and a further one above foot rim.

545 Tea cup with handle. Gilt rims. Outer border of blue ivy leaves with additional decoration of fronds and leaves in gilt. Gilt line above foot rim.

546 Tea cup with handle. Gilt rims. Outer border of single gilt line with intertwined leaf sprays. Gilt line above foot rim.

547 Tea cup with handle. Gilt dentil edge to inner rim. Green border in Vandyke style bisected with narrow border of ovoid lozenges overlaying each other, and each decorated with three dots placed vertically. Small reserves containing a tiny floret (number uncertain) complete this gilt border. Under the green Vandyke edge are placed vertical lines of feathers extending to line above foot rim.

548 Tea cup with handle. Gilt dentil edge to inner rim. Plain line to outer rim, below which is plain border in fawn, finished with gilt line. Simple but decorative gilt border immediately below. Gilt line above foot rim.

549 Tea cup with handle. Gilt rims. Deep outer border of classical design with pendant swags hanging from crescent moon shapes with intricate scrolls between each. Design in monochrome but marked 'red ground'.

550 Shown as tea cup with handle. Gilt rims. Border below outer rim (possibly in gilt) showing alternating leaf and seaweed fronds. Pale blue body colour to gilt line above foot rim.

551 Outline of tea cup with handle. No design inserted.

552 Tea cup with handle. Gilt rims. Ribands of gilt leaves interlacing ribands of cornflowers and leaves in natural colours extending from rim to line above foot rim.

553 Tea cup with handle. Gilt rims. Border of shapes looking exactly like stuffed olives with addition of gilt arrow motifs between each 'olive'.

554 Tea cup with handle. Gilt rims. Deep border to outer rim comprising vine leaves, grapes and tendrils (possibly in gold and brown).

555 Tea cup with handle. Gilt rims. Deep border below outer rim of leaves and stalks with buds. The whole design is carried out in grey monochrome with no indication of colour.

556 Tea cup with handle. Gilt rims. Narrow border of 'strong rose' to outer rim. Scattered sprigs over body of cup (no indication of colour).

557 Tea cup with handle. Gilt rims. Very deep border of undulating foliate fronds with tendrils and tiny red flowers interlaced with undulating continuous chain of red buds and gilt stalks.

558 Outline of tall tea cup. No design inserted.

559 Ditto.

560 Shown as tea cup with handle. Gilt rims. Outer border shows blue ribands joined by small chain of gold dots moving in opposite directions. Narrow gilt line above foot rim.

561 Shown as tea cup with and without handle. Deep outer border of leaf and seaweed design between two gilt borders.

562 Shown as tall tea cup with and without handle. Scalloped border to inside rim. Narrow gilt border to outer rim. Yellow body colour over remainder of cup terminating in gilt line just above foot rim.

563 Exactly as 562, but with bloom body colour.

564 Shown as tall tea cup with and without handle. Gilt rims. Narrow border of (indistinguishable) under which is a narrow gilt foliate border. Gilt line above foot rim.

565 Shown as tall tea cup with and without handle. Gilt rims. Outer border of upright ovals slightly leaning to the left, each containing a gilt floret and interspersed at intervals by a gilt oval reserve couchant, also containing a gilt floret. Between each of the upright ovals is a small gilt arrow – pointing downwards on the top line and upwards on the bottom line. The border is finished with a narrow gilt line, and there is a narrow gilt line above the foot rim.

566 Outline of tall tea cup with handle shown separately. No design, but the words 'Perple and yellow Ovals' have been inserted.

567 (See below.)

568 Shown as tall tea cup with handle shown separately. A dark blue line has been drawn round the outer border, under which is a narrower blue line. A dark blue line above the foot rim is also shown.

569 Shown as tall tea cup with handle shown separately. Gilt rims. Deep border of vine leaves, grapes and tendrils immediately beneath outer rim, finished with gilt line below. Scattered sprigs of vine leaves and grapes over body of cup. Gilt line above foot rim.

567 Shown as tall tea cup with and without handle. Gilt line to inner rim. Deep border of poppies and corn stalks with seaweed embellishments between two gilt lines. Gilt line above foot rim.

570 Tall tea cup with and without handle. Dark blue lines to inner and outer rims. Very narrow border of blue dots forming a chain, each connected by three smaller blue dots with very narrow blue line below completing border. Scattered sprigs in monochrome blue over body of cup.

571 Missing.

572 Shown as tea cup with handle. Gilt rims. Deep outer border of palms tied together. Between each palm is a fleur-de-lys in gilt, pendant from outer rim and upright from gilt line which finishes border. Note inserted: 'The Crop on the Palms White' (sic).

573 Shown as tea cup with handle. Very faintly outlined is a narrow border below outer rim, containing tiny leaf sprays at regular intervals. There appears to be a line round the middle of the cup with slight leaf decoration. No clue as to colour.

574 Missing.

575 No sketch. Words 'red Arrahbesk by Dodson and Torkington' appear alongside pattern number.

576 No sketch. Words 'new french ornament pattern by forester and Taylor' appear alongside pattern number.

577 No sketch. 'New Map by Taylor'.

578 No sketch. 'Same as 188 Except bottom Peacock yellow Instead of bloom and the top part strong Rose colour'.

579 No sketch. 'festoons of flowers and festoons of gold by Boys with a pale blue star'.

580 No sketch. '2 green borders with gold Laurell between [indecipherable].

581 Missing.

582 Vague outline of tea cup with oval reserve painted with 'Landskip on cup full 3 inches ditto on saucer full 3 inches' (sic).

583 No sketch. 'Red [indecipherable] Pattern'.

584 Faint outline of tea cup with deep outer border marked 'new blue bell'.

585 No sketch. Marked 'Roses and Cross bars. No inside border'.

586 No sketch. Marked 'same as 458 Except Green Ground instead of Yellow'.

587 Faint outline of tea cup with narrow red border below outer rim through which traverses an undulating line, possibly in gilt.

588 No sketch. Marked 'Red ball' (sic).

589 Faint sketch of cup with red ground with gilt enrichment. The pattern appears to cover the cup from rim to foot rim in stripes with gilt (or red) balls dividing each stripe.

590 Faint outline of cup with handle.

591 Ditto.

592 Faint outline of cup marked '19 cross bars inside the [indecipherable] 26 in saucer'. The 'bars' are outlined so that a criss-cross lattice effect is shown inside and outside the cup.

593 Faint outline of cup. Writing beside and below pattern number is illegible.

594 Faint outline of cup. Marked 'Same [indecipherable] as 592'.

595 Marked 'as 488 but red instead of yellow'.

596 Marked 'Blue pinks same as 567'.

597 Faint outline of cup with deep border of forms which resemble craggy mountains. Marked below 'yellow ground'.

598 Marked 'Gold and white flowers on red ground'.

599 No sketch but marked 'new Grape' (sic) and below 'Painted by Stanesby and gilt by Torkington'.

600 Faint outline of cup with deep border of ten spherical and ovoid shapes, each partially overlaying the other and each containing a spot. No information concerning colour but marked 'no landskip'.

601 Marked 'Dessert Pattern 313'.

602–10 Missing.

611 Shown as tea cup with handle. Deep borders to rim and foot rim in leaf and berry design between two gilt lines, with roses round the middle of the cup.

612–24 Missing.

625 Tea cup with handle shown at side. Deep border of dark blue leaves surrounded by gilt seaweed pattern. Gilt line above foot rim.

626 Tea cup with handle shown at side. Cross-banded in gilt to provide lozenge-shaped reserves from just below rim to foot rim. Each reserve contains one single rose in natural colours, and the whole design is repeated inside the cup.

627 Shown as tall tea bowl with handle at side. Gilt rims. Body entirely covered in black (blue?) with gilt enrichment ending just above foot rim.

628 Tall tea cup, handle shown at side. Deep border of bright red below heavily gilded rim. Border decorated with large white stars and small gilt stars. Gilt line above foot rim.

629 Gilt rims. Basket weave in the form of criss-cross bands of red decorated with gilt, yellow with gilt line through centre and, slanting in opposite direction, white bands with gilt enrichment of foliate design.

630 Shown as tall tea bowl. Heavily gilded rims. Body colour red with criss-cross bands of white and gold from just below rim to above foot rim. Gilt enrichment overlaying the red body.

631 Missing.

632 Missing.

633 Tall tea bowl, handle at side. Body covered with bands of gilt to form series of narrow borders, each alternate border decorated with slight foliate design in gilt. This foliate decoration is also carried out below gilt line to inner rim.

634 Tall tea bowl, handle at side. Gilt rims. Two-thirds of cup bearing gilt leaf sprays with flowers and leaves in natural colours.

635 Exactly as 627, but body colour appears to be fawn.

636 T/T handle at side. Gilt rims. Deep border of red with gilt enrichment below outer rim.

637 T/T handle at side. Gilt rims. Narrow blue border between two gilt lines below outer rim.

638 Tall tea bowl. Gilt rims. Wheat ear sprays in gilt pendant from lovers' knots in blue decorate the body, below a most unattractive border which resembles a doodle filled in with diagonal lines.

639 Tall tea bowl, handle at side. Gilt rims. Deep border with wheat ears alternating with leaves in continuous line. No indication of colour (if any).

640 Tall tea bowl with handle at side. Gilt rims. Inside and outside of cup look exactly like an unattempted crossword. No indication of colours used.

641 As 640, but crossword on outside of cup only.

642 Tall tea bowl, handle shown at side. Gilt rims. Body covered with crossed leaf sprays in manner of crossed swords. No indication of colour.

643 Tall tea bowl with handle at side. Extra deep border of seaweed pattern. No indication of colour.

644 Outline of tea bowl, but no sketch inserted.

645 Two sketches: the first showing an unusual octagonal reserve painted with 'Coloured flowers on olive ground', the second showing leaf sprays over the body of the cup and marked 'A circle of the Ornament in the saucer betwixt the Edge and the octogan compartment' (sic). This pattern also carries the note: 'Solid handles'.

646 Tea cup with handle shown at side. Heavy gilt rims. Body of cup dark blue containing 'white ovalls' with additional gilt decoration within each oval.

647 Tea cup with handle. Gilt rims. Red border below outer rim decorated with gilt leaves and tendrils.

648 Tea bowl with handle at side. Black border between two gilt lines to inner and outer rims. The entire body of the cup is covered in horizontal gilt borders, each separated by the black and gilt border described above.

649 Tall tea bowl. Deep border (two-thirds of height) below gilt rim, comprising blue ovals spaced at regular intervals with gilt enrichment overlaying blue and decorating border between ovals.

650 Missing.

651 Tall tea bowl, handle at side. Gilt rims. Deep border of Greek key pattern in gilt on black/dark blue, below which is a marbled decoration in gilt over body of cup.

652 Exactly as above, but Greek key design on red ground.

653 Slight sketch of tall tea bowl. Body colour dark blue with (possibly) three reserves, as sketch is marked '2 Landskips 1 flowers'.

654 Faint pencil outline of tea bowl marked '2 flowers 1 Landskip'. Body appears to have some sort of foliate design between reserves.

655 Indecipherable.

656 Faint outline of tea cup with handle. Blue ground colour from rim to just above foot rim. No other decoration.

657 Pencilled sketch of tall tea bowl marked 'border 628', below which is a further notation 'Marp ground'. Against the pattern number is the word 'Phillips', and at the side of the sketch 'handle solid'.

658 Faint outline of tea cup with handle. Border of deep blue to outer rim.

659 Marked 'Same as 588 only Blue Balls instead of Red'.

660 Missing.

661 Faint sketch of tall tea bowl. Deep border of blue ground with diamond-shaped reserves, each containing a 'star red and gold'.

662 Faint outline of tall tea bowl marked 'strong fawn border'.

663 Very faint pencilled outline showing pattern very similar to 626 but without the gilt enrichment in the trellis.

664 Tea cup with handle. Deep border of dark blue below gilt rim with additional gilt decoration below.

665 Exactly as 664 but with narrow blue border at outer rim.

666 Very faint pencil outline of cup with deep border marked 'Blue oak leaf' (sic).

667 Deep blue border to rim of cup.

668 Cup with handle. Deep border of criss-cross bands forming diamond trellis effect. Each diamond contains a rose in natural colours and the half-diamonds appear in blue/green overlaid with gilt enrichment.

669 Missing.

670 Tea cup with handle. Deep border of acanthus leaves with borders on three sides, the 'open' side alternating with the leaves which point upwards and then downwards, the border finished with a thick gilt line, below which is a scroll decoration of leaves and flowers in gilt. Broad gilt line at foot rim.

671 Tea cup with handle. Gilt rims. Very unusual sloping turret effect over body of cup in blue with gilt 'shadow' interlaced with vine leaves and tendrils. Gilt line above foot rim.

672 Shown as waisted coffee can with kick handle. Deep border of blue with sunflower medallions alternating with gilt classical scrolls. Border finished with broad gilt line just above base of handle, below which is a further border of wheat ears and leaves and a further broad gilt band at foot rim.

673 Coffee can (straight sides) with kick handle. Deep border of vertical linked chains, each complete link containing a flower. No indication of colour.

674 Coffee can, straight sides, kick handle. Gilt rims. Round the centre of the can are five bands over which hang large acanthus leaves – two leaves shown in sketch are marked: '(1) White and gold; (2) Not done fawn.' Broad gilt line to foot rim. Gilt handle.

675 Faint outline of tea cup with handle marked 'French pattern done by Taylor Junior'.

676 Tea cup with handle. Faintly marked 'Barley Corn [sic]. by Talkington'.

677 Coffee can, straight sides. Gilt rims. Alternate stars and dots in formal lines cover the body of the can between slightly decorated borders at rim and foot rim. No indication of colour(s).

678 Lightly sketched in and numbered. Marked indecipherably.

679 Faint outline of cup. Numbered. No sketch.

680 Tea cup with handle. Gilt rims. Leaf sprays from foot rim to rim over body of cup. Three different leaf spray designs shown (probably repeated twice to cover remainder of body). Design carried out in a terracotta monochrome, but no indication as to whether this is true colour.

681 Tea cup with handle. Gilt rims. Extra-deep border of ferns, leaves and berries, possibly executed in red and gold.

682 Very similar to above, but fern leaf pattern laid on a marbled background.

683 Tea cup with handle. Gilt rims. Deep border of passion flowers, leaves and buds. Colour possibly red and gold.

684 Tea cup with handle. Gilt rims. Deep border with large gilt arrow heads in continuous line round the middle, decorated with tiny red florets and gilt leaves overall.

685 Tea cup with handle. Gilt rims. Deep border of ferns and leaves – probably carried out in gilt.

686 Tea cup with handle. Gilt rims. Gilt dots in uniform rows over body of cup, graduating in size towards gilt line above foot rim.

687 Tea cup with handle. Gilt rims. Very ornate large wheatsheaf motifs extending upwards from foot rim to rim (possibly four in all).

688 Tea cup with handle. Gilt rims. Greek key pattern border below outer rim, probably in gilt.

689 Tea cup with handle. Gilt rims. Border as 670, but without additional border below.

690 Tea cup with handle. Deep border of gilt seaweed pattern with pink roses (possibly six).

691 Tea cup with handle. Deep border of ferns and leaves, possibly carried out in gilt.

692 Tea cup with handle. Gilt rims. Very bold Greek key border extending half-way down cup.

693 Tea cup with handle. Gilt rims. Deep border comprising large five-pointed leaves with smaller leaves and florets, possibly carried out entirely in gilt.

694 Tea cup with handle. Gilt rims and very ornate gilt inside border. Very ornate decoration also from rim to foot rim, consisting of vertical lines of leaves alternating with vertical lines of three roses in natural colours.

695 Tea cup with handle. Gilt inner rim. Narrow border of fawn between two gilt lines at rim and foot rim. Criss-cross lines of tiny laurel leaves forming diamond trellis effect over body of cup, possibly all in gilt.

696 Tea cup with handle. Deep border of bold Greek key pattern, possibly black on pink or red.

697 Tea cup with handle. Gilt rims. Border of nine acanthus leaves, alternately upright and pendant, possibly on a pale blue ground.

698 Tea cup with handle. Gilt rims. Deep border of red ground with Greek key pattern in gilt, marked '8 Keys in Cup'.

699 Faint outline of tea cup with handle. Number inserted but no sketch.

700 Tea cup with handle. Design appears to be an exact copy of 674 shown on coffee can.

701 Tea cup with handle. Gilt rims. Incredibly *avant-garde* geometric design over body of cup, carried out in black/dark brown and gilt. Continuous line of 'turreting' round middle of cup with tall 'turreting' extending from foot rim to rim, overlaying each upright.

702 Intricate scroll pattern in gilt and blue over body of cup. Diamond-shaped medallion on side opposite handle, with formal gilt motif within frame.

703 Tea cup with handle. Gilt rims. Deep border of pale blue with leaves and flowers in natural colours. Ornate inner border shown separately.

125

The Graces adorning Pan, decorated in colours typical of the period. The modelling may be reasonably attributed to Stephan. Incised number 196. William Duesbury & Co. *c.* 1775. 27.9 cm. *Victoria & Albert Museum, C307 – 1940.*

126

Pastoral group finely modelled on a rocky base. Note the small heads of the figures and the amusing disinterestedness of the dog. Patch marks, no factory mark. William Duesbury & Co. 1775–80. Approx. 14 cm. *Ronald W. Raven Collection.*

127 ▷ ▷

Seated figure of a woman with a cat. William Duesbury & Co. *c.* 1770–75. 12.7 cm. *David John Ceramics, Woodstock.*

128 ◁ ◁
Group of figures dancing, after a
Meissen original by J. J. Kandler. Patch
marks. William Duesbury & Co.
c. 1775. 18.5 cm. *Herbert Allen
Collection. Victoria & Albert Museum,
C254 – 1935.*

129
Group, one of a pair representing
'Autumn' and 'Summer'. Incised
number 68. William Duesbury & Co.
c. 1775. 22.1 cm. *Schreiber Collection.
Victoria & Albert Museum, 414/417 –
1885.*

131
Biscuit group of 'Three Graces distressing Cupid' (see black and white plate 132 for later model with source of both groups). Crown, crossed batons, dots and 'D', number 235 and triangle of repairer Joseph Hill all incised. William Duesbury & Co. *c.* 1790. 36.4 cm. *Victoria & Albert Museum, C768 – 1936.*

132 ▷ ▷
Group of 'Three Graces distressing Cupid', modelled from an engraving, 'Etiam Amor Criminibus Plectitur', by W. W. Ryland after the painting by Angelica Kauffmann. Incised number 235, large 'B', patch marks. William Duesbury & Co. 1775. 39 cm. *Victoria & Albert Museum, C194 – 1926.*

133
Fine figure representing 'Touch' from a set of 'Senses', possibly number 59 in Haslem's list. William Duesbury & Co. *c.* 1780. Approx. 17.8 cm. *Robert & Elizabeth Allport, Corner Antiques.*

130 ◁
Pair of groups, copied from two Sèvres groups known as 'La Bergère des Alpes' and 'L'Oracle ou le Noeud de Cravate' modelled in 1766 by Etienne Falconet after designs by François Boucher. It is interesting to compare the first group with its biscuit version (see colour plate 16). Incised numbers 256 and 257 and on each a cross. William Duesbury & Co. *c.* 1775. 30.5 cm and 29.8 cm. *Schreiber Collection. Victoria & Albert Museum, 414/420 and 414/420A – 1885.*

704 Tea cup with handle. Gilt rims. Extra deep border covering two-thirds body of cup with geometric turreting which contains at intervals a large acanthus leaf pendant from rim; 'frame' finished with pendant pineapple.

705 Tea cup with handle. Gilt rims. Geometric turreting overlaying turreting with additional decoration in the form of small laurel wreaths and tiny laurel wreaths within outlines of turrets (shadow lines in heavy gilt).

706 Tea cup with handle. Gilt rims. Leaf and fern design border which appears identical to 685. No colour change mentioned.

707 Tea cup with handle. Gilt rims. Marbled body. Oval reserve.

708 Faint outline of tea cup with handle.

709 Faint outline of tea cup with handle. Oval reserve.

710 Tea cup with handle. Deep border in red with twin Greek key patterns overlaying each other.

711 Tea cup with handle. Gilt rims. Body appears to be completely covered with gilding, over which large leaves have been painted in blue and white. These extend from just below the rim to a line above the foot rim.

712 Tea cup with handle. Gilt rims. Deep border of ovals overlaying each other, through the middle of which is a continuous line through which leaves and berries protrude.

713 Tea cup with handle. Gilt rims. Deep border of 'stuffed olives' slightly overlaying each other. No indication of colour.

714 Tea cup with handle. Gilt rims. Deep border of 'Orange leafes' (sic) with smaller leaves and acorns.

715 Tea cup with handle. Gilt rims. Deep border of purple uncurled leaves with additional leaf and tendril decoration in gilt.

716 Tea cup with handle. Gilt rims. Entire body of cup is covered with 'stuffed olive' shapes overlaying each other. No indication of colour, but probably in gilt only.

717 Tea cup with handle. Gilt rims. Painted with '2 birds Colord in Centre of Cup by Brewer' (sic).

718 Tea cup with handle. Gilt rims. Large and very ornate leaf and flower spray extending from foot rim upwards to rim of cup.

719 Tea cup with handle. Gilt rims. Oval reserve painted 'single bird on a tree' (sic).

720 Tea bowl. Gilt rims. Outer border comprising two parallel lines between which is a continuous undulating leaf garland. Gilt line below. No indication of colour, but probably carried out entirely in gilt.

721 Tea cup with handle. Gilt rims. Deep border of bold leaf pattern executed in black and red with gilt enrichment. Marked '8 leaves in cup'.

722 Tea bowl. Gilt rims. Deep border of dark blue, possibly with added decoration, but this is difficult to determine.

723 Tall tea bowl. Gilt rims. Ground of gilt dots over which is a very bold leaf design in red from rim to foot rim.

724 Tea cup with handle. Gilt rims. Deep border finishing at base of handle, but sketch not filled in – only gilt line denoting depth of border.

725 Tea cup with handle. Deep border of purple leaves with gilt berries and tendrils.

726 Tea cup with handle. Deep border of gilt seaweed pattern overlaid by continuous line of blue leaves round the middle of the border.

727 Tall tea bowl. Gilt rims. As 723, but leaves blue instead of red.

728 Tea cup with handle. Gilt rims. Very deep border – possibly fawn – with six-pointed star medallions, each with sunburst decoration inside and to outside edge of star. Seaweed and leaf fronds in gilt over remainder of cup to foot rim.

729 Tea cup with handle. Gilt rims. Very deep border of blue with marbled effect overlaid in gilt.

730 Tea cup with handle. Deep border of red overlaid with turret design in gilt, each opening containing vertical gilt line.

731 Tea bowl with handle. Deep border of blue leaves with additional leaf and tendril decoration in gilt.

732 Tea cup with handle. Gilt rims. A narrow border in red surrounds outer rim, and there is a similar narrow red border round the middle of the cup.

733 Tea cup with handle. Deep border of vine leaves in blue with grapes and tendrils in gilt. Single gilt line through middle of this border.

734 Tea cup with handle. Gilt rims. Deep border of red wheatsheaves at intervals, joined by trailing blue ribbon.

735 Tea cup with handle. Gilt rims. Border two-thirds way down cup of bold leaf design in red on background of gilt dots.

736 Faint outline of tea cup with handle. No design inserted.

737 Tea cup with handle. Gilt rims. Simple border of single gilt line with red leaf and gilt berry motif.

738 Tea cup with handle. Gilt rims. Deep border of 'Dark Green border under the Glaze Autumnal Leaves' (sic). These appear on a ground of gilt dots.

739 Tea cup with handle. Gilt rims. Border of yellow ground with simple leaf design in shape of horseshoe with additional gilt decoration.

740 Tea cup with handle. Gilt rims. Turret-style decoration in red and black from rim to foot rim, with large gilt leaf motif in base of turret (possibly repeated twice or three times).

741 Tea cup with handle. Gilt rims. Deep border of bold acanthus leaf design in yellow and brownish black with additional leaf decoration in gilt.

742 As 741, but large leaves in blue and brownish black.

743 Faint outline of tea cup with handle. No design inserted.

744–66 Missing (but 753 described from actual piece).

753 Shallow tea cup. Gilt rims. Narrow border in deep pink to outer rim with lace scallops and tassels in gilt. Inside cup nine heart shapes overlaid with crimson decoration and outlined with wide gilt band. Additional decoration in gilt.

767 Tea cup with unusually shaped handle. Gilt rims. Simple border of scroll motif with undulating garland of tiny red leaves.

768 Tea cup with handle. Gilt rims. Narrow border of tiny laurel leaves to outer rim and above foot rim. Remainder of cup divided into square reserves with two vertical stripes and jewels forming frame. Reserve from corner to corner diagonally contains two blue leaf motifs and leaf sprays in gilt. At the other corners of the square are fan shapes in two shades of red within closely placed vertical lines.

769 Outline of tea cup with handle. Marked 'Whitaker's pattern' (sic).

770 Outline of tall tea bowl. Marked 'Fawn border top and Bottom Coloured Arabisque by J. Lead and J. Mossop' (sic).

Plate Book

1 Border consists of one broad and one narrow band of blue at top and bottom of rim. Large cornflower sprays scattered over centre of plate. (Frequently found with basket-weave moulded rim.)

2 Gilt rim with narrow gilt line about three-eighths of an inch below outer border, below which are scattered sprays in gilt. Gilt spray in centre of plate within gilt circle.

3 Very bold Kakiemon design in iron red and blue. Deep outer border containing cloud-shaped reserves outlined in blue with varying decoration in each reserve.

4 Blue line to outer rim with gilt loops at intervals from which hang pendant swags of husks. Scattered sprays of roses and other flowers over centre of plate, all executed in 'dirty turquoise'.

5 Gilt dentil edge with narrow gilt line immediately beneath. Festoons of turquoise flowers pendant from ornate gilt hangings with spray of turquoise flowers in centre of plate.

6 Similar to 5, but flowers are executed in natural colours, with roses predominating in festoons.

7 Gilt dentil edge. Deep border of dark blue with gilt enrichment. Scattered sprays of flowers in natural colours.

8 Gilt dentil edge, below which is a narrow blue border with gilt enrichment from which, suspended by gilt loops, are pendant swags of husks with small spray of flowers in natural colours beneath each loop. Spray of flowers in centre contained within blue circle.

9 No sketch.

10 Gilt dentil edge, below which is a narrow border in pale lilac with deeper lilac decoration. Pendant swags of husks suspended from gilt loops hang from this border. Plate is scattered with small sprays of flowers in natural colours with large flower spray in centre.

11 Exactly as 10, but with green(?) border instead of lilac.

12 Gilt dentil edge, below which is a most attractive border composed of husks making a continuous chain, and in the middle of each 'link' is a rose painted in natural colours. Below, scattered sprays of flowers in natural colours.

13 Border of celeste blue broken at intervals by tiny florets from which are suspended pendant swags of husks. Further decoration of scattered sprays of flowers in natural colours.

14 Most attractive deep border in the oeil-de-perdrix manner with 'cloud-shaped' reserves, each containing a small spray of roses. Scattered rose sprays painted in natural colours complete design.

15 Plain gilt rim, below which is a narrow dark blue border with gilt enrichment. Sprays of flowers in natural colours scattered over plate with central spray within a blue circle complete design.

16 Gilt dentil edge, below which is a narrow dark blue border with gilt enrichment. Flower sprays in natural colours scattered over plate and central spray surrounded by blue circle.

17 Mid-blue border with slight decoration in darker blue, border broken at intervals by vertical rectangles from which hang tiny pendant swags of husks. Single flower spray in centre within circle of husks – all executed in shades of blue.

18 Narrow blue border to rim overlaid with vertical lines in gilt, and finished with continuous line of gilt dots immediately below. This border is repeated about an inch below without the gilt dots. The centre of the plate has a flower spray in natural colours surrounded by a border of large blue dots outlined in gilt with additional gilt decoration and a gilt circle surrounding the border.

19–25 Missing.

21
Exceedingly rare coffee cup and saucer with entwined handle, painted with fruit and flowers by William Billingsley. Crown, crossed batons, dots and 'D' in puce, gilder's number 2. William Duesbury & Co. 1785–90. Cup 6.3 cm. *Major G. N. Dawnay Collection.*

22 ■
Teacup, coffee cup and saucer, commonly known as a trio, painted with tea pattern number 118. Landscapes at the bottom of the cups and on the saucers are by Zachariah Boreman. Crown, crossed batons, dots and 'D' in puce, various gilders' marks. William Duesbury & Co. 1785–90. Teacup 6.2 cm. *Mr & Mrs White Collection.*

23
The Chedworth Jug, known as such because it was bought at a house sale there. Lygo's letters of 1790 state, 'Mr Eames found Baptiste's prints with large flowers but not all of them in baskets; also four other prints with horses, and a battle print with figures on horseback.' (Mr Eames was a London dealer in prints.) This very important jug, which is painted with a battle scene with such figures on horseback, by Zachariah Boreman, is otherwise gilt with simple, typical motifs of the period. Crown, crossed batons, dots and 'D' in puce. William Duesbury & Co. *c.* 1790. 21 cm. *Mary Field Collection.*

24
Coffee can and stand, painted by George Complin, with pendant festoons of birds, fruit and flowers. The can has an inside border and the cavetto of the stand has a Greek key motif. Pattern number 325 states, 'fruit & birds & flowers by Complin'. Crown, crossed batons, dots and 'D' in puce. William Duesbury & Co. 1790. Can 6.3 cm. *Formerly in the Brayshaw Gilhespy Collection. Private collection.*

25
Coffee can (stand not illustrated), painted with a fruit and bird panel by George Complin. Pattern number 259. Crown, crossed batons, dots and 'D' in puce. William Duesbury & Co. 1790. 6.4 cm. *Royal Crown Derby Museum.*

26
A fine pair of ice cups in Sèvres style, the foot rim carrying a blue 5 for the ground layer, a puce 1 for Thomas Soar and a long-tailed 7 for William Billingsley. These cups numbered six to a tray and an example may be seen in black and white illustration 212. It should be noted that Billingsley was making a direct copy here and thus the painting does not resemble his normal style (see black and white plate 250). Crown, crossed batons, dots and 'D' in puce. William Duesbury & Co. 1790. 6.7 cm. *Royal Crown Derby Museum.*

26 Gilt dentil edge. Two narrow blue bands containing a border of laurels in turquoise(?) on an (indistinguishable colour) ground, with additional gilt decoration in the form of tiny dots, comprise outer border. Flower spray (? landscape) in centre surrounded by blue circle intertwined with gilt florets.

27 Gilt dentil edge. Narrow dark blue border immediately below has slight gilt enrichment with further border of the same width in gilt. In addition to the flower sprays shown as being scattered below the gilt border, the plate is annotated 'Flies'. A further blue border with different, but equally slight, gilt enrichment surrounds the flower spray in the centre of the plate.

28 No appreciable difference between this pattern and no. 26, except that the border may have a different ground colour.

29 Identical to the famous pattern 86 in the Tea Book. Gilt dentil edge to plate and deep border comprising a single blue line intertwined with gilt foliate sprays between two narrow gilt borders. Landscape by Boreman in centre of plate, surrounded by blue circle with intertwined gilt garland.

30 Gilt outer rim, below which are two narrow gilt borders separated by a foliate garland of undulating form. Landscape in centre of plate framed by gilt border.

31 Deep border of yellow ground (?) between two narrow borders of blue and overlaid by continuous line of laurels in turquoise. Spray of flowers in centre executed in natural colours and framed by single blue line circle intertwined with gilt garland.

32 Deep border comprising two narrow gilt borders decorated with husk motif, between which is a continuous border of Chantilly sprigs in natural colours of pink and blue. Scattered sprigs over remainder of plate.

33 This corresponds to pattern 50 in the Tea Book. Executed in gilt overall, it has a narrow border below plain gilt edge with lovers' knots at intervals, from which are suspended swags in husk form. Below this is a thick gold line intertwined with slight foliate garland of undulating form. A circle of large dots surrounds the central flower spray.

34 Gilt rim. Chantilly sprigs in pink and blue with green leaves form deep border between two narrow gilt lines with further gilt line underneath. Scattered sprigs over rest of plate.

35 Gilt dentil edge. Deep border in dark blue with highly ornate gilt enrichment broken at intervals by cloud-shaped reserves, each containing a single rose in natural colours. In the space between the border and the central landscape the sketch is annotated 'Flies'.

36 Narrow dark blue border with gilt enrichment and gilt loops from which pendant swags of husk-form are suspended, also in gilt. Tiny gilt florets scattered below the swags, and in the centre of the plate the latter are surrounded by single blue line with undulating leaf garland intertwined.

37 Gilt edge. Deep border comprising a single gilt line intertwined with leaf and berry motif of undulating form contained within two gilt lines with a further single gilt line immediately below. Gilt sprays of flowers in natural form over remainder of plate with central flower motif in gilt surrounded by two gilt lines.

38 Missing.

39 Narrow dark blue border between two gilt lines and overlaid with gilt decoration in chain pattern, each link containing a single gilt dot. Immediately below is a tassel-type border in gilt. There is a further border of one thick gilt line intertwined with slight foliate garland of undulating form, and then a single blue line surrounds the floral motif in the centre of the plate.

40 Gilt dentil edge, below which is a gilt border comprising a single gilt line intertwined with an undulating continuous line of gilt dots in one direction and a foliated garland of leaves in the other. Below this is another border of large dots in a continuous line, and surrounding the central spray is a circle of tiny cornflowers.

41 Gilt dentil edge with border of harebell sprays immediately beneath. Below this a further border of gilt dots alternating with shapes like tiny Christmas trees. Central spray also in gilt surrounded by border of tiny floret heads.

42 Very dark blue border to rim with gilt dentil edge overlaying blue. Immediately below is a further border of blue between two gilt lines and overlaid with gilt flower heads and white dots. Gilt flower spray in centre of plate surrounded by scalloped border in gilt comprising one wide band and one narrow band of gilt, the latter embellished with tiny florets.

43 Gilt dentil edge. Deep border consisting of two gilt lines intertwined with garland of tiny floret heads in one direction and leaf sprays in the other, the border being broken at intervals by cloud-shaped reserves, each containing a large cornflower spray in gilt. Sepia landscape in the centre of the plate framed by a single gilt line around which is intertwined a foliate festoon.

44 As 18, but with gilt emblematic star motif in centre of plate.

45 Narrow blue border with gilt dentil edge overlaying at rim. A further slightly deeper border in blue, overlaid with foliate design in gilt. Emblematic star motif in centre of plate surrounded by blue line with gilt leaves intertwined.

46 Gilt dentil edge. Deep chintz border. Cornflower spray in natural colours in centre surrounded by narrow border of chintz.

47 Plain gilt border shown. No other indication of decoration for this pattern number.

48 This is exactly as pattern 54 in Tea Book. Smith's blue border with scattered flower sprays in gilt.

49 This appears to be exactly the same as 48, but instead of Smith's blue the border appears to be celeste.

50 Gilt dentil edge. Deep blue border overlaid with gilt enrichment of foliate design. Landscape in centre of plate framed by blue border and a further gilt border of leaf sprays.

51 Gilt dentil edge. Very deep border of chintz pattern with gilt motifs at regular intervals placed centrally in border. Sprays in centre of plate (these appear to be in natural colours) are surrounded by a narrow border of chintz.

52 Missing.

53 Gilt rim. Deep border of flower sprays in natural colours alternating with crossed fern leaves in gilt. Flower sprays in natural colours in centre of plate surrounded by foliated border in gilt.

54 Missing.

55 This appears to be similar in most respects to 45 except for the addition of some blue highlights to the starburst motif in the centre.

56 Narrow border of 'Green 176' to rim enclosed within two gilt lines and with added gilt enrichment underneath. This border appears to be repeated towards the centre of the plate, but there is no indication as to whether the central motif consists of a landscape or flower spray.

57 This pattern is almost exactly similar to 32; it varies only in that the two narrow gilt borders contain a laurel motif instead of husks.

58 Narrow dark blue border to rim overlaid by gilt dentil edge. Underneath, a wider dark blue border overlaid with gilt foliate pattern with white dots added at regular intervals. From loops on the underside of this border hang pendant swags of husks in gilt. Gilt sprays in centre of plate are enclosed within a blue circle decorated with undulating leaf motif in gilt.

59 Gilt dentil edge. Deep border of gilt in formal design, below which is a row of blue dots between two gilt lines. Immediately below this is a deep border of body colour (turquoise or green) with added gilt enrichment on underside. Large flower spray in natural colours in centre of plate.

60 Gilt rim. Deep border of Chantilly sprigs in natural colours between two gilt lines with added decoration of gilt dots. A further line of gilt is below this border. Scattered sprigs over remainder of plate in natural colours.

61 It is almost impossible to determine how this differs from pattern 40 without examples of each. They appear in the pattern book to be identical.

62 Gilt rim, under which is a deep border of blue, lavishly decorated with gilding. The flower spray in the centre, carried out in natural colours, is surrounded by a blue circle with a line of gilt dots on the underside and a sun-ray border on its outer edge.

63 Gilt dentil edge. Deep border comprising single dark blue line interwoven with gilt foliate decoration in undulating form contained within two narrow gilt borders each with chain motif. A further border is shown towards the centre of plate – blue line with added gilt – but not enough of the sketch remains for identification of the central motif.

64 Gilt dentil edge, below which is a deep border of blue between two gilt lines and heavily decorated with gilt. Below this a further border in delightful wheat ear pattern carried out in gilt. The landscape in the centre of the plate is framed by a narrow blue border between two gilt lines and a further border in gilt of foliated design.

65 Narrow border in bloom or fawn between two gilt lines with added gilt decoration on underside. The central motif (impossible to say whether this is landscape or flowers) is surrounded by a continuous line of gilt dots.

66 Gilt rim. Narrow gilt border from which are suspended swags of husks pendant from lovers' knots. The sepia landscape in the centre of the plate is surrounded by a single gilt line through which is intertwined a garland of tiny gilt ferns.

67 Missing.

68 It is impossible from the sketch to determine how this pattern differs from no. 32. They appear to be identical.

69 Narrow blue border to rim overlaid with gilt dentil edge and gilt line underneath. A further border of blue below between two gilt lines overlaid with gilt floret heads with additional decoration of tiny white dots. The flower spray in the centre of the plate is surrounded by a blue and gilt foliate border.

70 Missing.

71 Narrow blue border to rim overlaid with gilt dentil edge and having a gold line to under edge. Underneath is a deep border of formalized acanthus leaves, pointing downwards, carried out in gilt and finished with gilt line beneath. No indication of any further decoration on this plate.

72 Blue border to rim overlaid with gilt dentil edge with gilt line beneath and further slight gilt decoration below this. Scattered flower sprays in gilt above and contained within a blue line decorated with tiny gilt leaves.

73 Missing.

74 Gilt rim. A deep border of tiny blue flowers and gilt leaves in a continuous undulating line is contained within two narrow borders comprising a continuous line of gilt dots contained with gilt lines. The (apparently) large and important landscape in the centre of the plate is framed by a single gilt line and outer border of tiny gilt laurels.

75 Gilt rim under which is a deep border of single cornflowers in formal rows alternating with gilt stars, finished with gilt line.

76 Narrow border of tiny laurels in blue between two gilt lines. Blue sprays of flowers in centre of plate contained within single gilt band.

77 Missing.

125

134
Figure representing 'Smell' from a set
of 'Senses'. William Duesbury & Co.
c. 1780. 17.8 cm. *Robert & Elizabeth
Allport, Corner Antiques.*

135
Figure representing 'Sight' from a set
of 'Senses'. William Duesbury & Co.
c. 1780. 17.8 cm. *Robert & Elizabeth
Allport, Corner Antiques.*

78 Gilt rim. Scattered sprigs of cornflowers in natural colours but of varying size over the whole of the plate.

79 This pattern seems to differ from 78 only in that the cornflower sprigs seem to be of more or less uniform size and to be placed more regularly over the plate.

80 Gilt rim with large flower sprays in natural colours immediately below. The sketch in the book is quite exquisite, consisting of three roses, a dog daisy, blue flowers (probably gentians) and what appears to be an opium poppy.

81 Gilt dentil edge. Narrow border of light and dark blue zigzag lines with gilt enrichment of tiny leaves undulating between the zigs and the zags. This border is repeated in narrower width towards the centre of the plate.

82 Gilt dentil edge. Deep border contained within two gilt bands comprising tiny cornflower sprigs in natural colours in formal lines alternating with two gilt stars. Scattered sprigs over centre of plate.

83 Missing.

84 Gilt dentil edge, beneath which is a narrow border comprising single gold band intertwined with cornflower sprigs in natural colours with gilt leaves and stems. Scattered Chantilly sprigs over remainder of plate – in natural colours, but leaves and stems in gilt. Marked '5d. Gilding 6d. Painting'.

85 As 84, but with addition of one thick and one thin band of gilt beneath border.

86 Gilt rim. Narrow border giving scroll effect but containing tiny blue flowers and leaves in natural colours between two gilt bands. Scattered sprigs over remainder of plate – flowers in natural colours, leaves executed in gilt.

87 Very narrow border in fawn overlaid by gilt dentil edge. A deeper border beneath containing a scallop shell with scroll motif in blue and gilt contained within two gilt lines. Scattered sprigs over plate – flowers in blue and pink and stems and leaves in gilt.

88 Narrow border to rim in fawn contained within two gilt lines with additional border of gilt beneath in the form of pendant acanthus motifs and a further single gilt line completes border. Large and very beautiful flower sprays in natural colours over remainder of plate.

89 Gilt rim. Border, contained within two gilt lines, comprises scrolls made up of tiny blue leaves and each containing a small blue floret in centre. Described from a numbered lozenge-shaped dish in the author's collection: gilt rim, below which is a narrow border of mid-blue leaf motifs with tiny blue buds on gilt stems. Below, a deep border of upright stems with flower sprays in natural colours, the stems appearing to spring from the pointed tips of the scalloped edge of a dark blue border immediately beneath, this border being enclosed within gilt lines – one straight and the other following the scalloped edge of the border. Spray of pink roses in centre enclosed within blue circle which is decorated with gilt ribands. The scrolls alternate in travelling clockwise and anti-clockwise directions. There are '6 Sprigs in the plate' (*sic*) of cornflowers in natural colours.

90 Marked 'Tea Pattern 137'.

91 Missing.

92 This pattern corresponds exactly to 45, except that the deeper of the two outer borders is overlaid with tiny gilt flower heads instead of leaves.

93 Missing.

94 Gilt rim. Deep flower border with leaves and stems in natural colours. Three single gilt lines on underside of border.

95 Missing.

96 Missing.

97 Missing.

98 Missing.

99 Missing.

100 Gilt rim with narrow Smith's blue border beneath. Decorated with large flower spray in natural colours in centre of plate. Marked '1/¼d. Gilding'. (This pattern is invariably ascribed to Billingsley, but his name is not mentioned in pattern book.)

101 Gilt rim below which are two gilt lines, then a deep border (possibly in some ground colour) outlined in gilt to simulate open-fan effect, followed by a deeper border between two gilt bands of five rows of blue dots with sunburst gilt decoration alternating with small gilt stars and decreasing in size on each row. Central motif?

102 Gilt rim. Deep border of vertical lines of deep rose-pink broken at regular intervals by oval medallions, each containing emblematic star in blue and gilt. This border is contained within two narrow dark blue borders, each decorated with a continuous line of gilt dots, with additional gilt embellishment on the underside. Sepia landscape(?) in centre of plate within gilt circle and added circular frame of broad gilt band with gilt embellishment.

103 Gilt rim, below which is a narrow border of dark and light blue zigzag pattern enriched with intertwined gilt leaf garland. Deep border of yellow ground below, under which the zigzag border is repeated. A further border in gilt in chain design and a sunburst centre in blue and gilt.

104 Gilt rim. A narrow border consisting of a dark blue line decorated with tiny gilt dots above and below. A wider border of vertical lines in gilt, below which the narrow blue border is repeated. A further very deep border of dark blue ovals overlaying each other, each oval decorated with

tiny gilt dots, is finished with three single gilt lines. The central motif is a daisy shape of dark blue petals with gilt petal surrounding.

105 Gilt rim. Deep border of gilt oval hoops overlaying each other with a dot-dash-dot motif to each hoop. A further and much deeper border of chintz contained within two gilt lines with formal gilt motif in centre of plate.

106 Gilt rim with border of leaves and flowers in gilt and blue in scroll form – the scrolls alternating between clockwise and anti-clockwise directions. A deeper border below, contained within two gilt lines shows scattered floret heads and single leaves in profusion. Tiny gilt laurel leaves border the central star-shape motif carried out in blue and gilt.

107 Gilt rim. Deep border of festoons of small flowers and leaves undulating in serpentine fashion. A further deep border in (indistinguishable) ground colour. Central motif (landscape?) surrounded by gilt circle.

108 Gilt rim. Deep border carried out in gilt overlaid with blue and flanked by two narrow borders of gilt laurel leaves. A very deep border of alternating light and dark blue sun-rays extends to centre of plate where there is a formal central motif in blue and gilt surrounded by a slightly decorated gilt border.

109 Narrow gilt border to rim decorated with vertical lines, overlaid with scrolls, and finished with band of gilt immediately underneath. This border is repeated but with the gilt band above. A further border of leaf and berry motif is finished by three single gilt lines. Landscape in centre of plate.

110 Gilt rim and deep border of dark blue heavily gilded by large leaf sprays and a chain motif, with oval medallions at regular intervals, each decorated with a different motif in gilt. A narrow border of scrolls and flowers between two gilt lines below and a central landscape contained within a gilt circle.

111 Gilt rim below which is a single dark blue line. Border has a background of vertical lines in gilt overlaid with medallions of ovate form conjoined horizontally and each containing a blue dot in the centre with alternating emblematic star and flower-head motifs. A narrow border of gilt contained between two dark blue lines is followed by a very deep border of sun-ray effect comprising gilt lines interspersed with lines of tiny blue dots. The gilt border between two blue lines is repeated. Landscape in sepia(?) in centre of plate.

112 Gilt rim below which is a single dark blue line. Border has background of gilt dots and stars and medallions of ovate shape placed vertically at regular intervals, each containing blue dot in centre with gilt enrichment. Single blue line, below which is a yellow ground border with partridge-eye pattern used to form geometric shapes. The landscape(?) in the centre appears to be executed in a peculiar shade of purple.

113 Gilt rim. Deep border comprising large upright leaf motifs, each with leaf tips turning over, carried out in gilt on rose-red background colour. A narrow border below is marked 'this breadth' three-tenths of an inch in gilt and the remainder of the plate is scattered with large flower sprays in natural colours.

114 Missing.

115 Gilt rim. Deep gilt border of alternating leaf and harebell spray motifs and large sprays over remainder of plate; it is not possible to determine whether these are executed in gilt or in natural colours.

116 Gilt rim with a second gilt line below, followed by another gilt border of pendant leaves. Sepia landscape in centre of plate is surrounded by a narrow gilt line, a narrow border of fawn, a narrow line of sepia and a pale gold line, and finished with the gilt leaf border inverted (i.e. upright instead of pendant).

117 Gilt rim. Gilt border of small laurel leaves above very deep border of yellow ground between two gilt lines. A further and narrower border of gilt laurel leaves, the centre of the plate containing scattered flower sprays in natural colours.

118 Gilt rim below which is laurel leaf border in gilt. Deep border of yellow ground between two gilt lines and a further border of laurel leaves below finished with gilt line. The central motif in gilt is composed of berries and leaves and is surrounded by a very delicately drawn border of gilt leaves.

119 Gilt rim. Narrow borders of 'pearls', between which are undulating garlands of small blue flowers with gilt stems and leaves. Scattered sprays of similar form over the rest of the plate.

120 Gilt dentil edge. Deep outer border consisting of single gilt line interwoven with blue and pink cornflower heads with trailing foliage. Scattered sprays of similar form over the rest of the plate.

121 Gilt rim, under which is a narrow border of blue flower heads alternating with large gilt dots. Underneath, a single blue line with grapes, vine leaves and tendrils intertwined. Border of flower heads and gilt dots repeated. Single gilt line with added gilt decoration in the form of pendant trefoil leaf sprays under which is a further border of single blue line with gilt leaves. A further single blue line with slighter gilt decoration, below which the flower and gilt dot border is repeated once more. Remainder of plate decorated with (indistinguishable design).

122 Gilt rim. Narrow border of gilt dots between two gilt lines under which is a deep border of florets and leaves in natural colours forming a zigzag pattern, this border finished with a further border of gilt dots between two gilt lines. The central motif of (indistinguishable) is surrounded by a

136
Group known, from Haslem's list number 81, as 'Shoeblack'. This Chelsea-Derby version was re-issued later by Robert Bloor on round, pierced bases both in biscuit and colour. No mark. William Duesbury & Co. *c.* 1780. 17 cm. *The Hermitage, Leningrad, USSR, no. 19871.*

137 ▷
'Large Fountain Vase'. An identical vase is described in Messrs Duesbury & Co's list dated about 1774 (quoted in full by Bemrose):

A truncated vase in lapis lazuli blue veined with gold, with white and gold scollop'd and leaved pediment zone and top; round the vase are four Cupids, two holding a festoon in gold, fixed to two gold faces of satyrs, and two riding on dolphins forming the anses. On the cover is a genius vanquished by Cupid. The body of the vase is supported by 2 naiades, or sea gods, and the pedestal answering the vase has four sphynxes for its supporters, the emblem of wisdom.

Bemrose attributed the modelling to Rossi but it appears that it was copied, faithfully, from an unsigned etching by Jacques Saly (1717–76) (see *Ceramics of Derbyshire*, p. 28). Gold anchor on the plinth and incised number 19 (see Bemrose list). William Duesbury & Co. *c.* 1773–5. 40.7 cm. (It is interesting to note the Bemrose list vase measured 16½ in, i.e. 41.8 cm.) *Delomosne & Son, London.*

138
Vase and cover, painted *en grisaille* in black and decorated with gilding. The cover is fitted to the vase by means of a pierced ormolu band. The front and rear panels show a river-god and a female figure threatened by a cupid with an arrow. No mark, incised number 36 (not included in the Bemrose list). William Duesbury & Co. *c.* 1785. 25.4 cm. *Schreiber Collection. Victoria & Albert Museum, 414/411 – 1885.*

139
Rare Chelsea-Derby coffee cup and saucer, the centre of the saucer and the body of the cup decorated in the typical style of the period. The borders, however, are tastefully decorated in the Adam style predominantly in plum, pale blue and green. Gold anchor. William Duesbury & Co. *c.* 1770. Saucer diameter approx. 13 cm. *Private collection.*

continuous line of gilt dots forming a circle which has zigzag pattern of single gilt lines overlaid with tiny gilt leaf between each zig and zag.

123 Gilt rim. Narrow gilt border of pendant leaves and ferns. Broad border comprising five rows of gilt dots alternating with gilt stars. Sepia landscape in centre surrounded by four bands (colour uncertain) with further border of ferns and leaves in upright instead of pendant form.

124 Gilt rim with additional decoration in the form of tiny trefoil leaves, below which is a border of blue leaves with garlands of tiny intertwined florets in natural colours intertwined. A further gilt line is decorated with tiny trefoil leaves in upright form and the remainder of the plate is covered with minute flower sprigs in natural colours alternating with motif of partridge eye in gilt and blue.

125 Gilt dentil edge. Deep border of dark blue overlaid with chain pattern in gilt, each link containing a gilt flower head, the chain being outlined top and bottom by a continuous line of tiny white dots, with further outlining in gilt leaves forming small swags. This border is finished by a row of vertical gilt lines overlaying the base of the blue border. A further border of large blue dots with gilt enrichment and a small gilt floret head within each dot. Nearer the centre of the plate is a single blue line with gilt leaves and ferns intertwined, and the central motif in two shades of blue and gilt is surrounded by gilt stars and enclosed within a broad dark blue circle overlaid with vertical gilt bars and contained within two gilt lines.

126 Gilt rim. Page very badly torn, but what little remains suggests large sprays of flowers – probably in natural colours.

127 Gilt rim. Narrow border in gilt comprising spheres with a dot in centre of each (giving the appearance of small oranges), alternating with trefoil leaf motif and background of vertical lines contained within two narrow gilt lines. Below, a deeper border of pink ground colour overlaid with three rows of stars alternating with dots, all carried out in gilt between two gilt lines. This border is repeated but has greater depth and carries five rows of stars and dots. A further narrow border in gilt with oranges, alternating with tiny floret heads, contained within two narrow gilt lines. Centre of plate appears to have landscape in natural colours.

128 Gilt dentil edge. Deep border of leaf and fern motif; leaves in claret and turquoise colours, ferns in gilt between two gilt lines decorated with alternating small gilt circles and dots. Immediately below, a narrow gilt border of scrolls, below which is a very deep border of gilt ovate shapes overlapping each other, each decorated with a tiny border of dots. Through the centre of the ovals is a continuous line of small gilt circles, the whole border contained within two gilt lines. No indication of any central motif.

129 Gilt dentil edge. Deep border of fawn ground colour overlaid with gilt stars and dots, which is broken by alternating oblong and scalloped circular reserves, each containing pink roses with leaves and buds. A further border of trailing harebell and leaf sprays in gilt. Central motif of roses in natural colours surrounded by a fawn border between two rows of gilt lines and overlaid with gilt(?) dots.

130 Gilt dentil edge. Deep border of roses in natural colours interwoven round narrow border of gilt dots between two gilt lines. Remainder of plate is covered with scattered flower sprays interspersed with gilt leaves and stars.

131 Dentil edge with added gilt decoration. Deep border of dark blue flower heads decorated with gilt against a background of vertical lines shading from celeste down to a very pale blue, below which is a deep blue inverted dentil border with added gilt. A further gilt border of delicate trailing leaf design (pendant). This border is repeated, but the leaf design is upright and enriches the dark blue dentil border which surrounds the landscape in the centre of the plate.

132 Gilt dentil edge. Below, a narrow gilt border, followed by a further narrow border of floret heads in natural colours against a blue background. Deep border of gilt leaves and garlands and the centre of the plate marked '[indecipherable] of flowers [indecipherable] Pedestal'.

133 Gilt rim below which is a narrow border of fawn ground finished with scalloped edge in gilt with added gilt decoration below. Large sprays of flowers in natural colours over remainder of plate.

134 Gilt rim, with single gilt line decorated with tiny gilt dots underneath. Narrow chain-type border with a single gilt star in each link, under which are five rows of gilt stars alternating with gilt dots. 'Landskip by Boreman' in centre of plate, which is surrounded by two narrow borders of uncertain ground colours (possibly fawn inner and dark blue outer) with gilt enrichment.

135 Gilt rim. Deep border comprising undulating band containing pearls with delicate leaf sprays in gilt above and below the bends. Deep border of bloom ground colour under which is a narrow gilt border surrounding the central flower painting of 'Moses [sic] with some [indecipherable] Yellow flowers [indecipherable] a faint Brown [indecipherable] Ground by Billensley [sic]'.

136 Gilt rim. Narrow gilt border of chain design. Very deep border of bloom ground colour. Gilt chain border is repeated as surround for 'Fruit by Complin upon Landskip background'.

137 Narrow dark blue border to rim overlaid by gilt dentil edge. Border of leaves and harebells in natural colours between two gilt lines. Central spray of flowers in natural colours is surrounded by blue lupin-type flowers with gilt leaves.

138 Gilt rim. Gilt border of trailing leaf and harebell design. 'Fruit by Complin' in centre of plate, surrounded by narrow gilt border of leaves and berries.

139 'Margrave of Anspach' service. Executed in gilt and, with a crown and monogram 'AE' beneath. It is very disappointing when one considers the importance that was attached to its being delivered on time, and Duesbury's fall from grace as a result of failing to achieve this. (See chapter 7.)

140 Gilt rim. Marked 'this border in the Manner of 126' (and just as loosely sketched in, so we are no wiser). 'Fruit by Complin' in centre of plate, surrounded by simple gilt border.

141 Gilt rim. Simple gilt border of laurel leaves. Marked 'Botanical Plants'.

142 Gilt dentil edge. Border as 130. Marked 'Single Plants from the Botanical Magazine'.

143 Gilt rim. Very striking border of roses in natural colours on a black ground. Remainder of plate scattered with gilt stars (with black dot in centre) and gilt dots.

144 Gilt rim, below which is a single narrow gilt line decorated with a continuous line of tiny gilt dots. Border in gilt has a chain pattern with a star in each link, under which are two rows of gilt stars alternating with gilt dots. Centre of plate has 'Groop of Colord flowers by Mr. Billensly'.

145 Gilt rim with two narrow borders below of uncertain colour – possibly grey and fawn. Further border of leaves and flowers pendant in same undetermined colours. Possibly landscape in centre surrounded by circle of gilt dots with further decoration of ferns and leaf sprays tied with ribands in lovers' knot design at intervals.

146 Gilt dentil edge. Deep border consisting of a single gold line interwoven with cornflower heads in natural colours and gilt leaves and stems. Large cornflower sprays with gilt leaves scattered over remainder of plate.

147 Gilt rim. Narrow border of laurel leaves between two gilt lines. Wider border of blue flowers and gilt leaves, under which the narrow border is repeated. Large sprays of blue flowers and gilt leaves over remainder of plate. (NB it is noted that the workman received 1d. for the gilding!)

148 This appears in all respects to be exactly similar to 128; there is, however, a 'slice' of the centre which suggests this was carried out in dark turquoise and was possibly a 'landskip'. There is a note to this effect on the opposite page, suggesting that the landscape replaces a convolvulus on 128.

149 Gilt rim, below which is two very narrow borders of gilt dots between gilt lines, finished with additional decoration of trefoil leaves below second line. Central reserve has flowers in natural colours surrounded by single narrow gilt border with gilt dots and added trefoil leaves.

150 Gilt rim, below which is a single gilt line intertwined with leaf motif. Deep border of corn-sheaf motifs in blue and gilt surrounded by blue dots and gilt stars. The flower painting in the central reserve is surrounded by a simple narrow border of gilt leaves.

151 Missing.

152 Narrow gilt border to rim. Deep border of four rows of two gilt stars alternating with one blue dot. Flower painting in centre surrounded by same narrow gilt border as on rim.

153 Marked '153 Pattern in Portfolio', but is executed on next page of pattern book. Gilt rim. Deep border of alternating red and gold vertical lines with large medallions at intervals. Each medallion has a gilt border outlined with tiny gilt dots and laurel leaves tied with lovers' knot at base; a further gilt line is decorated with tiny gilt dots, in the centre of which is a cherub's face. Underneath, a border of pendant swags of leaves and gilt balls.

154 Missing.

155 Missing.

156 Gilt dentil edge. Deep border shows two rows of feather-like fronds in dark blue on a lighter blue background, broken at regular intervals by a scroll-type reserve containing gilt dots of graduated size. The underside of this border is decorated with grapes, vine leaves and tendrils in gilt. Gilt circle in centre of plate.

157 Narrow border to rim in fawn(?) ground colour between two gilt lines with additional gilt decoration below. Centre of plate appears to be painted with flowers in natural colours.

158 Gilt rim. Deep border of mid-blue heavily enriched with gilding and broken at regular intervals by oval medallions, each containing gilt flower heads surrounded by a gilt line decorated with tiny dots. Below, a very narrow border of gilt dots with added gilt decoration to underside of border. Beneath this, a border of gilt dots alternating with two rows of gilt stars and finally a narrow border of mid-blue overlaid with gilt spots between two gilt lines.

159 Gilt rim. Two very narrow gilt borders, each containing gilt spots, decorated with gilt dots and additional gilt decoration on the underside of the second border. Centre painted with 'Birds and Landskip by Complin' framed by same narrow gilt border as previously described.

160 Narrow gilt border to rim. Deep border of three rows of blue spots and gilt stars. Gilt border repeated round central reserve – possibly a landscape.

161 Narrow border to rim between two gilt lines in green no. 2. Remainder of plate decorated with green flowers and leaves, marked 'Green N.176'.

162 Gilt rim with narrow blue line below. Border of gilt and black lozenge

shapes in a continuous line, each lozenge containing a pearl. Gilt and blue lines beneath this border. Gilt circle in centre of plate.

163   Gilt dentil edge. Border between two gilt lines of trailing leaves and pink harebells intertwined through a gilt riband. The pattern is marked 'Green 847', but there is nothing to indicate whether this refers to the colour of the leaves or the ground colour.

164–171   Missing.

172   Gilt dentil edge. Deep border of ovoid shapes formed by graded gilt dots, each containing a red and a blue flower head and a palm in blue and gilt. Between each oval is a blue ribbon extending vertically from rim to base of border, below which are two gilt lines. A further narrow border of palms in red, blue and gilt, and the centre of the plate contains a 'Groop by Billensley' (sic) of roses, harebells, etc, in natural colours.

173   Gilt rim, below which is a border containing twenty-four medallions at regular intervals formed by wreaths of blue and gilt leaves, each medallion containing an emblematic star in gilt; the spaces between the medallions are decorated top and bottom by red and blue flower heads, the colour alternating between each medallion. The central painting depicts '1 flying bird in Center – 3 smaller ones in Colors' (sic) and this is framed by one broad and one narrow gilt line with a further border of an undulating garland of leaves in blue and gilt, each undulation containing a blue or red flower head, placed alternately.

174   Gilt rim. Deep border of medallions of laurel wreaths, each containing a small blue flower head with added leaf sprays either side of the medallions. Between some medallions is a gilt lovers' knot, from which is draped a crimson swag enriched with gilt which passes over the top of the blue florets. Centre, painted with '2 rich Gold Cornucopia; fruit and flowers by Billensley', is surrounded by a gilt line broken at intervals by seven gilt stars.

175   Gilt rim. Deep borders of gilt leaves and harebells in scroll design and immediately below a narrow border of gilt florets and green dots. Remainder of plate decorated with '1 Bell in Center 5 round'.

176   Gilt rim. 'Roses and Lillys of the Valley By Billensley' form the deep border of this plate, with an additional gilt border of leaves in scroll form immediately below. Remainder of plate decorated with harebell sprigs – '6 round' and one in the centre.

177   Gilt rim. Two narrow gilt borders of gilt spots above deep border of mid-blue overlaid with three rows of gilt circles alternating with gilt stars, and two further narrow gilt borders below with additional gilt enrichment under second border. Centre painted with 'Cupid on a Basket of flowers in the Clouds by Askew'.

178   Gilt rim. Border of red, blue and yellow flower heads and gilt leaves forming continuous undulating design. Centre painted with 'Landskip near Critch by Boreman', surrounded by single gilt line with tiny gilt trefoil leaves to outer edge.

179   Gilt rim. Typical harebell and gilt leaf border with narrow gilt border of laurels below. Five single harebell sprays round the plate and one in the centre.

180   Deep border of mid-blue between two broad gilt bands, each decorated with tiny trefoil leaves in gilt. The blue border is overlaid with three rows of gilt circles alternating with gilt stars, and the central decoration is of 'Cupit Painted by Askew flowers basket Clouds &c by Billensley'.

181   Gilt rim. Narrow gilt border of leaves above, and below deep border of mid-blue overlaid with croquet-hoop design in gilt. Centre painted with 'Palemon & Lavinia by Askew in Colors', surrounded by a single gilt line with trefoil leaf enrichment.

182   Gilt rim. Gilt border of pendant single leaves of fern-like design. Centre decorated with 'Landskip in Colors 3½ Inches'.

183   Gilt dentil rim. Deep border of undulating sprays of blue flowers with gilt leaves and stems. Large sprays of similar flowers and leaves over remainder of plate.

184   Gilt rim. No border inserted, but marked '1 Sprig in centre 3 round'; these are shown as slight Chantilly sprigs in blue, pink and gilt.

185   Gilt dentil rim. Deep border of fourteen 'Prentice plate' roses in natural colours. Green ground colour to central reserve which is also painted with roses in natural colours.

186   Narrow blue border to rim between two gilt lines with added gilt enrichment on underside. The centre of the plate shows a single rose and is marked 'same as 65'.

187   Exactly as 186, but border is in mid- or dark blue.

188   Missing.

189   Missing.

190   Narrow border in green no. 2 between two gilt lines. Very slight gilt border of 'broken chain' effect surrounds the central motif, which appears to be a sprig of some sort.

191   Gilt rim. Deep border of plain yellow ground colour marked 'Ground rather strong'. Centre painted with 'Moses in Bush very Pale' (sic). Also annotated 'Circle near 3¾ Inches wide', but it is uncertain whether this refers to the reserve or the depth of the border.

192   Marked 'Same as 162 Except the pale Blue Lines'.

193   Missing.

194   Missing.

195   Marked 'Same as No. 161 Except the sprig – 3 small ones'.

196   Missing.

197   Gilt rim. Marked 'Colord Plants'.

198   Missing.

199   Missing.

200   Narrow celeste border between gilt lines. Marked '3 sprigs round', but no indication of size or colour.

201   Deep border to rim between two gilt lines on which the ground colour appears to shade from yellow to green overlaid with star-shaped leaves in mauve, broken at intervals by cloud-shaped reserves each containing a small sprig. Pattern marked '3 sprigs round' (probably in gilt).

202   Deep border to rim between two gilt lines with undulating sprays of blue flowers with gilt leaves and stems, broken at intervals by cloud-shaped reserves, each containing a spray of blue flowers and gilt leaves. Further scattered sprigs round the central painting of 'Black Landskip on Moon Light ground'.

203   Very narrow celeste blue border to rim between two gilt lines. A further simple border of gilt laurel leaves. Centre painted with 'Landskip in Colours' and a surrounding border in bloom with gilt decoration.

204   Deep border to rim between two gilt lines containing continuous line of backward-sloping oval shapes in yellow(?), each containing a tiny floret and with additional gilt decoration of tiny trefoil leaves between each oval at top and bottom. The border is broken at intervals by cloud-shaped reserves, each containing a simple flower spray. There are further sprigs over the remainder of the plate, and the centre is painted with 'Black Landskip on Moon Light Ground'.

Not numbered: this pattern is not numbered but follows 204. Gilt dentil edge. Bloom border between two gilt lines marked 'this must be the Breadth of the Plate Brim'(?). Centre painted with 'Landskip 3 inches'.

206   No sketch. Marked 'French Grey border same as Pattern 65 Except Grey Instead of fawn and a Groop of Colord flowers Instead of the rose without the gold beads'.

207   Gilt rim. Deep border of cornflower sprigs in natural colours, alternating with leaf sprays in gilt contained between two very narrow borders of bloom ground with gilt enrichment. Five cornflower sprigs over the remainder of the plate with gilt leaf sprays scattered between.

208   Deep border to rim between two gilt lines containing continuous line of gilt leaf and wheat-ear pattern overlaid with undulating ribands in 'soft purple 28 twists round the table plate' (sic) with small blue flower heads in the 'hollow' of the twists. There are three sprigs round the centre of the plate and one in the middle.

209   Gilt dentil edge. Deep border of flowers and leaves in continuous line intertwined with a riband – 'Yellow finished with red-brown and new Olive equal' – contained within two narrow blue (green?) lines. Three sprigs of flowers and leaves in natural colours round the plate, and one in the centre.

210   Gilt rim. A deep border of green ground colour overlaid by eight rose sprays in natural colours. 'Three Bunches of Bird Eyes' over the remainder of the plate and one in the centre.

211   Gilt rim. Deep border of nine convolvulus flowers alternating with small sprigs of pink harebells. '3 round – one in Centre' (again with added pink harebell sprigs).

212   Gilt rim. Deep border of bloom ground between two gilt lines. Marked 'Colord Plants' signifying botanical service.

213   Gilt dentil edge. Deep border of flower garlands in natural colours intertwined with undulating palm leaves in green. Remainder of plate has three flower sprigs round and one in centre, all in natural colours.

214   Narrow border of bloom colour between two gilt lines at rim. Further border of laurel leaves in gilt. Centre of plate painted with 'Single Rose with 3 Blue Convolvulus' and finished with circle of gilt.

215   Gilt rim. A deep border of fawn ground overlaid with eleven oval medallions in a continuous horizontal row, each medallion decorated alternately with an emblematic star in gilt with a blue centre and a flower head in gilt, also with blue centre. A deep border of ground colour marked (somewhat astonishingly) 'Some Yellow Grounds, some straw, some Bloom Some Green No.2 and some French Grey' (possibly the first harlequin set?). Paintings in the centre marked '2 Doz. Done Landskips, 2 Doz. Done flowers 1 Doz. Fruit'.

216   Yellow border between two gilt lines at rim. Further border below of gilt laurel leaves. Marked 'Colord Plants'.

217   Ten borders from rim to centre, alternating gilt and celeste blue, each separated by a black line. Marked 'Centre ball ⅞ of inch', and there is an interesting note to this effect: 'Ground celest from the Princes Plates Cupid with storch [sic] & 2 Doves'!

218   Ten borders exactly as described for 217, including 'Centre Ball ⅞ Inch', but with addition of flower heads (these appear to be purple heightened with black) in the blue borders only as follows: (1) six large flowers round with '2 small ones betwixt'; (2) ditto; (3) ditto; (4) six large ones round with '1 small one betwixt'; (5) three large ones round with '1 small one betwixt'.

219   Gilt dentil edge, below which is a border of uncertain ground colour somewhat curiously described as 'Distance for Hills 1189'. Centre painted with 'Handsome Groop of flowers by Withers'.

220   No sketch. Marked 'same as 205 Except Ships Instead of Colord Landskips'.

140

A most elegant pair of draped vases, painted in enamel colours and gilt, illustrating the neo-classical vases of Derby at their best. They are incised with the number 38, and from Bemrose's list we find that figures are listed under this number. It should be noted that at the time of writing there appears to be no satisfactory explanation of the fact that some numbers do not appear in either Haslem's or Bemrose's list. The latter, of course, does include a greater number of other wares than the former. The models are adapted from Sèvres. These and other such vases are discussed in detail by M. C. F. Mortimer in the *Antique Collector*, August 1972. Gold anchor marks on plinths. William Duesbury & Co. 1773–5. 32.5 cm. *Delomosne & Son, London.*

141

Pair of vases from the antique, the decoration of which is *en grisaille* and is taken from the Pompeii and Herculaneum frescoes. It is believed that Duesbury had the plates copied from *The Antiquities of Herculaneum* by Martyn & Lettice, London, 1773. The Morley College guide to the *Ceramics of Derbyshire* also states that Duesbury's name appeared, together with those of Matthew Boulton and Josiah Wedgwood, in the list of subscribers. A similar pair were sold at Christie's on 5 May 1778. Incised number 68 which does not agree with Bemrose's list. Note number 67 is 'Small Term Vase'. William Duesbury & Co. c. 1775–80. 25.4 cm. *Victoria & Albert Museum, C240 and C241.*

142

A deep trembleuse chocolate cup and stand, with wide dark blue borders gilt with *oeil de perdrix* and painted with three landscape panels, reserved upon the cup and stand, probably painted by Zachariah Boreman. Incised 'N'. William Duesbury & Co. 1775–80. 10.2 cm. *David John Ceramics, Woodstock.*

143
Pair of figures, number 363, 'with
Dead Bird', modelled by Jean Jacques
Spängler. Ducret in his *Zurcher
Porzellan* illustrates on page 23 a similar
pair in biscuit (*c.* 1790), wrongly
attributed to Chelsea. William
Duesbury & Co. *c.* 1790. 20.3 cm.
Andrew Dando Antiques, Bath.

144
Biscuit group of the virgins awakening
Cupid (Haslem's list 195). Ducret in his
Zurcher Porzellan illustrates on page 25
a similar group entitled 'Schlafender
Amor', modelled in 1775–80 in Zurich.
This group has no tree supports nor
flowers applied to the base, and is
attributed to J. J. Spängler.
Traditionally this group is accepted as
the work of Pierre Stephan, also of
Swiss origin. William Duesbury & Co.
1775. 31.6 cm. *Victoria & Albert
Museum, C274 – 1935.*

145
Group of cupids as sportsmen. The style of modelling is that of the Tournai factory and it is conceivable that these were modelled for Duesbury by Nicholas François Gauron, who would have been about 40 years old at the time of modelling. It is documented that a highly paid modeller or repairer of that name was working for Duesbury at the Chelsea works (Jewitt, *Ceramic Art in Great Britain*, vol. 1, p. 186). William Duesbury & Co. *c.* 1775. Approx. 21.1 cm. *Victoria & Albert Museum, C61 – 1924.*

147
Pair of biscuit cupids with falcon and dog, each with incised number 213. The central figure of 'Summer' is from the French set of 'Seasons' attributed to Stephan, although it seems likely that Coffee remodelled this set on a round base *c.* 1790. Incised number 123. William Duesbury & Co. Cupids *c.* 1775–80. Cupids 12.5 cm and 13 cm, 'Season' 18 cm. *Dr J. Freeman Collection.*

146
Pair of biscuit vases, each with an incised number 116, which does not correspond to either Haslem's or Bemrose's list. Repairer's marks for Joseph Hill and Isaac Farnsworth. Crown, crossed batons, dots and 'D' incised. William Duesbury & Co. *c.* 1785. Approx. 16 cm. *Formerly in the collection of Mr Arthur Rokeby Price. Herbert Allen Collection. Victoria & Albert Museum, C294 and A – 1935.*

221 Narrow border of yellow ground between two gilt lines, below which is a further border of laurel leaves in gilt. Scattered sprigs of blue flowers with gilt leaves and stems – central sprig(s) surrounded by a blue circle with slight gilt decoration above and below.

222 Gilt dentil edge. Deep border of bloom ground colour between two gilt lines, below which is a border of gilt leaves and buds. Centre painted with 'Ships in Colors full 3 inches Robertson'.

223 Gilt rim with narrow gilt line below. No sketch, but marked '6 Flies round the Brim', and towards the centre '3 feathers round the bottom one in centre'. NB the 'feathers' mentioned here should be taken to mean bird feathers and not the feathers defined in the glossary.

224 Deep border of wide stripes of yellow alternating with leaf sprays intertwining a dark blue line, this border being contained within two gilt lines. Remainder of plate has '3 sprigs round' in yellow, blue and gilt and '1 sprig in Center'.

225 Deep border of soft yellow ground overlaid with bold design of tulips in 'hard Rose', a dark blue leaf motif and brown seaweed-type fronds with black scrolls connecting each motif. Remainder of plate has '3 sprigs round' and one in centre, these comprising small blue and rose-coloured flowers with gilt leaves.

226 No sketch. Marked 'same as 227 Except Yellow instead of Bloom'.

227 Narrow border of bloom ground at rim between two gilt lines. Undulating leaf sprays below in 'fine blue', and further narrow border of bloom between two gilt lines. '3 Sprigs round – 1 in Center' – these are quite small and consist of pink and blue flowers.

228 Gilt dentil edge. Deep border of bloom ground bound around with ribands in 'fine blue' and with small flower heads spaced at intervals between the ribands, the border contained between two gilt lines and a further gilt line below. The remainder of the plate contains 'blue shells done slight' ('three round one in Center') with 'Sea Weed faint Rose'.

229 Deep border contained within two gilt lines comprising '18 bends in the black Laurel' with the addition of 'blue Red and Purple flowers alternately in the bordr' (sic). A tiny blue sprig is shown and marked '3 of these buds round 1 blue 1 red 1 purple'. A further note states 'Green Leafs Dresden Yellow'.

230 Deep border contained within two gilt lines comprising bends of black laurels intertwined with ribands, the underside of which are rose-coloured and the outside described as 'filling in green and Dresden Yellow Green equal' (colour in pattern book exactly like khaki!). Remainder of plate scattered with tiny sprigs of leaves.

231 Deep border contained within two gilt lines of alternating flowers and upright lozenge shapes. The lozenges appear to be a uniform blue, but the flowers are rose, green and yellow in that order repeated round the border, each having a gilt spot at each side. Small sprays of flowers are scattered over the remainder of the plate.

232 Narrow border to rim between two gilt lines. Writing here almost illegible, but I have been able to decipher 'Green No. 8 but with White Enamell Equal but laid over with Green Gold [indecipherable]. Underneath, a simple border of gilt laurel leaves. Centre painted with 'Groop of 3 Roses with 2 buds Wardle'.

233 No sketch apart from slight sprig below number. Marked 'from Dodson's Tea Pattern No. 3' (no sketch for this appears in Tea Books). Underneath the outlined sprig it is noted '4 sprigs in bottom of the plate from the Brown [indecipherable] in the border'.

234 Gilt rim on what must be a fluted plate since it is noted there are '16 Bunches in the plate'. A 'bunch' comprises three small blue leaves tied together by their stems laid sideways, between which are two spots with black centres placed vertically, these spots coloured 'Yellow shade with new Olive'. Small blue sprigs over remainder of plate.

235 Number marked in but crossed out.

236 Deep border of 'Common fawn Ground' (sic) between two gilt lines. The border has twenty-one oval reserves, each formed by a continuous row of gilt dots which are graduated in size, and each containing a leaf spray in gilt. Between the ovals are vertical ribands in dark blue with tassels at each end. A gold line round the centre of the plate, but no mention of a central motif.

237 Deep border of dark blue ground with '15 palms crossed', coloured purple(?), which form ovoid shapes in the centre of each of which is a purple star. The border is also decorated with tiny floret heads in black. Centre of plate decorated with 'Earls coronet Gold finished with Brown'.

238 Deep border of celeste ground between two gilt lines. Twelve diamond reserves round the border, each containing an emblematic star in gilt with pearl in centre. Plain gilt circle round centre, but no indication given of a motif.

239 Deep border of sloping vertical stripes of blue alternating with flowers in natural colours against a background of gilt(?) dots, the border contained within two gilt bands. A narrow border below of undulating laurel leaves and 'flowers by Peg', which are shown as very slight sprays of roses, hollyhocks and daisies, marked 'these three round'. More flowers in the centre surrounded by two gilt lines with added gilt enrichment.

240 Deep border of 'fawn ground' heavily gilded with oval reserves containing floral festoons in natural colours. This is also marked 'flowers

by Peg', which again consist of very small sprays of red, blue and yellow flowers marked 'these three round'. Further spray in centre surrounded by gilt line.

241 Deep border of fawn ground between two gilt lines and overlaid with flowers marked 'Roses selest shaddowd with soft Rose' (*sic*); between each rose is a large leaf spray of uncertain colour but possibly gilt.

242 Gilt rim. Deep border of uncertain ground colour finished with a line of gilt below. Marked '5 Black sprigs Round 5 gold ditto' and 'One Black groop in Center'.

243 Gilt rim. Deep border of sixteen 'bunches' of blue leaves with gilt wheat-ears spaced at regular intervals. Gilt line below. Remainder of plate decorated with '5 flies'.

244 Gilt rim. Deep border of fifteen blue and fifteen fawn linked ovals, each decorated with gilt stars and having central gilt spot. Gilt line below. Plain gilt circle round the central motif.

245 Gilt dentil edge. Deep border of bloom ground colour between two gilt lines, finished with narrow gilt line below. A further border of gilt leaves and buds and a central square reserve marked 'Colord Shipping 3 Inch Square by Robertson'.

246 Gilt rim. Yellow(?) ground colour to deep border gilded with tiny dots to form background to '10 Different Flies' with additional decoration of gold stars and corn stalks and heads. This pattern is also annotated with amusing if somewhat obscure remarks which appear to read as follows: '245 Gone to London', 'But must be 246'. 'Gilt circle 3¾ Inches Inside'.

247 Gilt rim below which is deep border of yellow ground with formal scroll-type design in black, gilt line beneath, and gilt circle round centre of plate.

248 Gilt rim. Plate entirely covered with sprigs – '3 in the Brim', '4 Sprigs in bottom' and (possibly) one in centre. The sprigs are possibly blue and gilt and are in the form of small sprays of leaves with (in some cases) tendrils.

249 Gilt rim. Deep border of yellow ground overlaid with undulating leaves and flowers in brown shadowed with black (?). Below this border eight gilt stars alternate with gilt leaf sprays and a 'Circle 3¾ Inches' in centre of plate.

250 A special green border to rim between two gilt lines. Green is defined as 'two parts No. 2 ditto White Enamell mixt together'. Below, a narrow gilt border and remainder of plate painted with 'Variety of Avunculas Not Numbered but may take 250'.

251 No sketch. Marked 'Same as 216 Except a Circle instead of a Plant'.

252 Gilt rim. Narrow border of blue spots and gilt dots in continuous line. Underneath, an ornate border of red and purple scrolls between circular reserves, each containing a single rose painted in natural colours. Narrow border of blue spots repeated and two gilt lines below. Marked 'Dresden Green. Pattern from french broth [indecipherable] Cover'.

253 Gilt rim. Deep border of dark blue, heavily gilded with eighteen ovals with additional decoration of gilt stars and dots. Circle in gilt, 3½ in diameter, in centre of plate.

254 Gilt rim. Deep border of green finished with gilt band and a narrow gilt line below with carried further gilt enrichment. Square reserve in centre painted with '3 Inch Square Colord Shipping Robertson'.

255 Marked 'Same as 72 Except Plain brimd' (*sic*), and no sprig in centre ring.

256 Very narrow dark blue border to rim between two gilt lines. Below, slightly wider border of dark blue overlaid with small floret heads in gilt with three gilt dots above and below. Blue line with simple intertwining gilt leaf motif forming a circle of 3½ in diameter round centre of plate.

257 Gilt rim. Deep border of dark blue heavily gilded with a foliate design entwining a band of gilt; the border finished with a scalloped gilt line below. A gilt circle round the centre of the plate 'rather better 3½ inches'.

258 Narrow green border to rim between two gilt lines. Slight border of gilt laurel leaves below. Centre painted with 'Groop of flowers by Withers' (*sic*).

259 Gilt rim with narrow gilt line below. Heavily gilded border of leaves and buds with scalloped gilt line below. Centre painted with 'Ships in Colors', contained within gilt circle with further gilt foliate border surrounding.

260 Gilt rim. Deep border of shaded gilt stripes. Centre painted with 'Coloured Plants'.

261 Gilt rim with narrow gilt line below. Deep border of yellow ground, finished with gilt band and narrow gilt line below. Circle of 3½ in diameter round centre in gilt with narrow gilt circle surrounding.

262 Gilt rim. Deep border of 'fine Dark Blue' with heavily gilded ovals 'every other flute'. Additional decoration of gilt stars, black spots and white enamelled dots. Centre painted with 'Colord Landskips by Hill 4½ inches', surrounded by narrow blue border between two gilt lines with additional gilt enrichment above.

263 No sketch. Marked 'Same as Tea Pattern 187'.

264 Missing.

265 No sketch. Marked 'Clollord Groops' (*sic*) and 'Same Border as 250'.

266 No sketch. Marked 'same as [indecipherable] to fill the Brim of the Plate and four Sprigs in the Bottom' (*sic*).

267 'Same as 216 Except Bloom border instead of Yellow'.

268 Narrow green border to rim between two gilt lines. This border is marked 'Green Mint for the Set with [crossed out] &c' and underneath 'see Brewers sett' (*sic*). Wider gilt border below, heavily gilded in scroll-

type leaves with fern leaves added, below which is a very deep border in 'Green Mint' between two gilt lines and with further gilt band below. Centre painted with 'Annimals in Colors' (*sic*).

269 No sketch. Marked 'Same as 262 Except the Landskip [indecipherable] Instead of 4½ and the Gold Ornament round one third less'.

270 Gilt rim from which are pendant 'bunches' of leaves in gilt with half-circles of gilt between each 'bunch'. On the underside of the border is a gilt line with the same pattern of bunches of a smaller size and in an upright position. Centre painted with 'Colord Landskips 3¼' surrounded by single gilt band with additional gilding to outer edge.

271 Gilt rim. Thirty-seven diamond shapes in continuous line, each containing a pearl with gilt line under this border. Gilt circle to centre, 4 in diameter.

272 Gilt rim. Twenty-two red ribands round edge of plate. Three red and gilt sprigs scattered below, and one large sprig in centre.

273 Gilt rim. Bloom border overlaid with trellis design in gilt, with gilt leaf enrichment and black dots added. Below, a richly gilded border of leaves and ferns, and a further border of trellis design below this.

274 No sketch. Marked 'Same as 100 except no flowers'.

275 Gilt rim. Narrow border of blue ground between two gilt lines. Gilt circle round centre of plate, 3¾ in diameter.

276 No sketch. Marked 'Tea Pattern 58'.

277 Yellow ground border to rim between two lines of gilt with stripes of an undetermined colour. Narrow gilt line below, from which are suspended sprays of seaweed alternating with bell-shaped motif, all carried out in gilt. Centre reserve, 3 in square, painted with 'Shipping' – two gilt lines frame this reserve with added gilt enrichment to the outer line.

278 Gilt rim. Border of twenty-six harebells painted in blue and pink in scroll form with leaves in natural colours, gilt line below. Scattered cornflower sprigs over remainder of plate, '4 in bottom' and one in centre.

279 Gilt rim. Heavily gilded border of leaves over a background of seaweed fronds described as '16 turns in the Table plate 14 in the Desert' (*sic*). A large flower spray in gilt of assorted flowers is also shown, but it is impossible to determine whether this is the central motif or whether it is repeated round the 'bottom' of the plate.

280 Yellow ground border to rim between two gilt lines with a further narrow gilt line below. The centre of the plate is painted with 'Colord Landskips 3 inches by Robertson' in a reserve which appears to be of hexagonal form, surrounded by a yellow ground border following the lines of the hexagon and finished with a band of gilt with a narrow gilt line above.

281 Gilt rim. Simple border of twenty leaves and buds in continuous line, all carried out in gilt. Gilt circle to centre.

282–97 Missing.

298(9) Broad band of gilt round rim. Border of bloom ground decorated with black rectangles, each containing dots giving the appearance of dominoes, and from the side of each 'domino' is a double scroll giving the appearance of a Greek 'E', the border contained within two black lines. The centre is painted with 'One figure with a Serpent Entwining a Tree in Red Brewer'; this painting is surrounded by a narrow bloom ground border decorated with black leaves and contained within two very narrow black lines.

300–29 Missing.

330 Broad band of gilt to rim. Deep border of green ground marked 'Green for Annimalls with Enamell' (*sic*), finished with band of gilt under which there is a continuous design of gilt scallops. These are filled in with narrow vertical lines and have a gilt flower in the centre with a gilt spot each side of the flower, and a small pendant trefoil leaf motif between each scallop. Gilt circle to centre.

331 Broad band of gilt to rim. Deep border of 'Common Red shaddowed with Shaddow Color' and overlaid with bold Greek key design in darker red, with broad band of gilt below. Gilt circle to centre.

332 Broad band of gilt to rim. A very deep border which extends to the centre gilt circle comprises a narrow red border between two gilt lines with large trailing leaf garlands intertwining.

333 Broad band of gilt to rim with narrow gilt line below. Border of large undulating leaf sprays intertwined with festoons of smaller leaves, all executed in gilt with one narrow and one broad gilt line below. Gilt circle to centre.

334–6 Missing.

337 Deep border of dark blue ground to rim contained within two gilt bands and containing thirteen small oval reserves alternating with diamond lozenge shapes each outlined in gilt. The ovals contain emblematic stars in gilt, and the lozenges have a seven-pointed star in red. Gilt circle to centre.

338–56 Missing.

357 Broad band of gilt to rim. Deep border of orange-red ground decorated with red and black turret designs finished with broad band of gilt below. Gilt circle to centre.

358 Gilt rim. Deep border of vertical gilt lines with oval medallions of 'strong rose', each containing a gilt flower head with additional gilt decoration above and below the narrowest part of each oval. Gilt circle to centre.

359 Broad gilt band to rim. Deep border of stripes alternating green, gold, wider stripe containing leaf garlands in gilt, and fourth stripe marked

'silver' – this sequence repeated round the rim. Three further borders below, all exactly alike and repeating the leaf garland motif in the stripe in horizontal instead of vertical habit. Deep band of gilt between each border.

360 Deep border of orange-red ground containing sixteen six-pointed stars, each containing another star at centre executed in red and shaded olive green. Between each large star there is a gilt ball with additional decoration in gilt of half-moon shapes to the two bands of gilt enclosing the border. Directly below, 'marbling' covers the plate from the border just described to the centre gilt circle, within which is a large double-petalled flower head in red.

361 Deep border of roses in natural colours by Loton against an orange-red background. Remainder of plate scattered with dozens of tiny sprigs in monochrome red or gilt.

362 Gilt rim. A narrow border of green no. 5 (shown as a rather dirty olive) between two gilt lines. Below, a wide border of this ground colour extends to the centre which is painted with 'Groop of Collord flowers Loton' (sic), within a gilt circle.

363 Broad band of orange-red to rim. Below, is an exceptionally deep border of gold geometric shapes carried out in red and shadowed with black. The placing of the geometric lines leaves cruciform reserves which are decorated with leaves and scrolls, and additional leaf decoration is shown above the cruciforms and round the bottom edge of the border which is finished with a narrow red border between two black lines with a further line of red below.

364 A deep border of large green aspidistra-type leaves alternating with harebell sprays in red contained within two broad bands of gilt. The centre is painted with '3 Inch Collord Landskip' surrounded by gilt circle.

365 Deep border of trailing leaves and ferns contained within two gilt lines (the border itself may be gilt but it is not possible to determine this without an example). Centre painted with 'small Groop of Roses'.

366 Marked 'the same as Pattern No. 362 but fawn instead of Green'.

367 Marked 'the same as 362 but straw Color instead of Green'.

368 Gilt rim with border of vine leaves, grapes and tendrils. Marked 'tea pattern 554'.

369 Deep border of red ground decorated with black Greek key pattern contained within black lines.

370 Deep border of formal leaf motifs alternating in upright and pendant habit. Ground colour uncertain but border probably in gilt between two broad gilt bands. Centre painted with 'Collord Landkips' within gilt circle.

371 Sketch shows two bands of gilt forming border but no ground colour or design inserted. Pattern marked 'Bronze figure 3 inches', and it may be assumed that this is the central motif.

372 This pattern is pencilled in so faintly that it is impossible to describe it with any degree of accuracy. There appears to be a fairly deep Greek key border and the word 'Longdon' below. A central circle is also shown.

373–7 Missing.

378 (1) Gilt rim. Slight sketch of a daisy head and marked 'Slight white and gold border' with gilt line below. Also annotated 'Key and Clark' and 'Circle in Center'.
(2) Gilt rim. Border in gilt of turret form with large acanthus leaves in each section against a background of horizontal lines. Centre painted with 'Bird and Landskip Loton 3½ Inches' surrounded by border of flower heads and scrolls between two gilt bands.

Not numbered: Broad gilt band to rim with slight foliate border below, followed by '4 flies Largest Size 2 betwixt small ones' and narrower gilt band. Centre painted with 'Bronze Landskip Gold Ground 3 Inches' in hexagonal reserve surrounded by plain gilt band and a further border of linked chain pattern in gilt.

Not numbered: Gilt band to rim. Two very large leaf sprays crossing each other form deep border (possibly in gilt) finished with continuous row of gilt balls with white centre spot and a gilt band below. Centre painted with '1 Bird on a tree with Landskip 4½ Inches by Lawton'.

386 Gilt rim. Deep border comprising a gilt rope intertwined with undulating garland of leaves and flower heads between two gilt lines. A further gilt line below. Gilt circle in centre.

388 Sketch in pencil, but writing difficult to decipher though the name 'Whittaker' is legibly written.

392 Gilt rim with broad band of gilt and a narrow gilt line below. Gilt border of palm leaves and buds in a continuous line and a note 'Plants and Gold border by J. Lead'.

393 Number pencilled in with a note which appears to read 'Big [indecipherable] of [or by?] Keys'.

394 Number pencilled in and annotated 'Flys Gold Edge [indecipherable]'.

395 Marked 'Tea Pattern 741'.

396 Number pencilled in and marked 'Red and Gold [indecipherable] &c'.

398 Gilt band to rim with narrow blue line running through. Blue and gilt seaweed pattern over remainder of plate.

399 Very faint outline of main border between two narrow borders of red contained within two gilt lines suggests that this carries green, gold and red stars in varying sizes. Gilt circle round centre.

List of Patterns Given by Gilhespy, and Extracted from Lygo's Letters

DESSERT PATTERNS

Number	Date	Remarks
52	1787	
65	1786	
84	1789	Sold: may have been out some time.
87	1789	Just out.
116	1793	'Sent some time back for Mr. Boreman to do.'

TEA PATTERNS

Number	Date	Remarks
18	1787	
69	1784	Mr. Eliot, double shape.
82	1788	Hamilton shape.
84	1787	
100	1789	
109	1789	New tea pattern.
115	1789	
116	1789	Just out.
117	1789	Should be 41 pieces. French shaped cups.
190	1792	
321	1794	
395	1796	

5

Useful Wares
Including Blue and White

Although little useful ware has been recorded from the Andrew Planché period (c. 1748–56), a great variety of both useful and ornamental ware was produced during Duesbury I's time, as is shown by the large number of illustrations in this book, which cover most aspects of production of the Old Nottingham Road Works.

There has been much speculation about the blue and white products of the Derby Factory. The ratio of biscuit blue colour weight to glaze weight often caused the blue to run, which might account for this type of production being limited in comparison to that of other factories. It is worth mentioning that the running blue caused problems even in recent times at Osmaston Road, but they were rectified by in-glaze firing of the blue. This book includes only blue and white pieces which have polychrome counterparts made by the Derby Factory. For years Derby has become the dumping ground for pieces which are not readily attributable to other factories. However it has now become clear that a good deal more blue and white Derby exists than was previously thought.

The inspiration for the early period was Chinese export porcelain, and this type of decoration is very often seen. The rare and interesting coronation mug, dated 1761, suggests that Richard Holdship had arrived in Derby from Worcester earlier than 1764, as was originally believed. He was to teach the Derby hands the art of copper-plate printing and was to be paid, according to Jewitt, £100 down and £30 per annum as long as the firm of Duesbury and Heath used his process. He agreed to supply them with a 'secret' process for making china according to proofs already made by him at Derby. This would have been a soap-rock porcelain, since, according to Franklin Barrett, Holdship owned the rights to mine soapstone at Gew Graze in Cornwall.

Returning to blue and white porcelain, it seems reasonable, as has already been stated, that it was produced in larger quantities than was at one time believed. Printing was not popular with Duesbury, who had previously used painted decoration under blue, and there are references to Holdship's letters bemoaning the lack of work.

It is interesting to note that at the first recorded sale of Derby porcelain, a notice of which appeared in the *Public Advertiser* during December 1756, the items were described as: 'A Curious Collection of fine Figures, Jars, sauceboats, Services for Deserts, and a great variety of other useful and ornamental Porcelain, all after the finest Dresden models, all exquisietly painted in Enamel, with Flowers, Insects, India Plants &c....'

The following is a note of consignment of wares in 1763, reproduced from Jewitt:

The manufacture of china under the first William Duesbury must have rapidly risen into eminence, for in 1763 in an account of 'goods sent to London', no less than forty-two large boxes appear at one time to have been despatched to the metropolis, and the proceeds, I presume, of the sale of a part of them, on the 2nd of May, in that year, amounted to no less a sum than £666 17s. 6d. It is very interesting, at this early period of the art, to be

148
Fine biscuit group of the 'Seasons' from the French set (Haslem's list 123) remodelled on round bases perhaps by William Coffee. See colour plate 32 for a fine coloured set from the Indianapolis Museum of Art and compare black and white plate number 110 for the original set on pierced scroll bases. Crown, crossed batons, dots and 'D' incised. William Duesbury & Co. c. 1790. 21.1 cm. *Christie, Manson & Woods.*

149
A pair of groups entitled 'Renaldo & Armida' and 'Cephalus and Procris', incised with numbers 76 and 75 (Haslem's list). William Duesbury & Co. c. 1775–80. 21.6 cm. *Victoria & Albert Museum, 180 – 1874.*

151
Andromache weeping over the ashes of Hector. William Duesbury & Co. 1775. Approx. 21.6 cm. *Victoria & Albert Museum, C234 – 1922.*

152
Vase and cover of large proportions with biscuit winged female demi-figures. The central panel is painted with Celadon and Amelia, from *The Seasons*, book ii, by James Thomson. The panel is flanked by natural flowers and the predominant ground-colour is a rich blue. The figure subject is probably the work of Richard Askew and the source print would be after Angelica Kauffmann, engraved by F. Bartolozzi. Incised number 86, gold anchor on plinth, patch marks. William Duesbury & Co. 1775–80. 38.5 cm. *Victoria & Albert Museum, 825 – 1882.*

150 ◁ ◁
A group of nuns. William Duesbury &
Co. *c.* 1775. 12.7 cm. *Victoria & Albert
Museum, 2964 – 1901.*

153
Two large vases and covers, with
handles formed by biscuit female demi-
figures, identical in shape to the vase
shown in plate 152. The landscapes are
generally accepted to be the work of
Zachariah Boreman and the figure
subjects, which are in the reverse
panels, the work of Richard Askew. It
is interesting to note that the two vases
illustrated here are not exactly a pair,
and the author confirms that the two
vases of similar shape in the Field
Collection, and also the two in the
Victoria & Albert Museum, do not
form pairs with each other. It may
therefore be suggested that they might
be centre pieces for garnitures of three
or, more likely, five vases. This theory
is further assisted by the size of the
known pieces. William Duesbury &
Co. 1775–80. 40 cm. *Delomosne & Son,
London.*

154
A pair of ice-pails, covers and liners
(for the purpose of chilling the fruits),
decorated in the French taste. A similar
patterned dessert service was sold by
Christie's in May 1782, 'A very
beautiful Seve-pattern compleat desert
service, enamel'd with roses, fine
mosaic border, richly finished with
chased and burnish'd gold.' This
particular service did not include ice-
pails. The flower painting here may be
strongly attributed to Edward Withers.
Crown over 'D' in blue. William
Duesbury & Co. *c.* 1780–85. Approx.
23 cm. *Delomosne & Son, London.*

155
Teapot decorated in neo-classical style
with green swags pendant from Smith's
blue and gilt borders. Crown over 'D'
in puce. William Duesbury & Co.
c. 1780. 13.4 cm. *Royal Crown Derby
Museum.*

enabled to say of what varieties of goods the assignment to London consisted, and I therefore give the list of contents of some of the boxes entire, and also a few items from others. I do this the more readily because it has been recently said by the writer to whom I have already alluded [Alfred Wallis, a former editor of the Derby Mercury *], 'We doubt very much whether the higher sorts of fine porcelain (figures, vases, &c.) were made upon the Nottingham Road until the purchase of the Chelsea Works in 1769 and the commencement of what is called the Chelsea-Derby period, which lasted until 1785 or 1786.'*

The term 'Chelsea Derby' is used for the period 1770–84, when William Duesbury I was directing the Chelsea Factory in London at the same time as the Derby Works. See chapter 14, where a clarification of the products of the two factories is presented.

BOX NO. 41 CONTAINED –
>*8 Large Flower Jarrs, at 21s.*
>*3 Large Ink Stands, at 42s.*
>*1 Small ditto, at 24s.*
>*4 Large Britanias, at 36s.*
>*6 Second-sized Huzzars, at 12s.*
>*4 Large Pidgeons, at 7s.*
>*12 Small Rabbets, at 2s.*
>*12 Chickens, at 2s.*
>*16 Small Baskets, at 2s. 6d.*

BOX NO. 29 –
>*4 Large Quarters, at 40s.*
>*2 Jupiters, at 68s.*
>*2 Junos.*
>*5 Ledas, at 36s.*
>*1 Europa, at 36s.*
>*2 Bird-catchers, at 10s. 6d.*
>*12 Sixth-sized Solid Baskets.*
>*18 Second-sized Boys, at 1s. 6d.*

BOX NO. 31 –
>*4 Large Quarters, at 40s.*
>*4 Shakespears, at 42s.*
>*6 Miltons, at 42s.*
>*24 Bucks, on Pedestals, at 2s. 6d.*

BOX NO. 11 –
>*24 Enammelled, round, fourth-size, open-worked Baskets.*
>*12 Blue ditto.*
>*12 Open-worked Spectacle Baskets.*
>*9 Second-size Sage-leaf boats.*

There were also, of various sizes, blue fluted boats, Mosaic boats, sage-leaf boats, potting pots, caudle cups, blue strawberry pots, fig-leaf sauce boats, octagon fruit plates, vine-leaf plates, coffee cups, flower vases, standing sheep, feeding sheep, cats, sunflower blows, pedestals, honeycomb jars, coffee pots, blue guglets and basins to ditto; butter tubs, Chelsea jars, tea pots, honeycomb pots, figures of Mars and Minerva, sets of the Elements, Spanish shepherds, Neptune, the Muses, bucks, tumblers, roses, Jupiter, Diana, boys, garland shepherd, Spaniards, Chelsea-pattern candlesticks, Dresden ditto, jars and beakers, polyanthus pots, &c., &c.

On Monday 23 May 1785[1] Mr Christie offered Derby porcelain in a six-day sale at the Great Room, Pall Mall. This was Duesbury's annual sale; Nightingale's extracts from the catalogue of this sale are given below in full.

One pair of figures, Harlequin [2] and Columbine, 1 pair flute and cymbal, and 2 pair of sitting Cupids ditto 1l. 3s., Senior
A large and complete desert service, elegantly enamel's with different landscapes, finished with a beautiful laurel and buff border with fine blue and gold lines &c. 19l. 19s. Col. Thompson
A beautiful pair of caudle or cabinet cups, covers and stands, peacock pattern, richly enamel'd with the fine blue and gold 2l., ditto
A pair of broth basons, covers and stands, beautifully enamel'd with fine blue and gold 1l. 5s. Lady Fitzwilliam
Three flower beakers, fawn colour ground an gilt 18s.
A complat desert service of the fine old Japan pattern 43 pieces 15l.
A beautiful gallon punch bowl enamel'd with fine ultramarine *borders, highly enriched with pearls and burnished gold* 1l. 7s.
An elegantly finished set of 5 VASES, the centre one about 11½ inches high, the other pieces to correspond, beautifully enamel's in compartments on one side with pastoral groups, and on the other landscapes, in a pure self colour, elegantly ornamented with fine blue and gold 9l. 19s. 6d. Morgan
A very elegant desert service enamel'd with bouquets of flowers and fine blue and gold field–de–suc pattern, 43 pieces 17l. 17s.
A Derbyshire milk pail and ladle and 6 egg cups white and gold 1l. 14s.

159
Cabaret sucrier and cover, painted in the French manner by Richard Askew in puce camieu, with trophies and cupids. The panels are reserved upon white ground gilt with lines, the cover has a floral finial. Crown over 'D' in blue. William Duesbury & Co. 1780–85. 8.25 cm. *The Donovan Collection.*

160
A cup and saucer with typical gilt blue border and random flower painting in the Sèvres style. It is interesting to note the large size of the cup and unusually shaped handle. Crown over 'D' in blue. William Duesbury & Co. *c.* 1780. Cup 7 cm, saucer diameter 15 cm. *Victor Spenton Collection.*

A pair of neat butter tubs, covers and stands, basket work border, gold edge and ring 18s. Lady Weymouth

A beautiful group of 2 Bacchants dressing Pan with a garland of flowers in biscuit 2l. 4s. Lady Mary Duncomb

A beautiful small *CENTRE VASE elegantly enamel'd, on 1 front a TAMBORINE BOY* from C. White's beautiful plate, *on the other a landscape, and 1 pair of* ewer shape *VASES* enamel'd in compartments with pastoral figures, *richly gilt with burnished gold stripes* 8l. 8s. Lady E. York

A very capital *DESERT SERVICE highly enamel'd with landscapes of a* pure self color, *and richly finished with borders &c. in burnished gold, 43 pieces* 26l. 5s. Sir T. Wentworth

A very *elegant complete* set of tea china, *new shape cups, enamel'd with festoons of gold* husks, *fine* ultramarine *blue border*, richly finished with *pearls and burnished gold, 41 pieces* 6l. 16s. 6d. Price

Six very elegant caudle cups, covers and stands, highly finished with pearls and burnished gold, on a fine ultramarine blue ground 3l. 9s. Price

Eight fine old blue and gold Japan pattern fruit dishes 2l. 2s. Lady Cornwall

A superbly elegant cabinet cup, cover and stand, peacock pattern, *fine mazarine blue ground, enriched with burnished gold and one pair toilet boxes* 1l. 10s.

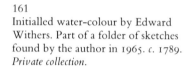

161
Initialled water-colour by Edward Withers. Part of a folder of sketches found by the author in 1965. *c.* 1789. *Private collection.*

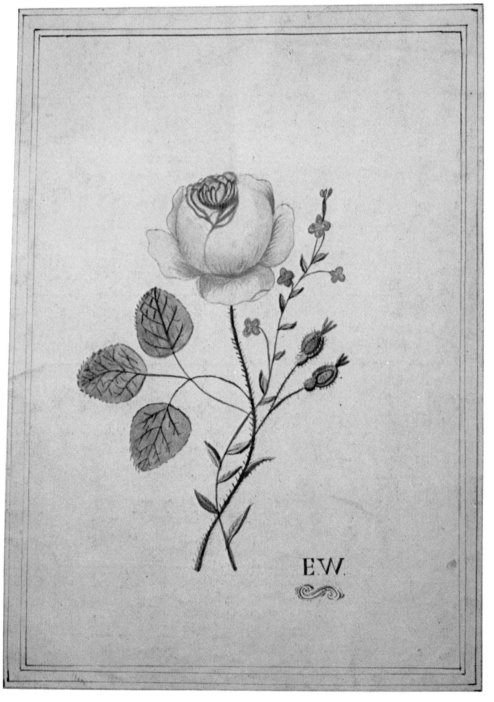

165 ▷
An interesting ice-pail of pattern 35, the panel showing a view of the silk mill and the cathedral over the Derwent, Derby. This appears to be one of the first topographical scenes, although not named, which were later to become so popular and to make the Derby factory the first porcelain works in Britain to use topographical paintings. Crown, crossed batons, dots and 'D' in puce. William Duesbury & Co. c. 1780–85. Approx. 22 cm. *George Woods Collection.*

167 ▷ ▷
Feather-edged Chelsea-shaped plate painted in botanical style by William Billingsley. Evidence for the attribution is given by the statement made by Samuel Keys in his account of the Old Works. Crown, crossed batons, dots and 'D' in puce, number 7 on foot rim for William Billingsley. William Duesbury & Co. c. 1792. Diameter 22.7 cm. *Major G. N. Dawnay Collection.*

162 ◁
Two botanical studies by Edward Withers executed on hand-dried paper of the period. Dated 1789 and initialled. This was the year Withers was re-engaged by Duesbury (see Lygo's letters 1789). *Mary Field Collection.*

163 ◁ ◁
A wine-cooler from a service made for James, 8th Duke of Hamilton, 5th Duke of Brandon. It bears an inset mark which is very rarely seen. William Duesbury & Co. c. 1780–85. 24 cm. *Private collection.*

164 ◁
The four 'Quarters' gathered round an obelisk. Australia is omitted. Incised number 295, patch marks. Duesbury & Kean. c. 1795. 25.4 cm. *Royal Crown Derby Museum.*

166
Pair of Chelsea-Derby chocolate cups, covers and stands. Interlaced anchor and 'D' in gold. William Duesbury & Co. c. 1775. Saucer: diameter right 17.8 cm, left 15.7 cm. *Sotheby's, New Bond Street.*

28 ▷▷
Fine tureen and cover, showing the pre-Adam shape and decorated with named pattern 159. The old pattern books have the lettering 'Birds and Landskip by Complin' on this pattern. Crown, crossed batons, dots and 'D' in puce. William Duesbury & Co. 1790. 12 cm. *Mary Field Collection.*

168
An important pair of ewers which seem to complement the Kedleston Vase, now in the Royal Crown Derby Museum, being identical in decoration except that they are painted on both sides with landscapes. The left ewer has a scene called 'View in Dovedale, Derbyshire', the other 'View near Matlock, Derbyshire'. Crown, crossed batons, dots and 'D' in blue with descriptions. William Duesbury & Co. *c.* 1790. 28 cm. *Indianapolis Museum of Art, gift of Mrs Herbert R. Duckwall in memory of her husband.*

A very elegant large bowl, beautifully finished with pearls and burnished gold, on fine ultramarine blue borders 3l. Temple

A group representing Music and 2 pairs of Cupids in biscuit 1l. 10s.

An elegant finished set of FIVE VASES, the centre one full 12 inches high, hath on one front a beautiful landscape, and on the other a figure of Sterne's Maria, the two side pieces to correspond, on one is represented a group of Damon and Delia, on the other a group of Paris and Oenone, and 2 ewer shape Vases to complete the set, ornamented with fine green and richly finished with burnished gold 14l.

A pair of very beautiful Caudle or Cabinet Cups, enamel's in compartments with rose coloured Cupids, richly finished with fine burnished gold stripes 2l. 15s.

A beautiful large group of 3 graces distressing Cupid, in biscuit 2l. 14s. Lady Monson

A beautiful BASON and EWER, elegantly enamel'd, with a fine blue and gold pearl and fringe border 2l.

A beautiful large DEJUNEE, with 2 cups and saucers, enamel'd with vases, neat festoons of husks, and pink and gold borders 3l. 10s.

A beautiful complete DESERT SERVICE, enamel'd with landscapes highly finished and decorated with entwined borders, &c. of a fine ultramarine blue and burnished gold, consisting of 24 plates, 13 comportiers of the newest and most fashionable forms and sizes, a pair of cream bowls, stands and spoons 26l. 5s. Dutchess of Portland

148

27
Rare teacup and saucer with wide
borders of rose trellis and gold lines,
upon which are reserved two landscape
panels by Zachariah Boreman. The
trellis roses are attributed to William
Billingsley. Crown, crossed batons,
dots and 'D' in puce. William
Duesbury & Co. 1790. Teacup 6.5 cm.
Major G. N. Dawnay Collection.

29
The celebrated Kedleston Vase, said to
have been commissioned by Lord
Scarsdale. The vase is surmounted with
a fixed cover upon which are snake
handles modelled by J. J. Spängler. One
panel depicts 'Virgins awakening
Cupid', by James Banford, the other a
view of the south front of Kedleston
Hall by Zachariah Boreman. William
Billingsley painted the swags of pink
roses. It is interesting to note that the
two ewers in the Indianapolis Museum
(see black and white plate 168), which
were also dispersed in the United States
of America, appear to belong to this
garniture. In the Bemrose sale of 1909 a
similar garniture was sold, except that
the ground was a translucent blue, and
the panels were decorated with marine
views which the author attributes to
John Brewer. These are now in the
Mary Field Collection. No mark,
incised number 131, also 'A'. William
Duesbury & Co. 1790. 36.5 cm. *The
Lords Scarsdale. Samson Selig, New York.
Royal Crown Derby Museum.*

30
The celebrated 'Bemrose' chocolate cup and stand, with Dovedale views on both cup and stand reserved within simulated pearl borders. The views are by Zachariah Boreman, although in the Bemrose sale catalogue of 1909 they were said to be by Brewer. Crown, crossed batons, dots and description in blue. William Duesbury & Co. 1790–95. Cup 7.7 cm. *Bemrose Collection. Anthony Hoyte Collection. George Woods Collection. On loan to the Royal Crown Derby Museum.*

31
The celebrated 'Prentice Plate' was painted by William Billingsley for the specific purpose of showing the apprentices his manner of painting his famous roses. After the close of the Old Works, Haslem found this important documentary piece in a London shop where it was priced at two shillings. Like the 'Thistle Dish' (see colour plate 41), it was on loan at South Kensington from 1871–5 and in the Derby Exhibitions of 1870 and 1877. Crown, crossed batons, dots and 'D' in puce, pattern number 138, gilder's number 10. William Duesbury & Co. 1790–96. 22.3 cm. *John Haslem Bequest. City Museum & Art Gallery, Derby.*

32
A fine set of 'Seasons' comprising 'Spring', 'Summer', 'Autumn' and 'Winter'. The author believes that this set, which originally would have had pierced scroll bases and have been modelled by Pierre Stephan in the 1770s, was remodelled by William Coffee between 1791 and 1795. His evidence comes from *Royal Crown Derby* (p. 33), and an extract from the old King Street factory catalogue illustrates 'Spring' and 'Autumn' and calls them 'Coffee Seasons'. No mark. William Duesbury & Co. 1791–5. *The Indianapolis Museum of Art.*

34
Very fine pair of chocolate cups painted with the border pattern number 351. 'Ground of coloured flowers by Billensley [*sic*] filled in with Gold'. Crown, crossed batons, dots and 'D' in puce. Duesbury & Kean. *c.* 1795–6. 8.5 cm. *Henry Lloyd Roberts Collection. Phylis Wilson. Royal Crown Derby Museum.*

33
Rare plate painted with pattern number 378 by Cuthbert Lawton, the 'bird in landscape' being a traditional type of decoration at the factory and to be found throughout the remaining years of its history. The pattern book states, 'I Bird on a tree with Landskip $4\frac{1}{4}$ Inches by Lawton'. Crown, crossed batons, dots and 'D' in red near the foot rim. Duesbury & Kean. 1795. 24 cm. *Alison Rose Collection.*

35
Circular plaque with a view of Darley Grove, Derby, painted by 'Jockey' Hill. This documentary piece was given by the painter to his friend, who was father of Erasmus Horsley of Pye Bridge in Derbyshire. *c.* 1795–1800. *John Haslem Bequest. City Museum & Art Gallery, Derby.*

152

A figure of Andromache and 2 pair of figures   1l. 13s.

Six large scollop'd shells and 2 pair sauce boats blue and white 9s.

Twelve coffee cans and saucers, enamel'd fine blue and white   1l. 4s.   Lady Mary
 Duncombe

*A French pattern group, a pair of Mars and Minerva and 2 pair shooting Cupids, in
 biscuit*   1l. 11s.

*An elegant finished set of Fine Vases, highly ornamented with figures of a pure Self
 colour and enriched with chased and burnished gold*   12l. 1s. 6d.   Jones

A set of figures on pedestals representing the 4 seasons, in biscuit   1l. 2s.   Lady M.
 Duncombe

An inkstand enamel'd green and gold   10s.   Lady Payne

A pair of elegant ice pails, *basons and covers, enamel'd with groups of flowers, fine
 mazarine blue ground, richly gilt*   3l. 18s.

*A beautiful model'd CENTRE VASE (about 9½ in high) decorated with fine
 untramarine blue, enriched with chas'd and burnished gold, in a very striking and
 brilliant stile, with on one front a landscape delicately enamel'd, and on the other a
 figure of UNA* (vide Spencer's Fairy Queen)*, together with TWO VASES
 finished to correspond, the front of one represents the* Birth of Shakespear*, the
 front of the other* Shakespear's Tomb*, admirably finished from those sublime
 compositions of A. Kauffman ; TWO EWER FORM'D VASES to complete
 the set, the front of one represents an enamel of the* Tamborine Boy*, the front of
 the other the* Cymbal Girl*, delicately finished from C. White's beautiful
 plates*   15l. 15s.   Simson

*A most capital compleat DESERT SERVICE, beautifully enamel'd in the centre with
 boys and girls, in different action, enriched with fine blue and gold, the border highly
 enriched with pearls and burnished gold, on a fine ultramarine blue ground,
 43 pieces*   40l. 19s.   Lewis

A pair of double ice pails ditto, and a pair of single ditto   13l. 2s. 6d.   Lewis

A pair of neat pint mugs, enamel'd fine blue and gold   10s.   Lady How

*A set of 3 vases and a pair of candlesticks, mounted with cut glass, enamel'd in compartments
 with groups of flowers, fine blue ground ornamented with burnished gold*   5l. 5s.

A breakfast set   2l. 5s.   Dutchess of Devonshire

A pair of Madona groups   1l. 8s.

A pair of small size tureens and covers, enamel'd fine blue and gold, &c.   1l. 10s.
 Lord Percy

A figure of Diana and 4 seasons   1l. 9s.

*A small size punch bowl, enamel'd with fruit and fine mazarine blue and
 gold*   6s.   Lord Grimston

A pair of elegant tripods, *supported by three* therms, *in biscuit, enamel'd with a fine
 blue ground, richly ornamented with burnished gold*   3l. 4s.   Lady Mary
 Duncombe

*A complete desert service, enameled blue and white Chantilly pattern, consisting of 24
 plates, 13 comportiers of the newest shapes and sizes and 1 pair cream bowls, covers
 and stands*   5l.   Lady Walpole

*An elegant compleat set of tea china, peacock pattern, enamel'd with a colour'd
 honeysuckle border and richly gilt, 41 pieces*   3l. 13s.   Lord Grimston

*A pair of figures, sportsman and companion, 1 pair Harlequin and Columbine and 1 pair
 sitting Cupids, in biscuit*   1l. 3s.   Lady Mary Duncombe

*A pair of superbly elegant caudle or cabinet cups, covers and stands, beautifully enamel'd
 with roses and landscapes, fine yellow ground, richly ornamented with burnished
 gold*   4l.   Price

*Six ice cream cups and covers on a stand, enamel'd with festoons of green husks and
 purple and gold border*   1l. 4s.   Dutchess of Portland

*A very elegant pair of ice pails, basons and covers, enamel'd with figures and highly
 finished with fine ultramarine blue and gold*   5l.   Lord Bessborough

*A complete set of tea china (except the tea-pot) highly enriched with festoons of gold
 husks and gold borders, 38 pieces*   5l. 15s.   Mrs Crewe

A beautiful dejunee richly enamel'd and highly finished with fine burnished gold,
 &c.   3l. 19s.   Dutchess of Devonshire

An elegant set *of 5 VASES, enamel'd in a peculiar and uncommon stile of richness
 and beauty, with groups of* natural flowers *and inlaid with a chased and burnished
 gold ground, fine ultramarine blue borders enriched with pearls and burnished
 gold*   14l. 14s.   Gandasque

36
Water-colour sketch, signed by
Thomas Martin Randall, showing what
appears to be a grouping of flowers in a
basket, such as might have been used to
decorate Derby coffee cans (see black
and white plate 180). *c.* 1795–1800.
9 × 6 cm. *John Twitchett Collection.*

37
Cabaret or déjeuner tray with rich
gilding upon a rich blue ground and a
central panel of a virgin disarming
Cupid, painted by John Brewer after
Angelica Kauffmann. Crown, crossed
batons, dots and 'D' in blue. Duesbury
& Kean. *c.* 1795–1800. Approx. 40 cm.
Nigel Kirk Collection.

153

169
Large oval dish of pattern 178, the border with gilt-linked coloured florettes between two typical gilt motifs. The central oval landscape, inscribed 'Bridge of Narni Italy' in blue on the foot, was probably painted by George Robertson. The Old Derby Pattern Books state, 'Landskip Near Critch by Boreman' but this dish was painted after he had left the Works. When making attributions, care should be taken to determine that the date of a particular piece coincides with the dates of the attributed painter's stay at the manufactory. This service, and possibly other services of the same pattern, has erroneously been referred to as 'The Blenheim Palace Service' but there seems little, if any, evidence to support the title, as the author has discovered after a search through relevant papers in the Muniments room, Blenheim. Duesbury & Kean. *c.* 1797–1800. 42.5 cm. *David John Ceramics, Woodstock.*

170
Two dessert plates. On the left, a plate from pattern number 178, possibly painted by 'Jockey' Hill, with a named view. Crown, crossed batons and description in blue. Duesbury & Kean. *c.* 1795–1800. Diameter 22.9 cm. The plate on the right is from pattern number 43 and the unnamed river landscape is the work of Zachariah Boreman. Marks as above but in puce. William Duesbury & Co. *c.* 1785. Diameter 22.9 cm. *Sotheby's, New Bond Street.*

Six breakfast basons and stands enamel'd with flowers and fine blue and gold border
    2l. 6s.   Imperial Ambassador
A pair of beautiful tripods, ornamented with natural flowers, fine crimson ground,
    enriched with burnished gold   2l. 9s.
A set of 3 elegant Vases enamel'd in compartments with groups of coloured flowers, fine
    blue ground enriched with burnished gold and a pair of vase candlesticks   4l.
    Montague
A beautiful complete DESERT SERVICE, highly enamel'd with landscapes in the
    centre and finished with a green laurel and buff border and fine blue and gold lines,
    43 pieces   23l. 12s. 6d.   Lady Churchill
A pair of double ice pails ditto   5l. 2s. 6d.   Lady Churchill
A beautiful group of figures, of 2 *Virgins awaking Cupid, in biscuit   1l. 16s.*
A cheese stand and 2 salad dishes, enamel'd fine blue and white   17s.   Imperial
    Ambassador
A toy dejunee, enamel'd gilt and 2 half-pint mugs, white and gold   10s.   Lady Payne
A beautiful pair of groups representing *Poetry* and *Music, in biscuit   2l. 1s.*   Imperial
    Ambassador
An elegant formed CENTRAL VASE (about 9½ in high) finished in a peculiar
    uncommon stile of richness and beauty, with on one front a landscape, *and on the*
    other Sewin's so justly admired figure of MEDITATION enamel'd with the
    utmost delicacy, together with 2 VASES (about 8½ in high) finished to correspond,
    one front of each is occupied with a landscape; the other fronts, one represents the
    Birth of Shakespear, *and the other* Shakespear's Tomb, *admirably finished from*
    those sublime compositions of A. Kauffmann (*in possession of Lady Rushout*)

and 2 EWER FORM'D VASES to complete the set, the front of one represents the Tamborine Boy *and on the other a* Cymbal Girl, *from C. White's beautiful plates 1*6l. 5s. 6d.   Nixon

A very capital large BOWL, beautifully enamel'd in the centre with a landscape, highly finished with borders of fine burnished gold 3l. 7s.

A pair of elegant ice pails, basons and covers, richly enamel'd with figures and fine blue and gold 5l. 5s.   Lord Gore

A figure of Time, 2 pair shooting Cupids and 4 small figures on pedestals in biscuit 1l.

A punch barrel, enamel'd with oak leaves, acorns, &c. 3l. 2s.   Price

A pair of beautiful cabinet cups and saucers, richly enamel'd in compartments with figures, green mosaic ground, enriched with chas'd and burnished gold 3l. 10s. Jones

Six beautiful double handle chocolate cups and saucers, *enamel'd with festoons of coloured flowers, entwined with blue ribbons and highly enriched with chas'd and burnished gold 2l. 10s.* Jones

*A very elegant TABLE SERVICE with richly finished blue and gold sprigs and fine blue and gold border, consisting of 60 table plates. 2 tureens, dishes, &c. in all 94 pieces 4*8l. 6s.   Farrar

A grand CENTRE VASE (full 16 in high) magnificently enriched with an ornamental ground of natural flowers inlaid with burnished gold and fine blue and gold pearl borders, on one front is displayed a Landscape *and on the other is a fine enamel of* Damon *and* Musidora *from Thompson's Seasons, to which is added 2 side VASES about 10 in high, and 2 antique ewer forms to complete the set, each of which has on one front figures representing the 4 periods of the day, MORNING from* Shakespear's Cymbeline, *NOON from* Gray's elegy in a Country Church-yard, *EVENING from* Shakespear's Twelfth Night, *and NIGHT from* Shakespear's Merchant of Venice *34l. 13s.*   Price [3]

A figure of Diana, a pair Mars and Minerva and a pair Jupiter and Juno, in biscuit 1l. 19s.

FINIS

This sale was to be followed by a most revealing sale of blue and white Chinese Derby porcelain in 1788, announced in the *Derby Mercury* on 20 March:

LATELY IMPORTED FROM CHINA

By Mr. Richard Wright & Nephew to Messrs. Richard and Joseph Wright.
And now selling by Hand at Mr. Wrights
opposite the New Inn, Derby.

A COLLECTION OF

FINE NANKEEN BLUE-AND-WHITE CHINA

Consisting of Table Services, Teatable Services,
Urns, Ornamentals, Jars & Bakers, Goglets and Basons,
Bowls and Basons, Mugs, Jugs etc.

The Messrs Richard and Joseph Wright were the brothers, Dr Richard Wright and Joseph Wright, the artist. A later advertisement omitted Dr Wright's name, presumably as a matter of ethics. The residence was that of the painter.

As a footnote to this chapter the author again refers to the attempts to make earthenware a commercial proposition for the Nottingham Road Works. But, as can be seen from Alfred Wallis' note below, from *The Pottery and Porcelain of Derbyshire* (1870), little success was achieved:

At the close of the 18th Century the manufactory of Faience was seriously contemplated and various experiments were made. It is said on good authority that when the new China Works [Calver Close] were built about 1800 it was Duesbury and Kean intention to make earthenware similar to that made by Wedgwood; and that for some months 'trials' were made of a ware similar to Wedgwood's Queens Ware and that a member of the Wedgewood family was at the works assisting. As the works did not proceed to the firms satisfaction they abandoned the idea and removed the China hands from the Old Works which was situated nearer to St. Mary's bridge, some of the boys were apprenticed as earthenware hands, but afterwards took to China making.

6

Ornamental Wares

The following notice given by Bemrose in *Bow, Derby and Chelsea Porcelain* offers a clear indication of the ornamental and useful wares produced by the Derby and Chelsea Factory *c.* 1773–4. Although there were changes in the styles of decoration during later years, the type of ware produced was more or less constant – dinner, dessert, tea and coffee services dominating the useful wares and figures, and urns, vases, etc., the ornamental production.

Mess. DUESBURY and Co.

Proprietors of the DERBY and CHELSEA Porcelane Manufactures,

Most Respectively Beg Leave

To acquaint the NOBILITY, GENTRY, and the PUBLIC in general, that they have now opened a commodious Warehouse in Bedford Street, Covent Garden, with large Assortments of the following Articles, specified in this Catalogue:

THE ORNAMENTAL PART

chiefly consisting in

Jars, Vases, Urns, Tripods, Altars, &c.

Designed in the antique and modern Taste, with great Choice of richest and most elegant Decorations of *Figures*, *Emblems*, and *Histories*, taken from the ancient History and Mythology, adapted for the Embellishment of Chimnay-Pieces, Cabinets, Toilets, Consoles &c.

AND

THE USEFUL PART

Furnishing an extensive variety of rich and select *Table* and *Desert Services*, elegant *Tea*, *Coffee*, and *Chocolate Equipages*, *Caudle* and *Cabinet Cups* and *Dejeunes*, from new patterns, in the most approved Taste.

TO WHICH ARE ADDED FOR DESERT SURTOUTS,

Great Choice of Biscuit Groups and Figures in a grotesque Stile, from accurate Designs, elaborately finished even to the minutest Imitation of Lace.

There followed a list of Derbyshire spar[1] pieces, 'so deservedly admired Abroad', which the company were also hoping to sell.

It is important to discuss the cylindrical cans known as coffee cans, which were produced during the late eighteenth century and were inspired by the Sèvres Factory. Normally, a 'Dejeune' or 'Cabaret' set would have two cylindrical cans rather than tea cups, and it was upon these wares, just as at Sèvres, that elaborate decoration was executed. The Derby Factory was versatile and would produce to

171
A very fine cabaret or déjeuner set, consisting of a tray, teapot and cover, sucriers and cover, cream jug and cup and saucer, painted with puce camieu landscapes by Zachariah Boreman with finely gilt borders. Taken from plate pattern 30. Marks in puce, no descriptions. William Duesbury & Co. *c.* 1785. Tray diameter approx. 30 cm. *Mary Field Collection. Sotheby's, New Bond Street.*

172
Dessert plate, pattern number 35, with an elaborate Sèvres-style border, reserved upon which are six panels each containing a single rose by William Billingsley. The central landscape is typical of the style of its painter, Zachariah Boreman. Crown, crossed batons, dots and 'D' in puce, gilder's number 8, 5 in blue for ground-layer, long-stemmed 7 in red for Billingsley. William Duesbury & Co. *c.* 1785. 22.2 cm. *Private collection.*

173 ▷ ▷
A shaped dessert plate with a blue celeste border, divided by gilt paterae from which is suspended a neo-classical chain. Central floral painting is by Edward Withers. Crown, crossed batons, dots and 'D' in puce, gilder's number 2 for Joseph Stables, red 6 probably for Withers. William Duesbury & Co. *c.* 1790. Diameter approx. 21.5 cm. *Andrew Crompton Collection.*

174
A square dish from the celebrated 'Hafod' service made for Mr Johnes, as a present for the Chancellor Lord Thurlow. Thomas Johnes was a rich man who made his estate in Cardiganshire a showpiece and invited many eminent people to his Gothic style Hafod (summer house in Welsh). Haslem said that the service was made for the Chancellor, and Thorpe & Barrett mistakenly believed that it had been made for use at Hafod, and that the landscape subjects had been taken from Warwick Smith's engravings of 1792. Lygo's letters, however, state that Mr Johnes had admired his dessert service, a present to the Chancellor. This was in 1788 and some 'Hafod' pieces carry pattern number 67 which was left blank in the pattern books. It would seem that the original service was made and largely decorated by Zachariah Boreman, but additions were made later and executed by John Brewer. The dish has a scene described in blue on the reverse 'Cold bath Hafod'. Crown, crossed batons, dots and 'D' in blue. William Duesbury & Co. *c.* 1788. 22.2 cm. *Mary Field Collection.*

175
Large dish by Richard Askew with floral border and central cupid subject which is symbolic of matrimony. No mark. William Duesbury & Co. *c.* 1785. 33 cm. *Dr Freeman Collection.*

176
Chocolate pot and cover painted with pattern number 111. Crown, crossed batons and 'D' in puce. William Duesbury & Co. *c.* 1785–90. 22.5 cm. *Paul Holborough Collection.*

177
A fine ice-pail, one of a pair, cover and liner decorated in Sèvres style, with borders of a translucent bright blue with chased gilding. The floral painting is attributed to William Billingsley. See W. D. John's *William Billingsley*, plate 30, for a plate of this pattern in the Alison Rose Collection. Crown, crossed batons, dots and 'D' in puce. William Duesbury & Co. *c.* 1785. 23 cm. *Victor Spenton Collection.*

178
A saucer dish of pattern number 86 painted with a river landscape by Zachariah Boreman. Crown, crossed batons, dots and 'D' in puce. William Duesbury & Co. *c.* 1785–90. Approx. 17 cm. *Ronald & Sylvia Edgley Collection.*

order individual coffee cans, as can be seen by pattern nos 301–13 in the Tea Book, which carry views for Lord Winchelsea.

In the very early days decoration was inspired by the Oriental taste, which had arrived in Europe early in the eighteenth century, and had dominated porcelain adornment, but 'India Flowers' (*cf* Meissen stylized *Indianische Blümen*), birds from the Sèvres Factory and figure subjects were also popular. Landscape painting was romantic, but by the 1780s the topographical scenes which were first used in Britain at the Old Derby China Works had spread to other English factories. Marine subjects were very much in vogue, and all of these can be seen in the illustrations in this book. By the late eighteenth century the Japan or Imari style patterns, which were later to become such an important part of Derby's history, were becoming more dominant. It was Robert Bloor who, in order to expand this field where labour and, in particular, female labour, was so much cheaper, saw a ready and constant source of income, and this type of pattern, which so suited the candle lighting of the day, was always in demand. No factory has ever made this part of the market so very much its own, and indeed even today these patterns are still synonymous with the name Derby. The Derby Factory also produced very fine flower painters, such as Billingsley and Pegg, and fruit painters like Thomas Steele, whose craftsmanship can be appreciated from the illustrations.

7

Figures

There is evidence of a considerable number of figures being produced at the china works in the Planché period – namely the *chinoiserie* groups and figures, as well as animals like the boars which show a sophistication of modelling not found in the more statuesque models of the 1760s. Although undocumented, it is likely that Andrew Planché did much of the earlier modelling work, since he had been apprenticed to a goldsmith, and Samuel Keys Senior confirmed the tradition of modelling small animals.

The main figure production in these early days comprised sets of Elements, Seasons and Senses, Street Vendors, classical subjects, and animals and birds. It is quite possible that some of the early versions of the *Commedia dell'Arte* figures were produced towards the end of the Planché period. The pair of figures in dancing position, the Harvesters, and St Thomas and St Philip are from this era. The 'dry edge class of figures' (Planché) which includes those mentioned above, are so called because during this time of production the glaze used was very thick and glassy, and when the figures were dipped a narrow, glaze-free band was left to prevent glaze running beneath the vase. If this method failed, it was necessary to grind the base smooth, which was a time-consuming operation. From the Duesbury I London account books references have already been extracted to 'Large Darby figars', and this is sufficient indication that they were by no means all small models.

After the Duesbury and Heath partnership was formed more subjects appeared and the so-called 'patch mark' period began. These marks were produced as a result of the pieces being rested on three balls or pads of clay during firing. References to this as the 'pale' period are rather misleading, since the predominant colours were quite a strong puce, a lettuce green colour, and a reasonably strong yellow.

After the Chelsea merger in 1770, the so-called Chelsea-Derby period began. Barrett and Thorpe state that Duesbury gave preference to Chelsea in his sale catalogue of 1771, but later, after the opening of the London showroom, we notice the reverse:

Messrs. Duesbury & Co.
Proprietors of the DERBY and CHELSEA
Porcelane Manufacturies.

Modellers such as Gauron, who had been the highest paid man at Chelsea, earning 8s. 9d. daily, became available to Duesbury. The factory at this period became the largest manufactory for figure production in the country, which is apparent from Haslem's list in chapter 3, and very many examples have survived in good condition. The bases were now scrolled and sometimes pierced. It is generally assumed that some of the early figures were still in production, the predominant enamel colours being a turquoise (somewhat improved and less drab than its original appearance), brick red, primrose yellow and a shade of puce, which were generally used in decorating the cloaks and other apparel. Sometimes the

179
A fine teapot, pattern number 401, painted with Derbyshire views by 'Jockey' Hill. This is the normal shape for its period and has the traditional French sprig and star ground decoration. Crown, crossed batons, dots and 'D' with descriptions in blue. Duesbury & Kean. 1795–1800. 16.5 cm. *Royal Crown Derby Museum.*

180
Two coffee cans (stands not illustrated). The right-hand can is painted by James Banford, with a mother and child described in the Old Derby Pattern Books as 'Happy and Tender Mother', pattern number 225. The left-hand can is painted with flowers in a basket, reserved in a panel on star and spotted ground. This can was once thought to have been painted by Billingsley but the author suggests that there is the possibility that Thomas Martin Randall was the painter, albeit that he was not more than 14 years old at the time, as the subject is so similar to his signed sketch (see T. M. Randall's biography). Crown, crossed batons, dots and 'D' in puce, various gilders' numbers. Duesbury & Kean. Can 1, 1790, Can 2, 1795–1800. Approx. 6.2 cm. *Mary Field Collection.*

181 ◁ ◁
Trembleuse beaker and stand (not illustrated), painted by James Banford, with a figure subject in a panel reserved upon white ground with sprig decoration. Crown, crossed batons, dots and 'D' in puce. William Duesbury & Co. 1790–95. 9 cm. *Brayshaw Gilhespy Collection. Mary Field Collection.*

182
Dessert plate, pattern number 80, decorated with three flower sprays by William Billingsley. Crown, crossed batons, dots and 'D' in puce, pattern number 80, number 7 on foot rim in red. William Duesbury & Co. 1785–90. 24 cm. *Major G. N. Dawnay Collection.*

162

183

Fluted dessert plate painted by James Banford with a figure subject in puce camieu. Crown, crossed batons, dots and 'D' in puce. William Duesbury & Co. 1790. 21.5 cm. *Royal Crown Derby Museum.*

184 ▷ ▷

Rare Derby plate probably made as a replacement for the 'Duke of Clarence' service originally got up at Worcester. The painting is *en grisaille* and is strongly attributed to James Banford. Crown, crossed batons, dots and 'D' with the inscription 'Griselda' in blue enamel. William Duesbury & Co. 1790. 24.1 cm. *Sotheby's, New Bond Street.*

185

Two-handled chocolate cup, cover and stand, finely gilt by Thomas Soar. Crown, crossed batons, dots and 'D' in puce, gilder's number 1 for Thomas Soar. William Duesbury & Co. *c.* 1790. 12.7 cm. *Alderman Edward Robson, JP, loaned to Hull Museum. Charles Littlewood Hill Collection. David John Ceramics, Woodstock. Photograph by courtesy of Neales of Nottingham.*

186

Derby bough pot and pierced cover, with gilt ground and borders with deep orange bands. The central landscape panel is by George Robertson with a named view 'Near Naples'. Note the angular-shaped handles, typical of the period. Crown, crossed batons, dots and 'D' with description in blue. Duesbury & Kean. 1797–1800. 15.2 cm. *Major G. N. Dawnay Collection.*

163

187
Pair of coffee cans (stands not illustrated), from a cabaret set, painted with two figure subjects upon rich blue ground finely gilt. The date of these would indicate that they are the work of John Brewer, but it should be noted that Askew and Banford also used such subjects for decoration. See Askew's biography for the following: 'a cadle cup, with a woman & a Lion, tow days . . . ' [sic] (1794). Many other such subjects are listed. Crown, crossed batons, dots and 'D' in blue, gilder's mark 'V'. Duesbury & Kean. 1800. 7.4 cm. *Nigel Kirk Collection.*

188
Cabaret or déjeuner tray with a fine animal subject, probably by John Brewer, depicting a fox with its prey. Crown, crossed batons, dots and 'D' in blue, gilder's number 6. Duesbury & Kean. 1795. 34.3 cm. *Anthony Hoyte Collection.*

189
Fluted dessert plate, pattern number 392, the border with a bold gilt design and the entire well covered by a yellow prickly poppy. Although the pattern books state 'plants and gilt border by J. Lead', the author firmly believes that the botanical subject is the work of William Pegg, the Quaker, and that only the border is by J. Lead, who was a gilder and who later worked at Pinxton. Crown, crossed batons, dots and 'D' and plant description in blue. Duesbury & Kean. 1800. 23.5 cm. *George Woods Collection.*

190
Derby plate, pattern number 100, from a service formerly in the possession of the Rothschild family. There were some ninety plates in this service and one could trace at least five or six hands. This example, however, is very strongly attributed to William Billingsley. Crown, crossed batons, dots and 'D' in puce, gilder's number 8. William Duesbury & Co. *c.* 1790. Diameter 21.5 cm. *Mr & Mrs W. H. Mordecai Collection.*

waistcoats, bodices, breeches and skirts were enamelled with flower sprays, and there was a more liberal use of gold.

Biscuit Body

'Biscuit groups and Single Figures' is how we find this celebrated biscuit body described in the early catalogues of the 1770–3 period. Bemrose tells us that the documents stated 'in 1770 ten bags of boneash sent to Derby'. Analysis has shown the presence of bone-ash from this date.

There has been much discussion regarding the body used after the Chelsea take-over in 1770 both at Derby and at the Chelsea works. Chelsea documents include a note

> *April 21–28 1770*
> *48 Comptiers made with Derby Clay*
> *24 Ornement Plates made with Derby Clay*

but to add to the confusion we find the same series of weekly Chelsea bills

> *2 tons of fine Clay Shipping to Darby . . . 2 7 0*

Biscuit porcelain falls into four periods. Originally the wares carry no marks other than the patch mark of the period. But from about 1784 they usually bear the crown, crossed batons, dots and 'D' mark. By about 1790 the ivory appearance of the body could, as Dr Hedges hints in chapter 12, indicate the presence of some surface treatment, which results in the ivory sheen which is so typical of the biscuit body of the period. J. J. Spängler modelled perhaps some of the finest figures in English ceramics, which had the body finish of this period. It is regrettable that later, and in particular during the Bloor period, the biscuit body declined into what was no more than unglazed porcelain with its normal chalky appearance.

Later, in the Bloor period, the figures were decorated elaborately. Dark blue and a deep, rich burgundy colour were frequently used, and there was far more decorative detail on waistcoats, hose, etc. Samuel Keys Senior was celebrated for his work in decorating figures. The faces and skin tints became much stronger to meet the demand for more colourful pieces, and, of course, the heavy enamels were useful for diguising blemishes!

It is interesting to note that a very wide survey of Derby figures reveals a majority with similar distinctive facial decoration. In eye colouring the irises are brownish-purple and the pupils black. The mouth is usually red, with a straight line through, and the eyebrows are tinted to match the hair colouring.

A further study of Haslem and Bemrose's lists (given in chapter 3) will reveal the Nottingham Road Factory's production of more than five hundred models. Below is a list of figures which can reasonably be attributed to their respective modellers.

List of Modellers with Their Known and Attributed Models

JOHN BACON RA   Four Seasons, Large, by Bacon (Bemrose list). Attributed three Royal Groups after Zoffany. Arts and Sciences (Haslem, pp. 39–45). Other models attributed, with little or no authentication.

ROBERT BLORE   Sleeping Endymion, biscuit, after Canova. (Not at Nottingham Road.) See biography (chapter 11).

COCKER   Nothing known at Nottingham Road.

191
Plate with gilt lines, three oval landscapes and a central round river scene probably painted by John Brewer *c.* 1795–1800. Smaller fluted dessert plate painted with pattern number 219, allocated to Edward Withers, although the later work of Withers is often attributed to Billingsley *c.* 1790–95. Both plates: crown, crossed batons, dots and 'D' in puce. William Duesbury & Co. Diameter 21.6 cm and 19 cm. *Brayshaw Gilhespy Collection. Sotheby's, New Bond Street.*

193
Figure of a shepherdess, one of a pair, finely modelled by J. J. Spängler, incised 395. William Coffee modelled the other figure of the pair, after the antique, because Spängler had absconded from Derby. Based upon 'Adelaide' by J. Hogg after Francis Wheatley. Number 395, crown, crossed batons, dots and 'D' and a curious 'N' with an incised triangle, four large patch marks. Duesbury & Kean. *c.* 1795. 27.5 cm. *Victoria & Albert Museum, C9 – 1975.*

192
Silhouette of the Derby modeller, William Coffee. 1833. *Christie Collection*. Photograph by courtesy of Mrs Sue McKechnie.

LOUIS BRADLEY   Two dancing figures (Haslem).

CATHERINE   Modelled busts for Duesbury. Also copied Sèvres china. Was a mould-maker. See Lygo's letters, 1787.

WILLIAM COFFEE   Haslem lists 335–59 as by Spängler and Coffee. Jewitt reports that Lygo did not think much of Coffee's 359: '359 is very vulgar about the bosom.' It would seem likely that attributions could be made between nos. 380 and 390. See Spängler entry for traditional attribution to Seasons.

JOHN DEARE   See Lygo's letters, 1786. No figures attributed.

N. F. GAURON   No figures attributed.

JAMES GOADSBY   Nothing attributed.

THOMAS GRIFFIN   Grimaldi as Clown *c.* 1830–5.

FRANÇOIS HARDENBURG   Yeoman figure attributed (see plate 363). Figure of George III is in the National Portrait Gallery, London.

CHARLES HOLMES   Seated set of Seasons not identified.

GEORGE HOLMES   Figure of youth in the Leverhulme Collection, inscribed on base, 'George Holmes did this figer 1765'. As Barrett and Thorpe point out, it is likely that he was the 'repairer'. It also seems certain that he was the man who applied to Wedgwood saying that he had worked at Derby for twenty-eight years.

HORWELL   See Lygo's letters, 1787. Possibly Zephanis and Flora.

EDWARD KEYS   See chapter 3 for a large list given by Haslem.

SAMUEL KEYS JUNIOR   See chapter 3 for details of this modeller also, who was the brother of Edward Keys.

JOHN MOUNTFORD   No attributions.

JOHN PERKINS   No attributions.

JOHN CHARLES ROSSI   Female Sacrifice figure and probably its companion (Lygo). Burning of Cato, Anatomy, bas-relief of the Philistines, Salamis, and Aphrodite; Aesculapius and Hygeia. Cherubs for Vulliamy's clocks.

J. J. SPÄNGLER   Belisarius and Daughter, 370; Palemon and Lavinia, Bemrose 366; The Russian Shepherd and Companion, Bemrose 393. The Dead Bird (two figures burying a dead bird, 363 (illustrated in *Zürcher Porzellan*, plate 9). Haslem: 335–59 listed as by Spängler and Coffee; Bemrose List II New Lace figures; Bemrose: 123–4 vase Spängler, also 126 and 130; Bemrose lists 396 Shepherdess; 371; 373; 381; Lygo's letters, 1793, Spängler to model Rosina; two girls with poultry not identified. Gilhespy wrongly suggests Haslem 360, but this is Johnny Wrapstraw and Companion! Jewitt tells us of 'Figure with Vase (morning) and Figure with Vase (noon)' for which Spängler was paid seven guineas each. Duesbury paid him ten guineas for 'Astronomy modelled in 1790 London'; Jewitt also reports 'Meditation' and finally 'Three Graces'. Another item has caused controversy, as there was mention by Nightingale of a sale entry 'a fine group of two virgins awaking Cupid in biscuit £1 19s'. Again, in plate 10 of *Zürcher Porzellan* Ducret illustrates Sleeping Love, which is in fact virgins about to, if not in the act of, 'awaking Cupid'. As Spängler seems to have been away from the Swiss factory during the years 1777–83, it is possible, but not yet confirmed, that he might have worked earlier for Duesbury in London, possibly at Chelsea. Three Graces Distressing Cupid, advertised in 1782, again makes us wonder. Several of the later numbers may have been modelled by Spängler or indeed by Coffee.

PIERRE STEPHAN   The Elements (Haslem, 3). Attributed French set of Seasons

167

194
Figure of a shepherd modelled by William Coffee as a companion for Spängler's shepherdess. It was based on an antique figure of 'Antinous' in the collection of Joseph 'Wright of Derby' and in spite of Lygo's disapproval (Jewitt) and that of the Works' manager, Charles King, it proved a worthy pair. Incised number 396 with crown, crossed batons, dots and 'D' and a triangle for the repairer. Duesbury & Kean. 1790–95. 35 cm. *Victoria & Albert Museum, 384–1896.*

(Haslem, 123). Three Graces Distressing Cupid (Haslem, 235). Two Virgins Awakening Cupid (Haslem, 195). Bacchantes Adorning Pan (Haslem, 196). The last three attributions must be questioned in the light of the Spängler details from Jewitt and Ducret. To add to the complication Stephan was a French-speaking Swiss and possibly could have worked at the Swiss factory. Research into the movements of these two fine modellers might throw light on the problem. The statuettes of National Heroes are attributed to Stephan and include Wilkes, Conway, Chatham, Charles Pratt and Admirals Howe and Rodney. Some signed in Dorset clay are in existence. Group of Cupids (Haslem, 234); two groups of Elements (Haslem, 48). Stephan is accused of modelling with over-large heads, and it may well be that the Seasons on pierced scroll bases are by Stephan (see plate 110); again, however, the set of Seasons illustrated in colour plate 32, which differ only in that they have round bases, may have been remodelled *c.* 1791 by William Coffee, as tradition passed down through the factory to the King Street Works ascribes them to Coffee. (See *Royal Crown Derby*, page 33, and illustrations 63 and 64, Coffee Seasons, Spring and Autumn.)

JOHN WHITAKER Between 1830 and 1847: an Eastern Lady, Guitar Player, Child in Armchair, Virgin Mary, an Angel, Boy and Dog, Girl and Dog, Sleeping Nymph, Mazeppa on Wild Horse, Boy with Greyhound, Girl with Falcon, Bust of Queen Victoria, Bust of Duke of Wellington, Group of Stags, Group of Dogs, Leaping Stag, Peacock among Flowers,[1] and Parrot.

168

8

Special Productions and Commemoratives

The wares mentioned in this chapter date mostly from the nineteenth century, but the George III and Queen Charlotte printed mug (1761) illustrated in plates 36, 37 and 38 is an important exception. On 22 June 1776 Queen Charlotte purchased[1]

'A compt set of Tea China new embossed blue & gold 49 pieces £7 7s'			
2 Sallet Bowls enamd with flowers blue and gold border	£2	2	0
,, Less ,, ,, ,, ,,	£1	16	0
,, Japan patt	£1	11	6
3 Small shell pickle stands enamel	£1	11	6
6 Ice cream cups enamd with an antique border & gilt	£1	10	0
6 Egg cups wt & gold		15	0

The above is what was bought by the Queen the first time she was at the warehouse and at that time was attended by the Dutchess of Ancaster which is now Dutchess Dowr and I believe it was from her Grace representing the warehouse to the Queen that occasioned the first visit.

The above passage was taken from the Bemrose papers, which continue to describe wares purchased by the royal family until September 1786. In most cases, as is still the custom, purchases were of normal, set factory patterns, and they would seem to confirm the date of 'Royal Appointments' in 1775 as Joseph Lygo had written. Duesbury II seemed a little uncertain about the date, as appears in a letter to Lord Rawdon of 25 February 1791: 'I believe it may be about thirty years since my Father was appointed "China Manufacturer to the King" paying the customary fees, after his death I succeeded him paying the fees again . . .'

The Rodney Jug was made to celebrate the famous victory of Admiral Rodney over the French fleet, under the Comte de Grasse, on 12 April 1782. There appear to have been at least two examples of the jug, one of which had been used by a club of loyal painters from the factory. It is important for the dating of the introduction of the crossed batons between the crown and 'D', being the earliest known use of them.

A service was got up for the Margrave of Ansbach, sometimes referred to in the pattern books as 'Anspach', or 'Heanspoch' in the Bemrose list of wares. Lygo's letters state 'A most expensive service . . . Ward & Silver are doing silver covers for the plates.' There were considerable problems over this order in 1793, and on 23 May the firm of Green and Ward[2] of London wrote to Duesbury urging delivery of a set of china for 'The Margrave'. They wrote again on 12 July:

We are extremely sorry to be again troublesome on the subject of our China but indeed there is an absolute necessity. We are just informed that the Margrave gives a Dinner at Brandenburg House to a very large Party on the 21st. and [as] the Gilt Plate is left here for the Summer they will be greatly at a loss without the China.

These retailers were still pressing for results in September! We are not told of the

195 ◁ ◁
The figure of Fame, with incised number 302, which has Mercury as its companion. Incised crown, cross batons, dots and 'D', and a triangle, the mark of the repairer Joseph Hill. William Duesbury & Co. *c.* 1785–90. 21 cm. *Dr J. Freeman Collection.*

200 ▷ ▷
Bullet-shaped teapot and cover, with heavily gilt peacock-feather pattern, above which are pendant flowers in blue. Crown, crossed batons, dots and 'D' in puce, gilder's numeral 1 for Thomas Soar and 7 in red for William Billingsley. William Duesbury & Co. *c.* 1785. 11 cm. *Major G. N. Dawnay Collection.*

196
Biscuit piping shepherd, modelled as a clothed adaptation of the antique 'The Piping Faun'. Incised number 369, the double triangular mark of Isaac Farnsworth. Duesbury & Kean. *c.* 1795. 25.5 cm. *Dr J. Freeman Collection.*

197
Dessert plate, pattern number 159, 'birds in landskip' by George Complin. Crown, crossed batons, dots and 'D' in puce. William Duesbury & Co. *c.* 1790. Diameter 21.5 cm. *Ashworth Collection. Colin & Elizabeth Liley Collection.*

198
Soup plate from the service formerly in the possession of the Duke of Northumberland. Twenty of these were sold by His Grace, together with the residue of the earlier service in Sèvres style (see black and white plate 156). The soup plates were all enamelled with roses by William Billingsley. Crown, crossed batons, dots and 'D' in puce, gilder's number 1 for Thomas Soar. William Duesbury & Co. *c.* 1790. Approx. 22.5 cm. *Royal Crown Derby Museum.*

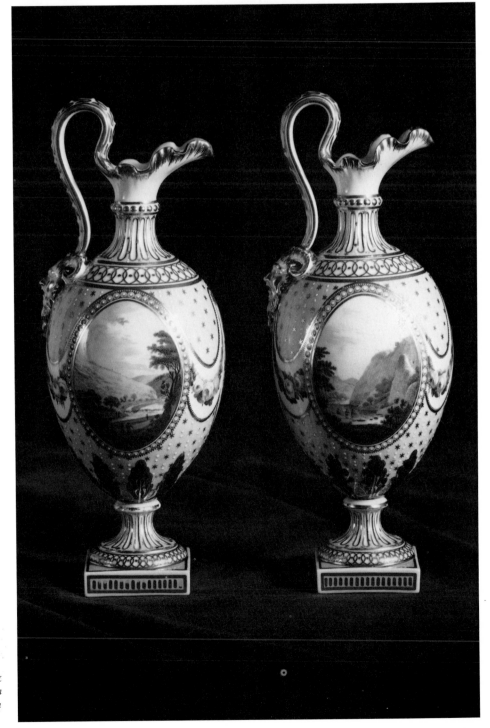

199
An important pair of ewers, as shown in plate 168, illustrating the reverse views. The left ewer has a scene called 'Straights of Dovedale', the other 'View of Matlock High Torr'. Crown, crossed batons, dots and 'D' in blue with descriptions. William Duesbury & Co. *c.* 1790. 28 cm. *Indianapolis Museum of Art, gift of Mrs Herbert R. Duckwall in memory of her husband.*

outcome or the Margrave's reaction to the delay. The pattern used is listed in the Old Derby Pattern Books as plate pattern 139. Further reference to the Lygo letters gives details of other services and commissions too numerous to mention here.

Haslem records that about 1820 a large service was produced which consisted of 365 bowls and several dozen plates. The pattern was gold 'in & out', being burnished inside, and a figured pattern executed in chased gold on the outside. Some of the pieces had pale rose groundlay with a narrow dark blue border and chased flowers on the ground. The centres were inscribed in Persian characters in black. The service was displayed at the London warehouse, 35 Old Bond Street, before being despatched to Persia.

Sir Charles Abney Hastings commissioned a piece of china in the form of a castle resting on the backs of four elephants. This group was designed to contain valuable gum brought back from India. It was about seven or eight inches in height and was presented to George IV.

In about 1830 a very expensive service was got up for John, sixteenth Earl of Shrewsbury. It consisted of some 250 pieces which were laid with a rich dark green

202
Two coffee cans (stands not illustrated), with views of Burley, commissioned by the Earl of Winchilsea. Pattern number 305, painted by Zachariah Boreman. Crown, crossed batons, dots and 'D' with description in blue. William Duesbury & Co. 1791. 6.4 cm. *Earls of Winchilsea. Steele & Garnett Collection. Mary Field Collection.*

203
A fine pair of ice-pails, covers and liners, the floral painting by William Billingsley. Crown, crossed batons, dots and 'D' in puce, number 2 for gilder, long-tailed 7 in pink. William Duesbury & Co. *c.* 1790. 24.3 cm. *Leeds City Art Galleries.*

201 ◁ ◁

Bullet-shaped teapot, as illustrated in black and white plate 200 clearly showing the puce gilder's factory mark and number 1 for Thomas Soar, and the very important number 7 in red for William Billingsley.

204

Chocolate cup and stand with green ground and bird and fruit decoration in the manner of George Complin, probably painted by John Brewer. Crown, crossed batons, dots and 'D' in puce. Duesbury & Kean. 1795–1800. 10.4 cm. *Mary Field Collection.*

205

Double-handled cup with a fine panoramic view and a peasant figure subject by John Brewer. Crown, crossed batons, dots and 'D' in blue, descriptions in blue 'Peasants' and 'Near Leicester'. Duesbury & Kean. 1796–1800. Approx. 10 cm. *Samson Selig, New York. London Exhibition, Derwent House, 1973. Ronald & Sylvia Edgley Collection.*

206 ▷ ▷

A cabaret cream jug well painted with a view near Thorp, Derbyshire, perhaps by Zachariah Boreman. Crown, crossed batons, dots and 'D' in blue, pattern number 137, inscription in blue 'Near Thorp'. William Duesbury & Co. *c.* 1785–90. 8.5 cm. *The Hermitage, Leningrad, USSR, no. 26760.*

ground and painted with six small groups of fruit by the celebrated Thomas Steel.

A pair of large vases was made for presentation by the workers to King William IV (see Haslem, pages 36–7) in 1832, but for political reasons the king was advised by his ministers to decline the gift. The notice quoted in chapter 2 from the *Derby Mercury* 3 August 1825 certainly refers to the Lord Ongley service mentioned by Haslem as having been got up about 1820–1. It is interesting to note that Haslem records William Corden returning to the factory to paint the figure subjects, and that the cost of the plates averaged about five guineas each.

During 1841–2 a royal service was executed for Queen Victoria, as already mentioned in chapter 2. The border was of chrome green, with six small panels on the border. These panels contained painted birds, insects and small groups of flowers, most of which were by the brush of Horatio Steele (see plate 396 for an example).

At some time in the 1840s a 'pair of large and splendid vases' was manufactured for Cardinal Wiseman, for presentation to Pope Pius IX to commemorate the opening of the Derby nunnery designed by Pugin.

The appendix gives some further details on special orders.

9

The Pegg and Randall Sketches

When the author was first approached by the present owner of these sketches, a descendant of Thomas Martin Randall, his anticipation was tremendous because of his belief in the very great importance of documentary evidence in the attribution of painters' works. The sketches are not only relevant to Derby, because during his working life Randall was concerned with the London Studio, where so much Nantgarw porcelain was decorated, and later at the Madeley Works in Shropshire, and, because of this, reappraisal of previous attributions is necessary.

When eventually author and owner faced each other, the owner revealed that William Pegg met Thomas Martin Randall when Randall went as a young lad to the Derby China Works at the end of the eighteenth century. They were to be great friends, and both became Quakers. When Pegg finished work, he gave Randall (who was younger) his 1813 sketchbook (water-marked Trevarno Mill, 1811), together with nine loose sketches, and these descended through the female line of Randall's wife, together with Randall's own sketches.

The Pegg sketches cover flower, fruit, landscape and insect subjects, and the book contains more than 112 different sketches, which are listed here since there are too many to illustrate.

Pegg's Sketches

1	Peak district landscape	26	Cannia Indica
2	Mary Duke cherries on a plate	27	Asslapins Corneso
3	Bunch pea	28	Grisley Grape
4	Canterbury bell	29	Rosa lutea
5	Double Larkspur	30	Honeysuckle
6	Evening primrose	31	Nasturtium
7	Carmine Sweet-William	32	Double lichness
8	Moss Rose	33	Bewberry bramble
9	Perrenial Snapdragon. Spartling poppy	34	Pottatoe
10	Holy Thistle	35	Ragwort yellow
11	Turnip, Raddishes etc	36	Wild tansey
12	White convolvulas	37	Ferraria Pavonia
13	Seedling Major	38	Tiger Iris
14	Ragged Spartling	39	[No subject]
15	Floral sketch (pencil), including Black rose, Moss Rose & Monkshead	40	Tulip
16	Picatee carnation	41	Daffodils
17	Everlasting Pea	42	Cerastium
18	Dwarf sunflower	43	French marigold
19	Alpinium Fringum	44	Olianda (rose)
20	Rose-pink poppy	45	China rose
21	Rose-pink poppy	46	Pansies
22	Rose-ball	47	Heartsease
23	Chrysanthemum Tricolour	48	Heartsease
24	Cape marygold	49	Carnation
25	Spoke-Leavd Loves Strife	50	Sunflower
		51	St John's wort

207

A green-ground coffee can and stand decorated with a rectangular panel of fruits, the can with an inside border of foliate gilding, repeated at the edge of the well of the stand. The stand and rectangular panel have a border of vertical lines. The pattern books do not document this pattern number 211 to George Complin, who arrived in Derby in 1789, but it is possible that it is his work. Crown, crossed batons, dots and 'D' in puce, with pattern number 211. William Duesbury & Co. *c.* 1790. 7.3 cm, diameter of stand 13.5 cm. *The Hermitage, Leningrad, USSR, no. 26648.*

208

An interesting trio of teacup, coffee cup and saucer, pattern 320, painted with river landscape panels by Zachariah Boreman. The pendant chains from gilt paterae are by Billingsley and the natural ground is painted with very pale blue and purple branches with gilt dots. Probably part of the service sold at the Derby Fine Arts Exhibition for the benefit of the Exhibition funds, 1877. A trio in the Exhibition sold for 10 guineas but in June 1978 at the Neales sale of the above collection the price was £1,650. Crown, crossed batons, dots and 'D' in puce, pattern number 320 in puce and gilder's number 3 for William Cooper. William Duesbury & Co. *c.* 1790–95. Saucer diameter 14 cm. *Charles Littlewood Hill Collection. Neales of Nottingham.*

There survives, in the Royal Crown Derby Museum, the documentary Pegg sketch, which has come down to us via John Haslem (see colour plate 39 and Haslem, page 96). It indicates the style of Pegg's first period (1796–1801), and these later sketches (see above) illustrate the differences between his first and second (1813–20) period at Derby.

The Introduction to this book gives an account of the author's long struggle to put the facts about Pegg into proper perspective. We can now look at this very fine flower painter's work with a good deal more certainty than before.

Among the Randall sketches which have come to light are floral, botanical, landscape and figure subjects. These are interesting insofar as they show the development of Randall's career. Of particular importance are the floral sketch, so similar to the coffee can discussed in Randall's biography in chapter 11, and the

38
Large coffee can and stand with green ground, painted with a military encampment scene, known from the Old Derby Pattern Books as a 'camp' scene. The scene, like most of such subjects, is the work of John Brewer. It depicts some form of military discipline, possibly with regard to a deserter or defaulter. Crown, crossed batons, dots and 'D' in puce. Duesbury & Kean. 1795–1800. Can 7.6 cm. *Anthony Hoyte Collection.*

40 ▷ ▷
Chocolate cup with a military encampment scene by John Brewer. The ground is yellow, with scrolling *en grisaille* and two bands of Sèvres-style gilding and jewelling. Crown, crossed batons, dots in puce. Duesbury & Kean. 1797–1800. 8.5 cm. *Mary Field Collection.*

39
A sketch which survived when William Pegg, the Quaker, burnt his sketches on giving up painting in 1801. Although the sketch has faded somewhat, it still gives great assistance in attributing Pegg's first-period work. This sketch was formerly in the possession of John Haslem, who bought it at the Unwin Sowter sale (see Haslem p. 96). 1796–1801. 40 × 32 cm. *Caroline Twitchett, at present on loan to Royal Crown Derby Museum.*

209
Very fine pink-ground bough pot and domed, pierced cover. It has solid gilt snake handles and simple gilding around the panels and at the top and bottom. The central panel after Angelica Kauffmann is strongly attributed to James Banford; the side landscapes may not necessarily be by the same painter. Crown, crossed batons, dots and 'D' in puce. William Duesbury & Co. *c.* 1790. 15 cm. *Private collection.*

41
Square dish known as the 'Thistle Dish', painted by William Pegg, the Quaker, and kept at the Old Works for many years. John Haslem recalled how Pegg personally told him how he had gathered a lady thistle on Nun's Green one Whitsun holiday, and that when he first sketched it his mother could make nothing of it. 'I'll shew thee then', he said, and coloured it. Later at the Works, Thomas Soar gave him the above dish on which to paint the sketch. This use of colour is further demonstrated in the later 1813 sketch-book which is made so powerful by the colour and shading, whereas some of the pencil sketches are somewhat lifeless when left uncoloured. On the close of the factory, this dish came into the possession of Horatio Steele who, unlike his father and brothers, had remained at the Old Works, and he sold it to John Haslem for four shillings on 1 January 1850. It was later part of Haslem's bequest to the City Museum & Art Gallery in Derby. It was also exhibited at South Kensington from 1871–5 and in the Derby Exhibitions of 1870 and 1877. No mark. Duesbury & Kean. 1798–1800. 21.7 cm. *City Museum & Art Gallery, Derby.*

42
Botanical study of a pink rose by Thomas Martin Randall. *c.* 1800. *Private collection.*

210
Dessert plate with small panels of roses, reserved upon a cobalt blue ground border. The well of the plate is painted with three natural flower sprays and a single central rose, all the work of William Billingsley. Crown, crossed batons, dots and 'D' in puce. William Duesbury & Co. 1790. 20.4 cm. *Major G. N. Dawnay Collection.*

211
A table setting reproduced from *Manufacture de Sèvres* showing a dessert service of that manufactory, the shapes of which usually constituted similar services made for the nobility by the Derby Works. It is important to note the ice-pails, the wine-coolers and the small-sized seaux for refreshing the liqueur glasses; the ice-cups on their stands; the preserve or honey pots fixed to their stands; and the use of biscuit figures on decorated plinths for table decoration. *c.* 1795.

212
A set of six ice-cups with their stand
decorated with pattern number 185.
The green ground is edged with
borders of pink roses and the tray has a
central group of roses by William
Billingsley. The shape of the tray is
taken from Sèvres (see black and white
plate 211). Crown, crossed batons, dots
and 'D' in puce with pattern number
185. William Duesbury & Co.
c. 1790–95. Tray diameter approx.
25.5 cm, cups 6.7 cm. *George Woods
Collection.*

213
Dessert plate with grey border and
monochrome landscape attributed to
McLacklan. Monochrome flower
sprays on border. Crown, crossed
batons, dots and 'D' in blue. Duesbury
& Kean. *c.* 1800. 22.9 cm. Right-hand
plate, decorated with pattern 66, with a
central landscape by Zachariah
Boreman. Crown, crossed batons, dots
and 'D' in puce. William Duesbury &
Co. *c.* 1780–85. Approx. 24 cm.
Sotheby's, New Bond Street.

sketch of Derby from across the Derwent. This sketch depicts the shot-tower (used
for making lead shot), which was not built until 1809, this adds weight to the
opinion that Randall was at Derby until 1813 or 1815. We must, therefore, consider
his botanical studies in relation to those by Philip Clavey (see chapter 11) and Pegg.
Randall's rose sketch is fine but lacks, perhaps, the natural look of Pegg's. His figure
subjects are well executed, and his landscapes are of a high standard. The later
sketches show a somewhat less romantic influence and were most probably done
when he lived at Shropshire. His bird studies are most accurate, as are his shells,
which again suggests that such Derby pieces painted between 1810 and 1815 were
by Randall, who might well be considered for bird and shell decoration.

Whatever the reaction to this major discovery, it certainly should cause much
discussion and search for relevant pieces.

Randall's Sketches

1	Floral sketch, flowers in basket	9	Derby from across the Derwent
2	Figure painting	10	Romantic landscape
3	Figure painting of a child	11	Romantic landscape
4	Botanical Rose	12	View near the Wrekin
5	Shells	13	Buildwas Abbey Salop
6	Birds	14	View above Ironbridge
7	Birds	15	View above Ironbridge
8	Dead finches		

10

Gilding

'Honey gilding' was the term given to a practice carried on until the end of the eighteenth century at the Nottingham Road Works. Twenty-four carat gold was ground in honey and applied with a brush. Because it was far less durable than the later mercury gilding, it would not allow burnishing to any high degree, but did enable the gilder to execute *cisele* or tooled work and therefore to obtain great detail. As honey gilding was applied thickly, it is quite easy to detect and, of course, serves as a guideline for dating pieces. Coffee cans decorated between 1790 and 1798 (approximate dates only) usually show the earlier method, and those after about 1798 the mercury method. See *Royal Crown Derby*, chapter 5, for an explanation of mercury gilding.

Chapter 1 of this book gives a list of gilders with numbers they were allocated, which may be considered reliable for the period *c.* 1785–95. However, the reader must be warned of the dangers of taking workmen's marks too seriously. Painters and gilders would leave the works, sometimes returning at a later date, and numbers were passed on to other workmen, so the correlation cannot be guaranteed for long periods. Enthusiasts have frequently been baffled by seeing a number on a flower piece and have not been able to break the code.

In the early days of numbers two gilders' names are outstanding – Joseph Stables and Thomas Soar – and it is interesting to note that Soar's 1 is always at five minutes past the hour on a foot rim, while Stable's 2 is at half past the hour. Sue McKechnie, an authority on silhouettes, has done many years of research into the gilding on Derby porcelain, which have helped to show that because it is normally the gilder himself who puts the mark and description on a piece one can trace individual gilders' marks as one might handwriting. All the roman numeral gilders are, unfortunately, unknown, but it is better to accept the facts as they are than to attempt to attribute pieces without sufficient evidence.

In conclusion, the arabesque gilding influenced by Islamic design, which was done during the first quarter of the nineteenth century, and which is seen on so many fine dessert services, has done much to enhance the international reputation of the Derby factory.

A list of nineteenth-century gilders is given below as being relevant *c.* 1820, and certainly in the case of Sam Keys, Clark, Torkington and Simpson the numbers would have been used from *c.* 1800.

1	Samuel Keys	18	John Moscrop
2	James Clark	19	Mundy Simpson
7	Torkington	21	James Hill
8	John Beard	27	George Mellor
14	Joseph Brock	33	Thomas Till
16	Joseph Broughton	37	John Whitaker

As with the eighteenth-century list in chapter 1, great care must be taken to check periods from which the gilders' numbers are taken.

214
Pair of covered bowls with enamelled roses by William Billingsley. Simple gilding. Crown, crossed batons, dots and 'D' in puce. William Duesbury & Co. *c.* 1790. 10.5 cm. *Major G. N. Dawnay Collection.*

215
Cabaret set, consisting of a teapot and cover, creamer, sucrier and cover, teacup, saucer and tray. The named views are: 'On the Trent, Derbyshire' and 'In Dovedale, Derbyshire' on the teapot; 'On the Trent, Derbyshire' on the creamer; 'On the Trent, Derbyshire' on the sucrier; 'Near Anchor Church, Derbyshire' on the cup; 'Near Belper, Derbyshire' on the saucer and 'View in Dove Dale, Derbyshire' on the tray. All views are painted by Zachariah Boreman and are reserved in gilt panels upon a pale pink ground. Crown, crossed batons, dots and 'D' in blue with inscriptions and pattern number 231. William Duesbury & Co. *c.* 1790. Diameter of tray 33.7 cm. *Bemrose Collection. Herbert Allen Collection. Victoria & Albert Museum.*

216
Plate from a service, pattern number 204, most pieces of which carry on the underside an unusual gilder's mark in the form of a 'T'. The coastal scene would certainly seem to have been painted by John Brewer and is painted in monochrome upon a yellow wash and known as 'Black Landskip on Moonlight Ground'. It is interesting to note that one source for the decoration of a plate from this service has been identified as coming from 'Liber Veritatis', a collection of 195 drawings by Claude Lorrain, formerly in the Dukes of Devonshire's collection but now in the British Museum. These were later engraved by Richard Earlom and published by John Boydell, Cheapside, London 1772. The particular print was of a 'Harbour Scene' entitled Napoli 1636. Crown, crossed batons, dots and 'D' with pattern number in puce. William Duesbury & Co. *c.* 1790–95. 23.5 cm. *Mr & Mrs W. H. Mordecai Collection.*

11

Biographies of Modellers, Painters and Gilders

217
Plate, painted with pattern number 182, with the central landscape, 'Near Curbar Edge Derbyshire', probably painted by Zachariah Boreman, although this is not typical of this painter's work. Crown, crossed batons, dots and 'D' in blue with description of the scene. William Duesbury & Co. 1790. Approx. 23 cm. *David John Ceramics, Woodstock.*

RICHARD ABLOTT Ablott was born during the first half of the nineteenth century – more accurate information is not available – at Fort Garry, Manitoba, Canada, where his father was a British soldier. His great-grand-daughter, Mrs Olive Hendrickson, relates his early background. After the soldiers had landed in Hudson's Bay and were making their way by river down to Fort Garry, a young baby was stolen by an Indian but, happily, restored to his irate mother a few hours later. Ablott's father did not see active service, and the family returned to England.

Ablott was a late apprentice at the Nottingham Road Works, and painted landscapes which were obviously inspired by Daniel Lucas, a leading landscape painter. After leaving Derby, he worked in Staffordshire and then for a while at the Coalport Works in Shropshire. According to John Haslem, he was working for the Davenport Factory in 1875 and was said by Dr Gilhespy, but without any reported evidence, to have worked at the King Street Factory. Some of his signed plaques – not on Derby porcelain – are noteworthy for his ability to convey the effect of distance (see plate 397). His great-grand-daughter possesses a fine example, and other members of the family living in Africa have good specimens of his work. In the Midland Counties' Exhibition[1] in Derby in 1870 a Mr Carter of Derby showed a dessert service made at Coalport, painted with Derbyshire views by Ablott.

RICHARD ASKEW It is not clear in which year this painter was born, although Mackenna stated in his *Chelsea Porcelain* that it was about 1730. The Chelsea Poll Books record him in 1761 at Church Lane West and in 1764 at Kings Road, Chelsea. One may assume that until 1764 he continued to do work for Sprimont and Duesbury, later going to Derby in 1772. He was principally a figure painter, and his accounts, reproduced here in full from Jewitt, give an idea of his versatility. It has been said that his figures, and particularly Cupids, have heavy limbs and jowls, and this may help in differentiating between Askew's work and that of James Banford, whose figures do not show these characteristics. Reference to the Derby Pattern Books, described in detail by Betty Clark in chapter 4, gives further evidence of his work.

Caution should be used when attributing the bowl made for the Coopers' Company to Richard Askew. It is true that the bowl is dated 1779 and that Askew had returned to London and was recorded in the St Pancras Poll Books as living at Coy's Gardens, Tottenham Court Road, in 1781. Whether he worked as a freelance or, as suggested by Tapp, for Thomas Hughes, is uncertain. In *Faulkner's Journal*, Dublin, in 1786 he was advertising himself as 'ASKEW Miniature Enamel Painter from London'. By 1793 he had returned to work at Birmingham, where he is recorded as living with his brother James at 8 Friday Street. In 1794 from the same address he bound himself 'to work by the piece in lieu of the day, and at the prizes mentioned in the adjoining list' to William Duesbury II. Although the list has never been found, the Askew account, mentioned earlier, is given below. The statement by Tapp that Askew was probably at Derby between 1762 and 1763 and again in

1765 seems to have no foundation. The *Derby Mercury* in its edition of 12 July 1798 records his death at Bilston.

Mr Wilm. Duesbury, Deptur to Richd. Askew, July 1794.

	£	s.	d.
a coffe can, with the King of France, one days work	0	5	3
a coffe can, with the Queen of France, one day	0	5	3
a coffe can, with a woman spining, one day	0	5	3
a coffe can, with the head of the Duke of York, one day	0	5	3
2 coffe cans, with cupeds, tow Days & a half	0	13	1
a cadle cup, with a woman & child, tow days	0	10	6
a coffe can, a woman holding flowers siting, a day & a half	0	7	10
a flower Pot, with a woman & child, tow days	0	10	6
a cadle cup, with a woman & a Lion, tow days	0	10	6
2 coffe cans, figuors of fath & hope, to days & a half	0	13	1
a cadle cup, with the fourting-teller, three and a half days	0	18	4
a coffe can, with the head of the Prince of Wails, tow days	0	10	6
a coffe can, with a Girl & bird, one Day & a half	0	7	10
2 coffee cans, with cupids, tow Days and a half	0	13	1
a cadle cup, with a woman siting at Woark, tow days	0	10	6
a cadle cup, with Doatage and beauty, three days	0	15	9
a cadle cup, with Age and youth, three Days	0	15	9
2 coffe cans, with cupieds, tow Days and a half	0	13	1
a coffe can, with a man & woman offiring to Cuped, 3 days & a half	0	18	4
a coffe can, with cupied chiding Venus, 3 days & a half	0	18	4
2 cadle cups, first & scount lasson of love, Eaght Days	2	2	0
a plate, with a head, half a Day	0	2	7
a cup & scarcer, with landsceps, one Day	0	5	3
a coffe can, with a Girl & a Rabbet, tow Days	0	10	6
a coffe can, with hebe & Eagle, tow Days	0	10	6
2 coffe cans, with the Prince of Wails & Dutchess of York, 4 days	1	1	0
a coffe can, with maid of Corinth, four Days	1	1	0
a coffe can, with love sleeps, four Days	1	1	0
a coffe can, with sapho & cuped, 3 Days & a half	0	18	4
a coffe can, with a offering to cuped, 3 Days & a half	0	18	4
for Drawings, tow Days & a half	0	13	1
a cup & sacer, in brown, half a day	0	2	7
a Plate, with Plamon & lavinea, 3 days	0	15	9
2 coffe cans, with single figuars, tow Days	0	10	6
a Plate, with a cupied & Emblems, tow Days & a half	0	13	1
8 coffe cans, single figuars, Eight Days	2	2	0
4 coffe cans, with the four Elements, 4 Days Each	4	4	0
to three weekes Drawing of cupieds	4	14	6
4 coffe cans, with figuars, a Day & half Each	1	3	7
4 coffe cans, with figuars, a Day & half Each	1	10	6
a coffe can, with the Duke o York, tow Days	0	10	6
a Pair, with figuars, 5 Days	1	6	3
2 chamber Pots, with cupieds in the inside, 4 days	1	1	0
a coffe can, with the Prince of Wails	0	10	6
to Drawing of cupieds, 5 Days	1	6	3
a stand, with cupieds, in Rose couler, Day & half	0	7	10
a cram Pot, in Do, half a Day	0	2	7
a cram Pot, with figuar in brown, half a Day	0	2	7
4 coffe cans, with dancing figuars, 5 Days	1	6	3
4 coffe cans, with the Elements, 4 Days	4	4	0
a cadle cup, with a woman & children a brakefarst, 3 Days & half	0	18	4
a cadle cup in Do, at supper, 3 Days & a half	0	18	4
a stand, a tay Pot, 2 coffe cans, a sugar Bason and cram Pot, work warry heily & neatly finishd by Pertickler Desier, 5 weekes	7	17	6
5 cups, in landskips, 2 Days	0	10	6
	£61	0	5

the subjects on the stad, 3 womans & cupied tyde to a tree.
on the coffe cans, to woman offereng to Pan & to woman awaking of cupied.
on the Tea Pot, maid of Corinth & love sleeps.
on the sugar-Bason, Euphorsnay & cuped.
on the crame Pot, a flying cupied.

Delevered October the 3, 1795.

		£	s.	d.
1	2 coffe cans, with the King & Queen of France	0	10	0
2	1 Do, with the duke of Yorks	0	5	0
3	1 Do, with the spining weele	0	3	0
4	2 Do, with cupets	0	10	0
5	1 cadle cup, with a woman & child	0	7	0
6	1 do, with Begar Girl & child	0	7	0
7	1 coffe cup, with a woman siting	0	5	0
8	a flower Pot, with a woman & cupet	0	9	0
9	a Cadle cup, with Hosea & a Leon	0	7	0
10	2 coffe cans, with hope & fath	0	10	0
11	a cadle cupe, with the fortin teller	0	14	0
12	a coffe can, with a head of the Prince of Wales	0	7	6
13	a coffe can, with a Girl & bird	0	5	0
14	a cadle cup, with a woman siting at work	0	7	0
15	a cadle cup, with doatage & beauty	0	12	0
16	Do, with age and youth	0	12	0
17	2 coffe cans, with cupets	0	10	0
18	2 cadle cups, first & secont leson of love	1	8	0
19	2 coffe cans, with venus and cupet & sacrafise to love	1	10	0
20	a Plate, with hand	0	2	0
21	a cup & saucer, with Landsceps	0	6	0
22	2 coffe cans, hebe & the child & rabbet	0	18	0
23	2 coffe cans, with heads of the Prince of Wales & Dss of York	0	15	0
24	a coffe can, with the maid of corneth	0	15	0
25	a coffe can, with love slepes	0	15	0
26	a coffe can, with sappho to Phaon	0	15	0
27	a coffe can, with offering to cupet	0	15	0
28	for Drawings	0	12	0

Deliverd. November the 26, 94 £15 11 6

RICHARD ASKEW.

JOHN BACON, RA   This famous sculptor, who was born in 1740 and died in 1799, is mentioned in a letter to John Haslem from Henry Duesbury, great-grandson of William Duesbury I, and a London architect who had been responsible for the old Derby Town Hall.

> *1862.*
>   *What you told me about the 'Rodney' Club[2] and the origin of it interested me much, and I think it would be very desirable to record all facts concerning it.* [Haslem to Duesbury]

> *London, 27 November 1862:*
>   *I am much obliged by your letter, although I regret that you have found out so little about the old hands. Coffee (three of whose busts I have in the house) was one of the modellers, and I see by an old mem. book now before me (of my great grandfather) that he paid Bacon, the first sculptor of the day, £75. 7s. 2d. in 1769 for models; this is a point worth noting, as showing his determination to have the best that could be got.* [Duesbury's reply to Haslem]

Bacon, together with other celebrated sculptors, worked for the Misses Coade (see the biography of William John Coffee, page 221) He was reported by Lane to have become manager. It is controversial to attribute figures that were made at

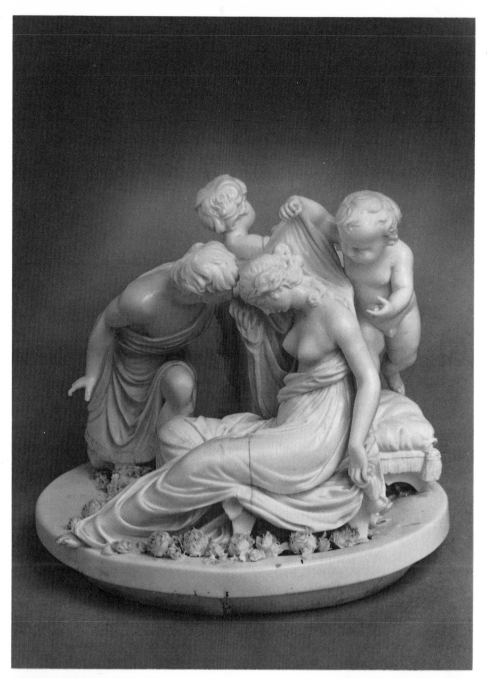

218
A rare biscuit group modelled by
J. J. Spängler. This group would appear
to fit into a plinth. It has the smooth
appearance of semi-glazed biscuit.
Crown, crossed batons, dots and 'D'
with the number 373 and a script 'V'
all incised. Duesbury & Kean. 1795.
17 cm. *Royal Crown Derby Museum.*

219
Dessert plate with fluted edge painted
with a botanical plant centre. Crown,
crossed batons, dots and 'D',
description of plant and pattern
number 197 in blue. Duesbury & Kean.
c. 1800. Approx. 22.9 cm. *David John
Ceramics, Woodstock.*

220
A fine pair of bough pots with pierced covers, reserved upon the salmon ground of each of which are five views which were probably the work of George Robertson. Crown, crossed batons, dots and 'D' in blue with descriptions. Duesbury & Kean. *c.* 1797–1800. 16.5 cm. *Delomosne & Son, London. Mary Field Collection.*

221
A pair of dessert plates with green borders and central square panels, containing maritime views by George Robertson. Tapp refers to *Boydell's Collection of Prints* for a likely source of the scenes painted here. The pattern number of the plates is 254, '3 Inch Square Coloured Shipping Robertson'. Crown, crossed batons, dots and 'D' with description in blue. Duesbury & Kean. *c.* 1797–1800. 22.9 cm. *Christie, Manson & Woods.*

222
Yellow-ground cabaret tray and two coffee cans with interesting handle shapes; reserved in oval and circular panels are animals, birds and butterflies, believed to be the work of John Brewer, the more versatile of the Brewer Brothers. Crown, crossed batons, dots and 'D' in puce. Duesbury & Kean. *c.* 1800. Tray width 40 cm, cans 6.2 cm. *Christie, Manson & Woods.*

223 ◁

Green-ground cabaret set consisting of tray, teapot and cover, sucrier and cover (missing ring finial), can and stand and creamer. All painted with maritime views, which are described in blue on the base, reserved in rectangular panels. Crown, crossed batons, dots and 'D' in blue, including descriptions. Duesbury & Kean. c. 1797–1800. Tray width approx. 33 cm. *Christie, Manson & Woods.*

225

Dessert plate, white ground, with a central river landscape, unnamed, reserved within a circular panel. The border is gilt, with a connected circular motif and edged with dentil. The painting would seem to be the work of John Brewer and this is one of the missing pattern numbers 194 from the plate book. Crown, crossed batons, dots and 'D' in puce with pattern number. William Duesbury & Co. c. 1790–95. 22.7 cm. *The Hermitage, Leningrad, USSR, no. 18966.*

224 ◁

Yellow-ground teapot, cover and stand painted with named views strongly attributed to 'Jockey' Hill. Note that the shape of the teapot was probably not used before c. 1795. Crown, crossed batons, dots and 'D' with description in blue. Duesbury & Kean. c. 1795–1800. Teapot approx. 14 cm. *Private collection, USA. Photo by courtesy of Christie, Manson & Woods.*

226

A double-handled chocolate cup, cover and stand painted with small and irregular panels of pink roses, reserved upon strong salmon ground, which is gilt with stars and dots in white enamel. Possibly the work of Edward Withers. Crown, crossed batons, dots and 'D' in carmine. Duesbury & Kean. 1800. 11.5 cm. *Major G. N. Dawnay Collection.*

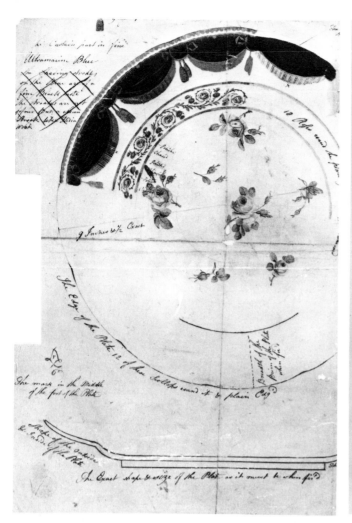

Derby, but the large Seasons in the Bemrose list are allotted by the modellers to Bacon.

THOMAS BAKEWELL

This man is listed by Barrett and Thorpe as having been, according to lists of voters and freemen, firstly 'Potman' and secondly 'Chinaman'. The latter could refer to a retailer, but in view of the designation 'Potman' it is possible that Bakewell worked at the factory. One must remember that there were certainly former employees who set up on their own.

This Bakewell should not be confused with the Bakewell (1725–95) who gave letters of introduction to François de la Rochefoucauld (see chapter 2). This man lived near Loughborough as was a friend of Arthur Young.

JOSEPH BANCROFT

Born in 1796. He only stayed in Derby for a short while after the completion of his apprenticeship and, according to Wallis, left to work for a firm in London before going to Staffordshire. Wallis also stated that he had worked for Smith and Mansfield in Liverpool.

Besides being a flower painter, Bancroft, according to Haslem, painted shells during his time at the Old Derby Works. Both he and Thomas Martin Randall, a most excellent shell painter, would have been at Derby together from 1810 until 1815. It is possible that when Bancroft went to London he worked with Robins and Randall, but there is still a great deal of information to be unearthed regarding the outside decorating establishments.

It is certain, though, that Bancroft was at Minton's as a leading flower, fruit and feather painter by October 1831, as Geoffrey Godden quotes, in *Minton Pottery and Porcelain of the First Period: 1793–1850*, from the wage book entries. 'Bancroft's strings of flowers in Sèvres style' are listed in 1837. It is interesting to note that a documentary Derby dish, illustrated in plate 247, shows the first use of the Bourbon rose decoration, or 'Rose barbo' as it became known at Derby.

Bancroft is said to have died in 1857, but according to Godden his name continued in the Minton estimates until the late 1850s, so it would seem that he died while in their employment.

229

Dessert plate painted with a Derbyshire view, perhaps by John Brewer. The pattern is often known as 'Chatsworth pattern' as there remains a part service of this pattern, number 148, at Chatsworth House in Derbyshire. Crown, crossed batons, dots and 'D' with pattern number and description of scene in blue enamel. William Duesbury & Co. *c.* 1790. 22.4 cm. *M. K. Nielsen Antiques.*

228
Rare biscuit group attributed to J. J. Spängler. Duesbury & Kean. 1790–95. Size not known. *His Grace the Duke of Devonshire.*

Two great-nieces of Joseph Bancroft told how they were related to him and also to William Corden (q.v.). The Corden Shakespeare pieces were originally in their possession.

JAMES BANFORD Born at Berkeley, Gloucestershire, on 7 May 1758, and was, according to Tapp, the son of Thomas Banford, 'Mariner'. James was apprenticed to Richard Champion at the Bristol Factory on 19 January 1773:

19/1/73, to Richard Champion, China Manufacturer, and Judith his Wife, for 7 years to be educated as a China Painter, Friends to find Apparal and washing, James Banford, the son of Thomas Banford, late of the Parish of Berkeley in the County of Gloucr, Mariner, doth put . . .

Banford excelled in painting floral garlands, so typical of the charming products of the Bristol Factory. However, Champion's financial difficulties, brought on largely by the American War of Independence which prevented shipments leaving Bristol for the Americas, and also because of his very costly lawsuit over Josiah Wedgwood's objection to his application for an extension of Cookworthy's patent for hard-paste porcelain, caused Banford, together with his friend Henry Bone, to leave for London in August 1778.

230
Shell dish from the service made for HRH the Prince of Wales, the central panel containing his crest and motto 'Ich Dien'. Crown, crossed batons, dots and 'D' in puce. Duesbury & Kean. 1795–1800. Approx. 20.2 cm. *Christie, Manson & Woods.*

232
Teacup and saucer, with bloom-ground, reserved upon which are two gilt-framed square panels painted with maritime views by George Robertson. Crown, crossed batons, dots and 'D' with pattern number 447 in puce. Duesbury & Kean. *c.* 1797–1800. Cup 6.2 cm. *Lawrence Fine Art of Crewkerne.*

233

Dessert plate with fluted border and central plant subject. Most of these named plants are taken from *Curtis Botanical Journal*, a set of which appears to have arrived at Derby in 1792 (Lygo). It is interesting to note that on earlier pieces the border pattern of gilt lily of the valley is more restrained. This can apply to other border patterns and especially to the inside borders on coffee cans, chocolate cups and similar articles. Crown, crossed batons, dots and 'D' with description and pattern number 115 in blue enamel. Duesbury & Kean. *c.* 1795–1800. 22.7 cm. *Private collection.*

234

Plate with fluted border of bloom-ground colour, painted with a central named landscape, 'Near Matlock Derbyshire', by John Brewer. Crown, crossed batons, dots, and 'D' with pattern number 205 and description of scene in blue enamel. William Duesbury & Co. *c.* 1790–95. 21 cm. *Tony Varnam Collection.*

231 ◁ ◁

Dessert plate of pattern number 142 painted with a named plant, the border of roses by William Billingsley. It is not certain whether he executed the central plant subject. Some pieces of this pattern are almost certainly by John Brewer, whose accounts to Duesbury include plant services and also plates with rose borders. Crown, crossed batons, dots and 'D' with the pattern number and plant description in blue enamel. William Duesbury & Co. *c.* 1795. 22.3 cm. *Major G. N. Dawnay Collection.*

Bone was later to become a very well-known miniature painter. According to Tapp, he and Banford visited Wedgwood and Bentley's decorating establishment in Soho, and it was there that Banford met his future wife, Bernice Glisson, whom he married in July 1783. Before the marriage Banford and Bone both lived at 6 Queen's Row, Islington, obviously near to Thomas Hughes Junior's establishment, where work might possibly have been available. One thing is fairly certain, that Banford learnt figure painting from Bone, who encouraged him to turn to it. Henry Bone married Elizabeth Vandermeulen at St James's Church, Clerkenwell, on 24 January 1779, with Banford acting as his best man. They both returned to Bristol when Champion reopened his factory at Castle Green. Both painters were released from apprenticeship and made burgesses of the city of Bristol on 9 February 1781.[3] 'James Banford. China Manufacturer, is admitted to the Liberties of this City for that he was apprentice to Richard Champion and hath taken the Oath of Obedience and paid 4/6.' Both painters were again listed in London in 1781: 'Coldbathfields, St. James Clerkenwell, London'; and in 1784, 'Great Bath Street, St. James's Clerkenwell, London'.

It is interesting to note that both Bone and Banford had been described in their burgess entries as china manufacturers. This may indicate that both painters were engaged in decorating china at an outside decorator's kilns. Tapp suggests George Randall, whose kilns had apparently belonged formerly to the Hughes and Weston families. More research may reveal the details of these outside decorators and perhaps link the name of George Randall with that of Thomas Martin Randall, later to work at Islington in premises used by the Hughes family.

In 1789 Banford went up to Derby to work at Nottingham Road where he was to execute some very fine figure and landscape subjects. He holds the record of having sixteen patterns assigned to his name. Unfortunately, records do not show a very successful or, indeed, harmonious relationship between employer and employee. Several letters, including one to Duesbury II on 18 June 1792, indicate the problems:

> *Dear Sir,*
>
> *The Mannaer of your conduct towards me last week has awakened some sensations of the Dignity of Human Nature (which I am sorry to say has been for some time dormant in me) and has held up a mirror which reflects how wretched and abject a man may become by deviating from the path of rectitude – for had I pursued the Ideas which was early inculcated in me I should not now have been Dependant no man perhaps feels more pleasure in his sober moments in pursuing the laudable and Social Occupations of life than myself and no-one more wretched after a deviation from them . . . I do not blame you, Sir, for witholding your friendship for by the message sent by Mr. King [Manager] you must have thought that if I was lent a little money for a good purpose I should dissipate it . . . but it would not have been so . . .*
>
> *Yours humble Servt.*
>
> *J. Banford.*

Other letters were written with good intentions but with protestations of poor pay: 'How can you think that five people can live seven days on eleven shillings . . . through Complin and Withers [painters] being so much in debt people is pressing with me therefore have resovlved [sic] to leave the place as there is no probability of paying them . . .' That was written on 13 March 1795. Tapp mentions a letter written to James Henry Duesbury on 1 October 1793, in which Bernice Banford reveals her plight with her husband who was 'behind the Green Rails at the Centrey the House from the Gates' – doubtless for debt and drunkenness – and indicates her love for Duesbury, which is 'as Brother and Sister untill I may be set free'. Tapp further explains that James Henry Duesbury[4] belonged to the Fifth Regiment of the Northumberland Fusiliers. (It seems quite obvious that he was a member of the family.)

In a more business-like manner Bernice Banford wrote to William Duesbury to thank him for arranging work for her to paint at home, in spite of the earlier notice from the workers, given in full on page 32, objecting to female employment in decorating. This letter was undated, but it indicates that Banford had returned to Derby by 1793.

> *Sir, I hope you will excuse me for takeing the liberty to trouble you again, as my motive for writeing is to Return you thanks for the Favour you was pleased to confer in allowing me some work. I have only painted 4 Dozen and 3 plates, at 3d. each, which I believe is Charged Right, but know not whether I am so happy to merit your approbation in the Performance. Mr. John Duesbury would have sent me more work, but Mr. Banford Declin'd it till your return, as all the man (Mr. Bilinsley and Mr. Complin Excepted) treated him in a very unbecoming manner, and even threaten'd him if the work was continu'd to me, which would at this time be of the greatest service to my Family, and should be very happy to contribute to its support. Pardon me, Sir, if I presume to say I am certain one work from you would ease their Doubts and effectually silence them. I am, Sir, with the greatest Respect, your Obliged, Humble Servt., BERNICE BANFORD. – March ye 3.*

James Banford was certainly a most accomplished painter, and a careful comparison of his work with that of Askew will reveal differences of style, colour and manner of execution. It is reported that rather high eyebrows and aquiline noses are a feature of Banford's figure painting. He probably died at Bilston in 1798.

BANKS A modeller of this name is mentioned in a letter of Lygo's written in 1797: 'Mr Vulliamy states that "Mr. Banks is the modeller just in the same way as Mr. Bacon."'

W. BARKER Described by Jewitt as 'formerly of London, was employed between six and seven years at the Derby Works, and left them in March 1795'.

JAMES BARLOW Senior A potter who was to take charge of the useful ware department in 1837 until he died in 1842.

JAMES BARLOW Junior A son of the potter of the same name, he was a gilder who, according to Haslem, painted birds and insects. In 1848 he went into the Potteries and became in 1875 foreman at Allerton and Sons, Longton.

JOHN BEARD Given by Haslem in the list of gilders *c.* 1820, using the number 8, and he may well be one of the two workmen at Minton listed by Geoffrey Godden in *Minton Pottery and Porcelain of the First Period: 1793–1850*. His date would seem to agree with the painter and gilder born in Derby in 1787, making him about thirty-three in 1820.

WILLIAM BILLINGSLEY Born in Derby in 1758 and baptised on 12 October at St Alkmund's church. He was the son of William and Mary Billingsley, who were married at St Werburgh's church on 9 October 1757.

William (Senior) had been a flower painter at the Chelsea Factory and, according to W. D. John, his name was listed in the ratebook for Chelsea (area two) in 1756, as paying rent and rates equivalent to six shillings per week. His brother, Samuel

45
Extremely rare cabaret set in fine condition, and in its complete form, comprising tray, teapot and cover, sucrier and cover, cream jug and two cups and saucers. Pattern number 626. The central floral spray and the individual rose paintings could be attributed to John Brewer, but the author feels that with all Brewer's versatility, he may well have done less flower painting at this time. Later, i.e. after 1800, there were so many flower painters, such as Stanesby, Brentnall, Webster, Wheeldon and Hall, to mention but a few and it is still quite difficult to attribute flower painting around 1800. Crown, crossed batons, dots and 'D' in puce. Duesbury & Kean. 1800. Tray 40 cm. *Major G. N. Dawnay Collection.*

46
A fine sketch of bird subjects by Thomas Martin Randall. *c.* 1800–20. *Private collection.*

236 ◁ ◁
Ice-pail and cover with set pattern decoration carrying the crest of Cusac Smith. Crown, crossed batons, dots and 'D' in puce. William Duesbury & Co. *c.* 1790. Approx. 23 cm. *Private collection.*

239
Beaker with an oval named landscape, near Breadsall in Derbyshire, strongly attributed to 'Jockey' Hill, the panel reserved upon bloom ground with simple gilding. Crown, crossed batons, dots and 'D' in blue with named Derbyshire view. Duesbury & Kean. 1795–1800. Approx. 11 cm. *Private collection.*

237
Large size can and stand with salmon ground, reserved upon which are two river landscapes by Zachariah Boreman. Crown, crossed batons, dots and 'D' with descriptions in blue enamel. William Duesbury & Co. *c.* 1790–95. Can approx. 7.7 cm. *Private collection.*

238
A pair of coffee cans and stands, the ground of salmon colour, reserved upon which are irregular panels of pink roses. The oval panels are painted with classical subjects, the inside border and stands gilt with lily of the valley. The bold lily of the valley gilt pattern indicates a later date. The author attributes the painting of figures and roses to John Brewer. Crown, crossed batons, dots and 'D' in carmine. Duesbury & Kean. *c.* 1795–1800. Cans 6.5 cm. *Christie, Manson & Woods.*

240
Trio, consisting of teacup, coffee cup and saucer, with bloom-ground, upon which are reserved panels of maritime subjects by George Robertson. Crown, crossed batons, dots and 'D' in puce. Duesbury & Kean. *c.* 1797–1800. Teacup 6.2 cm. *Christie, Manson & Woods.*

241 & 242
Rare and documentary mug made to commemorate the victory of Lord Nelson of the Nile, 1 August 1798. Haslem tells us that Alexander Davison is reputed to have had two such mugs made for his friend Lord Nelson and these were later sold at the sale of effects of Sir W. Davison at Swarland Park in 1873 and purchased by a Mrs Ablot of London. Haslem suggested Askew or Banford for the figure of Peace and the portrait of Nelson. Gilhespy suggests Robertson and possibly Michael Kean for the Nelson portrait, but the author believes that the complete decoration is the work of the very versatile John Brewer.

243
Inscription in enamel on base of mug. Duesbury & Kean. *c.* 1798. 11.4 cm. *Brayshaw Gilhespy Collection. Christie, Manson & Woods.*

Billingsley, was a printer and publisher of small educational books in the Ludgate Hill district. From this we may assume that Billingsley's forebears came from London.

According to W. D. John again, Billingsley (Junior's) father could well have set up as an independent painter of porcelain and as a japanner in his home at Bridge Gate, Derby, after leaving Duesbury's employment. When he died in March 1770, he left the Nottingham Arms alehouse to his widow and son (there were in fact six children from this marriage), and certainly this indicates that Billingsley Senior had met with some success.

William was apprenticed by his widowed mother to William Duesbury I at the Nottingham Road Works on 20 September 1774 at the age of sixteen. He was to serve for five years at five shillings weekly for the whole period, rather than at increasing wages which was more usual. In 1780 William married Sarah Rigley. An extract from St Alkmund's register reads: 'William Billingsley of this parish, artist, and Sarah Rigley of the same parish were married in this church by Licence this fourth of November One thousand seven hundred and eighty by me Manlove vicar.' There were to be three children: Sarah, born 1783; James, who died in infancy in 1793; and Lavinia, born 1795.

The work of this most celebrated flower painter is not as commonly encountered as many people believe. He is possibly the most wrongly attributed painter in the history of ceramics. In the Old Derby Pattern Books his name is spelt 'Billensley'. When Joseph Lygo, the London agent of the China Works, heard of Billingsley's intended departure in 1795, he wrote to Duesbury urging him to prevent Billingsley from leaving:

> I hope you will be able to make a bargain with Mr. Billensley for him to continue with youm, for it will be a great loss to lose such a hand and not only that, but his going into another factory will put them in the way of doing flowers in the same way, which there at present ignorant of.

Billingsley used his brush to wipe out the highlights. Earlier painters, such as Edward Withers, had used the uncoloured porcelain to mark the palest highlights in their flower painting.

Considerable effort has been taken here to illustrate only work which can most certainly be attributed to Billingsley. For instance, the celebrated Pendock Barry service, illustrated in W. D. John's book *William Billingsley*, and once believed to be by Billingsley, could not in fact have been painted by him. The body more correctly dates from between 1800 and 1805, by which time Billingsley had left Derby.

The two chocolate cups illustrated in colour plate 34 show Billingsley's contrived and stylized method, which he also used on coffee cans, beakers and sometimes on bough pots. At other times he painted in a natural watercolour style such as in colour plate 31. This is, of course, confusing, but a modern example of the work of Cuthbert Gresley, who worked during the first half of this century at Royal Crown Derby, shows a similar conflict in style. One piece is a slight painting done with few burnings, and another is unrecognizable as coming from the same hand, but both are signed. The 'Prentice plate' bequeathed by John Haslem to the City Museum and Art Gallery at Derby shows Billingsley's second method of painting as well as any piece.

An interesting reference to Billingsley's botanical style of painting, and his close friendship with Zachariah Boreman, the painter, is made by Samuel Keys in his account of the old Nottingham Road Works (see page 40). Pattern no. 246 in the Old Derby Pattern Books (Tea Book I) is 'Rue-Leaved coronilla plant by Billensley', another example of his floral versatility.

In the list of gilders Billingsley was allocated number 7, which seems strange since he was really the only accredited painter in the list. To support this claim for authenticity, the author must confirm that whenever he has come across the 7 in the period of Billingsley's stay at Derby, when the factory mark should appear either in puce or blue, this 7 normally appears in red.[5] The Royal Crown Derby Museum contains a pair of ice cups copied from an original Sèvres pattern (see colour plate 26). On the base of these is a 5 in blue for the groundlayer; a puce figure 1 for the gilder – Thomas Soar; and a red 7 for William Billingsley. The rose painting is exactly like the Sèvres pattern, and the usual flowing style of Billingsley is missing, which is obviously intentional.

244
Rare diamond-shaped dish, one of a pair, painted with Etruscan figures probably by John Brewer. Pattern number 326, possibly adapted from Duesbury's subscriber copy of *The Antiquities of Herculaneum*, London 1773. Crown, crossed batons, dots and 'D' in carmine with pattern number. Duesbury & Kean. *c.* 1800. Width 28.3 cm. *Royal Crown Derby Museum.*

245 ▷ ▷
Square dish with central panel of enamelled pink roses by William Billingsley, reserved upon a strong yellow ground. Crown, crossed batons, dots and 'D' in puce with gilder's number 4. William Duesbury & Co. *c.* 1795. 22.2 cm. *Major G. N. Dawnay Collection.*

246
Sucrier and cover in brilliant condition, pattern number 401, with a ground covered with gilt stars and enamelled Angoulême sprigs. Reserved upon the ground in a large oval panel is a named view, 'Near Matlock, Derbyshire', painted by 'Jockey' Hill. Crown, crossed batons, dots and 'D' with pattern number and named view in blue enamel. Duesbury & Kean. *c.* 1800. 14 cm. *John Twitchett Collection.*

247 ▷ ▷
Square dish which forms the first appearance of 'Rose Barbo' as it was known at Derby and which was taken from the French Bourbon Rose. Pattern number 328, 'French pattern done by Bancroft and Taylor Jnr. and gilt by Shepherdson', is used. It was to become a most popular pattern used at Nottingham Road and later at King Street. Crown, crossed batons, dots and 'D' in puce with pattern number. Duesbury & Kean. *c.* 1800. 22.2 cm. *Mary Field Collection.*

248
Pair of seaux à bouteilles and dish from the 'Three Friends of Good Fortune' service, the pine, the prunus and bamboo. Decorated in a dark royal blue, orange-red and gilt. Crown, crossed batons, dots and 'D' in puce enamel and simulated Chinese marks. Duesbury & Kean. *c.* 1800. Sizes not known. *Formerly in John Twitchett's Collection.*

249
Coffee can and stand, pattern number 401, the ground gilt with stars and enamelled with the Angoulême sprigs. The rectangular panel on the can is painted with a named view by 'Jockey' Hill. Crown, crossed batons, dots and 'D' with the pattern number and named view in blue enamel. Duesbury & Kean. *c.* 1800. Can 6.5 cm. *Andrew Crompton Collection.*

250
Square dish from the service formerly in the possession of the Camden family. The pink roses are by William Billingsley, reserved upon an unusual translucent green ground. Crown, crossed batons, dots and 'D' with the pattern number 185 in puce, gilder's number 1 for Thomas Soar. William Duesbury & Co. *c.* 1795. 22.2 cm. *Private collection.*

The number 7 has been identified on plates from the Plate Book, pattern numbers 65, 80, 100 and others, and similarly on the botanical plates made as Chelsea replacements. (See A. L. Thorpe's article in the *Antique Collector*, August–September 1965, on 'Some Unusual Derby Plates'.) Billingsley decorated replacements for Chelsea pieces – plate 167 illustrates one of these plates, which were described by Samuel Keys in his recollections as mentioned in chapter 1.

It appears that Billingsley executed his finest work at Derby when under the direction of Duesbury. His work consisted mainly of floral subjects and obviously included many fine cabinet cans as well as services, but probably no landscapes until he went to Pinxton, as there were always very competent landscape painters at Derby during Billingsley's period. He left Derby in April 1796 to work with Mr John Coke, in whose partnership he established the Pinxton China Works. The following letter written in October of the same year is interesting, but one should remember that there is no documentary evidence available that William Billingsley returned to the Derby Works, and we might well assume that Duesbury did not even reply to the letter:

> *Sir, – From the circumstance that occurr'd when I was last in Conversation with you, I am induc'd to take this mode of informing you of my opinion on the subject then in question. My opinion is, that I have fulfill'd the warning [notice] I gave (my reasons in support of which it is not necessary to advance at this time). But as I am inform'd that you believe I have some further time to work for you before the warning is fulfill'd – namely, to make up the time I lost in the six months I was under warning, and as it is my wish to leave no ground for dissatisfaction, I take this opportunity of informing you that I am willing to come and Work that time according to that opinion of the case. If the foregoing is according to your opinion and desire, your being so kind as to send me advise to that effect at any time in the course of a week, and likewise the time I have to work according to the rule and opinion above stated, I will attend your works accordingly. If I do not hear from you in the course of the time above stated, I must then conclude that you are satisfy'd, and the information that I have receiv'd is without foundation. I am, Sir, your Humble Serv., Wm.* BILLINGSLEY. *– Derby, Oct. 14, 1796.*

Having left the Pinxton China Works in April 1799, Billingsley moved to Mansfield in Derbyshire, and details of his life here (1799–1802) and at Torksey in Lincolnshire can be found in W. D. John's *William Billingsley*. Here he decorated porcelain bought in the white, although a small quantity of earthenware and porcelain was claimed by Exley to have been made at Brampton in the parish of Torksey.

Billingsley's movements in 1808 seem to concentrate on an unsuccessful visit to Wales, and by October 1808 he had arrived at Worcester with his two daughters and his future son-in-law George Walker, who later married Sarah at Claines parish church, Worcester, on 22 September 1812. Billingsley had parted from his wife at Mansfield, although she was reported by her niece, a Mrs Fletcher of Derby, to have gone to see the family at Brampton. It was believed by the Wheeldon family, relatives of the painter, that it was from Torksey that Billingsley left, adopting a new name from a village near Chatsworth called Beeley.

Billingsley and Walker were engaged at Worcester by Martin Barr, a proprietor of the Worcester Works, and are reported to have been largely responsible for the improvement in the Worcester body. The Nantgarw Works were started by Billingsley and Walker in mid-November 1813, and details of their stay may be obtained from W. D. John's works on the two Welsh porcelain factories of Swansea and Nantgarw. After the failure of this great project and the loss of his very devoted and loyal daughters, Billingsley spent the last years of his life working for John Rose at Coalport. W. D. John tells us that in 1820, accompanied by his son-in-law, Billingsley walked the 100 miles from Wales to secure employment with John Rose, who was certainly to benefit from his misery. No longer were they able to supply white porcelain direct to the London decorating establishments, thus taking a proportion of John Rose's own London market.

Billingsley died on 16 January 1828, aged seventy, and was buried in an unmarked grave in the churchyard at Kemberton, near Coalport. Soon after his death, Samuel Walker went to America with his children, where he established a

251
Low teacup and saucer, brick-red ground, gilt with the 'tree of life' pattern, reserved upon which are oval panels of natural flowers painted with a bright palette. It is interesting to note that this tea pattern shows the use of the low teacup, but is missing in the book. Crown, crossed batons, dots and 'D' with pattern number 603 in carmine. Duesbury & Kean. 1800–5. Cup 4.8 cm, saucer 13.5 cm. *The Hermitage, Leningrad, USSR, no. 20756.*

252
Oval portrait plaque said to be of William Corden. It comes from the family of Edwin Trowell, who was a leading painter at Osmaston Road at the close of the nineteenth century, and it has been passed down with this information. However, there exists no further evidence at present to support the claim that it is a self portrait of William Corden *c.* 1835. *Private collection.*

254
Vase of rare shape, painted just above its waist with a panoramic view and with handles used on the campana-shaped vases of the early nineteenth century. A broad band of Smith's blue colour is heavily gilt with foliate and scroll design. Above the landscape, the neck is again gilt with lines and foliate scrolling. The landscape appears to be the work of 'Jockey' Hill, as it has similarities to the documentary plaque of 'Darley Grove' which is in the City Museum & Art Gallery, Derby. Crown, crossed batons, dots and 'D' in blue. Duesbury & Kean. *c.* 1795–1800. Approx. 20 cm. *Alison Rose Collection. Photograph by courtesy of Sotheby's, New Bond Street.*

253

Bough pot with ram's head handles, painted with peacock-feather ground in dark blue and gold, reserved upon which is a large central panel of fruit and birds, flanked on either side by smaller oval panels of game birds and waterfowl. The attribution is to John Brewer. His painting, as comparison shows, was influenced by that of George Complin. Complin's work has a jewel-like quality unsurpassed by other fruit and bird subject painters. Crown, crossed batons, dots and 'D' in puce. Duesbury & Kean. 1795–1800. Approx. 12.6 cm. *Mr & Mrs J. S. Buxton Collection.*

255

Teapot and cover of pattern number 654, with floral and landscape panels reserved in panels upon rich dark blue ground with foliate gilding. The floral painting has been attributed in the past to Billingsley but the lateness of the pattern number may preclude this artist. The whole may be the work of John Brewer but no certain attribution may be given in this case. Crown, crossed batons, dots and 'D' with pattern number in carmine. Duesbury & Kean. *c.* 1800. Approx. 16.5 cm. *David John Ceramics, Woodstock.*

256

Ice-pail and cover painted with named botanical plants strongly attributed to William Pegg, the Quaker. Crown, crossed batons, dots and 'D' with description and pattern number 197 in blue enamel. Duesbury & Kean. *c.* 1795–1800. Approx. 27.5 cm. *Mr & Mrs J. S. Buxton Collection.*

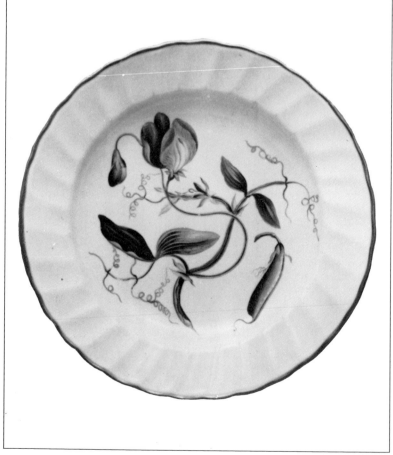

Fine pair of chocolate cups and covers with angular handles. The canary-yellow ground has reserved upon it panels of 'camp scenes' painted by John Brewer, who was the more versatile of the two brothers. Pattern number 453 states, 'Large New Chocolate' and pattern number 454 mentions covers and stands, which gives some idea of the date. Crown, crossed batons, dots and 'D' in puce, impressed number 73. Duesbury & Kean. *c.* 1797–1800. 10.2 cm. *Charles Littlewood Hill Collection. Photo by courtesy of Neales of Nottingham.*

258 ◁ ◁
Illustration reproduced from *Curtis Botanical Journal.*

259 ◁
Dessert plate with fluted edge, upon which the design illustrated in black and white plate 258 is adapted by William Pegg, the Quaker. Crown, crossed batons, dots and 'D' with plant description and pattern number 197 in blue enamel. Duesbury & Kean. 1796–1800. Approx. 21 cm. *Private collection.*

260
Plate with green ground, pattern number 268, known as 'The Animal Service'. The central panel is painted with a named subject 'Arabian Camel' by John Brewer. It is interesting to note that written on pattern number 268 in the plate book is 'see Brewer's set' and we know that John Brewer was engaged to paint figures, animals, landscapes and flowers by the piece: 'Animals to be half the price of adult figures' (extracted from manuscripts in the City Library, Derby). Crown, crossed batons, dots and 'D' with description and pattern number in blue enamel. Duesbury & Kean. 1795–1800. 23.3 cm. *The Hermitage, Leningrad, USSR, no. 18992.*

pottery named the Temperance Hill Pottery. He died about 1880 at the age of nearly a hundred.

JOHN BLOOD   A gilder to whom number 10 was allocated and who was reputed to have been among the earliest apprentices. He married Elizabeth Clayton at All Saints church,[6] Derby, on 9 March 1784. Like many of the gilders he was later responsible for the painting of arabesque borders.

A reference to John Blood appeared in the *Derby Mercury* on 17 August 1786:

Derby August 16th. – On Sunday night, about nine o'clock, as Mr. Blood, (China Painter of this Town) was on his Return from Nottingham, he was stopped by two Footpads who robbed him of 28s. One of them struck him across the Shoulders with a Bludgeon.

Another reference in the local Derby press (10 September 1811) was to a dissolution of partnership at the Belper Pottery where the senior partner was one John Blood. As yet there seems no evidence that this is the same John Blood.

A painter named W. Blood[7] worked at Osmaston Road until 1909, which again illustrates the frequency with which the names reappear.

ROBERT BLORE   No relation of Robert Bloor, this man was apprenticed at the Nottingham Road Works but appears to have left early on to work for Minton. He did not, however, stay long and returned to Derby where he went into business on his own account in his father's yard, modelling vases, ewers, figures and animals. In about 1835 he went to work for Mason's of Lane Delph and then later to Isaac Wilson & Co. There are examples of his work in the Derby City Museum.

BOLLAND   A gilder whose name appears faintly by tea pattern 617.

JONATHON BOOT   This modeller is reputed to have been employed at the Nottingham Road Works. A documentary Derby frill vase, incised in script 'Jonathon Boot 1764', appeared as Lot 133 in a Sotheby's catalogue dated 18 April 1967. The catalogue noted that he had worked as a 'modeller at Cobridge in Staffordshire' and that he is said to have learnt his trade at Derby. Thorpe and

261
Plate with green ground, pattern number 268, known as 'The Animal Service'. The central panel of dairy cows is painted by John Brewer. Crown, crossed batons, dots and 'D' with pattern number 268 in blue enamel but without description. Duesbury & Kean. 1795–1800. 23.3 cm. *The Hermitage, Leningrad, USSR, no. 18985.*

263
Dessert plate with fluted edge gilt by John Lead, a gilder who, according to Haslem, was at Pinxton with Billingsley. The central painting of 'Heartsease' is easily attributed to William Pegg (see colour plate 41 of the 'Thistle Dish'). There is controversy about this pattern number which some people believe should read 392 'Plants and Gold border by J. Lead'. The author feels that it means 'Plants, Gold border by J. Lead'. Crown, crossed batons, dots and 'D' with pattern number 392 and plant description in blue enamel. Duesbury & Kean. *c.* 1796–1800. 21.5 cm. *Leslie Hill Collection.*

Barrett state that his apprenticeship papers do not survive among factory documentation, but the author feels that the vase is sufficient evidence of him working at the factory in 1764.

ZACHARIAH BOREMAN According to the registers of St Martin in the Fields for 1738, Boreman was born in Falconer Alley, Aldersgate, London. It is thought that he was apprenticed to the Chelsea Factory but the actual date is unknown. Richard Barton's Chelsea accounts dated 1770 contain an entry: 'Dec. 1/8 Boarman 6 days at 5/3 – £1-11-6.' And again in 1773: 'June 19/26 Boarman 5 & ¼ days at 5/3 – £1-7-7.' From this we can see that over three years Boreman was receiving the same rate of 5s 3d per day. He also managed a little extra by way of overtime. The accounts are mainly for seals, thimbles and mottoes, but it is almost certain that by this time Boreman was trying his hand at landscape painting, the subject which was later to make him so very famous in the ceramic world. It is quite definite that he came under the influence of Paul Sandby, who was reported to have been the chief drawing instructor at the Royal Military Academy at Woolwich from 1768 to 1799, even though he may not personally have known the painter.

The agreement (given on the next page) between William Duesbury and Boreman is dated August 1783 and precedes the closing of the Chelsea Works in 1784, and Boreman's arrival at the Nottingham Road Factory. Reference to the Old Derby Pattern Books, together with the illustrations in this book, will give evidence of Boreman's work at Derby.

Reports from various sources indicate that while at Derby Boreman was a likeable man who had the respect of both his colleagues and management. Of course there always seemed to be wage problems! Joseph Lygo wrote to Duesbury on 9 July 1787: 'Sorry to hear Mr. Boreman has decided to leave Derby – I think it may be a try on.' It is easy to see that the agreement previously mentioned was due to run out in 1787, three years after his arrival 'at the said Manufactory at Derby', and Lygo may well have been right.

In 1790 Lygo writes: '. . . Mr Eames [a print dealer] found Baptist's prints with large flowers but not all of them in baskets; also four other prints with horses, and a battle print with figures on horseback.' It was difficult to procure prints with horses for the workmen to copy. The jug illustrated in colour plate 23 is from the Field Collection and was sold at a sale at Chedworth, Gloucestershire, in the 1960s. It provides a very rare subject, although sea battles are more frequently seen.

The last reference to Boreman in Lygo's letters is in December 1794. 'Mr. Boreman back from Derby – behaved as cool as usual but would not discuss business.'

After leaving Derby Boreman worked at Simm's decorating establishment, Five Fields Row, Pimlico, where he continued painting until his death in 1810.

GEORGE BRADBURY Jewitt gives details (see Bibliography) of Bradley's apprenticeship 'to learn the Art of Repairing China or Porcelain Ware', beginning on 10 March 1765, to last for seven years.

LOUIS BRADLEY A clever modeller in the later Bloor period. Named in Haslem's list.

THOMAS BRENTNALL This flower painter, born in 1803, is possibly one of the most underestimated. A plate in the Derby City Museum is said to be by Brentnall (see plate 345), and it is not difficult to see why his work has, in the past, been confused with that of Moses Webster or even Thomas Steel. Haslem stated that 'Brentnall excelled as a flower painter'. There were two fine plaques by him in the Haslem collection, measuring 13 in × 10 in, painted with vigour in the manner of Van Huysum and harmoniously coloured. One can at times see the influence of William Pegg, the Quaker.

Owing to the retraction of business, Brentnall was discharged together with Jesse Mountford, William Hall, William Cresswell and James Farnsworth. With the exception of Mountford, who was a landscape painter, these men were all flower painters and, according to Haslem, the Coalport Factory, where they subsequently became employed, benefited by their services at the expense of the Derby Works. Geoffrey Godden, in his *Coalport and Coalbrookdale Porcelains*, gives details of Brentnall, stating that he believed that much ware bearing the 1820 Society of Arts

262 ◁ ◁
Rare dated Jug, painted with pattern number 554, the front panel containing the name of Robert Sidley 1801. This is the latest dated puce-marked piece so far recorded. Crown, crossed batons, dots and 'D' together with the pattern number in puce. Duesbury & Kean. 1801. Approx. 17 cm. *D. Sulley Collection.*

Articles of Agreement made concluded upon and entered into this twnty sixth day of August in the year of our Lord Christ one thousand seven hundred and eighty three Between William Duesbury of Derby in the County of Derby China or Porcelain Manufacturer of the one part and Zachariah Boreman of the Parish of Saint Luke Chelsea in the County of Middlesex China or Porcelain Painter of the other part.

Whereas the said William Duesbury hath engaged the said Zachariah Boreman to serve him the said William Duesbury his Executors Administrators or Assigns in the painting of China or Porcelain at the Manufactory of the said William Duesbury in Derby aforesaid for the Term of three years. It is therefore covenanted and agreed upon as follows

First the said Zachariah Boreman for the considerations hereinafter mentioned Doth hereby for himself covenant promise and agree to and with the said William Duesbury his Executors Administrators and Assigns in manner following (that is to say) That he the said Zachariah Boreman shall and will for and during the Term of Three years to commence from and immediately after he the said Zachariah Boreman shall begin to work at the said Manufactory at Derby aforesaid and that within One month from the date hereof serve abide and continue with the said William Duesbury his Executors Administrators or Assigns as his or their Covenant Servent and duly diligently and faithfully according to the best and utmost of his skill and knowledge exercise and employ himself in the art of painting China or Porcelain ware to and for the most profit and advantage of the said William Duesbury his Executors Administrators or Assigns And also shall and will keep the secrets of the said William Duesbury his Executors Administrators and Assigns in all matters and things and no ways wrongfully detain imbezzle or purloin any monies goods or wares belonging to the said William Duesbury his Executors Administrators or Assigns And further that he the said Zachariah Boreman shall and will find and provide for himself Meat Drink Washing Lodging and all other necessary's during the said Term In consideration of the premises and of the several matters and things by the said Zachariah Boreman to be done and performed he the said William Duesbury for himself his Executors and Administrators Doth hereby Covenant promise and agree to and with the said Zachariah Boreman that he the said William Duesbury his Executors Administrators or Assigns shall and will well and truly pay or cause to be paid unto the said Zachariah Boreman weekly and every week during the said Term of Three Years (commencing as aforesaid) for every whole week thereof which he the said Zachariah Boreman shall work according to the usual hours of painting at the said Manufactory the sum of Two pounds two shillings of good and lawfull money of Great Britain But if the said Zachariah Boreman shall at any time or times during the said Term wilfully neglect or by sickness or other inevitable accident be rendered unable to paint china or porcelain ware for the said William Duesbury his Executors Administrators or Assigns according to the true intent and meaning of this Agreement Then and in either of these cases the said William Duesbury his Executors Administrators or Assigns shall not be obliged to pay unto the said Zachariah Boreman more in proportion than after the rate aforesaid for such parts and so much of every week as he the said Zachariah Boreman shall actually paint for the said William Duesbury his Executors Administrators or Assigns as aforesaid And for the true performance of all and every the Articles Covenants and Agreements aforesaid each of the said party's by these presents bindeth himself unto the other in the penal sum of One hundred pounds In witness whereof the said party's have hereto interchangeably set their Hands and affixed their seals the day and year first above written.

> Sealed and delivered by the said
> William Duesbury having been first duly stamped in the presence of FFRAN JESSOP Atty at Law Derby.

Wm DUESBURY. (L.S.)

> Sealed and delivered by the said Zachariah Boreman having been first duly stamped in the presence of JOSEPH LYGO.

ZACHh BOREMAN. (L.S.)

264
Bough pot and pierced cover of small bombé shape with an oval named landscape by John Brewer. Crown, crossed batons, dots and 'D' with description in blue enamel. Duesbury & Kean. c. 1795–1800. 11.5 cm. *Graham & Oxley, London.*

265
Large plate with wide very dark blue border, gilt by Samuel Keys with hunting horns, foliate gilding and the crest of the Dukes of Rutland. The central hunting scene is thought to be the work of Robert Brewer and shows the hounds at the kill. Crown, crossed batons, dots and 'D' in puce with gilder's number 6 in puce. This was the mark used by Keys before he became number 1 gilder early in the nineteenth century when he used to paint his 1 in red. The author has referred again to Sue McKechnie for this information. The mark used here is identical to the mark used in his red period, i.e. the crown, crossed batons, etc. Both Sue McKechnie and the author firmly believe that it was normally the gilder who marked and described the piece on its reverse. Duesbury & Kean. 1800. 25 cm. *Royal Crown Derby Museum.*

266 ▷ ▷
Rare miniature teapot and cover with broken ring handle decorated with orange bands and gilding. Crown, crossed batons, dots and 'D' in puce. Duesbury & Kean. 1795–1800. 7 cm. *Royal Crown Derby Museum.*

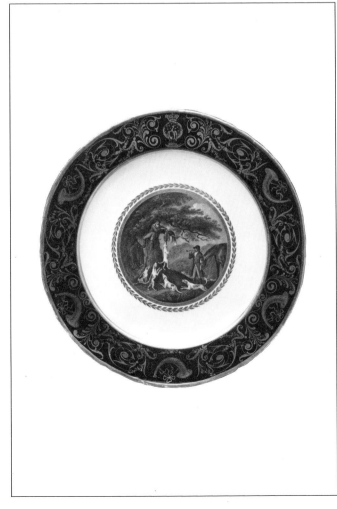

mark was his work. On leaving Coalport, Brentnall worked in Staffordshire, and the latter part of his career was spent at Ridgway's of Cauldon Place. He died in 1873, aged seventy.

JOHN BREWER

JOHN BREWER John was the elder of two brothers who both worked at Derby. Their parents were both artists and from 1762 to 1767 had studios in London at Rupert Street (a street which joins Brewer Street, stated by Tapp to have been so called because of its proximity to the Brewers' studio); they were later at Duke Street (1768–78), and finally Mercers Street (1779–86). The family are said to have come from Madeley, Shropshire, where in fact the talented modeller Francis Brewer (son of Robert Brewer) is said by Jewitt to have worked for Thomas Martin Randall. John Brewer Senior and his wife, formerly Ann Warburton, both exhibited at the Free Society and the Society of Artists.

John Brewer Junior was born in 1764 and became a talented watercolourist, exhibiting paintings of butterflies and insects. Although Jewitt states that Brewer had previously worked for Duesbury, a letter dated 17 April 1793, from Duesbury II's brother-in-law Nicholas Edwards, clearly indicates that he was to take up painting on porcelain 'tomorrow week'. Brewer was a watercolourist and 'had never applied his art to porcelain painting'. Brewer had stated that he would need time to get used to the new techniques before his rate of pay was agreed.

> *Were you in Brewer's case you would not be willing to tie yourself down to the execution of work in colours you are a stranger to at the same terms that you could venture to agree to with those that were familiar to you . . . I showed him the plate with the hand and dagger [Nelthorpe service], I asked the time he would require for that, his answer was 'Twenty minutes, I should think would be amply sufficient.'*

Strangely, although the above letter was quoted in Thorpe and Barrett, they stated in Brewer's biography that he did not come to Derby until 1795, and continue on the assumption that Brewer might have worked at Derby for Duesbury, which seems to this author totally illogical.

As can be seen in the Old Derby Pattern Books no distinction is made between the Brewer brothers, and so there have always been controversial attributions. John Brewer's accounts listed below,[8] for work done for Duesbury II, contain forty-six landscapes, twenty-four plant and flower subjects, ten bird studies, seven shipping scenes, two figure subjects and twenty plates with rose borders. It has long been the author's opinion that the military encampment scenes were executed by John Brewer.

Finished from April 29th.

			In hand.	
2	Coffee cans and stands, Shipping N	1	2	Comports of plants.
6	Plates of plants	2	4	Plates of do.
4	Comports of Landscapes	3	4	Coffee Cans of flowers.
6	Comports of plants	4	1	Dejunee of Ships.
2	Comports of plants	5	1	Comport of Landscape, finished
2	Coffee Cans Moonlight and fire	6	1	Cream jug Birds
2	Coffee Cans and stands Birds	7	1	Tea pot Do.
2	Tea pots Landscapes from Gilpin	8	12	Saucers Landscapes.
1	Dejunee of Birds	9	2	Cans shipping.
20	Plates of Rose border	10	1	Cream jug Do.
1	Cream jug of Birds	11	1	Sugar Bason Do.
1	Sugar bason Do.	12	—	
2	Cabinet cups 1st and 2nd Lesson of Love	13	30	Sept. 8th.
12	Coffee cups of Landscapes	14		
12	Plates of Landscapes	15		
3	Comports Do.	16		
1	Tea pot of Birds	17		JNo. BREWER.

83 Pieces to Septbr. 8th.

Although he became a drawing master in the town, he did not cease to work for the china factory entirely. Advertisements were inserted by him in the *Derby*

49

This remarkable vase, complete with its dragon handles and eagle-surmounted cover, is a lesson in the use of numerous techniques such as marbling, scrolling, gilding and green spot raising. The vase has two named views and the author believes it to be the only one of its kind to survive in its complete form. The painting is by John Brewer. Crown, crossed batons, dots and 'D' with description in red. 1810. 40 cm. *Captain & Mrs C. Liley Collection.*

Mercury between 1808 and 1815, soliciting the favours of 'the Nobility, Gentry, and the Public of Derby.' Here is a typical example:

> Mr Brewer most respectfully informs the *Nobility*, *Gentry*, *Clergy*, and *others* in Derby and its vicinity, that he has arranged for their inspection his Specimens of Water-colour Paintings as an Exhibition, consisting of more than two hundred different Subjects, many of them quite new, and the whole designed and painted by himself, which he hopes during the interval of time not given to the festival will afford agreeable change of amusement. May be viewed from 8 in the morning until dark at his house near St. Mary's Bridge, Bridge Gate, Derby. *Admittance* – Ladies and Gentlemen 1s., Children half price. Mr. Brewers pupils free, also purchasers of Drawings.

The notice of John Brewer's death in the *Derby Mercury*, 16 April 1816, ends: '. . . the modesty of his character in his own pretensions, and for his candour respecting the merits of others: He has left a family in the deepest affliction.' He had a son, Frederick William, baptised on 13 September 1800, according to St Alkmund's registers. Wallis refers to one of his mother's (formerly Miss Wightman) pensioners, the same Miss Charlotte Brewer, who used to bring 'silken watch guards and other articles to the doors of well-to-do Derby families' to earn a rather precarious living.

ROBERT BREWER The younger of the two Brewer brothers who worked for the Duesburys was born in 1775, and died in 1857, aged eighty-one, at Great Barr, Staffordshire.

Before joining John at Derby in about 1797 Robert lived at 5 Duke's Street, Bloomsbury, London, and had a picture entitled *A View of Finchley Common* exhibited at the Royal Academy. Later, in 1817 in the *Derby Advertiser*, he solicited favours as a student of Paul Sandby RA. One interesting advertisement that appeared in the *Derby Mercury* in 1816 said that he was the brother of the late John Brewer and that he 'purposes that the Widow and Daughter of his much lamented Brother shall derive a certain profit therefrom'. In view of what was said about the daughter, Charlotte (see John Brewer's biography), this may not have proved successful!

Robert had two daughters, Matilda and Emma, and three sons: George Henry, baptised on 15 December 1802, who became an artist and plumber; James, baptised on 14 June 1810; and Francis, baptised 12 December 1813. Francis became a well-known modeller at the Madeley Works. Later he worked at Shelton from about 1840 to 1856, and at Tamworth Pottery from 1856 to 1875.

In August 1820 Robert Brewer was still advertising for work from Burton Road, Derby. Certainly most of his attributed work on porcelain at Derby is landscape painting.

His wife, Mary, is recorded by Tapp as having worked in Worcester, and the entry in Graves' *Dictionary of Artists* which lists Mrs Brewer as at Worcester 1848–53, and gives her six exhibits at the Royal Academy, would suggest that Robert went there with her in 1848 after the close of the factory, or perhaps a short while before it closed.

The author refutes Tapp's statement that Robert Brewer was the more versatile of the brothers. In his booklet *The Brothers Brewer* Tapp writes: 'His name appears seven times in the Derby Patterns.' This statement is based on the incorrect assumption that the old Derby patterns clearly stated John or Robert Brewer against patterns allotted to them. As stated in John Brewer's biography, no such distinction was made. John Brewer's accounts[8] show the diversity of subject matter, and strongly suggest that John was indeed the more versatile.

There is in a private collection a campana-shaped vase with a large rustic scene in a hayfield, depicting figures in the foreground and a barrel which is clearly initialled 'R.B.'. The author takes this to be a signature much in the manner of O'Neale or Fidelle Duvivier, who inscribed their names on obelisks or other similar objects; the signatures are not immediately obvious because painters were not usually allowed to sign their works during this period, and therefore one does not expect to find these initials.

267
Green-ground cabaret set consisting of
tray, teapot and cover, sucrier and
cover (missing knob), cream jug and
two coffee cans and stands all painted
with named maritime views by George
Robertson. Crown, crossed batons, dots
and 'D' with description of scenes in
blue enamel. Duesbury & Kean.
c. 1800. Tray diameter 40 cm.
Sotheby's, New Bond Street.

268 ◁ ◁
Dessert plate with fluted yellow
border painted with a named plant
'Sweet Briar Rose' possibly by John
Brewer. Crown, crossed batons, dots
and 'D' with description and pattern
number 216 in blue enamel. Duesbury
& Kean. 1795–1800. 22.8 cm.
Mr & Mrs W. H. Mordecai Collection.

269
Plaque of William Pegg, the Younger
(1795–1867) (see biographies).
*Photograph by courtesy of descendants of
William Pegg in Canada.*

271
Water-colour sketch by Thomas
Martin Randall of an unidentified
stately home. Early nineteenth century.
Descendants of Thomas Martin Randall.

270
William Pegg, the Younger
(1795–1867), photographed in
Manchester as a successful business
man. *Photographs by courtesy of Mr W.
H. Barron, Canada.*

272 ▷ ▷
Water-colour sketch by Thomas
Martin Randall. Early nineteenth
century. *Descendants of Thomas Martin
Randall.*

273

Most interesting water-colour sketch by Thomas Martin Randall depicting a view of Derby from the meadows. It cannot be dated before 1809 as it includes the shot-tower which was erected in that year. This suggests that Randall stayed at Derby for about twelve years until 1813 when he left for London. *Descendants of Thomas Martin Randall.*

275

Tureen and cover, shell and diamond-shaped dish with salmon border, painted almost certainly by William Pegg, the Quaker, with bold plant subjects. Crown, crossed batons, dots and 'D' with pattern number and description in blue enamel. Duesbury & Kean. 1800. Standard sizes. *Sotheby's, New Bond Street.*

276

Rare oval-shaped vase on pedestal base with domed cover, the handles simulating bronze, dark blue ground gilt with a foliate design. No factory mark, repairer's incised *, number 2 (for second size), number 80 incised (Bemrose's list). Duesbury & Kean. 1800. 22.5 cm. *Mr Rowland Williams Collection.*

274
Figure subject sketch by Thomas Martin Randall. *c. 1800–25. Descendants of Thomas Martin Randall.*

JOSEPH BROCK   This gilder worked at the Nottingham Road Factory until 1825 and later at the Worcester Works. He died in 1870, aged eighty-eight. His gilder's number from the Haslem list was 14.

BENJAMIN BROCKLESBURY   According to Jewitt apprenticeship papers were taken out on 16 September 1783 for Brocklesbury to learn 'the Art or Business of Painting Porcelain or China Ware'. After Duesbury's death on 30 October 1786, he absconded the following August, and a warrant[9] was issued for him and endorsed to be executed in Middlesex and Westminster.

GEORGE BROUGHTON   Listed by Jewitt as a painter.

JOSEPH BROUGHTON   He was apprenticed at the Nottingham Road Works at the early age of eleven, and later specialized in Japan patterns. He was working at King Street for Sampson Hancock shortly before his death in 1875. See *Royal Crown Derby*, page 199.

THOMAS BROUGHTON   Listed by Jewitt as a painter, 1776.

JOSEPH BULLOCK   Listed by Jewitt as an apprentice painter, 23 September 1765.

CATHERINE   From Lygo's letters Gilhespy stated that in 1787 a man of this name made moulds of boys, etc. See Lygo's letters for 1787 and later.

SEBASTIAN CLAIS   A Frenchman employed as a painter 1772–9, according to Jewitt.

JAMES CLARK   A gilder, he was stated by Barrett and Thorpe to have worked at the Nottingham Road Factory for thirty years in the nineteenth century and to have been one of the early apprentices. He died about 1840 and during the red-marked period used the number 2. Like other gilders he later did much arabesque work.

PHILIP CLAVEY (or Cleve or Cleavey)   This painter is mentioned by Jewitt but he obviously mis-spelt his name either in his reference to Madeley (see Jewitt Vol. I, page 302, and Vol. II, page 108) or in the list of workmen that he gives. The first reference states that Thomas Martin Randall became the friend of two well-known painters, Philip Cleve and William Pegg. As both Randall and Pegg were devout Quakers it might be assumed that Clavey may well also have been one. Care should be taken when attributing botanical or plant studies, particularly those carrying the red mark, to Pegg the Quaker. The 1813 Pegg Sketch Book should be

277
Pair of navette or boat-shaped tureens and covers, pattern number 36, well painted with named views, the borders with celeste blue bands and traditional gilt motifs. The landscapes would appear to be the work of George Robertson. This pattern is similar to pattern number 56 but the coloured bands are broader and it is not clear whether there were landscapes in that pattern. Crown, crossed batons, dots and 'D' with description in black enamel, pattern number 36 in iron-red on some pieces. Duesbury & Kean. *c.* 1800. Approx. 14.5 cm. *Christie, Manson & Woods.*

278
Pair of blue-ground plant pots and
stands with large oval landscapes
named 'Ponty Glyn Duffid, Corwen,
Merioneth' and 'Besborough,
Kilkenny, Ireland' and strongly
attributed to George Robertson.
Crown, crossed batons, dots and 'D'
with descriptions of scenes in blue
enamel. Duesbury & Kean. 1800.
21 cm. *Christie, Manson & Woods.*

279
Important indenture of William Locker
apprenticed to Michael Kean in 1809.
Locker was later to become the chief
partner in the King Street factory,
which was firstly known as William
Locker & Co. Late Bloor. It is very
interesting to note the signature of
Robert Bloor as a witness when he was
a clerk in the office department of the
old Nottingham Road China Works;
this is the first mention of his name. *By
courtesy of William Locker's descendants.*

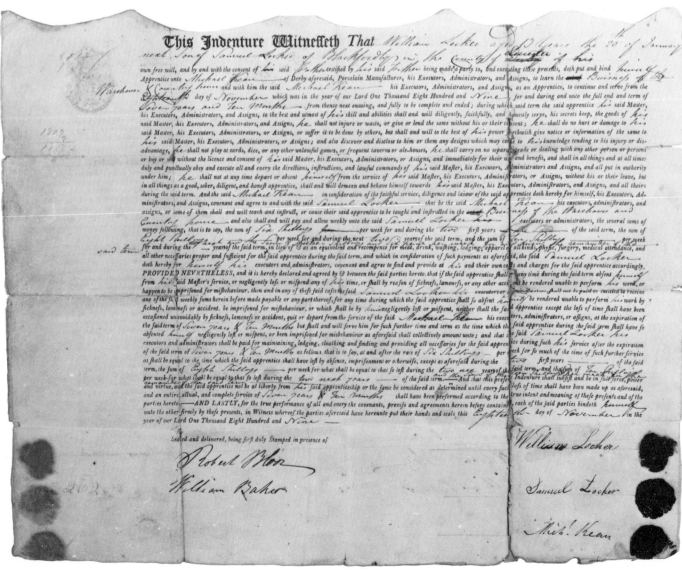

consulted, and so should documented pieces like the Thistle Dish in the Derby City Museum, since there may well be a similarity between the style of Pegg and that of Clavey. According to Haslem, Cleve (as he called him) kept a glass and china shop at the bottom of Sadler Gate, Derby, close to the bridge.

GEORGE COCKER Apprenticed to figure-making about 1808 at the Derby Works, and left about 1817, finding employment with John Rose at Coalport on raised flower work. He started a small business at Jackfield, but after six or seven months it closed and he lost his capital. After having worked for a short time at Worcester, Cocker returned to Derby in 1821 and was employed at the Nottingham Road Works again until 1825, when together with John Whitaker Senior he started making china figures in Friar Gate. Whitaker, however, remained little more than a year and Cocker carried on, firing his goods in a yard opposite his shop, until 1840. A notice appeared in the local press during Whitaker's partnership with him.

DERBY

NEW CHINA WORKS

For the Manufacture of Porcelain Figures Ornaments, &c

Messrs. COCKER and WHITAKER beg most respectfully to inform the nobility, gentry and the public, that they have commenced the above business in FRIAR GATE, DERBY, where they manufacture, and have now ready for inspection, and sale, a numerous assortment of Goods in Biscuit and Enamel, such as they hope will be found not inferior to anything of the kind at present produced in this kingdom.

Messrs. C. and W. have also a variety of *Tea* and *Dessert Services* of modern and approved patterns; and by arrangements already made, and a strict attention to the orders with which they may be favoured, they hope to obtain the honor of that patronage they now venture to solicit, and which it will ever be their most earnest endeavour to merit.

N.B. Ladies or Gentlmen may have Figures Ornaments, &c, executed from models or drawings of their own.

Friar Gate, Derby, Feb. 28, 1826.

280
Octagonal plate from a service removed from Lowther Castle and formerly in the possession of Lord Lonsdale, decorated in oriental taste, the colourings being predominantly red, light blue, green and gold. Crown, crossed batons, dots and 'D' in red. Duesbury & Kean. *c.* 1807. Diameter approx. 21.5 cm. *Royal Crown Derby Museum.*

When Cocker left his shop, adjoining Schweppe's Soda Water Factory, he moved to Chenies Street, Tottenham Court Road, London, where he continued making figures until 1853 when his business declined and he left London and found employment at Minton's.

The figures produced by Cocker are not without merit, though being made in the ordinary china body they have a chalky, dry appearance. He also published some small busts of celebrated people of the day. Some articles were signed but many were sold without a mark. He died in 1868.

WILLIAM JOHN COFFEE A modeller whose father William worked at a Chelsea pottery; it was probably there, with his father, that he began his career. He moved to Coade's Artificial Stone Works, Pedlar's Acre, Lambeth. This firm had been established *c.* 1760 by the Misses Coade and produced statues, vases, monuments, church fonts, etc. An example of their work is the font at Debden church in Essex. The eminent sculptors Bacon, Banks, Flaxman, Rossi and Pauzetta modelled for them. It was, however, after a disagreement between Mr Sealey, the Misses Coade's cousin and partner, that Coffee left and entered into an agreement with William Duesbury II in about 1792.

Duesbury's London agent was not at all flattering about the new modeller:

> *I do not much admire Mr. Coffee's modelling from what I have yet seen. The figure 359 (gardener & comp) is one of the most stupid looking things I ever saw, and the figure of Apollo in group 379 [no details given] is very vulgar about the bosom, for sure never such bubbys was seen and so much exposed – the design is pretty enough.*

Shortly afterwards a new agreement was negotiated at 3*s.* 6*d.* for each ten-hour day at the works or 'at the rate of 7*s.* for any single figure of 6″ high, whether

282
Dessert plate with elaborate gilt border and central fish subject, named on the reverse in red, 'Dace or Dare', and attributed to Thomas Tatlow. This uncertain attribution is traditional and appears to be based upon the fact that he was a keen angler. Crown, crossed batons, dots and 'D' with description in red enamel. Duesbury & Kean. 1810. 22.9 cm. *Royal Crown Derby Museum.*

284 ▷ ▷
Fine campana-shaped vase with snake handles. One of a set of three vases, this one has periwinkle matt ground with quality gilding, reserved upon which is a fine panel showing a basket of flowers on a marble ledge. The floral painting is of a high standard and might well be the work of Hall, Brentall or Wheeldon. Crown, crossed batons, dots and 'D' in red. Robert Bloor & Co. 1815–20. 20 cm. *City Museum & Art Gallery, Derby.*

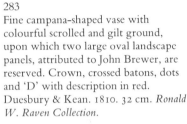

281
A remarkable grouping of a pair of vases and a single larger classical-shaped vase. The flanking pair are painted with landscapes possibly by William Cotton and have the ground enamelled with amatory and other trophies. The central vase has a celeste blue ground with a large canted-cornered rectangular panel depicting a basket of natural flowers, possibly by Thomas Martin Randall. Crown, crossed batons, dots and 'D' in red, gilder's mark 11 in red on large vase. Duesbury & Kean. *c.* 1810. Pair 36.7 cm, large vase 44.4 cm. *Anthony Hoyte Collection.*

standing or in any other action, which if standing would be 6″ high; and that all figures shall be roughed out naked in correct proportions before draped'. There were other agreements between the parties but Coffee left in 1795 to join Sir Nigel Gresley at the china works at Burton-on-Trent. After Coffee had returned to London, since there was no further work on hand, his father wrote to Duesbury asking him to have his son back at the Nottingham Road Works. This plea succeeded and William John returned to Derby. By 1810 he was advertising in the *Derby Mercury*:

W. J. COFFEE

Modeller & Sculptor

Having lately executed some Figure Monuments in Marble and Terra Cotta after his own Models, which have been much approved; he therefor begs leave to acquaint the Nobility and Gentry, that he now intends to carry on the business of

Sculptor in Marble, Alabaster, &c.,

W.J.C. flatters himself from his knowledge of the Antique, (beyond which he has not the vanity to aspire,) that he is capable of producing such designs as will meet with the approbation of the Amateur.

Bridge Street, Derby, Sept. 26th. 1810

283
Fine campana-shaped vase with colourful scrolled and gilt ground, upon which two large oval landscape panels, attributed to John Brewer, are reserved. Crown, crossed batons, dots and 'D' with description in red. Duesbury & Kean. 1810. 32 cm. *Ronald W. Raven Collection.*

Haslem tells us that Coffee went to London to carry on his business, and eventually left for America. His son remained in the business for some years. Plate 192 shows a silhouette of Coffee.

As a postscript it is interesting to note that the final success of Coffee at Derby was perhaps his finest model, which was made as a companion for the Spängler's Shepherdess. It was based on Wright of Derby's Antinous, and was among the fine collection of casts that the Nottingham Road Works had acquired after the artist's death in 1797. See plate 194, where the 'bubbys' are this time discreetly draped!

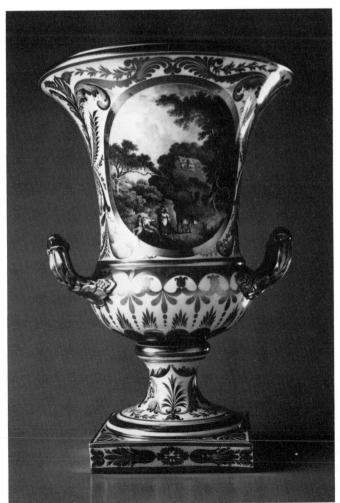

285
Signed water-colour sketch by William Dexter. *c.* 1835–40. *Royal Crown Derby Museum.*

287
Trio consisting of teacup, coffee can and stand, with blue ground gilt and a rich foliate design, each piece having panels of named landscapes painted by Robert Brewer. Note the sea-horse handles and simulated pearls on the coffee can. Crown, crossed batons, dots and 'D' with descriptions in red. Duesbury & Kean. *c.* 1810. Can 7 cm, saucer diameter 14 cm, cup 5 cm. *Victor Spenton Collection.*

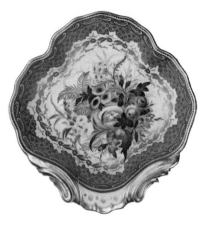

286
Shell-shaped dish with finely executed gilt border and central bird's nest group with flowers, previously attributed to William Dexter, who was not born until 1818. A plate of the same service is in the Royal Crown Derby Museum. Crown, crossed batons, dots and 'D' with number 12 in red. Duesbury & Kean. 1810. Width 25.4 cm. *Charles Littlewood Hill Collection. Neales of Nottingham.*

288 ◁ ◁
Rare pair of duck sauceboats, probably taken from the Old Bow moulds (Haslem). Crown, crossed batons, dots and 'D' in red. Duesbury & Kean. 1810. Length 13.9 cm. *Pegeen Mair & Angela Drayson Collection. David John Ceramics, Woodstock.*

289 ◁
Teapot, cover and stand decorated in Meissen style, with flower groups and single flowers in brown monochrome heightened with gilding. It has been suggested that this was a special service but in fact the pattern appears on a standard 1805–20 bun-footed teapot in the Royal Crown Derby Museum thus suggesting the pattern was in general use. Crown, crossed batons, dots and 'D' in red, with number 1 for Samuel Keys Senior. Duesbury & Kean. 1810. Teapot 13 cm. *Royal Crown Derby Museum.*

GEORGE COMPLIN   This fine painter is believed to have been French but he was certainly working at Battersea enamelling in 1765, since a documentary box carried a dedication to his wife Mary. It is possible that he worked at Chelsea, but that he had a trial on the white before going up to Derby in 1789 is documented by Lygo's letters. According to these, Withers, who was in London, is stated to have said that Complin was a better painter than Hilliard, another aspirant for the factory, who had worked with him at Chelsea but could make little of it. Jewitt quotes from a letter dated 18 September 1794 'I think my hair admits of more respect', and in the same letter he talks of '. . . the variety I do, and the variableness of the work'. He is justly famed for his coffee cans painted 'Fruit & birds by Complin', patterns 236 and 237 being documentary ones. The detailed quality of this type of decoration is most highly prized by collectors. See colour plate 25 and plate 207 for examples in the Hermitage, Leningrad, and in the Royal Crown Derby Museum. It should be pointed out that when attributing the work of this painter, later pieces were decorated in this style by (in the author's opinion) John Brewer. In Complin's work the birds are nearly always disproportionate to the fruit and other background details. In the red-marked period the celebrated Thomas Steel emulated Complin's work on vases, etc.

WILLIAM COOPER Senior   This painter was stated by Jewitt to have been a clever flower painter between 1770 and 1776 when he died.

WILLIAM COOPER Junior   The son of the painter mentioned above, he was put apprentice by his mother, Sarah, on 1 January 1777, to learn the 'Art of Painting upon China or Porcelain Ware'. He used the numeral 3 on the foot rim of his pieces between 1785 and 1795.

WILLIAM CORDEN   Born at Ashbourne in Derbyshire on 28 November 1797, and was apprenticed at the Nottingham Road Works in 1811. Although he was to be known later for figure and portrait subjects, he was a competent landscape painter, sharing this task with Mountford, Cotton, Robert Brewer, Robertson and possibly a few others. Shortly before Corden left the works *c.* 1825–30 he painted the greater part of a dessert service with subjects copied from Thurston's illustrations to Tegg's edition of Shakespeare's plays (1811). See colour plate 69 and plate 111. According to Haslem, who may well have been biased, Corden excelled as a colourist rather than in the manner of drawing.

On leaving Derby he set himself up as a portrait painter in London where he met with considerable success, exhibiting at the Royal Academy for the first time in 1826. In 1829 Corden went to Windsor where, although George IV promised to sit for him, the king's illness and subsequent death prevented this. However, as can be seen in the Royal Crown Derby Museum, he made up for this by painting William IV at Windsor. In about 1831 Corden was engaged to paint some of the subjects on the costly (£5,000) Rockingham service which was made for William IV, and was reputedly the downfall of this firm. Alfred Wallis in his unpublished notes wrote that his father sat for him soon after his return from Germany (Prince Albert had sent him to the Castle of Rosenau to copy various family portraits). 'He was a chatty good-humoured man,' he wrote, 'who did not object to a cheerful glass but I never saw him the worse for liquor . . . Corden was a stout-built man and I should think capable of holding his own in a bout of fisticuffs.'

Corden was recorded in the Tyrian Lodge of Freemasons after his initiation on 29 November 1825.

WILLIAM COTTON   This landscape painter was working at Derby during the first quarter of the nineteenth century, painting landscapes (plate 315 illustrates a signed plaque) and hunting subjects. The incensories in the City Museum, Derby, formerly in the Haslem collection, were stated by Haslem to have been painted by Cotton and the author sees no reason to doubt this documentation. It will be noticed that one of the three campana-shaped vases illustrated in colour plate 67 has the identical panoramic scene as one of the incensories mentioned above.

Haslem states that he left Derby for the Potteries in about 1821. He also painted Dutch subjects and was known as the 'Lady Killer' because of his appearance and dress. Haslem describes his clothes: '. . . black trowsers, buff waistcoat, and a blue coat with a black velvet collar and gilt buttons'.

WILLIAM CRESSWELL One of the painters discharged by Bloor in 1821, Cresswell was a flower painter whose work at Derby and later at Coalport is still to be discovered. Haslem tells us that on leaving Coalport this painter worked for some years at a manufactory in the south of France, but after the revolution of 1848, like many Englishmen, had to leave. He died in 1870, in the Potteries where he had been teaching dancing.

JOHN DEARE According to Jewitt, Deare, born in 1759, was a London modeller of considerable note and was employed by Duesbury in 1784. In 1785, according to Barrett and Thorpe, he was elected a travelling student of the Royal Academy and went to Rome where he remained until his death in 1798.

WILLIAM DEXTER Painted birds, fruit and flowers, and according to Haslem excelled in the superior Chinese and Oriental style of decoration. It would seem that he did not remain at the works for long after his apprenticeship. He went to Paris for the first time in 1839 to paint china, and again a few years later. He worked for George Mellor, a former Derby painter, in London, and by July 1847 was in Nottingham where he styled himself 'Chinese Enameller to Louis Philippe, King of the French, and M.M.S.A.R. the Duke de Nemours'. He later returned to London, chiefly executing watercolours, and found a ready sale for them at Ackermann's the printmaker's. In about 1851 Paul Jarrard of Fleet Street published a book called *Birds and Nests, from the original drawings by Dexter*. He exhibited this particular subject at the Royal Academy in 1851, and appeared at a soirée in Hungarian costume; Haslem records the surprise of not only himself, but of most of the guests who, influenced also by his beard, thought he was a foreign artist. The Royal Crown Derby Museum possessed a sketch of a nest signed by Dexter. He later went to Australia where he died shortly after 1860 in Melbourne, in the prime of life. His wife was celebrated for giving lectures on the 'Bloomer costume', and dressed in character. She joined her eccentric husband in Australia a few years before he died.

WILLIAM DIXON A figure painter who worked at Derby between about 1820 and 1823 and is best remembered for his grotesque figures which appear on large-sized porter mugs. These were taken from a 1773 book, *Human Passions Delineated, In above 120 Figures, Droll, Satirical and Humerous*, by Tim Bobbin Esq. (John Collier). These designs were in the 'Hogarthian' style, very useful for young practitioners in drawing. Plate 312 shows two of these porter mugs.

JOSEPH DODD A gilder listed in the late eighteenth-century list; during the period 1785–95 he would have used the numeral 13.

RICHARD DODSON Son of William Dodson,[10] a foreman painter, Richard painted birds – somewhat carelessly drawn, according to Haslem – but always brightly coloured and in landscapes. He had been apprenticed at the Derby China Works and was probably there from about 1813 until he left in 1820. He set up as a china decorator at premises which were to become the Plough public house on Nottingham Road. See plates 324 and 348 for examples attributed to Dodson.

There is documentary evidence that both John Brewer and Thomas Martin Randall painted bird subjects, and it is possible that, because of overlapping dates, some pieces are wrongly attributed to Dodson. Later there are Poulson's birds, but these pieces normally would carry the engraved mark. The Sèvres style of bird painting that was to be used by John Hancock Junior, William Dexter and others, often on plaques as well as on ornamental and useful ware, usually carried the mock Sèvres mark. See page 340, mark no. 13, for an example.

JOHN DUESBURY A relative of the famous Duesburys, he was in the late eighteenth-century list of gilders and used the numeral 12. He was later to hold a position of authority and the author believes that he may well have been responsible for drawing many of the patterns in the Old Derby Pattern Books, since in one place there is a signature 'Duesbury'.

FIDELLE DUVIVIER Cousin of the Tournai and Chelsea painter Joseph Duvivier, he was born on 6 August 1740 in the parish of St Brice in Tournai. With

290
Ice-pail and cover (liner missing), one of four from a service belonging to the Earls of Shrewsbury. The coastal shipping scene in puce camieu is almost certainly the work of John Brewer. The scattered flower decoration and ribbon panel are very typical of the Berlin factory and in fact these pails may well have been included in a Berlin service also in the possession of the Talbot family. Crown, crossed batons, dots and 'D' in red. Duesbury & Kean. 1805–10. 30.5 cm. *Formerly in the possession of The Earls of Shrewsbury. Royal Crown Derby Museum.*

291 ▷ ▷
An immaculate ice-pail, cover and liner, with highly worked-up and burnished gilding, which remains in unbelievably good condition. The two oval landscape panels are named 'In Llangollen Vale, Denbighshire' and on the reverse 'Nr Brosely Shropshire'. The author, who has known this item for some time, firmly attributes the landscapes to George Robertson. Crown, crossed batons, dots and 'D' with the descriptions of the scenes in red. Duesbury & Kean. 1810. 26 cm. *Royal Crown Derby Museum.*

292
Vase of campana shape with a broad band of green coloured scrolling of a foliate design, from which appears a horse and, on the reverse, a dog. The remaining decoration is executed in gilt. It would appear that this was originally part of a garniture of three vases and in fact one of a pair which would flank a central and larger vase of the same shape. Crown, crossed batons, dots and 'D' in red. Duesbury & Kean. 1810. Approx. 17.8 cm. *Mrs Margaret Taylor Collection.*

293 ▷ ▷
Large vase of campana shape with fine gilding on salmon ground, ram's head handles and a waist richly striped upon gold ground. The rectangular panel with canted corners shows a named view 'In Dudley Wood, Worcestershire', possibly the work of Robert Brewer. Crown, crossed batons, dots and 'D' with the scene description in red. Duesbury & Kean. 1810. 33.4 cm. *Geoffrey Godden.*

294

David Garrick (1717–99) in the role of
Richard III, modelled from an
engraving by J. Dixon and published in
1772 after the painting by Nathaniel
Dance, which was exhibited in the
Royal Academy in 1771. Listed in the
joint Chelsea and Derby sale catalogue
of 9 February 1773: 'A fine figure of
Garrick in the character of Richard the
Third, in biscuit, 1l. 10s.' (Nightingale).
The figure is listed number 21 in
Haslem's list and is stated to be Garrick
modelled by Bacon. A paper by
Babette Craven, who has much
researched Garrick, was read by
Donald Towner at the Victoria &
Albert Museum on 18 October 1975.
She believed that the heads of the
Derby figures of Richard III varied
according to the period in which the
figures were made. Firstly the head
of Garrick with neat hair was used,
secondly John Philip Kemble's head
and thirdly that of Edmund Kean. The
figure illustrated here is certainly
Garrick, dating from 1773–5, and
should be contrasted with the
Hermitage Richard III. William
Duesbury & Co. 1773–5. 28.6 cm.
*Victoria & Albert Museum, 414/205 –
1885.*

296 ∎

Edmund Kean in the role of Richard
III, thus completing the trio with the
previous plates. Here the painting of
the head would appear to change the
identity of the figure shown in plate
263. Robert Bloor & Co. 1815.
Approx. 29 cm. *Graham & Oxley,
London. Royal Crown Derby Museum.*

295
Figure of Richard III being played by John Philip Kemble, modelled from the original Garrick figure but with the changed head of Kemble with his hair blowing in the wind. It seems perfectly reasonable that as the hey-day of the various actors waned, so the shrewd Derby manufactory would appeal to current demand by substituting the head of the currently popular actor on the figure of Richard III. Hence the Bloor figure of Richard would seem quite appropriate with the head of Edmund Kean (who had a moustache). Time, however, seems to have disarmed all three, as they all lack the sword. No mark. William Duesbury & Co. 1790. 29.1 cm. *The Hermitage, Leningrad, USSR, no. 20894.*

297 ◁
Plate with asymmetrical floral decoration, the border with basketweave in the Meissen style. Not attributed. Crown, crossed batons, dots and 'D' in red, gilder's number 15 in red and 48 in puce near foot rim. It is interesting to note that numbers running up to about 100 often appear on early nineteenth century and early Bloor pieces in various enamel colours. To date no satisfactory explanation may be found, but the author feels that the numbers are more likely to be workmen's numerals rather than pattern numbers. It should be noted that only the late eighteenth century patterns survive and although these were used through to the Bloor period, no patterns established in the Bloor period have yet been found or brought forward. Duesbury & Kean. *c.* 1810. 24 cm. *Mr & Mrs W. H. Mordecai Collection.*

his family he attended the Huguenot church de la Barrière de Tournai et Armentiers. It is believed that he was apprenticed to Peterinck's factory in Tournai and there became a painter of some note. Being a Huguenot, it is very likely that he was tempted to come to Chelsea by Nicholas Sprimont who had already employed Tournai men, including Joseph Duvivier, who returned to Tournai as Directeur de l'Académie de Tournai. Certainly Fidelle came to London at this time, 1764, but whether he worked for Giles or Sprimont is not absolutely certain. What is, however, most certain is that this Frenchman entered into an agreement with William Duesbury I in 1769.

The agreement, duly signed by the two parties, and witnessed by John Bosher and S. Horrocks, is dated 31 October 1769, and is 'between Fidelle Duvivier of the borough of Derby China or Porcelain Painter', and 'William Duesbury of the same place China or Porcelain Manufacturer', and covenants that the former shall, for four years from that date, 'diligently and faithfully according to the best and utmost of his skill and knowledge, exercise and employ himself in the Art of Painting China or Porcelain Ware', for the weekly wages of 24s; Mr Duesbury agreeing, at the end of that time, to give him an additional five guineas 'in case he shall merit the same'. Jewitt informs us that Duvivier became the principal flower painter at the Derby Works, and that his style was much followed by the later painters.

Figure subjects and bird decoration also featured in this painter's work. There are some *trembleuse* chocolate cups which could be attributed to Fidelle Duvivier; one of them is illustrated in plate 114 and shows very typical French-style painting. We

229

298
Rare pair of vases of most unusual shape on square bases, with gilt cupids riding dolphins adapted as handles, and dark blue ground gilt with stylized gilding. The oval landscape scenes are named on the base and are possibly the work of William Cotton who used a predominant wash of puce colour in his foregrounds. The floral painting on the reverse panels is unattributed. Crown, crossed batons, dots and 'D' in blue with scene descriptions. Note that although these vases carry a blue mark they belong to the red-marked period. Duesbury & Kean. 1810. 32.5 cm. *Delomosne & Son, London. C. B. Shephard & Sons.*

299
Pair of ice-pails, covers and liners richly gilt and painted with named views, possibly by Robert Brewer. Crown, crossed batons, dots and 'D' with descriptions in red. Duesbury & Kean. *c.* 1810. 24.1 c. *Delomosne & Son, London.*

50
Covered urn, the shape of which is believed to be
unrecorded, with two floral panels by John Brewer.
Note the less common grouping of the flowers. The
ground gilt is by Samuel Keys Senior, whose number 1
appears on the foot rim. It is interesting to note the
simulated bronzed decoration above the snake handles
and on the base. Red crown, crossed batons, dots and
'D', gilder's number 1. Duesbury & Kean. 1810. 33 cm.
David Holborough Collection. Royal Crown Derby Museum.

51
Campana-shaped vase with an all-over
'Japan' pattern of good quality. One
can appreciate the attractive appearance
of such objects by candlelight. Crown,
crossed batons, dots and 'D' in red.
Robert Bloor & Co. 1810–15. Approx.
32 cm. *W. Garwood Collection.*

52

A vase of rare elongated campana shape, the blue ground heavily gilt and the reverse side showing the use of white enamel to heighten decoration. The oval landscape, of a scene at Linmore in Ireland, is strongly attributed to John Brewer. Crown, crossed batons, dots and 'D' with description in red. Robert Bloor & Co. 1812–15. 27 cm. *Royal Crown Derby Museum.*

are told that Duvivier remained at Derby until 31 October 1773, when his agreement terminated. Tapp tells us of news from Coalport that an elderly craftsman of theirs (aged eighty in 1932) remembered his grandfather telling him that his father had worked with Duvivier at Caughley in 1773–4. The signed Worcester teapot in the Dyson Perrins Museum is dated 1772 and has also caused concern, but this of course was almost certainly not decorated at Worcester. Duvivier is described in the Duesbury agreement as being of the borough of Derby; evidence of this is provided by the record of the baptism at St Alkmund's church on 20 March 1771 of Peter Joseph, the son of Fidelle and Elizabeth Duvivier. Fidelle is later reported as being at Sceaux, near Paris, in 1775. His movements from then until 1787 are uncertain, but in that year he painted a John Turner beaker which he signed 'Duvivier ft' and dated 'Lane-End, *Juin* 1787'. This beaker was probably made while he was a drawing master at Stone, as the following letter to Duesbury explains:

> *Hanley green, the 1 novebr 1790, Mr Dousbery, Sir – take the liberty Adressing you with a few lines, as mine Engeement in the new Hal Porcelaine manufatory is Expierd, and the propriotors do not intend to do much more in the fine lineof Painting, therfor think of Settling in new Castle under lime being engag'd to teech Drowing in the Boarding School at that place, one School I have at Stone, so as to haveonly three days to spare in the week for Painting, wich time Could wish to be employ'd byyou preferable to eany other fabrique, because you like and understand good work, as am inform'd, my painting now to what I did for your father is quit diferent but without flatering my Self, Hope to give you Satisfaction, In Case you Schould like to imploy me, Sir, – your anser will much oblige your Humble Servant, Duvivier. P.S. the conveyance would be much in fevoir for to Send the ware to and from as ther is a waggon Every week from darby to new Castle.*

The author feels that William Duesbury II, who had gathered round him one of the finest bands of painters and craftsmen ever working for an English factory, would not have cared much for the Duvivier suggestion and possibly declined the offer.

Duvivier was, like Duesbury and Corden, a mason, and his lodge in Tournai was known as *Les Frères Reunis*.

It is reported that Duvivier was a drawing master at the Orme School of Art in Newcastle-under-Lyme during 1791–6. After this date his movements are certainly not clear, but he appears to have died in 1817, aged seventy-seven, and was buried, it is believed, at Hanley Green parish church.

JOSEPH ECCLESHARE　He was born on 10 March 1793, and died on 6 June 1846. The author is indebted to Mrs Nina Copp for providing information about her forebear. She possesses three watercolours, one of which is reproduced on a china plaque; all are signed by Eccleshare. He is listed by Haslem[11] in the abortive subscription list for the present to celebrate the Reform Bill, and is listed as a gilder.

THOMAS EDLIN　Jewitt mentions an Elin (*sic*) as a painter and gilder from 1786 to 1795. He was quite possibly the same man mentioned by Barrett and Thorpe as having married at St Alkmund's, Derby, in July 1767.

JAMES FAIRBANKS　A potter who in 1822 succeeded William Porter as overseer of the useful wares department, where he remained until his death in 1837.

JAMES FARNSWORTH　He was one of the four flower painters dismissed by Bloor in 1821, and who were stated by Haslem to have found employment at Coalport.

ISAAC FARNSWORTH　He was a repairer of figures from about the mid-1750s until his death in 1821. As a repairer he would build up the moulded pieces and incise the final piece with his mark, an incised star. He was responsible for drawing up from memory the list of Duesbury moulds and models, with the co-operation of Soar, Longdon and Hardenburg. These dated from 1795, and were to

300
Large vase of campana shape with mask handles, the main body of which is covered with large natural flowers by William Pegg, the Quaker. Crown, crossed batons, dots and 'D' in red. Robert Bloor & Co. 1815. 39.4 cm. *Lady Lloyd. Anthony Hoyte Collection.*

be used in the Duesbury *v.* Kean litigation of 1818 (see chapter 1). Chapter 3 contains the full list, reproduced from Bemrose. Farnsworth was foreman of the ornamental department from the time of Duesbury II until he died.

JOHN FROST   Jewitt tells us that he was apprenticed to Edward Phillips on 16 April 1770 as a painter, but the following year was transferred, by fresh indenture, to Duesbury.

WILLIAM GADSBY   On 2 September 1772 he began a four-year apprenticeship as a mould-maker. Duesbury was to give 'William Gadsby a Waggon Load of Coals at the end of every year', so Jewitt tells us.

NICHOLAS FRANÇOIS GAURON   This modeller was born in Paris in 1736 and was apprenticed to his uncle Jacob, a silversmith. He worked at Mennecy and was later chief modeller at Tournai from 1758 to 1764. He is mentioned in the Chelsea work lists of 1773 as being paid 8*s.* 9*d.* daily, which was a very high wage. His son Nicholas worked with him and, according to Severne Mackenna, the two later went up to Derby. The elder Gauron is said by the same writer to have modelled many of the classical and allegorical figures which William Duesbury favoured.

JAMES GOADSBY   An ornamental potter listed by Haslem.

THOMAS GRIFFIN   A clever modeller or ornamental potter, described in Haslem's list as having modelled 'Grimaldi as Clown', which would be *c.* 1830. After Edward Keys left in 1826 he was foreman for a short while.

234

301
Large campana-shaped vase with mask handles and richly gilt body, painted with a canted-cornered rectangular panel of peacocks, a parrot and other birds. These are traditionally ascribed to Richard Dodson. Crown, crossed batons, dots and 'D' in red. Robert Bloor & Co. 1815. Approx. 48 cm. *David John Ceramics, Woodstock.*

WILLIAM HALL Born in 1800. Haslem mentions him as having been discharged in 1821 with Jesse Mountford, William Cresswell, James Farnsworth and Thomas Brentnall, and to have found work at Coalport. After he left Coalport he worked at Allcock's and Copeland's. While at Coalport he painted a plate with a basket of flowers in the centre, which he presented to Haslem's aunt, Mrs Thomason. This piece, which bears the painter's initials and is dated 1822, later passed into Haslem's collection.

JOHN HANCOCK John, son of George Hancock, was apprenticed for seven years on 29 September 1769, aged twelve.[12] He became a talented flower painter, according to Jewitt, and Haslem tells us that he worked for a while at Swansea, going on to live in the Potteries.

It is to this man that the credit for inventing the new method of gilding is given. Gilding had formerly been carried out with leaf gold ground up in honey, and, because of the soft glazes used then, very little flux was needed to make the gold adhere to the ware. The new method, known at first as 'brown gold', consisted of melting pure gold in a crucible; while the gold was still molten, the metal was poured into cold water. Five parts of mercury were added to every six parts of gold, and this mixture was then ground in turpentine on a glass slab with a glass muller until it was of a consistent fineness. A little flux was added to make the gold adhere to the ware, and afterwards the gilded piece was heated to a high enough temperature to bring the rose colour bright and clear. The mercury passed off in the firing, leaving the gold in a matt state ready for burnishing with a blood stone or silver sand. This method was found to be far more durable and allowed burnishing to a high degree.

Hancock was the first to discover silver and steel lustres, which he used at the

302 ◁
Reverse of vase in black and white
plate 301 with panel of fruit and birds
in the manner of Thomas Steele who
probably painted it.

304
Large campana-shaped vase painted
with a vulture and snake in a landscape.
Unusual horned mask handles, the
ground covered with a profusion of gilt
motifs and the interior decorated with
flowers and butterflies give an overall
opulent appearance which so readily
found custom in this period. Pieces of
this nature must of necessity have been
costly to decorate. Crown, crossed
batons, dots and 'D' in red. Duesbury
& Kean. 1810. 41.1 cm. *Leeds Art
Galleries*.

305
The reverse of the above showing a
bold floral painting.

303 ◁
Pair of figures known as 'Welch Tailor
and Wife', adapted from the Kandler
and Eberlein versions. According to
legend they were made in mockery of
von Bruhl's tailor who wished to be
present at a court banquet; he was
represented modelled as a table
decoration. The title does not denote
the Welsh nationality of the tailor but
merely a mistranslation of the German
'Schneider, welcher auf einem
Ziegenbock reutet' (Tailor, who rides
on a goat) (*Ceramics of Derbyshire*).
Robert Bloor & Co. 1815. Sizes not
known. *Fox Collection*.

306
A garniture of three campana-shaped vases with natural birds in panoramic landscape painting possibly by Richard Dodson, although Thomas Martin Randall was still active up to 1813. The vases have snake handles. Crown, crossed batons, dots and 'D' in red. Robert Bloor & Co. 1812–15. Centre vase 20.8 cm. *Sotheby's, New Bond Street.*

307
A most impressive pair of ice-pails and covers, painted with a wild profusion of flowers including lilies, passion flowers, roses, morning glory and sweetpeas by William Pegg, the Quaker. Crown, crossed batons, dots and 'D' with plant names in red. Robert Bloor & Co. *c.* 1813–15. 23.5 cm. *Christie, Manson & Woods.*

308
Four coffee cans with 'Japan' patterns. From left to right: Greek-shaped handle, Hamilton fluted plain loop handle, wishbone handle and ear-shaped handle. Pattern names not known. Crown, crossed batons, dots and 'D' in red, various workmen's marks. Robert Bloor & Co. 1810–15. Average height 6 cm. *John Twitchett Collection.*

309
Four coffee cans with 'Japan' patterns. From left to right: angular-handled can with 'Witches' pattern, wishbone handle with 'Derby Garden' pattern, same shape with 'Derby Rose' pattern and Greek-shaped handle (Spode London shape) with 'Old Japan' pattern. Crown, crossed batons, dots and 'D', various workmen's marks. Robert Bloor & Co. 1810–20. Average height 6 cm. *John Twitchett Collection.*

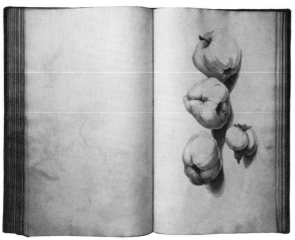

310 ◁ ◁
Facsimile of a page in the 1813 sketch-
book of William Pegg, the Quaker,
depicting apples.

311
Loose sketch discovered with the 1813
sketchbook of William Pegg, the
Quaker, showing an oval landscape
below which he wrote the following
verse. *Descendants of Thomas Martin
Randall.*

> ~~Yes~~ Rustics ~~acknowledge~~ my *so* sacred *thy* birth
> Thou need not fear the weather
> Then freely approach their humble hearth
> They will not touch a feather
>
> So bow thy head and wail thy wings
> and perk thy turned tail as ever
> Thou wont to do in beautious Spring's
> Most dear delighting weather
>
> Then come little warbler my favorite bird
> a Favorite why I cant tell how
>   without its being the first ever I heard
> on Chimney top or naked green bough
>
> or perhaps because thou welcome in spring
> just as Primroses beginning to peep
> For oft Ive been raptured to hear thee sing
> When sitting on these mossy banks steep

312
A pair of porter mugs painted with
subjects taken from *Human Passions
Deliniated* by Tim Bobbin and painted
here by William Dixon.

Left mug; plate 3, published June 1773:

> See here an emblem of a married life,
> When filthy lucre joins a man and wife:
> Each three times married, both expected
>   riches;
> Both sides are cheated, – thus fight for
>   th'breeches,
> Disorder reigns! – all pleasure flies
>   away;
> Chagrin the night, and fury rules the
>   day.

Right mug; plate 6, published June
1773:

> He miss'd at first, but try'd again,
> Then clapp'd his foot o'th chin;
> He pull'd – the patient roar'd with pain,
> And hideously did grin.
>
> But lo! – capricious fortune frown'd,
> And broke the clewkin string,
> And threw him backwards on the
>   ground,
> His head made floor to ring.

Crown, crossed batons, dots and 'D' in
red. Robert Bloor & Co. *c.* 1820.
12.7 cm. *Formerly in Brayshaw
Gilhespy's Collection.*

313
Bough pot and pierced cover of bombé
shape; the large rectangular panel is
painted with a landscape, probably by
Robert Brewer. Crown, crossed
batons, dots and 'D' with description of
scene in red. Robert Bloor & Co.
c. 1811–15. Approx. 13 cm. *Graham &
Oxley, London.*

314
Counter box and cover, decorated with
playing cards supported on dolphin
tails and surmounted with a dolphin
head finial on the cover. Crown,
crossed batons, dots and 'D' and 37 in
red. Duesbury & Kean. *c.* 1810.
13.4 cm. *Victoria & Albert Museum,*
C306 – 1935.

Spode Works. In 1816 Josiah Wedgwood realized Hancock's talents and employed him as a colourmaker and manager of their enamelling department.

John Hancock died – dubbed by many the 'Father of the Potteries' – on 18 July 1847. One of his sons, James, worked at Worcester as a colourmaker and groundlayer.

GEORGE and JOHN HANCOCK (sons of the above)   George Hancock worked at Derby from 1819 to 1835. He brought with him a number of women who were engaged to paint slight flowers and cheaper-class patterns. Women had been employed to paint earthenware and china in Staffordshire, but had been resisted at Derby in the eighteenth century (see Banford's biography and the list on page 191). Haslem tells us that the move was still not well received by the men. Some years earlier that part of the Old Factory on whose site the nunnery (mentioned in chapter 1) was built, had been closed, and it was now re-opened to accommodate these women.

Wallis writes of a sale by Mr Cross, the auctioneer, in 1822 in the Large Warehouse at the Derby Works:

I remember the appearance of the 'large warehouse' very well. It was situated to the right of the great entrance doors, and was approached by a short flight of stairs; was probably 50 feet long and 15 or twenty wide, lighted from the roof and sides; the ware was arranged upon benches under the side windows and the middle of the room, leaving space for visitors to walk between the rows of specimens. The side-windows looked out upon the Nottingham Road, passing through this room, you entered the girls' painting room which crossed it at a right angle and had a row of windows looking out upon a footpath which ran from the highway across the fields. The painting-table was arranged in front of this window which was like an elongated greenhouse.

About 1820 George's brother John (1777–1840), was engaged as a colourmaker and groundlayer; together with the women and a few other painters and gilders, he was superintended by George Hancock. John was one of the first to use the new method of groundlaying details, which Haslem reports.[13] He also painted birds in Sèvres style.

Returning to George Hancock, who had worked for a while with Billingsley at Mansfield, we find that, before coming to Derby in 1819, he had worked for Ridgway's and several other potteries, as well as living in London for a while, decorating on his own account. His style of painting was bold and somewhat heavy, and according to Haslem he loved painting on large pieces. The author had a large vase, referred to as a 'Long Tom', which he attributed to this painter. Haslem tells us that a large china jug of Derby manufacture, belonging to a Mr Alfred Lafone, was exhibited in the South Kensington Museum in 1871, and was described as: 'Large Jug – Crown Derby, richly painted with flowers. English, late 18th. or early 19th. century.' Haslem goes on to tell us that this jug was painted by George Hancock about 1822–3 and was in hand for a long while, receiving some finishing touches from his nephew, John Hancock Junior (1804–39). This delay caused a lack of lustre in its final appearance. George Hancock was responsible for teaching flower painting to John Haslem.

Hancock left Derby in 1835 to superintend the Burton-upon-Trent China Works, but by 1839 was employed in France at a manufactory near Lyons. His final engagement was as a painter of glass ornaments with Richardson of Wordsley, near Stourbridge, and he died there shortly after 1850.

The Hancock family contributed greatly to the history of ceramics, continuing the tradition until the death of Harry Sampson Hancock in Derby in 1934.

JOHN HANCOCK Junior   Born in 1804, he was the son of the second John Hancock. He too painted birds in Sèvres style, executed armorial bearings and painted fruit and flowers. The Earl Ferrers service (see plate 378) is attributed to him. He died in 1840.

FRANÇOIS HARDENBURG   There is evidence that this modeller worked at Tournai and later at Caughley. He appears to have replaced Coffee at the Derby Works but does not appear to have remained long. He manufactured figures and ornamental work for interior architectural decorations in marble and plaster at

315 ◁ ◁
Landscape plaque with strong puce undertones in the foreground, painted and signed by William Cotton. *c. 1810–15. Private collection.*

318
Rare large octagonal dish decorated in the 'famille verte' style. An old label states that this dish comes 'from the collection of Dr Taylor of Ashbourne . . . the friend of Dr Samuel Johnson'. Crown, crossed batons, dots and 'D' in red with number 24 also in red. Robert Bloor & Co. 1810–15. 47 cm. *Charles Littlewood Hill Collection. Neales of Nottingham.*

316
Shell-shaped dish, tureen with cover and stand and fluted dish painted with the traditional flower group surrounded by four single flower patterns. The standard of flower painting was very high during the first quarter of the nineteenth century and it is very difficult to make strong attributions because, as Haslem said, there was a family likeness in the style of the floral painters of this period. Crown, crossed batons, dots and 'D' in red with various workmen's numbers. Robert Bloor & Co. 1811–15. Standard sizes. *Sotheby's, New Bond Street.*

317
Pair of pierced baskets supported by three gilt owls standing on a three-sided base which has feet in the form of gilt shells. The author once possessed a basket which was identical except that it was supported by three gilt cats. Crown, crossed batons, dots and 'D' in red. Robert Bloor & Co. *c.* 1811–15. Approx. 12 cm. *Schreiber Collection. Victoria & Albert Museum, 414/419 – 1885.*

319
Garniture of three vases richly gilt with panels of garden flowers in baskets on marble slabs. Crown, crossed batons, dots and 'D' in red. Robert Bloor & Co. 1815–20. Flanking pair 22.2 cm, centre vase 31.5 cm. *Charles Littlewood Hill Collection. Neales of Nottingham.*

320
Pair of campana-shaped vases with rich blue ground, gilt in the romantic style of the painter William Watson. Crown, crossed batons, dots and 'D' in red. Robert Bloor & Co. 1815–20. 32.3 cm. *Christie, Manson & Woods.*

321
A pair of kidney-shaped dishes flanking a large fluted dish, forming part of a dessert service that was attributed to William Pegg, the Quaker, but which also brings the name Philip Clavey to mind. The flowers seem more contrived than natural. Crown, crossed batons, dots and 'D' in red. Robert Bloor & Co. *c.* 1811–15. Standard sizes. *Sotheby's, New Bond Street.*

241

extensive premises in Mount Street, Grosvenor Square, London. He was called upon to value the models and moulds at the Derby Factory in 1810, prior to leasing to Bloor, and again in 1818 for use in the Duesbury *v*. Kean litigation. The National Portrait Gallery in London contains a statuette of George III executed by Hardenburg in 1820, and the modelling bears a striking resemblance to the figure of a yeoman illustrated in plate 363. It may well be that this was modelled by Hardenburg, possibly while in London. Haslem records that one figure in plaster of Paris measured seven feet in height and that another was placed in the Derby Arboretum grounds and soon perished from exposure. These large figures, together with several smaller ones, were originally commissioned for Markeaton Hall, but for some reason were never placed there.

JOHN HASLEM

Born at Carrington, Cheshire, in 1808, arrived in Derby as a boy to live with an uncle, James Thomason, who was a most controversial character. Young Haslem was put apprentice to Bloor at the Nottingham Road China Works in 1822, aged fourteen, and for that very reason his knowledge of his contemporary painters was first-hand. His book, *The Old Derby China Factory: The Workmen and Their Productions*, is still regarded as a standard work and is the basis of modern scholars' research. Figure painting became his great interest and, although he left Derby in 1835 to work in the studio of E. T. Paris, a historical painter who worked for Queen Adelaide, he returned from time to time, to execute certain commissions for the china works, later to be managed by his uncle, James Thomason.

An April 1884 issue of the *Derby Mercury* had this to say of Haslem: 'Mr Haslem's genius was not long in asserting itself, and he painted portraits on enamel that are now historical.' Of course his stay in London, where he copied small portraits in the style of the seventeenth-century French artist Petitot, had later repercussions when they began to pass as originals. Haslem was honest enough to admit that a struggling artist would hardly be put off even were he to have known what would be the outcome. In 1844 he gained a Society of Arts medal for an enamelled portrait of the Duke of Wellington. The author's daughter, Elizabeth Anne, possesses a small miniature painted with a portrait of a little girl. It is inscribed on the reverse 'Eliza Anne Horsley painted by John Haslem 1854'.

Colour plate 79 illustrates a magnificent pair of miniature paintings of Queen Victoria and Prince Albert. These were executed in 1844 and the author has no doubt that they were the just cause for Haslem to receive his first royal patronage in 1845, and from this date he was employed almost continuously by the Queen and Prince Albert. One would think that the Great Exhibition of 1851 would have added to Haslem's reputation, but unfortunately the reverse is true. Prince Albert loaned five important Haslem enamels, the Duchess of Bedford four, and so did several other exhibitors, but none received mention. Bias was reported to have been responsible for the fact that out of the thirteen medals awarded for enamel painting on metal and china only one went to an Englishman. Thus Haslem's period as miniature painter to Queen Victoria came to an undeserved end.

He continued to enjoy much patronage, however, and the art world was surprised at his decision to leave London in 1857 and to return to Derby to live with his widowed uncle James Thomason. During his remaining years he wrote for the *Derby Reporter*, completed several catalogues and his previously mentioned standard work on the Nottingham Road Factory, *The Old Derby China Factory*, in 1876. He served on the Corporation Art Gallery Committee during 1883–4. In the Midland Counties' Exhibition 'row' in 1870 much unpleasantness came to light and clearly illustrates how petty jealousies can disrupt research.[14] The author discussed and reported matters relating to this 'row' in an article in the *Collectors' Guide* in February 1971, in which James Thomason was reported in a most unfavourable light.

JOHN HENSON

A potter who had been one of the last apprentices at the Nottingham Road Factory before going to King Street as one of its six founder members.

JAMES HILL

Born in 1791 and apprenticed at the Nottingham Road Factory, he became a flower painter and gilder. He was using the numeral 21 *c*. 1820, as listed by Haslem. Haslem described his pattern known as 'Hill's flowers': the pattern

322
The reverse of a rare elongated campana-shaped vase (see colour plate 52), shown here to demonstrate the skilful art of the gilder. Crown, crossed batons, dots and 'D' in red. Robert Bloor & Co. 1812–15. 27 cm. *Royal Crown Derby Museum.*

323 ▷ ▷
Figure of a cow and calf with bocage support, made during the Bloor ownership of the factory. A similar but earlier group is illustrated by George Savage in plate 141 of *Englische Keramik*, Wien, 1961. No mark but workmen's numbers 13 and 23 in red and incised cross. Robert Bloor & Co. 1811–15. 15.5 cm. *The Hermitage, Leningrad, USSR, no. 20885.*

324
A part dessert service consisting of two plates, a shell dish, a pair of tureens with covers and stands, flanking an oval dish and, in the foreground, a central basket with a larger pair of dishes, all laid with celeste blue ground with bird painting, probably by Richard Dodson. The panels and borders are edged with elaborate gilding. Crown, crossed batons, dots and 'D' in red. Robert Bloor & Co. 1815. Standard sizes. *Christie, Manson & Woods.*

243

328
Dessert plate painted with a central panel of birds in a landscape by Richard Dodson and a border of apple blossom and butterflies probably the work of Thomas Steel. The cavetto is gilt with a foliate design and the border edged with dentil. Crown, crossed batons and 'D' in red. Robert Bloor & Co. 1815. Approx. 23 cm. *Private collection.*

326
'Fury Group' depicting a man lying on a broken chair with a furious woman attacking him in great anger. The figure is adapted from a Frankenthal model and the decoration may well be the work of Samuel Keys, who excelled in this quality figure painting. Marked with number 89 (Haslem's list). Robert Bloor & Co. *c.* 1820–30. 14.3 cm. *Victoria & Albert Museum, 3016 – 1901.*

327
Derby coffee can and stand decorated with an anglicized oriental-type pattern, the predominant colouring being red, blue, green, purple and gold. Crown, crossed batons, dots and 'D' in red. Robert Bloor & Co. 1815. Can 6.2 cm. *Elizabeth Allnutt, Topsham.*

consisted of one large rose and a few small sprigs of different colours. Haslem was critical of the slight manner in which these groups were executed: 'The lights of his roses were taken out in a series of straight cutting lines, and there was no variety in the colouring of the foliage.' Hill is also stated to have modelled small animals, which, again according to Haslem, sold well. James Hill was one of the six founder members of the King Street Factory. He died in 1854.

JOSEPH HILL   A modeller believed to have been one of the earliest apprentices of William Duesbury I. He is reputed to have used an incised triangle as his mark.

THOMAS HILL   'Jockey' Hill, who was the son of Thomas Hill, the portrait and landscape painter, came to Derby about 1795 after working at Chelsea. The reason why he did not come to the Nottingham Road Works sooner is not known; he was recorded in the Chelsea rate books until the second half of 1794. He eventually arrived at Derby to replace Zachariah Boreman who was returning to London. He lodged with a Mr Horsley, a farmer at Pye Bridge near Derby, and obtained his nickname by riding to and fro daily on his pony, Bob.

Duesbury's terms of employment were as follows: 'To be employed in the painting of Landskips at the rate of $2\frac{1}{2}$ gns per week of not less than fifty-four hours, or seven shillings per day and over-hours at 1/6 per hour'.

Like Boreman, Hill was greatly influenced by Paul Sandby, and indeed there is much similarity between the two ceramic painters. Their palettes, predominantly greens and russet browns, are alike, but the drawing appears more detailed in Boreman's work. This is because Hill did not usually stipple but used brush lines to create his effect and obtained contrast by superimposing transparent paint, particularly in outstanding trees or clumps of bushes.

Also like Boreman, he could not agree with the manager and co-partner, Kean. Hill returned to Chelsea in 1800, to Paradise Walk. In 1801 he joined his father at 53 Great Marlborough Street, and from that address exhibited several Derbyshire views at the Royal Academy between 1805 and 1808. He concluded his working life as a government stores dealer, and died in Marylebone in 1827, aged seventy-four.

RICHARD HOLDSHIP   The Royal Crown Derby Museum has a commemorative mug (see plate 36) of considerable importance – firstly because it commemorates the coronation of George III and Queen Charlotte in 1761, and secondly because it bears the rebus for Holdship and strongly suggests that he was in Derby by this date, having left the Worcester Works in 1758. It is known that he was still in Derby in 1769.

HOLLAND   Jewitt lists him as a flower painter, but gives no dates.

CHARLES HOLMES   Described in the St Alkmund's register as 'China man' when he married there on 24 December 1765.

CHARLES HOLMES   Stated by Haslem to have been apprenticed in the late eighteenth century as a modeller. He modelled sheep and other animals, as well as a set of seated Seasons. From the date of his apprenticeship it would seem that he and the preceding Charles Holmes could not have been the same man.

GEORGE HOLMES   In the Leverholme Collection there is a figure of a youth, inscribed on the base 'George Holmes did this figer [sic] 1765'. He was obviously a figure repairer and would certainly seem to have been the workman mentioned by Wedgwood in his letter to Bentley, where it was stated that Holmes had worked at Derby for twenty-eight years.[15] This claim would place Andrew Planché's works around 1747 – and possibly this is why Jewitt claimed that he knew Planché to have been in Derby for eight years from 1748 to 1756.

EDWARD HOPKINSON   A gilder who had been apprenticed to William Smith, and whose sons were brought up at the Derby Works. William, the elder, was a figure-maker and was working for Sampson Hancock in the 1870s; Edward Junior, the second son, was a gilder and later, against his will, gave such satisfaction helping with painting a large floral service that according to Haslem he was much

329 ◁ ◁
Soup plate illustrating one of the many 'Japan' type patterns which, since the late eighteenth century, have been an important part of production in the city of Derby. Crown, crossed batons, dots and 'D' in red. Robert Bloor & Co. 1815. 24.5 cm. *Royal Crown Derby Museum.*

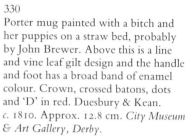

330
Porter mug painted with a bitch and her puppies on a straw bed, probably by John Brewer. Above this is a line and vine leaf gilt design and the handle and foot has a broad band of enamel colour. Crown, crossed batons, dots and 'D' in red. Duesbury & Kean. *c.* 1810. Approx. 12.8 cm. *City Museum & Art Gallery, Derby.*

331 ◁ ◁
Porter mug with random floral sprays, including roses and tulips, probably painted by Moses Webster. Crown, crossed batons, dots and 'D' in red. Robert Bloor & Co. 1815. Approx. 12.8 cm. *Ann Wise, Wreyland Manor Antiques.*

333
Porter mug in brilliant condition with a large rectangular panel of flowers in a basket on a stone slab, possibly by Edwin Steele. Bloor circular mark. Robert Bloor & Co. *c.* 1825. 12.9 cm. *Formerly in the Alison Rose Collection. Victor Spenton Collection.*

332
Teapot and cover of standard 1805–20 shape on bun feet. The rich dark blue ground is gilt with a foliate design, reserved upon which are two oval landscapes, probably by Robert Brewer, 'In Cumberland' and the reverse panel 'In Italy'. Crown, crossed batons, dots and 'D' with descriptions of the named scenes in red. Robert Bloor & Co. 1811–15. 15 cm. *Royal Crown Derby Museum.*

334
Pair of figures known as 'The Dresden
Shepherd and Shepherdess' on pierced
scrolled bases. The decorations might
well be by Samuel Keys. Incised
number 55. Robert Bloor & Co.
c. 1820. 24.6 cm. *Formerly in John
Twitchett's Collection.*

335
Four small figures; a grotesque cook, a
flautist and a pair of fruit- and flower-
sellers. Figures of this small size were
very charming and much in demand
during the Bloor period. Various
incised marks. Robert Bloor & Co.
1820–30. Average height approx.
11 cm. *Joan Neat Collection.*

336
A pair of cat and dog figures which
first appeared during the Chelsea-
Derby period but became popular
again in the nineteenth century. Incised
numeral 51; the woman also has
crown, crossed batons, dots and 'D'
with number 41 in red. Robert Bloor &
Co. 1820. He 13 cm, she 13.2 cm.
*Victoria & Albert Museum: C1298 –
1919 man; C1299 – 1919 woman.*

employed in flower decoration. He was also stated to paint in a similar manner to Edwin Steele, but with more cutting outlines. On the close of the works the Hopkinsons found work in the Potteries – William manufacturing figures, vases and other ornaments, some of which measured two to three feet in height, before returning to work at King Street for Sampson Hancock.

In Bemrose we read of an interesting encounter between William and the man destined to become prime minister – William Gladstone. This took place at an exhibition of workmen's craft in London. In fact the politician arrived after it had closed. The committee were asked to provide twenty working men to dine with him, each to take along some object which he had exhibited.

After the repast Mr. Gladstone took his visitors round his gallery of pictures and showed them various cabinets of china – English and foreign – for the ex-Chancellor of the Exchequer has a great love for old china. On coming to the splendid case of Dresden china, Mr. Gladstone remarked that he had been told that two vases, which he pointed out, ought properly to be placed in the next cabinet of Darby China. Hopkinson, who was a tall man, stood rather behind the rest and replied, 'Yes, sir, they are Darby.' Mr. Gladstone turned sharply round and said, 'Who said that? Let him come here.' So Hopkinson stepped forward, when the following conversation took place. Mr. Gladstone: 'How do you know they are Darby?' Hopkinson: 'Why sir! they were made in the same room where I worked as an apprentice at the Darby Works, and a man named Gadsby[16] made them, and they were painted by Lucas.' Mr. Gladstone: 'Now how old were you then?' Hopkinson: 'I was about 18 years of age.' Mr. Gladstone: 'Very good;' and turning to Mrs Gladstone, he said that 'the two vases were to be removed into the Darby cabinet, as Darby should not be robbed of any of its well-earned honours.'

MICHAEL KEAN   Kean was an Irishman who, when a student in Dublin in 1779, gained the medal of the Society of Fine Arts there. He had practised as a miniature painter in London. According to John Haslem his work was distinguished and could be compared to that of Cosway. He came to the Nottingham Road Works in 1795 to enter into a partnership with William Duesbury II, whose health was failing. After Duesbury's death he married his widow in 1798. The third William Duesbury was only ten years old when his father died in 1796, and was away at boarding school. His sister, Sarah Duesbury, was nine at this time. Both this lady and Mr William Wheeldon confirmed that this third William Duesbury never took an active part in running Nottingham Road, and in fact after an unsuccessful attempt at setting up a colourmaking establishment at Bonsall, near Matlock, he left in 1826 for America, where he stayed until he died.

The absence of a suitable adult Duesbury to inherit the reins left Kean to conduct the running of Nottingham Road from 1796, and though there was a gradual deterioration of the body, the decoration was maintained at a high standard. Bitter family quarrels caused Kean to withdraw in 1811. Lawsuits were continued, but the Nottingham Road Works was leased to Bloor in 1811. Michael Kean died in 1823; the *Derby Mercury* reported his death cursorily: 'A few days since in London, after a short illness, Michael Kean Esq, formerly Proprietor of the Porcelain Manufactory in this town'.

EDWARD KEYS   This son of Samuel Keys (q.v.) was a fine modeller, and according to Haslem was responsible for the fourteen figures illustrating the amusing antics of William Coombe's character Dr Syntax, and for many other figures (see Haslem's list on page 71). Edward Keys succeeded Isaac Farnsworth as foreman of the figure department in 1821, and kept that position until he left in 1826.

JOHN KEYS   Another son of Samuel Keys, he died at the early age of twenty-seven after a long and lingering illness. The *Derby Mercury* reported his death on 27 April 1825:

On Thursday (Ap. 21. 1825) aged 27, after a long and protracted illness Mr. John Keys of this place, flower painter. As an artist, though almost self-taught, he ranked high, and has left behind specimens of his superior abilities; his style which was entirely his own, is allowed to be chaste and masterly, all his studies and best pictures are from nature which he closely copied.

53
Portrait, believed to be a self-portrait by William Pegg, the Quaker. It was found together with the loose sketches, when the 1813 sketch-book was discovered. In 1812 Pegg wrote in his journal:

I often walked out for retirement in unfrequented places. During this time (1812) I wore my beard. I was not shaved within the year from the time that I neglected to do it; but it was not altogether neglect, it was intended for a testimony against effeminacy.

Haslem stated:

Pegg's appearance, on his return to his old employment, plainly indicated that he had undergone suffering and privation during his absence. He still wore his beard, and his shopmates, somewhat illnaturedly, perhaps, said it was because he was too poor to pay a barber to shave him. (1813)

54
An interesting sketch by William Pegg, the Quaker, showing his great versatility in flower painting. It might well have served as a sketch for a vase panel. c. 1813. Donated to *Royal Crown Derby Museum* from descendants of *Thomas Martin Randall.*

249

SAMUEL KEYS Was apprenticed to Duesbury in 1785 and proved to be one of the finest gilders of his day, excelling in gold arabesque decoration (colour plate 50 illustrates a vase, *c.* 1810, which bears Keys' number 1 in red). Haslem tells us how Keys' figure decoration in the Dresden style was unsurpassed. He left Derby some years before the close and went to work at Minton's.

SAMUEL KEYS Junior Another son of Samuel Keys Senior, he was a modeller and Haslem lists his models (see page 71). He succeeded Thomas Griffin as foreman of the figure department and stayed there until he left in 1830. Like his brother Edward, he worked for Minton's – the dates, according to Geoffrey Godden, *c.* 1831–42 for Edward and 1830–40s for Samuel Junior. By about 1850 Samuel Junior had joined John Mountford, who claimed to have been the discoverer of Parian body while at Copeland & Garrett's, and these two received an 'honourable mention' for their Parian ware at the 1851 Exhibition. Godden further states that in 1877 Lady Charlotte Schreiber remarked upon 'Poor Mr. Keys, a hearty old man of 72 or 73', whom she had found employed at Peterinck's factory at Tournai.

JOSEPH KIRKLAND Apprenticed under William Smith, Kirkland worked at Nottingham Road for a number of years.

JOHN LAURENCE A repairer whose incised name appeared on one of a pair of figures offered for sale by Sotheby's on 20 May 1969, as Lot 243. Barrett and Thorpe state that Laurence was working for Thomas Turner at Caughley on 11 April 1790 when he wrote to Duesbury at Derby.

CUTHBERT LAWTON Worked at the factory very early in the nineteenth century, and was said to be a landscape painter, and to have executed hunting and figure subjects. However, in the Old Derby Pattern Books he is allocated plate pattern nos 361 and 362, both of which are floral subjects, and 378 – a plate with a central panel of birds in a landscape. The author saw a plate of pattern 378 and was not impressed, and is not yet satisfied about the hunting and figure subjects which Haslem said he painted with 'agreeable freshness'. Perhaps in time a signed plaque or some documented piece may turn up to convince us.

LEONARD LEAD This flower painter was born in 1787, apprenticed about 1800, and worked for over forty years at Derby. His palette is extremely strong and his work is met with possibly more often after 1820 than that of any other flower painter. Mellor stated that both Leonard and John (his brother) worked at Pinxton before returning to Derby. John Lead was believed to have been a gilder. See pattern 392 in the Plate Book.

WILLIAM LONGDON A gilder and painter who was much engaged in painting the Chantilly pattern and who, according to Haslem, was most impressed with himself over this work. During the period 1785–95 it is likely that the gilder's number 8 would be his mark. A son of the same name was apprenticed to Duesbury on 5 July 1790 as a china or earthenware painter.

JOHN LOVEGROVE This man was named in a commitment for breaking his agreement with the proprietors of the Cockpit Hill Pottery in 1758, so Jewitt tells us. A gilder of the same name was apprenticed to William Smith at his enamelling works in a court in St Alkmund's churchyard, and found work at Nottingham Road in 1815. He later worked in London, but returned to Derby where he died in 1873, aged seventy-nine.

WILLIAM LOVEGROVE The son of John Lovegrove, he was a flower and bird painter who served his apprenticeship at the Nottingham Road Works.

DANIEL LUCAS Senior A landscape painter who came from the Davenport Factory about 1820 and became the principal painter of this subject. His painting has an opaque, oily nature and a somewhat dull and monotonous palette. He knew the art, however, of conveying light and shade. (See plates 369 and 377 for examples.) On leaving Derby in 1848 he painted Japan ware in Birmingham, where

251

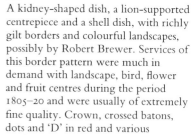

339
A kidney-shaped dish, a lion-supported centrepiece and a shell dish, with richly gilt borders and colourful landscapes, possibly by Robert Brewer. Services of this border pattern were much in demand with landscape, bird, flower and fruit centres during the period 1805–20 and were usually of extremely fine quality. Crown, crossed batons, dots and 'D' in red and various workmen's marks. Robert Bloor & Co. 1815–20. Standard sizes. *Sotheby's, New Bond Street.*

340 ◁ ◁
A pair of flower-sellers standing against tree-stump supports on pink and gilt scroll bases. Imitation Meissen crossed swords. Robert Bloor & Co. 1835. 26 cm. *Royal Crown Derby Museum.*

341
Plate with regimental badge of the 34th Foot Regiment, the King's Royal Border Regiment. The badge is decorated with battle honours won in the Peninsular War, written on the cross. Bloor circular mark. Robert Bloor & Co. 1825–30. 22.9 cm. *Royal Crown Derby Museum.*

337 ◁ ◁
Seated figure of a Turk sitting cross-legged on a cushion. The base is taken from a Chelsea mould and it is possible that the modeller was John Whitaker. Bloor circular mark in red. Robert Bloor & Co. 1825–30. 14 cm. *Victoria & Albert Museum, C1304 – 1919.*

338 ◁
Oval plaque painted and signed by George Hancock, son of John Hancock Senior, who worked with Billingsley at Mansfield and later taught Haslem the art of flower painting. He had worked for many factories before his death in about 1850. Plaque signed. Robert Bloor & Co. *c.* 1820–25. *Sotheby's, New Bond Street.*

342
Figures known as 'The French Shepherd and Shepherdess', decorated in the stronger colours of the period and standing on circular pierced and gilt bases. In the King Street list of 1934, however, they are described as 'English Shepherd and Shepherdess' (*Royal Crown Derby*, p. 34). Female has Bloor circular mark, both have incised number 57. Robert Bloor & Co. 1825–35. 14 cm. *Royal Crown Derby Museum.*

he lived until his death in 1867 in his eightieth year. He had three sons, all of whom were apprenticed at the Nottingham Road Works: John worked at Rockingham until his death in 1833; William excelled as a gilder and later worked for Minton's, but died young; and the third and youngest son – Daniel Junior – followed his father as a landscape painter, worked for Coalport and Copeland's and finally as an outside decorator, assisted by his sons.

McLACKLAN   Haslem stated that McLacklan's landscapes were of a slight character and in monotone, usually black, and Barrett and Thorpe rightly assert that as a consequence all such landscapes seem to be attributed to this painter. It must be pointed out that most of the late eighteenth- and early nineteenth-century landscape painters were known to use monochrome decoration.

M. MASON   Was apprenticed to Duesbury as a painter. He left Derby, so Jewitt informs us, and was engaged by Barr of Worcester in October 1792.

THOMAS MASON   A repairer apprenticed on 2 September 1772 'for four years to Mr Duesbury, at one guinea per week'. Jewitt reports that later on a Thomas Mason was a timekeeper.

GEORGE MELLOR   A gilder and Japan painter, he left Nottingham Road to go to Pinxton in 1796 where he worked under Billingsley until 1799. He later found work at Coalport but left again in 1811 to work in the Potteries, where he remained until his death in 1861, aged eighty-four. He had two sons: George, who had learnt to gild and paint Japans, left Derby in 1828 to work in London as an outside decorator; nothing is known of his other son, but we know that his aunt Sarah was employed at the Derby Works and later had a shop in Victoria Street, Derby, selling earthenware, glass and china. She died in 1873.

JOHN MORLIDGE   A repairer apprenticed for seven years on 21 August 1777.

JOHN MOSCROP   A gilder whose number was 18, and who is mentioned in tea pattern 770.

JESSE MOUNTFORD   Apprenticed at the Nottingham Road Works and became a very useful landscape painter. The Derby City Museum has a cup and saucer attributed to him by John Haslem, from whose collection it was presented. He was, as mentioned in other biographies, one of the painters made redundant by Bloor in 1821. He went to Coalport and later found work at the Davenport Factory, where he died in 1861.

JOHN MOUNTFORD   Jesse and John Mountford's father was one Thomas Mountford who was an enamel kilnman at the Nottingham Road Works and was

343
Large plate or plaque executed by George Mellor, the border of stylized design and the floral group on a shaded ground, signed. This was said to have been done *c.* 1830, or shortly afterwards, when he left the factory. Robert Bloor & Co. 38 cm. *Formerly in the Brayshaw Gilhespy Collection.*

345
Large plate with lime green border upon which are three groups of flowers, scattered flower heads and sprigs, the central landscape painted with a named view by Daniel Lucas Senior. The flower painting has been attributed to Thomas Brentnall but this seems unlikely as he was dismissed before 1825 when the Bloor circular mark was first used (Haslem's collection catalogue). Bloor circular mark. Robert Bloor & Co. 1825–30. 25.3 cm. *City Museum & Art Gallery, Derby.*

344 ◁ ◁
Small circular cabaret teapot and cover with pendant floral decoration. Bloor circular mark. Robert Bloor & Co. 1825. 10 cm. *Royal Crown Derby Museum.*

346 ◁ ◁
Figure of a white horse standing on a colour-washed base. Crown, crossed batons, dots and 'D' and number 52. Robert Bloor & Co. 1820. 10 cm. *Victoria & Albert Museum, C1305 – 1919.*

347
Large plate with gilt dentil edge and three brightly coloured floral sprays, painted in typical manner by Leonard Lead, who worked for many years at the factory. His floral works were somewhat slight but always strongly coloured and gay. Crown, crossed batons, dots and 'D' in red. Robert Bloor & Co. 1815. 25 cm. *Jean Rieger Antiques, London.*

said by Haslem to have a good knowledge of colourmaking. It is not surprising, therefore, to report that John Mountford, while trying to rediscover the old Derby biscuit body, accidentally discovered Parian body at the Copeland Works.

MULLINS Jewitt informs us that this man was engaged by Duesbury to come down from London to paint in enamel on porcelain by the piece. He was stated to have been a figure and landscape painter.

THOMAS PARDOE A flower painter who made his name at the Nantgarw Factory but who had been apprenticed at the Old Nottingham Road Works in the 1780s. No documentary pieces executed at Derby have yet been found.

THOMAS PEGG A gilder at the china works, and a brother of Quaker Pegg.

WILLIAM PEGG One of the finest natural flower painters ever to paint on china, he was born at Whitmore, near Newcastle-under-Lyme, on 10 May 1775. His father was a native of Etwall, near Derby, and worked for some years at Etwall Hall. John Haslem gives the most detailed biography with personal details of the painter's religious feelings which led to him giving up painting in 1801. At the age of ten he was put to work at an earthenware factory and by 1788 began to learn earthenware painting. In 1790 he was apprenticed to china painting, and wrote later:

I then began to turn my thoughts to study of the business. 'The Artist's Repository', in 36 parts, was purchased to assist my studies. I bought prints of various kinds, also colours and other materials for the use of drawing, &c. But I worked fifteen hours at the China business, so I had not much time for study. I improved the little I had. First-day was often made use of for that purpose, and the Meeting House and School neglected. In this manner I spent about four years.

In the autumn of 1796 William Pegg began his first period at the Nottingham Road Works, entering into an agreement with William Duesbury II to work for

348
A shell dish, tureen with cover and stand and a kidney-shaped dish richly gilt with their centres painted with brightly coloured birds by Richard Dodson. Crown, crossed batons and 'D' in red, various workmen's numbers. Robert Bloor & Co. 1815–20. Standard sizes. *Sotheby's, New Bond Street.*

349
A pair of jugs flanking a porter mug, all with typical gilding of the period, with oval panels of birds in landscapes on the jugs and a rectangular landscape panel, perhaps by Robert Brewer, on the mug. The bird panels are probably by Richard Dodson. Crown, crossed batons, dots and 'D'; the mug has the scene named in red. Robert Bloor & Co. 1815–20. Mug 12.8 cm, jugs 15.5 cm. *Sotheby's, New Bond Street.*

255

five years. At this period Pegg's work would normally carry a blue mark if there was a description of the piece painted; but if it was a piece from the patterns allocated to him in the Old Derby Pattern Books – plate patterns 239 and 240, and cup pattern 475 – it would normally carry the puce mark with no description. Plates 258 & 259 show a botanical plate and the Curtis botanical illustration from which the former is freely adapted. These are strongly attributed to Pegg the Quaker, and similar colourings appear in his sketches of the later period. John Haslem records two blue marked pieces in his collection which were painted by Pegg. He wrote in his journal:

About 1799 I was under excercise about fiving up the business of China painting, but I did not effect it till 1801, about the fifth month. About this time it was that I burned all my drawings, Books and all (except a few drawings of flowers)[17] even Watt's Hymns and Psalms I committed to the flames, as I considered them the engines of will-worship. On the 7th. day of the Fifth month, 1801, I left the China Manufactory, and betook myself to the business of making stockings.

Pegg joined the Society of Friends early in 1800. In 1806 he visited London and considered Kensington Gardens well suited for an evening walk. While in London Pegg stayed with an aunt who kept a small public house called The Jolly Sailor on the corner of Little Thomas Street, East Smithfield. Altogether Pegg's quarters were not what he would have wished for, but they were all he could afford.

In his thirty-ninth year he returned to work for Robert Bloor, because, he wrote, he had 'lost the feeling which induced me to give up china painting'. This was in April 1813. He still had a beard and his unkind shopmates ribbed him because they said he could not afford a barber. 'At this time,' he said, 'I again began to study the Art of Painting, and I spent much time in the study of that Art, tho' I had once burnt all my Drawings and Drawing Books. Thus I Built up that which I had once destroyed; but this I suffered for.'

It was a marvellous experience when the author discovered the very book that Pegg had started in July 1813, and which he had signed. Many of these fine sketches

256

350 ◁ ◁
Porter mug of standard shape, the body with elaborate gilding and coloured scrolls, and a rectangular panel depicting a harbour scene, probably by Robert Brewer. Crown, crossed batons, dots and 'D' in red. Robert Bloor & Co. 1811–15. 12.8 cm. *City Museum & Art Gallery, Derby.*

show a wild, erotic abandon, as if he were releasing his pent-up emotions. Some of the sketches illustrated here show great knowledge of plants. It must not be forgotten, however, that Pegg would have painted panels on vases, and indeed a sketch from the loose sketches (discovered at the same time as the 1813 book and presented to the Royal Crown Derby Museum) depicts an arrangement of flowers which might well fill a panel on a vase. There have been many plaques attributed to this painter; one signed one, formerly the property of Martin Abell of the Worcester China Works, was later owned by Lord Kinnaird and subsequently came into the author's possession. This fine work bore a signature that was identical to that in Pegg's letters. The vase of flowers is painted in Van Huysum's manner, but has all the magic of this very remarkable man.

In June 1814 Pegg married Ann Headley of Derby. Eventually, in 1820, he left the china works to run a small huckster's shop. Ann Pegg died there, to the great grief of her husband, in 1847. Pegg himself died there on 27 December 1851, aged seventy-six.

WILLIAM PEGG (the Younger)   This flower painter, who was no relation of Quaker Pegg, was born in 1795 and was apprenticed at the Nottingham Road China Works about 1810; according to Haslem he left about 1819.

W. D. John describes in *William Billingsley*[18] an exhausting journey made by the more famous William (Quaker) Pegg, whom he confuses with William (the Younger). He also writes: 'Mr. Bevington of the china works gave him some temporary lodging, but the part-time wages were but twelve shillings weekly. Pegg commented in a letter to his wife in Derby that the inactivity had however enabled his eyesight to improve considerably.'

I believe that this information is confusing and inaccurate, since, according to Bemrose, William (the Younger) and his wife, Margaret, were friends of Billingsley and decided to join him at Nantgarw: 'He and his wife often used to speak of the long and wearisome pedestrian journey they had to make to reach such a distant and out-of-the-way place.' Bemrose had these facts related to him personally by Pegg the Younger, who presented him with one of his drawings of

352
Dessert plate with typical richly gilt border and central square panel, by Thomas Steel, with canted corners and showing a wicker basket of fruit on a ledge. Crown, crossed batons, dots and 'D' in red with number 36 in red. Robert Bloor & Co. 1815–20. 22 cm. *Mr & Mrs W. H. Mordecai Collection.*

354 ▷ ▷
Coffee can with looped handle, decorated in Sèvres style. The flower painting is in the manner of Leonard Lead. Crown, crossed batons, dots and 'D' in red. Robert Bloor & Co. 1815–20. 8.4 cm to top of loop. *Dr J. Freeman Collection.*

353
A part dessert service with elaborate and richly gilt borders and central rectangular panels, by Thomas Steel, of wicker baskets of fruit on a stone ledge. Crown, crossed batons, dots and 'D' in red with some pieces marked in gold. Robert Bloor & Co. 1815–20. Standard sizes. *Christie, Manson & Woods.*

355
This is perhaps the most famous of all pairs of Derby figures. Originally known as 'Pair Grotesque punches', they were number 227 in Haslem and in the Bemrose list. They probably take their inspiration from the Callot engravings, but it seems likely they were modelled at Derby to commemorate the dwarfs which used to stand outside the Mansion House in London, with advertisements written on their large brimmed hats. Samuel Keys, with his figure painting skill, must have decorated many such dwarfs during his long period at the factory. The original price list gives their cost as 18/-. At Osmaston Road the cost was 90/- in 1878 and today, over one hundred years later, £154. Bloor circular marks. Robert Bloor & Co. c. 1825–30. 17.8 cm. *Sotheby's, New Bond Street.*

356 ▷
Plate with rare claret-ground laid border. This colour was seldom used during the Bloor period and indeed is not often to be seen on Derby Porcelain. The ground has raised and chased gilding. The floral decoration is pendant from inlets on the border, and points to the plate centre. It is interesting to note that two documentary patterns of William Pegg, the Quaker, numbers 239 and 240 in the Old Patterns plate book, have similar floral decoration, but they would have carried the mark of the period in puce. A service of this pattern was in the possession of the Dukes of Argyll at Inverary Castle and in 1817 the Duke and Duchess visited Derby (see chapter 12). Crown, crossed batons, dots and 'D' in red. Robert Bloor & Co. c. 1817. 24.1 cm. *Mrs Sue McKechnie Collection.*

357 ◁
Pair of campana-shaped vases with dark blue ground, richly gilt with large landscape panels, possibly by Lucas Senior. These pairs were in great demand and had flower, fruit, bird and occasionally figure subjects in the panels. The workmanship was of a very high standard until about 1825. Crown, crossed batons, dots and 'D' in red. Robert Bloor & Co. 1820. 32.3 cm. *Christie, Manson & Woods.*

358
Pair of plates with dark blue borders, gilt with a typical design and with the centres emblazoned with the arms of a Welsh family. Crown, crossed batons, dots and 'D' in red. Robert Bloor & Co. 1815. Approx. 25.4 cm. *Christie, Manson & Woods.*

359
A garniture of three vases, known at the factory as 'Long Toms', richly gilt, with continuous bands of fruit and flowers, possibly by Edwin Steele and not by his father Thomas, as normally suggested. Haslem warns that Hopkinson, a late flower painter, was very skilled in painting floral panels on such a set of vases, and that his best work could hardly be distinguished from that of Edwin Steele. Bloor circular marks. Robert Bloor & Co. c. 1825–35. Central vase 75 cm. *Christie, Manson & Woods.*

361 ▷ ▷
A garniture of three shield-shaped vases laid with lime green ground, upon which are groups of natural flowers and circular panels reserved within gilt circles. The landscape panels are named beneath as follows: 'Castle of Stirling'; 'Windsor and town'; 'Malvan Church Worcestershire' [*sic*]. Crown, crossed batons and 'D' in red. Robert Bloor & Co. 1825–30. Central vase approx. 30 cm, flanking pair approx. 23 cm. *Sotheby's, New Bond Street.*

flowers. A quotation from a letter written by Quaker Pegg corroborates the above evidence:

> *Swansea 1817. August 1.*
> *I have recovered my sight considerably since I have been here, and while I have been writing this letter my sight is so fallen off that I can scarcely see the pen with the left eye. Tho I could have seen that eye only when I began to write. I feel in usual health except that my ankles are weak, I have an objection against attempting to work as it would or will probably offend Mr. Bloor, and also if the painters allow the twelve shillings a week they will take that off and do right in so doing . . . .*

Pegg the Younger apparently stayed with Billingsley for several years before leaving to design prints in the Lancashire textile areas. He was, according to Haslem, working for Hoyle's and left to establish a successful business in the same line at Heaton Norris, near Manchester, in the name of Taylor, Hampton & Pegg. Plate 270 shows a portrait photograph of William Pegg taken in a Manchester studio, showing him to be a successful businessman. The porcelain plaque (plate 269) was painted a few years earlier, but regrettably is not signed.[19]

William Pegg the Younger died aged seventy-two in January 1867. Haslem remarks that he painted flowers in his retirement, which were executed with great neatness and taste, and that he retained the talents of his best days.

ROBERT PENNINGTON   A painter mentioned by Jewitt (1775).

JOHN PERKINS   This modeller and ornamental potter is mentioned by Haslem, and he probably started at the factory in 1820. He is recorded as having married at St Werbergh's church, Derby, on 9 May 1825.

360 ▷
Rare Derby vase of quite enormous size, elongated in shape, having dark blue ground richly and typically gilt and painted with a large continuous band of parrots, game birds and waterfowl in brilliant colourings by Richard Dodson. Robert Bloor & Co. 1820–30. 76.5 cm. *Collection of the late Jack Robinson. Phtograph by courtesy of Sotheby's, New Bond Street.*

EDWARD PHILLIPS   Apprenticed 2 September 1772 as a 'China or Porcelain Painter' at 25s weekly. Barrett and Thorpe report that he went to Pinxton in 1798 and that he worked afterwards in the Potteries. He may be the same painter mentioned in tea patterns 615 and 639, which, if Barrett and Thorpe are correct, would mean he had returned from Pinxton by 1805.

JOHN PORTER   Apprenticed on 7 April 1777 as a painter.

WILLIAM PORTER   This potter was at the factory in the days of Duesbury I and was said by Haslem to have been at Nottingham Road since 1756. He was foreman of the useful wares department from about 1818 until his death in 1822.

362
Rare standing monkey musician, well modelled and
supported by a tree-stump, dressed in a blue coat with gilt
pattern and a finely painted waistcoat. Bloor circular mark.
Robert Bloor & Co. 1825. 17.5 cm. *Susan Becker
Antiques, London. Royal Crown Derby Museum.*

HENRY LARK PRATT This landscape painter was apprenticed during the second quarter of the nineteenth century, and was much inspired by Daniel Lucas Senior, although his palette is rather softer. In a newspaper advertisement he styled himself:

HENRY L. PRATT,

LANDSCAPE AND ANIMAL PAINTER.

Paintings carefully cleaned and repaired.

8, LARGES STREET, FRIAR GATE, DERBY.

363
Rare unidentified figure of a short stocky man with a stick, carrying his hat under his arm. He has a green coat, fancy waistcoat and yellow breeches. The modelling would certainly seem to have been the work of François Hardenberg. The figure on the right is John Liston in the role of Paul Pry, modelled by Samuel Keys Junior. Robert Bloor & Co. 1820. Man 11 cm, Paul Pry 12.7 cm. *Man: collection of Mr & Mrs Temperton. Paul Pry: David John Ceramics, Woodstock.*

Pratt's obituary, which appeared in the *Staffordshire Sentinel* on 8 March 1873, said that he left Derby in 1830, firstly to work for Minton's. In 1844–5 he was employed by Chapman & Hall, a firm of London publishers, in making sketches of baronial halls in Staffordshire, Cheshire and Derbyshire. He received commissions from the nobility, and indeed enjoyed the patronage of Queen Victoria, 'who was pleased to purchase a tête déjeuner service, on which were views of Windsor Castle, Balmoral, &c'. The obituary described Pratt's achievements as a painter in oils and mentioned that many noblemen and gentlemen of the Midland counties had bought his paintings to hang in their private picture galleries.

Wallis records that Pratt's son, also Henry, worked at Coalport and that he (Wallis) possessed a teapot painted by him about 1860, and inscribed 'View of Stafenhill Ferry, near Burton-on-Trent'. This son died at Derby in January 1914, aged seventy-four.

EDWARD PRINCE This landscape painter was a late apprentice and was at the Derby Works until its closure in 1848. Haslem tells us that Prince worked in London after this and states in 1875: 'For more than the last twenty years he has been engaged at glass painting at Messrs. Wales's establishment, Newcastle-upon-Tyne.' The author feels that this statement is inaccurate, since quite a few King Street pieces carry Prince's signature together with the mark first used in 1863. One of these plates, signed and painted with a Matlock view, is in the Royal Crown Derby Museum. (See *Royal Crown Derby*, page 208.)

364
Plaque depicting the gypsy fortune teller, after Reynolds, painted by William Corden and signed and dated 1848 on the reverse. *Ronald Raven Collection.*

THOMAS MARTIN RANDALL Born at Broseley, near Coalport, Shropshire, in 1786, and, like his elder brothers Edward and William, was apprenticed at the Caughley Works. T. M. Randall's dates of apprenticeship are stated by W. D. John in his *Nantgarw Porcelain* to have been 1800–3, which was about the time of the merger with the Coalport Works; Randall is also recorded as having been apprenticed as a gilder. Jewitt informs us that he moved to Derby, where, he reports, 'He remained for some time, and became the friend of two of their famed painters, Phillip Cleve [Cleavey or Clavey] and William Pegg.' It was from Pegg that Randall was to receive the 1813 Sketch Book on Pegg's retirement in 1820. One reason – and a strong one – for their lasting relationship was the fact that both were devout Quakers.

The T. M. Randall sketches lead us to consider an interesting and very fascinating possibility: in the Mary Field Collection – the most representative and important collection of the blue- and puce-marked period – is a coffee can readily attributable to him. Its date is between 1796 and 1800 and the gilding is the work of Thomas Soar. Is it possible that Randall could have arrived at Derby and executed this work at the tender age of, say, twelve or fourteen? There certainly are precedents, since William Pegg was working at an earthenware factory when he was only ten, and by the age of fifteen was working for fifteen hours a day!

Jewitt informs us that in 1813 he left Derby for London, where, together with Richard Robins from Pinxton, he set up an enamelling business known as Robins & Randall. It was here in Barnsbury Street, Spa Fields, Islington, where Thomas Hughes had formerly worked, that much French china, Nantgarw and Swansea was decorated for London retailers such as Mortlock's, Baldock & Jarman, and Bradley & Co. Randall was stated to have been related to the Bradleys by marriage.

The discovery of the Randall sketches should help in establishing pieces decorated at Islington. As can be seen from the illustrations, he painted exotic and naturalistic birds, fine landscapes, and quite excellent figure subjects including cupids, floral and shell compositions; and, as we have already been told, he had been apprenticed as a gilder. Amongst others who were employed at Islington was another fine Derby flower painter, Moses Webster. Much work previously attributed to other talented London enamellers, such as James Plant, must now be reconsidered in the light of these new finds.

In 1825 Randall dissolved his partnership with Robins and went to Madeley in Shropshire, where Jewitt informs us that he used a box kiln with charcoal, but afterwards built an enamelling kiln which was wood-fired. In the early days much lightly decorated Sèvres porcelain was cleared with acid and redecorated. One of these plates, obtained from Randall's descendants, had retained the original mark and also the signature 'nq' for Niquet (a flower painter, 1764–92). This piece had been completely redecorated by Randall with border panels of exotic birds and a central fruit and floral composition, and this central painting underlines Randall's influence over both his nephew John and William Cook, who worked at Madeley and whose style was very similar. Perhaps it was Randall's strict Quaker morals which prevented this 'bastard' plate from ever being marketed. Randall is said to have later produced a soft-paste porcelain as fine as Nantgarw and the nearest to old Sèvres.

The Madeley Works closed in 1840 and Randall moved to Shelton, Staffordshire, where he continued to decorate fine-quality wares. These so impressed Herbert Minton that he tried to persuade Randall to join his firm, but to no avail, since Randall soon afterwards retired from business and went to live at Barlaston, near Trentham.

It was during these later years of his life that he met a fellow Quaker, Louisa West, whose second husband he became. He died in 1859 and was buried, according to Jewitt, 'in a spot he had chosen for himself'.

RICHARD ROBERTS   A Chelsea workman who had been a soldier and was a pensioner at the Royal Hospital in Chelsea. According to Jewitt he was allowed 'occasional furlough to paint at Derby'. Duesbury wanted him to stay permanently. Jewitt quotes the order concerning Roberts' work:

> *By Order of Sir George Howard, K.B., General of His Majesty's Forces, and Governor of the Royal Hospital at Chelsea. Permit the Bearer, Richard Roberts, a pensioner in the above-said Hospital to pass from hence to Darby in Darbyshire, for the space of Two Months from the Date hereof, and then to return to the above-said Hospital. He behaving as becomeith. Given under my hand this first Day of Decr, 1791.*
>
> *   L. Grant, Adjt.*

GEORGE ROBERTSON   According to unpublished material by Alfred Wallis in the author's possession, Robertson, born in 1777, came from Ayrshire (though Tapp states London), and settled in Derby about 1797. On 15 April 1798 he married Ann Yates, daughter of the painter and gilder John Yates. Sarah Yates and Minshull Birchall acted as witnesses. In 1801 Sarah married John Wallis, so linking the two families. Wallis tells how he remembered Robertson's widow, and explains that their son James was his father's cousin; the widow lived in St Alkmund's churchyard.

George Robertson was certainly one of the finest landscape and marine painters to have worked in ceramics. Many of his sketches have survived and one in the author's possession gives details for a south-east view of Dovedale and on the reverse Thorp Cloud, a well-loved Derbyshire landmark. Rather as in the case of McLacklan, to whom all monochrome paintings tend to be attributed, anything resembling autumnal tints seems automatically to be attributed to Robertson. Plate pattern numbers 222, 245 and 254 are all coloured shipping by Robertson, and teacup patterns 406, 416, 417 and 418 are all 'landskips' allocated to him. His work shows meticulous attention to detail and a fine sense of colour.

He later set himself up as a drawing master, but was admitted to the Nottingham County Asylum on 7 September 1830 and died there on 8 January 1833.[20] Haslem tells how, shortly before Robertson left the Derby Works, he executed two large oil paintings – one showed the Nottingham Road frontage, and the other showed the Large Warehouse with its numerous windows, and other buildings. These paintings were intended for the Old Bond Street showrooms and indeed hung on

365
Bloor group originally modelled by Spängler and known as 'Belisarius and Daughter' (no. 370), elaborately decorated and standing on a circular base, gilt with a broad band. Bloor mark. Robert Bloor & Co. 1825. Approx. 20.3 cm. *Formerly in John Twitchett's Collection.*

366
Exceedingly rare pair of Bloor musicians copied from the Chelsea red anchor period originals. The Chelsea female version is illustrated in Severne Mackenna's *Chelsea Porcelain, The Red Anchor Wares*, plate 147. It would seem that the original source was the Meissen factory, especially as the male has a Kändler-style face. Crown over Derby in red, number 32 also in red. Robert Bloor & Co. 1825. 16.5 cm. *Royal Crown Derby Museum.*

368
Pair of vases of extremely rare shape, being groundlaid in lime green and having highly burnished sea-horse handles with pierced and shaped necks. The landscape painting is by Daniel Lucas Senior. Bloor circular marks. Robert Bloor & Co. 1825–35. Approx. 21 cm. *David John Ceramics, Woodstock.*

the walls there for some years before being relegated to the cellar, where they rotted.

ROBINSON   Listed by Jewitt as a landscape painter.

JONATHAN ROSE   According to Jewitt this painter came to Derby from London in 1780, and was employed for some time.

JOHN CHARLES ROSSI, RA   This well-known sculptor modelled for Duesbury. Lygo wrote in a letter to Duesbury in 1788: 'The figure Mr. Rossi is modelling is a female sacrifice figure from a drawing Mr. Vulliamy gave from one of his books and he suggests a male figure to match.' According to Gilhespy the Lygo letters shed much new light on Rossi, because of the clockmaker Vulliamy's request for his cherubs and other small figures. Gilhespy states, too, that Rossi fashioned other figures: the Burning of Cato, Anatomy, Bas Relief of the Philistines, Salamis and Aphrodite, Aesculapius, and Hygea. Rossi also did work for the Misses Coade of Coade's Artificial Stone Works, Lambeth.

JAMES ROUSE Senior   Rouse Senior was the only painter to have worked at all three of the Derby factories. He was apprenticed at Nottingham Road about 1815, and Haslem informs us that he worked in the same room as Pegg the Quaker, Robertson, Cotton and Corden, among others. Haslem used to relate how kind 'the Quaker' was to him and the other apprentices; when work was over Pegg would invite them to his home for tuition in painting, and in return was happy to accept their sketches. A detailed biography of Rouse is given in *Royal Crown Derby* (page 209), and tells of his movements after he left the Nottingham Road Factory in about 1826. In later years Rouse signed much of his work, whether for a specific factory or as an outside decorator, and at times it is difficult to attribute some of the plaques which are merely signed 'J. Rouse', as one of his sons, who painted similar subjects, did not always use 'Junior' after his signature.

James Rouse Senior died when he had almost completed the floral reserves on the celebrated Gladstone service, in February 1888. He had a long and distinguished career, and was certainly one of the most versatile painters that Derby ever produced; his subjects ranged through flowers, fruit, figures, landscapes, sporting subjects and indeed anything that was required.

SARTINE   Jewitt tells us that Vulliamy, the distinguished clockmaker, recommended this modeller to Duesbury, who employed him to make models in 1790.

HENRY SHARPE   A late apprentice at the Nottingham Road Works, who after the closure in 1848 worked for Wales' Glassworks in Newcastle-upon-Tyne. He later went to New York where, Haslem says, he established a very important factory manufacturing painted windows for churches and other public buildings.

SHEPHERDSON   This gilder appears against Plate pattern 328, which was described in the books as 'New French pattern, done by Bancroft and Taylor Junior, and gilt by Shepherdson'.

THOMAS SIMES (or SIMS)   According to Jewitt this painter was apprenticed to Duesbury from the age of eleven to twenty-one. He absconded in 1792 and a warrant was endorsed for the county of Stafford. He might well have been related to the Sims mentioned below.

MUNDY SIMPSON   It appears that this gilder and Japan painter worked for a considerable time at the very beginning of the nineteenth century. He is allocated the number 19 as a gilder in the red-marked period. But, as previously mentioned, numbers were probably reallocated to others when workmen left the factory, and if the men returned – as did Moses Webster – a new number would probably be allocated to them. In modern times, both at the King Street and Osmaston Road Factories, this traditional practice has been continued. This would mean that the original list given by Jewitt should really only apply to the period 1785–95, when certainly the numbers and their factory marks (usually painted by the gilders) are

367
Rare screw-topped armorial toilet pot laid with rich blue ground, the box gilt with *oeil de perdrix* and the border of the cover with another carefully executed gilt motif. This piece refutes the claim that nothing good was made after 1830, although there was a gradual decline in general standards after the indisposition of Bloor forced the family to appoint Thomason to act as manager. Printed crown over the ribbon mark. Robert Bloor & Co. 1840. Diameter 8 cm. *Royal Crown Derby Museum.*

found to tally. After all, their work is really handwriting and would obviously show different characteristics. Sue McKechnie, well known for her knowledge of silhouettes, carried out much valuable work in this area some years ago. The red mark list given by John Haslem as being *c.* 1820 must be carefully used, since the number of painters and gilders would have grown, and the author believes that at one stage they were numbered through the list and certainly reached the nineties, because he found this on a fine coffee can, painted in about 1820. On the cup '33' in red is (for Thomas Till) just discernible, with '19' in red on the saucer for Mundy Simpson. Research has shown that the accompanying puce numbers must refer to the flower painter. This can has '65' in puce, which is the number on one of the Derby City Museum's Moses Webster plates, and the saucer bears '80' in puce. Using Sue McKechnie's research results to compare the two gilders' marks, we find they are similar, indeed identical to other pieces manufactured at about the time Haslem's list is given. Although it is sad to see yet another theory passing, it is important to state that at least it is known that the numbers which appear in puce and sometimes yellow, green or other colours refer to the floral painters, and the red numbers certainly apply to the gilders. Blue numbers or marks refer normally to the groundlayers.

Two of Mundy Simpson's sons were apprenticed at Derby. John, the eldest, left Derby about 1836 to work for Minton's where he proved to be a fine figure-subject painter. In 1847 he left Stoke for London to take charge of painting classes at Marlborough House. He worked on metal as well as porcelain, and received considerable patronage from Queen Victoria. He exhibited at the Royal Academy. There is no information about the career of the other son.

SIMS A painter who worked at Nottingham Road but left in the late eighteenth century to start his own decorating studio in Pimlico, London. Zachariah Boreman worked for him, as did James Turner, another Derby flower painter. A good deal of Welsh porcelain from Nantgarw was used by Sims.

JOSEPH SLATER Apprenticed at the Derby Works, he was a good heraldic painter and first-class gilder. After the works closed in 1848 he left Derby to work in Staffordshire. According to Haslem he worked at Minton's and was foreman of the paintresses and majolica hands between 1856 and 1875, but left to take charge of the enamelling department at another works in Longton. He had four sons: William (not to be confused with the two William Slaters mentioned below) started his career at Derby, but later worked as a fine painter for Minton's; Albert and John also worked for Minton's; and the fourth son, George, was working for Minton's in 1875.

WILLIAM SLATER This painter was apprenticed at Pinxton and, apart from a period working for Robins & Randall after the Pinxton Factory closed in 1813, he worked at Nottingham Road until 1848. He was versatile and painted insects, fruit and armorial bearings but also excelled as a fine gilder and gold chaser. Shortly after the Nottingham Road Works closed he went to the Davenport Factory, where he remained until his death in 1867, at the age of seventy-three.

CONSTANTINE SMITH Jewitt tells us that Constantine Smith was considered to be one of the best hands at Nottingham Road. He was a preparer of colours and a china painter and gilder. It is now believed that bright on-glaze blue known as 'Smith's blue' was Constantine's discovery rather than that of his son William. An outside decorating establishment was set up by Constantine, and a teapot signed in the cover 'Smith enammeller Derby', dated *c.* 1785, in the Royal Crown Derby Museum, provides interesting documentation.

Constantine was recorded, with another Derby man George Holmes, as a ratepayer in Clerkenwell in 1746 and 1747. Both probably joined the Derby Works late in 1747, and had possibly already met Andrew Planché whilst working for Thomas Hughes. Tapp further suggests that, like so many other early ceramic workers, they might well have been taught their trade by Thomas Hughes, possibly 'the father of the outside English china decorators'. Certainly there is much truth in his suggestions, since Planché would almost certainly have known of Thomas Hughes and his decorating establishments, even if he did not have first-hand experience of them.

59
Carmine Sweet William.

60
Oriental Poppy.

61
Turnip Raddishes, etc.

62
Rose.

(See also page 250.)

63 ◁ ◁

Dessert dish painted by William Pegg, the Quaker, with crown imperial, double red-hepatica and cuckoo-bud. Exhibited at the 'Quaker Pegg' exhibition held at 37 Bury Street, St James's, London, November 1977 (No. 26). Crown, crossed batons, dots and 'D' in red. *c.* 1813–15. 30.5 cm. *Albert Amor Limited.*

64

Dessert plate painted by William Pegg, the Quaker, with lilium martagon and purple-cupt thrift. Exhibited at the 'Quaker Pegg' exhibition staged by Albert Amor, London 1977 (No. 19). Crown, crossed batons, dots and 'D' in red, gilder's number 2 for James Clark. *c.* 1813–15. 22.1 cm. *Albert Amor Limited.*

65

Shell-shaped dish boldly painted with 'Ladies Thistle' by William Pegg, the Quaker. It is remarkable that another 'Thistle Dish' should come to light after so many years; see colour plate 41 for the documentary dish, painted with almost an identical subject by Pegg and described by him to John Haslem. Crown, crossed batons, dots and 'D' with description in red. Robert Bloor & Co. 1813–15. Diameter 23.3 cm. *Royal Crown Derby Museum.*

JOSEPH SMITH   Listed by Jewitt as a landscape painter. He is reported – again by Jewitt – to have received 7s per dozen for painting tea pattern 115 in 1792.

WILLIAM SMITH   William was apprenticed to his father, Constantine Smith, on 28 October 1773, as Barrett and Thorpe reveal,[21] 'in the same art or mistery of preparing colours, painting and enamelling Porcelain'. They make the very plausible statement that, as the indenture has survived with the Duesbury papers, it is evident that Duesbury took it over. William Smith used number 9 from the late eighteenth-century list of gilders.

THOMAS SOAR   Samuel Keys' notes on the history of the factory inform us that Soar was the principal painter in gold. During the period 1785–95 he would have used his numeral 1, which invariably appears at about five minutes past one on the foot rims of pieces gilt by him. His mark can be traced even to the 'crown over D' period, but his number would not have been used before the crossed batons were added. On 10 April 1810 he solicited the nobility, gentry and public at large for enamelling work. His advertisement from the *Derby Mercury* also stated that: 'His long experience in the Derby Porcelain Manufactory encourages him to look with confidence for support, which it will be his study to deserve and his pride to acknowledge. N.B. – Ladies instructed to Paint China at their own Apartments, on liberal terms.' At this time he lived in Navigation Row, near St Mary's bridge, Derby. As the advertisement also mentioned heraldic work we may well assume that a good deal of the late eighteenth-century work in this manner would have been executed by him. He was obviously highly respected, since in 1815 he was appointed Governor of the Poor in the parish of St Alkmund's.

THOMAS SOUTHALL   Apprenticed on Christmas Day 1772 for seven years as a china painter.

JEAN-JACQUES SPÄNGLER   This modeller's father was one of the chief men at the German Höchst Factory before going to Switzerland, where he became director of the Zürich Works. In his book *Zürcher Porzellan* S. Ducret gives details of the Spängler family and illustrates a pair of 1790 Derby figures, wrongly attributed to Chelsea, and captioned in English 'The Dead Bird'.[22] A very similar group to The Virgins Awakening Cupid is also illustrated,[23] but this time it is a Zürich model by Spängler, called *Schlafender Amor* and dated *c.* 1755–80. Both pieces are biscuit porcelain.

Jewitt gives much information regarding this rather troublesome modeller who caused Duesbury II much annoyance. He originally arrived in Derby in 1790 on the recommendation of Mr Vulliamy and not, as Wallis stated, on Michael Kean's instigation. The witnesses to the first agreement, dated 13 July, confirm this:

London July 13, 1790

A MEMORANDUM

That the Bearer, Mr. J. Spängler, has agreed to come down to the Manufactory at Derby, to work as a Modeller, &c., and to receive for the first month at the rate of three Guineas per week, and his expenses paid down by Coach. His hours of work to be from Seven o'clock in the morning till the rest of the People in the Manufactory give Over work in the Evening. It is further agreed on, that after the expiration of the first Month, if the parties like each other and they agree for a fixed time to come, The bearer, Mr. J. Spängler, is then only to receive after the rate of two pounds ten shillings per week from the first day he began to work in the manufactory.

Witness:	(signed)	For Mr. W. Duesbury
B. VULLIAMY.	J. SPÄNGLER.	J. LYGO.

Spängler was not unlike Banford in causing problems to his employer, and after getting into debt, and showing 'inattention to work' and being guilty of breach of contract he absconded in 1792. He was caught at Ramsgate and placed in the King's Bench Prison. After signing a very restrictive contract a friend of Spängler bailed him out so that he could complete the new contract, but by November the same year he had left again. The friend who had bailed Spängler out wrote Duesbury a

369
Oval dish with gadroon-edged border, blue band with stylized gilding and central landscape of Warwick Castle by Daniel Lucas Senior. Bloor circular mark and named description in red. Robert Bloor & Co. 1825. Length 28 cm. *Royal Crown Derby Museum.*

370
Small basket with gadroon edge, canted corners and double twig handles. The border is in pale blue and the landscape attributed to Edward Prince. Crown over Gothic 'D'. Robert Bloor & Co. 1835–40. Length 13 cm. *Royal Crown Derby Museum.*

371
Garniture of three bough pots and pierced covers, painted with rectangular panels of river landscapes. Robert Bloor & Co. 1825–30. Central pot approx. 13 cm. *Christie, Manson & Woods.*

372
Very rare pair of Bloor Derby
candlesticks of rococo design. Robert
Bloor & Co. 1825–30. Approx. 23 cm.
Christie, Manson & Woods.

373
Dessert plate, from the service made for
John, 16th Earl of Shrewsbury, with
dark green ground and fruit painting
on the borders by Thomas Steel, also
gilt butterflies and moths. The cavetto
is gilt and the central crest is that of the
Earls of Shrewsbury. Bloor circular
mark. Robert Bloor & Co. *c.* 1825–30.
17.8 cm. *David John Ceramics,
Woostock.*

most amusing and revealing letter which Jewitt was – understandably – unable to resist quoting:

Sir, – I received your favour of the 24th Inst only this day, in Answer I shall tell you that on the 7th. Inst I wrote to Spängler to know from him whether he had settled with you that I might know whether I was discharged from my bail, he answered me by the ninth that he was working indefatigably to bring under the pretended debt (as he call'd it) and that he was allowed out of his weekly wages barely to maintain himself upon this I thought he would continue to work 'till he had complately discharged your debt. But how great was my astonishment when last Saturday sen'night I saw him arrive, in the most pity full condition. I asked him immediately what brought him hither, and whether he had settled with you and cleared me of my responsibility, I recd no answer, but that nobody would ever ask me anything and that you owed him money; without saying any thing more he sate down to dinner with me, and after dinner he went up into my room to shave himself and dress his hair; a little while after my servant going up to make my bed found him in it she told him he could not remain in the house, all the rooms being engaged, he begged to be left to take a little rest (being very ill) and he would rise again. I good naturedly never intended to disturb him, and thought him really asleep in my room! 'till 11 o'clock when I went up to take a few things I wanted I found he was gone and on looking round I missed several things which he has made free with to the amt. of £4. 4s. Notwithstanding this I think he is still in London or its vicinity and that he will have the impudence enough to call on me or write: However I giveup everythought of making any good of him. Therefor must beg you to dispose to the best advantage of those things he left in yr possession, and to let me know what further sum is coming to you, without any more law proceedings. when I know your demand I shall endeavour to settle it with Mr. Lygo to whom you may give orders for the purpose I remain Sir Yr most obedt. Hble sevt H.

> *HURTER*

London 28th. Novr. 1792.

Spängler was very soon in prison again, and wrote a pathetic letter, in French as always, to William Duesbury. In 1794 it was agreed that he should work for Duesbury in London at Chelsea, where he was then living. Jewitt quotes from another letter dated 3 February 1795: 'Spängler will set off for Derby tomorrow, he intends walking it as it will not be so expensive and he may as well be walking to Derby as stay here doing nothing.' How long he remained at Derby is not certain, but after Duesbury's death he may not have found a relationship with Michael Kean compatible and probably he returned to the Continent.

JOSEPH STABLES Another fine gilder who worked for a long period at the factory. During the period 1785–95 he used the numeral 2 which invariably appeared at half past six on the foot rim. This loyal workman later rose to act as manager when Duesbury was away; one letter recorded by Barrett and Thorpe, written in September 1788, concerned several matters relevant to the running of the factory at Derby. Stables talks of a visitor to the factory: 'I fancy is a Lord . . . The supposed Lord seems to be a French man and says that the set of China should have a socket [in] the saucer to hold the cup fast and that the French China is [?] are all made so.' This type of saucer is still produced by Royal Crown Derby today and is called *trembleuse*.

JOHN STANESBY Born in March 1786, he was apprenticed at the Nottingham Road Works as a flower painter at an early age, and particularly excelled in painting roses. He was allocated tea pattern 599.

About 1808 he left for London where he executed some fine china painting and also, according to Haslem, worked extensively on glass. He subsequently took up portraiture, and was an occasional exhibitor at the Royal Academy. He returned to Derby in 1825. In 1832 he again went to London, where his children won many prizes awarded by the Society of Arts. He died on 18 December 1864, in his seventy-ninth year.

374
Circular plaque painted by John Lucas at the age of eleven, with a view of Rivaulx Abbey in Yorkshire. Haslem tells us that John, the eldest son of Daniel Lucas, learned the art of landscape painting but shortly after his apprenticeship left to work at Rockingham (Swinton) until his death in 1833. *c.* 1821. *City Museum & Art Gallery, Derby.*

375 ▷ ▷
Soup plate from the celebrated 'Trotter' service. The service was made for Mr John Trotter, of Dyrham Park near Barnet in Hertfordshire, and his name and residence is inscribed upon the rear of each piece together with the Derby mark, all in gold. The illustrated plate is painted by Moses Webster, presumably in about 1815 before he left Derby for London, or after he returned in about 1820. It would seen that the date lies between 1820–25 (Haslem's collection catalogue). A good deal of this pattern was done at the factory but whether it was made before Mr Trotter ordered his service or not is uncertain, especially as much of this pattern carries the red crown, crossed batons and 'D' mark, and the actual service carries a special gold mark. Robert Bloor & Co. 1820–25. 24.5 cm. *Royal Crown Derby Museum.*

376
Rare pair of large covered urns, with rich gilding and large continuous bands of flowers on the main body and covers, painted in the manner of William Pegg, the Quaker. Crown, crossed batons, dots and 'D' in red. Robert Bloor & Co. *c.* 1820. Approx. 36.5 cm. *Sotheby's, New Bond Street.*

377
Damaged plaque painted with a view of Spencer House in Regent's Park, London, by Daniel Lucas in his heavy style but illustrating good use of light and shade. During the Bloor period the Earl Spencer commissioned pieces to be painted with views of his London estate. As early as 1789 Lady Spencer had ordered items for Althorpe, Northants, some of which were painted with the cypher 'L.S.' (Lygo's letters). Green ground seemed prevalent. Robert Bloor & Co. *c.* 1820. *City Museum & Art Gallery, Derby.*

378
Dessert plate from the Earl Ferrers service, with the gadroon-edged border laid with blue ground and stylized gilding, reserved upon which are four panels, three containing flowers and the fourth the coat of arms of the Ferrers family. A larger grouping of flowers fills the centre of the plate. The armorial bearings and flower painting is believed to be by John Hancock Junior who was, according to Haslem, very proficient in these arts. Bloor circular mark. Robert Bloor & Co. 1825–30. 20.2 cm. *Private collection.*

THOMAS STEEL   This fine painter was born in 1772 and came from the Potteries to the Nottingham Road Works about 1815. His fruit painting is fresh and natural and much sought after by collectors. He decorated numerous dessert services with fruit arrangements on marble slabs, and gave them elaborate gilt arabesque borders. To boost his financial status he painted large numbers of plaques, some of which he signed. Two of these plaques were sold in Phillips' saleroom on 29 January 1975; one was dated 1838, signed, and gave his age as sixty-six, and the other was dated 1846. They measured $10\frac{3}{4} \times 11\frac{5}{8}$ ins.

It would seem that Steel worked with his son Edwin at the Rockingham Works some time after 1826, but by about 1832 he was working at Minton's, where many patterns were allocated to him. He died in Stoke-on-Trent in 1850, aged seventy-nine.

EDWIN STEELE[24]   With his brothers Horatio and Thomas Junior, Edwin was apprenticed at the Nottingham Road Works. Edwin, the eldest, worked at the Rockingham Factory, but later returned to the Potteries where, according to Haslem, he worked for Minton's and some other works. A very good flower painter, he died in 1871 at the age of sixty-eight.

HORATIO STEELE   A clever flower painter who remained at the Derby Works until its closure in 1848. During the early 1840s he was largely responsible for the flower, bird and insect panels in the service produced for Queen Victoria. During Christmas week, 1842, the service was exhibited at the showrooms in Bond Street (see plate 396).

THOMAS STEELE Junior   A landscape painter who, like his brothers Edwin and Horatio, was apprenticed at Derby. He died young, at Coalport.

PIERRE STEPHAN   Like Spängler, Stephan was a French-speaking Swiss; his first documented agreement with Duesbury is signed and dated 17 September 1770, and he agreed to model and repair china or porcelain ware for three years, for £2 12s 6d weekly. A letter to Josiah Wedgwood, in the Wedgwood Museum Archives, shows that he worked at the porcelain factory at Wirksworth, which was sold up in 1777.

> *Sir,*
> *I was informed some time agoe by sevral persons (particularly by Mr. Gardiner of Derby the Architect) that you gave great encouragement to Artists in the Modelling branch, at which time I was then Engagd with Mr. Duesbury of Derby, and since then with the China Factory at Wirksworth both which I am now disengagd from and have some thoughts of goeing to London, but first take the Liberty of informing you that if I could meet with agreeable Employment and that encouragement my work may deserve I should be glad to have an opportunity of being Employd by persons of taste and Merrit which I hear is the Character of your Manufactory but at the same time should chuse to have some part of my Employment in London on account of haveing a greater opportunity of improveing my Ideas in the Art of Modelling; but hope you will be so kind as to favor me with a line as soon as possible I shall leave this place in a fortnight or three weeks at the farthest which will much oblige Your Most Obedt Hble servt*
>
> *Wirksworth, 9th. May 1774.   P: Stephan.*
>
> *P.S. please to direct for me at the Post office in Wirksworth.*
> *N.B. I work in Figures, Vasses, or any sort of Useful as Business may require.*

He may well have acted as a freelance either before or after he joined Wedgwood. There is a Wedgwood basalt figure impressed 'Stephan' at Kedleston Hall in Derbyshire. He certainly worked for Champion's Bristol Factory. He did not have the brilliance of Spängler but was a more stable workman. Jewitt tells us that he was at Shelton in 1795 and that while there he modelled for Duesbury. Later he settled in Coalport where his descendants worked, and some still live today.

A grandson (William) is reported in *Royal Crown Derby*[25] as having entered into an agreement on 30 August 1876, to act for two years as 'Designer and Artificer for

Pottery Models and Shapes'. William Stephan had worked for Sampson Hancock at the King Street Factory.

THOMAS STRONG   Described as a 'china painter' when he married at All Saints' Church, Derby, on 22 December 1765.

TALKINGTON   Another gilder whose name is on pattern 310 in the Plate Book. He was using a 7 in the list given by Haslem, who then spelt his name 'Torkington'.

JOSEPH TATLOW   With his brother Thomas he was apprenticed at the Derby Works at the end of the eighteenth century. Joseph excelled in arabesque borders and was at Pinxton and Mansfield with Billingsley. He later worked for outside decorators in London.

THOMAS TATLOW   Haslem states that Tatlow was a clever painter of flowers, shells, etc, and that he painted in oils. A service with gold arabesque borders and named fish centres may be by him. Like so many of his contemporaries he was an expert angler. He kept the Seven Stars public house on the north side of St Mary's Bridge, and Haslem tells us that there was a popular bowling green here; on the green was a summer-house, the inside wall of which was painted with a view of Darley Grove by William Corden. The *Derby Mercury* recorded Tatlow's marriage to a Miss Simms on 19 November 1812 – 'both of this place'.

WILLIAM TAYLOR   Appears in the late eighteenth-century list of gilders, where he was given the number 11. He later painted arabesque and Indian patterns. Jewitt tells us that he decorated the centres of a service of plates for a Mr Digby in 1784. See Lygo's letters of 1791 for comment. A painter, Taylor Junior, was responsible for tea pattern 695.

THOMAS TILL   During the red mark period this fine gilder used the numeral 33 on the foot rim of the pieces which he gilt. He was not a native of Derby but possibly worked there between 1815 and 1825. Geoffrey Godden suggests that by 1831 a gilder of the same name was at Minton's, and it is likely, but not certain, that this was the same man.

S. J. or L. VIDAL[26]   A painter of floral subjects who exhibited in London at the Royal Academy from 1790 to 1792. Jewitt lists a painter of this name, who from August 1793 until May 1795 was living at 1 Grosvenor Row, near the Bun-house, Chelsea. In 1795 he arranged to leave London for Derby 'for six months every year from June to January'. He had previously sent samples of his flower painting and had told Duesbury that he had not painted on china in Britain, but that he wished to show him that he was master of the employment, 'having painted for about eleven years in the Porcelaine line &c'.

JAMES WANTLING   The son of a potter, he was brought up by his widowed mother, a native of Derby. He was apprenticed to Robert Bloor and was very soon noticed for his good health, strength and swiftness. At the age of sixteen he was recognized as a runner of great ability and on one occasion during his lunch break he took on a man called Shaw, who was held in high esteem in his native Staffordshire. Before the race Wantling pointed to a mole on the back of his neck and told his opponent that he would have a good view of it at the winning post. This prediction proved correct since Wantling won with ease. He was said to have run 100 yards in nine seconds, 200 in nineteen seconds and 300 in thirty seconds. He soon became champion of Derbyshire and Nottinghamshire. On his return race with Shaw he was heavily backed and again won easily, this time at Lane End, Staffordshire. He later took on Beddor of West Bromwich and again won three challenges with great ease. His trainer, a Mr Finney of Hanley, had brought him through all his early years.

In 1825 he went to London and on 31 January that year took on a wager to go over five Thames bridges in thirty-five minutes. The wager had often been attempted, without success, but in the presence of a large crowd James started from the Surrey side of Vauxhall Bridge, crossed Westminster Bridge, went up the steps

66
A fine flower piece painted and signed by William Pegg, the Quaker. The painting still shows very much the Dutch style of painting and in particular that of Van Hysum. *c. 1815. Martin Abell. Lord Kinnaird. Elizabeth and Caroline Twitchett. Now in a private collection.*

67 ▷ ▷
Campana-shaped vase with snake handles, part of a garniture of three, painted with panoramic hunting views outside Derby by William Cotton. Note the shot-tower and All Saints in the background. Crown, crossed batons, dots and 'D' in red. Robert Bloor & Co. 1815. 21.8 cm. *Ronald W. Raven Collection.*

68
Dessert plate painted with unusually bold fruit painting. The style and execution of the plate seem to be so typical of the work of Thomas Steel. Crown, crossed batons, dots and 'D' in red, gilder's number 2 in red. Robert Bloor & Co. 1815–20. 22.2 cm. *Anthony Hoyte Collection.*

69 ▷ ▷
Dessert plate from the Shakespeare service adapted from Thurston's illustrations to Tegg's edition of Shakespeare's plays (1812). Inscription on reverse: 'Fear not. The forest is not three leagues off; if we recover that, we are sure enough.' (*Two Gentlemen of Verona*: Act 5, Scene 1). Description and crown, crossed batons, dots and 'D' in red. Robert Bloor & Co. *c.* 1820. Diameter 22 cm. *The Gordon and Bancroft families. J. B. Green Collection.*

71
An unusual pair of Bloor Derby figures on square bases. Crown over Bloor mark in red and workman's number. Robert Bloor & Co. 1825–30. Approx. 11 cm. *Lita Kay Antiques, Lyndhurst.*

70 ■
An interesting group of three figures at a raree-show, indicating again the strong colourings of the Bloor period. A similar group, dated earlier and with only two figures, was lot number 56 in the Charles Littlewood Hill Collection sale at Neales of Nottingham on 22 June 1978. Red crown, crossed batons, dots and 'D', incised number 94. Robert Bloor & Co. *c.* 1820. 15.2 cm. *City Museum & Art Gallery, Derby.*

75 ▷
Small box painted with an all-over 'Japan' pattern known as 'Witches'. Bloor crowned ribbon mark. Robert Bloor & Co. 1835. Approx. 4.5 cm. *Margaret Martin Collection.*

72
Pierced plate with pink scale decoration and central group of flowers, painted in heavy oil colours, probably by Leonard Lead. Bloor circular mark. Robert Bloor & Co. 1825–30. 25.5 cm. *Royal Crown Derby Museum.*

73

A pair of Bloor Derby flower-sellers adapted as candlesticks with a central seated figure which is a direct copy of Meissen. The figures illustrate the demand for more colour at this period. Female: Bloor ribbon mark, incised number 8; male: no mark; seated figure: crown, crossed batons, dots and 'D' in red, gilder's number 1, incised number 314. Robert Bloor & Co. *c.* 1830. The pair 13.5 cm, seated figure 15.1 cm. *Joan Neat Collection.*

74

A fine set of Bloor Derby 'Elements', originally modelled by Pierre Stephan, who worked both at the factory and as a freelance modeller between 1770 and 1800. Imitation Meissen crossed swords mark, incised number 3. Robert Bloor & Co. 1830. 17.5 cm. *Royal Crown Derby Museum.*

76

Three spill vases of the late Bloor period, with raised and tooled gilt borders to the panels. The floral subjects are attributed to Horatio Steele, who remained until the close of the Works. The central figure subject is Lady Scarsdale in mourning for her monarch and her late husband. Pseudo Sèvres marks on floral spills and crown over Gothic 'D' on central spill. Robert Bloor & Co. 1837. 14 cm. each. *Private collection.*

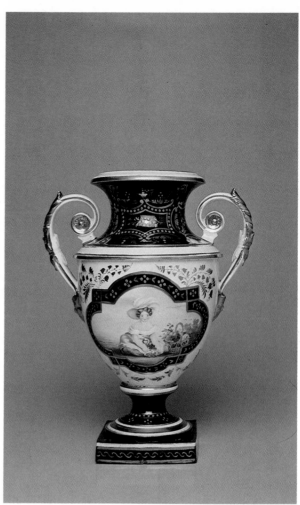

and over Waterloo Bridge, down Fleet Street and over Blackfriars Bridge along the Surrey side, and then over Southwark Bridge. His time was thirty-four minutes and twenty seconds! He was said in London to be swifter than the wind itself.[27]

WARDLE This painter, of whom little is known, was allocated pattern number 232 – a green-bordered plate with a centre 'group of three roses and two buds, by Wardle'. A later period tureen, cover and stand in this pattern, and bearing the red mark, is in the Royal Crown Derby Museum, but is considered too late for Wardle.

WILLIAM WATSON An eccentric gilder whose gilt figures, trees and mountains often appear in strange and unconventional places. He worked at Derby until about 1830. He then returned to the Potteries, where he had come from, but is reputed to have been found dead in a ditch. While at Derby, Haslem reports, he was known to perch in willow trees while eating his lunch and periodically shout out 'Georgie', which his workmates adopted as a nickname.

H. WEBBER This noted modeller was living at 4 Lisson Grove, near Lisson Green, Marylebone, in July 1795 when he wrote to Duesbury regarding his employment. He was to receive £100 per annum and a month's vacation without deduction; the stumbling-block was that he had to find a new tenant for his house. We are not told whether he was successful. Jewitt said that he had done work for Duesbury before, in London.

MOSES WEBSTER A very fine flower painter, Webster served his apprenticeship at Derby. He seems to have been working in London about 1817, where it is said he joined Thomas Martin Randall. Later he went on to Worcester, where Haslem tells us he was instructed by Baxter. Graves, in his *Dictionary of Artists*, records an M. Webster as having exhibited in London during 1818. Webster returned to Derby by about 1820 and was responsible for most of the flower painting on the John Trotter service made about 1825. John Keys had died in 1825 and Webster left to take on his position as a drawing master. Wallis quotes from the *Derby Mercury* of 13 July 1825, which confirms this:

MR. WEBSTER,

FLOWER PAINTER,

Castle Street, Derby.

Member of the Spring Gardens Association of Water Color Painters London.

Respectfully informs the Nobility and Gentry of Derby and its Vicinity, that he has commenced Teaching the Art of Flower Painting, of which he flatters himself that he has a perfect knowledge, and begs to refer them to specimens of his abilities, which are close copies of nature, and may be seen at the Mercury and Reporter Offices; and Mr Moseley's, Corn Market.

The most sedulous attention, joined to a practical and intimate knowledge of the above Art, will, he hopes, secure to him the favor and patronage of all who may honor him with their commands.

This painter was also responsible for the drawing of the Old Nottingham Road Works illustrated in plate 2; it was done from memory, in old age. He died on 20 October 1870, aged seventy-eight.

WILLIAM WHEELDON Was working with his uncle, Billingsley, at Mansfield in January 1801, but returned to Derby to be apprenticed to Duesbury and Kean in 1802, and remained as a flower painter until 1823 when he inherited a business at Bridge Gate. He died on his birthday, 19 December 1874. Wallis tells how he used to frequent the Lamb Inn in St Alkmund's churchyard, and loved to talk about his connection with the Old China Works; with 'pardonable pride' he would allude to the talents of his uncle Billingsley. His mother was Mrs Billingsley's sister.

JOHN WHITAKER This gilder served his apprenticeship at the Old Works,

379
Campana-shaped vase with richly gilt blue ground and a large rectangular panel of flowers in a wicker basket, painted by Moses Webster. Bloor circular mark. Robert Bloor & Co. 1825. 39.4 cm. *Sotheby's, New Bond Street.*

380
Dessert plate, two tureens with covers and a serving dish, decorated with a pattern much used at the factory between 1810 and 1825 and drawing its influence from the Japanese taste. This is just one of the many 'Japan' types of pattern, but certainly one of the most common. Crown, crossed batons, dots and 'D' with various workmen's marks in red. Robert Bloor & Co. 1820. Standard sizes. *Sotheby's, New Bond Street.*

using the number 37, but left in 1826 when, Haslem tells us, there was a turn-out of gilders and Japan painters.

JOHN WHITAKER   Grandson of Richard Whitaker, he was apprenticed as a boy in 1818 to learn modelling and figure-making. He stayed at Nottingham Road until it closed in 1848. He succeeded Samuel Keys in 1830 as superintendent of the figure-makers, and in 1842 was foreman of the whole potting department.

RICHARD WHITAKER   He was one of the first of William Duesbury's apprentices to rise as a figure-maker, beginning a family connection that was to continue for many years. In the mid-eighteenth century his father owned the mill at Little Eaton, near Derby, where he was able to grind some material for the china works.

JOHN WINROW   Apprenticed as a china painter on 6 June 1766 for seven years.

WILLIAM WINGFIELD   Apprenticed to figure-making, he died in March 1825 aged only twenty-nine. In his obituary, quoted by Haslem, the *Derby Reporter* stated that he left many specimens of his ability and spoke highly of his talents.

381
A pair of rare shaped vases with applied flowers and fruits surrounding landscape panels by Daniel Lucas. The pedestal and necks have gilt stripes and the ground colour is light periwinkle blue. Crown over Gothic 'D' in red. Robert Bloor & Co. *c.* 1840. 25.5 cm. *Royal Crown Derby Museum.*

EDWARD WITHERS Was from London. He certainly worked at Chelsea and may possibly have been related to Edwin Withers, the Staffordshire painter, and to his grandson Walter Withers, the well-known Australian landscape painter. He was born at Hansworth, Middlesex, on 22 October 1854, and died on 13 October 1914. This information was received from Noel and Carrie Fromholtz. There is a possibility that Noel Fromholtz's uncle, Arnold Shore – also well known in Australia as a painter – was related to Walter Withers, but the records have not yet been established conclusively. Graves mentions six painters named Withers who exhibited between 1829 and 1893. We may assume that Withers went to Derby from Chelsea in 1770, after William Duesbury had bought the factory. From Lygo's letters to Duesbury we know about Withers' time working at the Chelsea Manufactory.

1789. Mr Complin had a trial on the white before going to Derby, and Withers, who was in London, said that he was a better painter than Hilliard – another aspirant for the factory, who had worked with him on buttons at Chelsea but 'could make little of it'.

We also find Withers wishing to leave Mr Horwood, a china dealer, because he wanted to return to Derby. Doubtless Withers foresaw the financial crisis coming to his master, because Horwood was declared bankrupt in 1790!

We know that Withers approached Duesbury in 1789 and was re-engaged. In the agreement he was described as 'of London, porcelain or china painter'. The document was dated 8 May 1789 and the engagement was to commence in September at the rate of '3s 6d per day'.

While researching in the West Country a few years ago, the author made a most important discovery consisting of an old folder containing twelve watercolours by Edward Withers. They were said to have been in the possession of an old Derby family who did not really know anything about their origins. Two were initialled 'E.W.' and one dated 1789, and all were on paper of a similar type and quality to that of the Old Derby Pattern Books. The subjects were varied and included flowers, botanical specimens and birds, and there was one – albeit naïve – fruit study featuring a wasp. The variety was probably intended to show Duesbury that his earlier work on formal flower sprays was not his only talent. Bemrose illustrated a similar sketch of a single rose in his *Bow, Chelsea and Derby Porcelain*. Samuel Keys stated that 'very soon after Mr. Duesbury's death (1786) flower painting was at a very low ebb. Withers was then looked upon as the best flower painter on China in England.' Obviously the more naturalistic style of William Billingsley's brush had not yet made its full impact. Withers' earlier work left the highlights of the rose to be formed by the white porcelain, while Billingsley brushed his roses to give them their highlights.

It seems that Withers' relationship with his employer was at times strained; at one time he headed the list of painters opposing the employment of women at the factory: 'From the many injuries done to the trade by employing Women in Painting of China, &c., Particularly not being employ'd in London in any Painting or Gilding Shop whatsoever, we hope you will not withstand Granting us the favour of their not being employ'd here.' Apart from Withers' name, the list also included the names of Billingsley, Soar and Samuel Keys. Its date is about 1789.

Withers was likely to have been the instigator of the Loyal Club, a group of painters and workmen who formed a friendly club to give mutual aid in the event of need. A certain famous jug, known as the Rodney Jug, was kept at the Admiral Rodney public house and was most probably painted by Withers. The jug is noteworthy because it roughly marks the period before the introduction of the crossed batons in the Nottingham Road mark. The date of Rodney's victory was 1782 and from Lygo's letters of 1784 we see that tea pattern 69 was out. Research has shown the author that none of the numbered tea patterns ever has the crown over D mark.

Withers worked in Staffordshire and painted Japanned tea trays in Birmingham during his absence from Derby. He was given plate patterns 219 and 258, and tea pattern 451 and two others close by – curiously, not numbered. On one he has the unique claim over all other named painters of having 'Esquire' after his name!

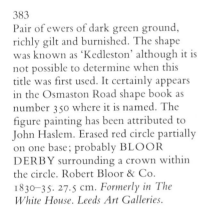

383
Pair of ewers of dark green ground, richly gilt and burnished. The shape was known as 'Kedleston' although it is not possible to determine when this title was first used. It certainly appears in the Osmaston Road shape book as number 350 where it is named. The figure painting has been attributed to John Haslem. Erased red circle partially on one base; probably BLOOR DERBY surrounding a crown within the circle. Robert Bloor & Co. 1830–35. 27.5 cm. *Formerly in The White House. Leeds Art Galleries.*

Because of the change in fashion most of the named patterns would have been in his more sophisticated style, and executed after his return to Derby in 1789.

Finally, below is a document concerning a dispute between Withers and William Duesbury II in 1795:

A dispute having arisen between Edward Withers & Mr. W. Duesbury respecting the value of painting Roses with their buds & leaves, such as now executing by E. Withers upon Mr. W. Duesbury's China & calld No. 269.

It is concluded between the said parties that the value shall be settled and absolutely determined by the Time which similar roses, buds and leaves, shall be found to take in executing on the back of this paper; upon condition that such Roses &c shall be executed as well as the Roses &c. on the porcelain executed by the said E. Withers & in the same style And in order that E.W. shall be satisfied that they actually take the time which it shall be stated they do – Mr E.W. shall (whenever he shall be required to do it) note with his own hand on this paper the hour & minute when such a design is intended to be began, & shall be informed in a clear and satisfactory manner of the time when the same is finished & ready for his inspection, & the determination of the business Agreed between the parties hereto this 28th. day of April 1795

WITNESS

The above was duly tendered to E: Withers agreeable to his engagement, but rejected by

384
Child in armchair modelled by John Whitaker after a portrait by Chalon RA. John Haslem painted a plate with the same subject (see colour plate 77). Imitation Meissen mark. Robert Bloor & Co. *c.* 1835–40. 11.4 cm. *Geoffrey Godden.*

385
Shell-shaped dish with the moulded border gilt with an unusual design and the centre painted with a view of 'The Leasowes' in Shropshire, by Edward Prince. 'The Leasowes' was a small estate of some thirty acres owned by William Shenstone (1714–63), a writer and landscape gardener, who in fact coined the phrase 'landskip gardener' in his posthumously published *Unconnected Thoughts* (*House & Garden*, November 1977). Crown over Gothic 'D' and description of scene in red. Robert Bloor & Co. 1835. 22.5 cm. *Stephan Nowacki.*

386 ■
Figure of George III (1738–1820) modelled by François Hardenberg. 1820. *National Portrait Gallery.*

E:W. who was determind he said not to work the remainder of his Term out with Mr. Duesbury according to his Engagement unless Mr. D. would pay E.W. such price as the said E.W. thought proper to fix Mr. D. also proposed that E.W. should draw up an engagement to the above effect with his own hands that he might be satisfied of the full import & meaning of it E:W. having express'd a fear of putting his hand to any paper drawn up by any other person This was also rejected by E.W. E.W. has repeatedly consented to the above mode of determining the fair value of the Roses &c.

Witness   CHARLES KING.

The sad conclusion to the story is that 'Edward Withers Esq' died in poor circumstances and was buried by his old shopmates.

JOSEPH WRIGHT   This celebrated English artist, known as Wright of Derby, probably supplied Duesbury II with drawings and advice, and obviously influenced the landscape painters of the late eighteenth-century period.

JOHN YATES   This gilder and painter was Alfred Wallis' great-grandfather. Wallis quotes his grandfather's account of the man:

A little fresh-complexioned old man with bright, keen eyes and cheerful manner. He usually wore a blue coat, with gilt buttons, knee-breeches and ribbed hose, shoes and buckles. His position in society was good and his manners and conversation indicated a superior degree of education. He came from Staffordshire. His daughter Ann was to marry the landscape painter, George Robertson.

Wallis also stated that this painter executed hunting scenes. He used the number 5 in the years 1785–95 when the mark of the factory would normally be puce or blue. He died in 1821.

WILLIAM YATES   A gilder who used the number 4 in the years 1785–95.

12

Paste Comparisons

The investigation reported here by Dr Robert Hedges was conducted in order to determine changes made in the composition of paste and glaze in the production of Derby porcelain over a period of time. These might arise from changes in the available raw materials, experimental variations in the glaze or body formulations, or during the gradual evolution of a technical process. This work is no more than a preliminary investigation in which a *prima facie* case can be clearly made for quite major changes in glaze and especially paste composition within a few years. A detailed account of the complete history of such changes would require a lengthy, although quite feasible, programme of analysis. An important feature of the analytical work described here is that it is entirely non-destructive. While, as explained below, this necessitates some loss of information, its advantages for this study are essential.

A list of objects analysed is appended below. The analytical technique used is that of X-ray fluorescence using an energy-dispersive spectrometer. In this method the levels of most of the major and minor elements occurring in a thin surface layer

387
Brilliant mazarine-ground cup and saucer decorated in Sèvres style, with birds in landscape reserved within raised and chased gilt panels. Much of this work was undertaken by Horatio Steele. Crown over Gothic 'D' in red. Robert Bloor & Co. *c.* 1835. Approx. 6.2 cm. *Joan Neat Collection.*

(0.1–0.01 mm) can be determined quantitatively and rapidly. Thus a glaze can be analysed *in situ*. For the paste, an area on the object must be found where the surface composition is the same as that of the body. If the analysis is performed in air it is not possible to analyse for minor elements lighter in atomic weight than potassium. Unfortunately this includes the technically significant elements of sodium, magnesium, aluminium and phosphorus. Any systematic study of the glaze and body compositions of soft paste wares would need a vacuum apparatus for the measurement of these elements by X-ray fluorescence, or else the removal of a small sample (eg 5 mg), followed by analysis by, for example, atomic absorption spectrometry. Nevertheless, the information gained in this study, while incomplete and of limited precision, is quite sufficient to establish the wide variations in composition of early Derby. The analysis was made in two groups, at two different times, with different spectrometers and somewhat different aims. Therefore the results are grouped into two, and detail somewhat different information. The results are commented on below.

Results (note: all values refer to the percentage of oxide present).

GROUP I	*Paste compositions*	
Cup (1783)	K/Ca ratio	1/25
	Pb	0.1–0.5%
	Ti	Strong
	As	Probably present
	Rb	Not detected
	Sr	Trace
Plate (Late 1815)	K/Ca	1/10
	Pb	0.1–0.5%
	Ti	Weak
	As	n.d.
	Rb	Strong
	Sr	Trace
Plate (early)	K/Ca	1/25
	Pb	5%
	Ti	Strong
	As, Sr, Rb	n.d.
Plate (1778)	K/Ca	1/8
	Pb	10%
	Ti, Rb, Sr	n.d.
Plate (late 1820)	K/Ca	1/25
	Pb	trace (0.1%)
	Ti	Weak
	Rb	Strong
	Sr	Weak

Group I glaze compositions were all very similar, containing about 20% of PbO, and a potash/lime ratio of between 1/1 and 1/2.

Comments

While the glaze composition is basically the same for all the objects examined, approaching the composition for a typical 'lead glaze' (in which the PbO is typically in the 30–40% region), the paste compositions vary considerably. The minor and trace elements, Ti, Rb and Sr, would be present as contaminants in the raw materials, so that their pronounced variation implies the use of different ingredients, even when the same overall composition is achieved. Unfortunately it is difficult in general, and impossible with the information obtained here, to reconstruct the original minerals used as raw materials. But we can be certain that they differed at different periods. While the trace elements give somewhat indirect evidence of changes in the source or type of raw material, the levels of K, Ca and Pb (potash, lime or bone ash, and lead) directly influence the properties of the ceramic, and so their variation must have been deliberate. It is not possible to determine the extent of bone ash incorporated since the technique cannot measure P (phosphorus)

388
Dessert plate, ice-pail, cover and liner and oval dish, all with moulded borders picked out as simulated pearls and daisy heads. Each piece has broad, bright apple green borders with plant centres in bright colours. Some of this later painting of floral subjects must have been the work of Horatio Steele, who remained at the factory until its close and was concerned with decorating the Royal service. Crown over Gothic 'D' in red with plant descriptions. Robert Bloor & Co. c. 1835–40. Standard sizes. *Sotheby's, New Bond Street.*

391 ▷
A remarkable grouping of monkey musicians on square bases, canted at the rear, adapted from the Meissen idea of animal musicians. It was not thought fit for the musicians to be on a level with the courtiers so they were demeaned by being made to wear masks. No mark. Robert Bloor & Co. c. 1830. Average size 10.8 cm. *Sotheby's, New Bond Street.*

389
Brilliant blue-ground coffee can and stand painted with flowers by Horatio Steele in panels reserved within gilt frames. Crown over Gothic 'D' in red. Robert Bloor & Co. c. 1835–40. Can 7 cm. *David John Ceramics, Woodstock.*

390
Teapot and cover painted with random sprays of flowers on the natural white ground. Crown over Gothic 'D' in red. Robert Bloor & Co. c. 1835. Approx. 14 cm. *Major G. N. Dawnay Collection.*

392
Figure of a milkmaid carrying a pair of
churns and a milk pot suspended from
a yoke. The decoration and round
circular base are typical of the period.
She is usually paired with a milkman
also carrying churns. Crown over
Gothic 'D' in red. Robert Bloor & Co.
1825. 13.8 cm. *Victoria & Albert
Museum, C1130 – 1924.*

393 ▷ ▷
Dancing group from the Meissen
original, finely decorated, probably by
Samuel Keys, with the boy in an
elaborate waistcoat and patterned
breeches and the girl a colourful skirt.
Incised number 17. Robert Bloor &
Co. 1820. 17 cm. *Victoria & Albert
Museum, 3015 – 1901.*

394
An oval dish, tureen with cover and stand and a shell dish, all gadroon-edged with stylized blue and gilt borders. The dishes depict birds in landscapes and the tureen has two small panels front and reverse of the same subject. The painting cannot be attributed to Richard Dodson because, according to Haslem, he left shortly after his father's death in 1820. Most painters, since Complin's pattern number 159 'Birds in Landskip', had painted their birds with this form of natural background, and therefore these pieces might have been painted by Poulson, who is reputed to have worked for a short time at the factory. Bloor circular mark. Robert Bloor & Co. *c.* 1825. Standard sizes. *Sotheby's, New Bond Street.*

395
Two groups representing 'Shoeblack', number 81, and 'Hairdresser', number 84, produced during the Bloor period, now placed on pierced scroll bases heavily gilt and decorated in the strong colourings of the period. 'Shoeblack': crown over Gothic 'D' in red; 'Hairdresser': Bloor circular mark with number 84 incised. Robert Bloor & Co. *c.* 1830–35. 'Shoeblack' 18.4 cm, 'Hairdresser' 17.6 cm. *Victoria & Albert Museum; C1303 – 1919 left; C1302 – 1919 right.*

396
A plate from the service made for Queen Victoria, having a bright chrome green border, reserved upon which are six small panels of birds, insects and flowers. The greater part of the service was decorated by Horatio Steele and the ground between the panels was gilded in embossed gold chased in Sèvres style. Crown over ribbon mark. Robert Bloor & Co. 1841–2. 20.3 cm. *Victoria & Albert Museum.*

with sufficient sensitivity. But one explanation for variations in the K/Ca ratio is through the addition of bone ash (calcium phosphate, $Ca_3(PO_4)_2$). If so, this addition seems to have been more common for the later pieces. The use of lead oxide would help vitrification of the body at lower temperatures. From this group it would seen to be commoner at early times. If any trend can be discerned, it is for increasing the Ca content (or decreasing the K content), and decreasing the Pb content, with time.

GROUP II		Paste	Glaze
Street Figure, 1750 (illustrated on jacket and plate 4)	K	4	5
	Ca	15	9
	(K/Ca)	1/4	1/2
	Pb	12	30
	Ti	0.06	0.03
	Fe	0.1	0.06
	As, Rb, Sr, Zr	n.d.	n.d.
Bowl, c. 1758 (Royal Crown Derby Museum)	K	3	3
	Ca	24	2
	K/Ca	1/8	1/1
	Pb	18	40
	Ti	0.04	0.03
	Fe	0.25	0.01
	As, Rb, Sr, Zr	n.d.	n.d.
Piper (illustrated in plate 75)	K	4	6
	Ca	8	6
	K/Ca	1/2	1/1
	Pb	8	30
	Ti	0.03	0.02
	Fe	0.2	0.1
	Sr	trace	n.d.
	As, Rb, Zr	n.d.	n.d.: Cu present in glaze.*
Shepherd and Shepherdess *La Bergère des Alpes*, (illustrated in colour plate 16)	K	5	5
	Ca	14	14
	K/Ca	1/3	1/3
	Pb	20	15–20
	Ti	0.02	0.03
	Fe	0.1	0.15
	As, Rb, Sr, Zr	n.d.	n.d.
Fame (illustrated in plate 195)	K	3	3†
	Ca	14	12
	K/Ca	1/5	1/4
	Pb	4	4
	Ti	0.05	0.8
	Fe	0.1	0.1
	As, Rb, Sr, Zr	n.d.	n.d.
Areas analysed	Street figure, ground base; white glaze on base and side. Bowl, base rime, white glaze on side. Piper, base (brownish area), white glaze on leg. Shepherd, base, glossy side (2). Fame, base, leg and back.		

* This piece was unglazed, but had a glossy 'sheen' from which analysis corresponding to the column marked † was made. It is seen that there is no important difference in composition.

† The same remarks apply as to the Shepherd. Note, however, the difference in Ti.

Usually two different areas were analysed for paste and for glaze to check for consistency. The accuracy of the quoted figures is reckoned to be within $\pm 20\%$ of the quoted value. ($<$ means 'less than'; n.d. means 'not detected'.)

Comments

Group II in general seems to differ from Group I in having somewhat higher lead contents and higher K/Ca ratios. This may be because the objects are of a different type, being much heavier and thicker. However, like those in Group I, the glazes are all much more similar to each other (and to the Group I glazes), while the pastes again show some very distinct variations. However, it is difficult to pick out any

397
Mountainous river landscape painted and signed by Richard Ablott. *c.* 1850. *Sotheby's, New Bond Street.*

399
A print of the nunnery erected in 1847 at a reputed cost of £10,000. The building was designed by Pugin and was built on the Duesbury family site known as the Old Works, which were closed in 1835, as opposed to the Calver Close site leased by Kean and later by Bloor. A pair of vases were said by Haslem to have been given to Pope Pius the Ninth to celebrate the opening of the nunnery, but the author was unable to obtain confirmation of this from the Vatican City. The nunnery was pulled down about 1863. In the Derby City Museum there is a mug painted with this view by Edward Prince.

398
Portrait of King William IV, painted
by William Corden at Windsor, and
signed by the artist. *c.* 1835. *Royal
Crown Derby Museum.*

trend either in the K/Ca ratios or in the Pb contents. It is interesting that Fame and
the Berger des Alpes, while so similar in appearance and in composition, should
nevertheless have lead contents that differ by a factor of five. There is no evidence
for a different composition on the surface of these biscuit pieces. The extra-
ordinarily high titanium content to be found on the surface of Fame could perhaps
be due to a surface treatment such as the painting of the white pigment titanium
dioxide. There is no visual evidence for this, and the high Ti is not confined to just
one area, but it seems doubtful that it could be due to a process involving the second
firing. The presence of copper in the glaze of the piper explains the faintly greenish
hue of the glaze, and may have been intentional. The occurrence of trace elements is
of less use in the Group II study, only one – strontium – being observed, and that
once. It has not been possible to estimate if this implies an overall difference in trace
element composition from the Group I objects, since different equipment was used
and the high lead content makes for difficulties in comparison.

Relation to previously published analyses

Analyses of Derby porcelain are to be found in *Derby Porcelain* (Barrett and Thorpe,
Faber, 1971, pp. 119–22) and *Crown Derby Porcelain* (Gilhespy, Lewis, 1951). These
were clearly by 'wet' chemical methods, involving the destruction of a sample, and
include more elements.

The same elements as measured in this study are repeated below. (Numbers refer to % of oxide of element.)

CUP, *c.* 1760 (Dr Gilhespy) (*Crown Derby Porcelain*)

K   2.5
Ca   16.3
K/Ca   1/7
Pb   9.1
Ti   0.2
Fe   0.4

FIGURE (1750–6) *Derby Porcelain*, p. 119
K   not measured but < 3%
Ca   20.6
K/Ca   < 1/7
Pb   2.1
other elements not measured.

PLATE (1770–1810) *Derby Porcelain*, p. 120
K   0.9
Ca   24.3
K/Ca   1/25
Pb   0.36

400
A large continental group spuriously marked with the crown, crossed batons, dots and 'D' mark in red, hard-paste. Possibly manufactured by Sampson of Paris. Late nineteenth century. Height 40.2 cm, width 40.2 cm, depth 27.9 cm. *Mr & Mrs V. H. Thomas Collection.*

In addition the 1760 cup had small quantities of phosphate, while the 1770–1810 period plate had very substantial quantities, indicating a very considerable fraction of bone ash as raw material. (The figure was not analysed for phosphate.)

While none of these results exactly corresponds to the analyses made in this study, in every one of the elements studied the range encountered is similar.

Conclusions

There is no doubt that the paste composition of Derby wares has gone through a variety of chemical formulations during the period from 1750 onwards. This is particularly clear from the potash/lime ratio and from the variation in lead content. These variations are surely deliberate, and would influence the technical properties (thermal and mechanical) of the body and the relationship to its glaze. Furthermore, trace elements variations support the contention that different raw materials were used at different times. On the other hand, the formulation of the glaze seems to have been remarkably stable.

While it is tempting to infer trends in the paste composition with time, the number of pieces analysed is far too small for this to be done. This preliminary work shows that a more systematic study would clearly be worthwhile.

To end with, the following notes from the Wallis manuscripts gives an idea of the jealousy with which industrial secrets were guarded:

The composition for the paste was ground at the Flint Mills, near the bottom of St. Michael's Lane and much secrecy was observed as to the method of operation. The clay was at one time obtained from a lead mine, near Brassington, in this County, but it proved not so even in quality as the imported article. In 1785, the following notice appeared:

>   Derby 20th July 1785

>   '*Whereas, on the night of Tuesday, the 12th of this Instant July, Person, or Persons, entered the Flint Mill situate upon the River Derwent, in the Parish of St. Michael, in Derby, and wilfully pulled out a plug whereby a large quantity of slip or composition for making Porcelain or China Ware, was let out and lost or rendered totally useless,*

>   NOTICE, THEREFORE IS HEREBY GIVEN,

>   *That if any Person, or Persons, will give information of the Persons concerned in the above Malicious Transaction, so that they may be brought to Justice, they shall receive*

>   A REWARD OF TEN GUINEAS,

>   *to be paid on conviction by Messrs. Duesbury's, China Manufacturers, in Derby, aforesaid.'*

13

Question and Answer

There are certain questions which ceramic historians are continually asked. Here is a selection of those most commonly raised, together with some questions and answers specifically on Derby wares.

1. What causes crazing?

A web of tiny fractures in the glaze surface is caused by unequal expansion and/or contraction of the body and the glaze. Normally these fractures occur over varying periods of time, depending on the degree of difference between the expansion/contraction characteristics of both body and glaze.

2. What are stress cracks?

These are cracks which develop at varying intervals of time, in some cases years after manufacture, which are caused by a higher than normal percentage of insufficiently ground bone-ash being present in the bone-ash content of the body.

3. At what temperature are porcelain and bone china bodies fired?

To give a simple, non-technical answer, porcelain is first fired at around 1,200 degrees Centigrade in the biscuit oven, and fired again after glazing at up to 1,400 degrees Centigrade. The temperature for soft paste or artificial porcelain such as that made at the Nottingham Road Factory would be in the region of 1,250 degrees Centigrade. The bone china body usually contains at least 50 per cent ox-bone. From 1770 Derby porcelain body contained at least 40 per cent ox-bone.

4. What does the expression 'groundlaying' mean?

After hand-painting of ground colours on wares ended about 1817, it became the practice to overlay the ground with a specially prepared oil carefully applied; colour in powder form was then dusted on to the oiled ground with cotton wool. This accounts for the rather uneven grounds on the wares.

5. What does the expression 'clobbered' mean?

According to Alfred Wallis it was Sir Woolaston Franks who coined this phrase in the nineteenth century. It is used for wares that have been redecorated or have added embellishment beyond the original factory-marketed production. The expression is often used where ground colour has been added at later dates.

6. What is meant by 'flaking'?

This term is applied where enamels flake away from the overglaze decoration. The Derby Factory suffered greatly from this fault about 1820, with the result that more heavy, oil-type colours were used in the landscape paintings of Robert Brewer, William Corden, William Cotton and, later, Daniel Lucas. The style of painting was altogether inferior to that of the late eighteenth and early nineteenth century, when washes in the watercolour style provided more definition. The later work of

George Robertson is much more difficult to separate from his 1797–1810 period because of this – as also is the work of Robert Brewer.

7. What is the difference between a repairer and a restorer?

A repairer works in the modelling department and assembles the moulded parts of a figure or vase. The original modeller's figure must therefore be judged from the repairer's finished work, and because everything is done by hand there are slight differences of, say, head alignment or position of arms. A restorer mends damaged china and sometimes needs to model a missing limb or a piece of a vase.

8. What is casting?

This is the production process of pouring liquid clay into moulds to produce shapes. Because the moulds are porous, water is absorbed from the liquid clay in immediate contact with the surface of the mould and solid clay starts to build up. When the desired thickness is achieved the surplus liquid clay is poured off, leaving a hollow cast in the mould. After a short drying time the clay cast shrinks sufficiently to allow it to be released from the mould.

9. What are screw-holes, in connection with the dry-edge class of figures?

Screw-holes are merely holes pierced through the base of a figure to allow steam to escape during firing. They seem peculiar to Derby. The name was possibly taken from the tool which was used to bore or pierce the piece. It is important not to confuse these with holes in the back of a base which could have been used to take metal and porcelain flower sprays.

10. What are patch marks?

These are the result of the piece having stood on little balls of clay while in the glost ovens (glaze kilns).

11. What are glost ovens or kilns?

These are kilns in which the wares are fired to develop the glaze surface, as opposed to the firing of clay wares to the vitreous, biscuit stage.

12. Who or what are Long Elizas?

These were elongated figures known at the Meissen Factory as *Lange Liszen*, and were adopted from the *chinoiserie* taste as a form of decoration on early useful wares.

13. What is meant by impressed marks and incised marks?

Impressed marks are stamped into the unfired body with a die stamp. They are generally accepted by ceramic historians as being used to indicate the potter's activity rather than that of the decorator. These marks can refer to firing bundle instructions or to date; the latter purpose was adopted at Osmaston Road, where a date stamp was used. Incised marks are scratched into the unfired body, and can indicate workmen's marks or again, as in the case of the Osmaston Road Factory in the Derby Crown Porcelain Company's time, the shape numbers. Note that figures produced at the Nottingham Road Works might well carry an incised repairer's mark, and after the Chelsea merger figures are incised with numerals.

14. What were the origins of the Japan or Imari patterns?

These patterns, as the names imply, were adopted from Japan via the European porcelain factories. The predominant colours were red, blue and later gold. Other colours were added, and towards the end of the eighteenth century patterns such as Old Japan and Witches were introduced. During the first quarter of the nineteenth century the Derby Factory increased its use of this type of decoration, bringing in female labour for cheapness. It is still produced today and is in great demand at Osmaston Road, surely a great test of public demand after so long a time!

15. What causes pitting?

The small black specks or marks in the glaze are caused by defects in firing. In the old wood-fired kilns wood sparking often occurred, which could ruin a whole firing. Also impurities can cause ware to be spoilt. In the days of coal-firing smoke stains sometimes occurred, and certainly modern electric kilns have done much to eradicate these problems.

16. What does the term 'scuffing' mean?

This word is used to describe scratch marks or wear on the ground colours. The marks are usually caused by cleaning china with abrasive materials or by standing items one upon another without protective sheets in between.

17. Does one find Derby-type productions with fake markings?

The short answer is yes! Certainly there are products from Europe – not necessarily those of the famous forger Samson of Paris – which bear the crown, crossed batons, dots and D in red. Some are even signed, in spite of the fact that painters did not sign ware decorated at the Old Nottingham Road Works!

18. Were Derby plaques, which appear from time to time in the salerooms, actually marketed by the factory?

Generally speaking, no. Certainly the majority were painted by men employed at the works, but usually they were sold by the painters to supplement their income and also as a lasting testimonial of their ability. It should be pointed out that plate centres must not be confused with plaques. Plate centres are usually cut out of damaged marketed ware, which would normally carry the factory mark.

19. On what grounds are attributions made?

Where no documentation exists, items are usually attributed on stylistic grounds. This is the policy adopted by the Royal Crown Derby Museum.

20. Why did Andrew Planché go to Derby to begin manufacturing porcelain?

There has long been discussion as to why Derby was chosen. The waterways had not been navigated by 1748–50, but Planché, who as we know was apprenticed as a goldsmith in 1740, may have heard of Heath who had an interest in the pot works at Cockpit Hill. Certainly, until research reveals some more evidence, answers to this question can only be supposition.

21. What is cobalt blue?

Cobalt was essential in the manufacture of blue and white china and is known in the trade as biscuit blue because it was often used as an underglaze colour. Originally an inferior blue was used underglaze, and it was found that the impurities in the cobalt ore damaged the colour properties. Derby, so Haslem tells us, were among the first to use cobalt oxide to obtain the colour which was to become the famous 'Derby blue'. A report in *The Gentlewoman* of 5 December 1891 reads: 'Here are glass cases filled with vases of every conceivable hue and lovely outline. Colour indeed! We were informed that the Crown Derby body admits of a treatment of colour unattainable elsewhere. Here are vases of the noted "Derby blue" . . . .'

22. What sources did the painters use for their subjects?

Most of the landscapes were taken from contemporary prints in such publications as *Middiman's Views*, *Harrington's Engravings of the Lakes*, and *Hazle's Tour to the Isle of Wight*, but they also used sketch books, of which examples survive in museums and private collections. Other papers and periodicals, such as *Curtis's Botanical Magazine*, were used for botanical subjects and, as reported in Lygo's notes, prints were obtained for the Duesburys if the cost was not prohibitive.

23. What were the most popular forms of decoration used at Derby?

Flower painting was foremost, but was closely followed by landscape subjects and set geometric or foliate decoration including the inevitable sprig. The rarer subjects were usually figure, marine and animal ones, and such pieces surviving from the late eighteenth century are highly prized by collectors and museums.

24. How important are shapes in the identification of factory products?

Shapes are of paramount importance because, although they were copied by other works, there are often small differences, for example in the knops on teapots or the handles of jugs.

25. To what does the term 'distance for hills' refer?

In the Old Derby Pattern Books it is used to describe a colour which appears in landscape painting, and is a literal title. Plate pattern 219 has a border in this greyish blue colour.

26. What do the terms 'black upon moonlight' and 'black upon fire' mean?

They refer to the use of black detail painted upon a wash of yellow and black upon a bright orange wash. These techniques were mostly associated with the work of John Brewer, but it is certainly possible that other landscape painters at the end of the eighteenth century used this type of decoration.

27. Did the Duesburys purchase any models made away from the Derby Factory?

It is known that they purchased models from many well-known sculptors, and details of these (incomplete, however) appear in Lygo's letters quoted in the Appendix.

28. What is bloom ground – a colour so often mentioned when discussing blue-and puce-marked Derby?

This refers to peach bloom ground, which is pink; it is often misunderstood because the word 'peach' implies a definite colour.

29. What was the purpose of gilders, painters and groundlayers numbering wares?

This was to ensure instant recognition of the worker responsible if a defect were seen while ware was being sorted. The system is still used today.

30. Why is it that most pieces c. 1797–1805 lack any workman's mark?

It seems that this was the period when Michael Kean was in control of the day-to-day running of the factory; it was a period of deterioration of the paste, which must obviously be connected with Kean. He does not seem to have found it necessary to enforce the practice introduced by the Duesburys.

31. To what extent was Derby porcelain exported from the Nottingham Road Factory?

In spite of strong competition and political unrest the Duesburys were successful in exporting to Europe and America. In the Lygo letters of 1790 we have 'Figures and Groups for Cadiz'; and in 1792 'Mrs Hope's order for Amsterdam' and 'Mr Jack services for America'. There were orders for the East Indies and other countries. It is not surprising, therefore, that many foreign museums have good collections of Derby porcelain. The Hermitage Museum in Leningrad, USSR, has an extensive uncatalogued collection of Derby porcelain, and attempts are now being made to discover in detail its contents. American museums have well-documented examples of Derby. The Indianapolis Museum were particularly helpful during the preparation of this book, and some of their fine pieces are illustrated.

32. What have you found most useful in researching for this book?

Apart from the tremendous assistance that I have received from the staff of many of the major museums, from collectors and dealers, I think that the largely unpublished material left by Alfred Wallis, who was editor of the *Derby Mercury* in the nineteenth century, has helped me greatly. However I am also grateful for the opportunities I have had of meeting people at Open Days at the Royal Crown Derby Museum, and I am well aware of the value of the resulting two-way exchange of information.

33. What is your personal attitude to previous writers on the subject?

This question takes me back to the Morley College Seminar of 1976, when the subject was 'The Pottery and Porcelain of Derbyshire', and the author was on the panel of lecturers answering the audience's questions. The author at that time put up a strong defence of his predecessors. Without them we would not be able to draw on what is now established scholarly documentation. Of course new evidence is always turning up to make students re-think and possibly change what has become accepted opinion.

34. Is it true that the manufacture of porcelain and china has continued longer in Derby than in any other town or city in Britain?

It has been continuously manufactured from about 1748, and is at present manufactured by the Royal Crown Derby Porcelain Company. The Old

Nottingham Road Works closed in 1848 and manufacture was continued, although on a reduced scale, at the King Street Works. Since the 1935 merger wares have been manufactured only at Osmaston Road. (See *Royal Crown Derby*.)

35. *How long did Duesbury keep the Chelsea Factory going after the merger with Derby?*

Duesbury closed Chelsea in 1784, and from a letter written by the then Chelsea foreman we can see that no new money had been ploughed into the factory, and Duesbury I's declining health may have contributed. It is well worth reading the letter published by F. Severne Mackenna in his series on the Chelsea Factory (*Chelsea Porcelain, the Gold Anchor Wares*, page 41), in which he tells of the 'Ion Kiln' being hardly worth sending to Derby.

36. *What benefits did the Duesburys receive from the Chelsea takeover?*

There were numerous gains to be made from taking over the factory that had once been the foremost in the land. By expanding the business Duesbury was able to eliminate many competitors. There were many technical advantages, such as improvements in body and decoration, but above all the availability of modellers such as Willems and painters of the calibre of Boreman, Askew, the Duviviers, Jockey Hill, George Complin – who had worked on enamels at Battersea, and many others. The increase in figure production was inevitable, since Chelsea, like Derby, had a large figure department, and the Chelsea moulds enabled Duesbury to extend his range. Finally it was of great use for him to have a London base, and he opened his London showroom at 1 Bedford Street, Covent Garden, in 1773, only three years after the merger.

37. *What evidence exists to show that porcelain was manufactured at the Cockpit Hill pot works?*

Most ceramic historians do not believe that porcelain or china were ever made at this works. In chapter 1 it was reported that 'the china works near Mary Bridge' was in existence by the end of 1752, and was certainly not on the Cockpit Hill site. F. Williamson, formerly curator of the Derby Museum and Art Gallery, claimed in his history, *Derby Pot Manufactory Known as Cockpit Hill Pottery*, that this works produced the small cream jugs made at Derby in 1750, but he offers no evidence. He also suggested that as Heath was interested in the Nottingham Road Works and Cockpit Hill there must be a relationship between the two. Heath was a banker, whose interest would of course have been largely financial. Williamson also claimed that Nottingham Road was certainly not the site on which porcelain-making began. Our evidence shows the works to have been close to St Mary's Bridge and, although it is not certain, the site offered for sale in July 1756 would appear to have been occupied by the original works and so, as in the *Derby Mercury* report of a drowning workman already quoted, 'close to Mary Bridge'. It is fair to state, in conclusion, that certainly no evidence exists to show that porcelain or china were manufactured or sold on a commercial scale at this works.

38. *Which of the two sites on Nottingham Road was never owned freehold by the Heaths, Duesbury, Kean or Bloor?*

The site known as Calver Close, which was to the east of the Old Factory site, was leased from the Liversage Trust by successive manufacturers. Kean in fact retained his lease, paying the rent until his death in 1823.

39. *What periods do you consider the best in Nottingham Road's history?*

The fine figures from the early period have much to recommend them, but certainly the paste, glaze and decoration of the Duesbury II period, c. 1785–95, have not been excelled, as can be seen from the illustrations in this book. Many superb and unique items were also produced at other times, including some exceedingly lavish and colourful pieces in the period of Robert Bloor, a much maligned proprietor of the works.

40. *Which interests you most, the pots or the people?*

This question is often asked, and the author can truthfully say that, as a ceramic historian, he tries not to neglect any side of the history, neither social nor commercial, but concludes that without people there would be no pots!

14

Marks

It is worthwhile reminding the reader that normally the marking of wares was done by gilders and, as stated in chapter 10, since the marks were made by hand, variations frequently occurred in the mark of any one individual gilder.

1–6

These marks date from the Chelsea merger and it is likely that 2, 3 and 4 were used at Chelsea, whereas 1, 5 and 6 would have been used at Nottingham Road.

1   2   3   4   5   6

It is the author's considered opinion that pieces so marked (with the entwined anchor and 'D' mark, gold anchor) refer to pieces decorated at Chelsea, and pieces marked crown over D would have been potted and decorated at Derby. Some early Chelsea Derby pieces may appear without any mark, but there would not seem to be a great quantity of them. With figures, however, there is room for speculation as to which were made at Chelsea and which at Derby, particularly as there seem to have been no distinguishing marks used between 1770 and 1784.

Note: mark 1 has been seen painted on blue and white pieces which could be a few years earlier than other pieces bearing this number. It is also found on early pseudo-Sèvres pieces, on which it is incised in script and accompanied by a small hole in the foot rim, and marks 5 or 6.

The marks at Chelsea (2, 3 and 4) were normally in gold. The Nottingham Road marks appear in blue and occasionally in puce.

7–9

These are the most frequently encountered marks of the period 1782–1825. The

7   8   9

marks are more carelessly drawn after about 1820. The normal colours are puce and blue until about 1806, when red became the usual colour.

These engraved marks were made firstly to counteract the careless drawings, and secondly to save man-hours, since the process was much quicker. Apart from the

King Street Factory, which normally used hand-painted marks, engraved marks have been used in Derby until the present day.

13

Used very late, on Sèvres copies.

14–16

These marks usually appear on figures and indicate a Bloor production. Mark number 16 is an imitation Meissen mark *c.* 1830.

Uncommon or infrequently seen marks

17

The author has seen this mark on a cup and saucer, *c.* 1790, in the Mary Field Collection.

18

Like John Haslem, the author has never seen this mark except for a very rare mug in the Victoria and Albert Museum, *c.* 1795, painted with a rainbow in a landscape.

19–20

Marks recorded by Haslem as having been used by William Slater Senior between

1825 and 1830. Haslem sat at the same table and therefore, as he reported, was able to testify to the variations.

21

This mark appeared on transfer-printed ware and is, of course, a rebus for Richard Holdship. (See plate 37.)

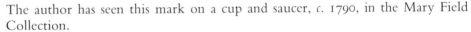

22

This 'potter's stool mark' may be found on genuinely Derby Manufactory potted pieces. The author has noted that they are often of inferior quality to the normal ware – possibly they were either seconds or ware sold to outside decorators.

Incised marks   (These are all potter's marks.)

23

Repairer's mark of Isaac Farnsworth.

23

24

Repairer's mark of Joseph Hill.

24

25

These impressed capital roman letters may relate to firing batches. Occasionally more than one letter may be seen. But, as Haslem states, these cannot now be conjectured. However, the author agrees that they were for manufacturing purposes and certainly not for dating.

25

B E   F H K V X Y Z

Note: quite fine Derby copies, executed in the eighteenth century, carry pseudo-Chinese marks which tally with their decoration. The word 'normally' has been intentionally used when talking about the colour of marks. Haslem, who was of course, like the author, well acquainted with live ceramic production, wrote about this:

The practises in marking were well known in the trade, though to others, from the stress laid on the subject, and the attempts which have been made to explain the variously coloured marks, and to establish some supposed relation between them and the quality of the articles, it would appear to be a mystery and much time has been wasted in endeavouring to account for it. No theories and suggestions can upset these facts; there will, however, probably be more believers in the theories than in the facts, simply because the many are as unacquainted with the matter as these speculative theorists, and are willing to believe any bold assertion, although the few know it to be absurd.

Marks alone must not be trusted, for they were copied on the Continent and not only by Samson of Paris. The shapes of potting, colours of decoration and paste help in attributing pieces, and specialist authorities such as museums will always offer advice.

Appendix:

Joseph Lygo's Letters to Derby

This appendix consists of Joseph Lygo's letters written to Derby from 1777 to 1797, while he was their London agent. They follow Dr Gilhespy's interpretation, with a little necessary editing and correction for the convenience of the reader.

When writing *Crown Derby Porcelain*[1] it was only after a good deal of consideration and with diffidence that I inserted the contents of sales and exhibitions which were difficult to acquire. This was favourably commented upon from America on behalf of people there without the facilities for research enjoyed by us. I am therefore tempted to give the result of my research into the correspondence between Joseph Lygo, the manager of the Derby showroom in London, and the successive Duesburys. This was partially embodied in a paper delivered to the English Ceramic Circle in 1952 and I am grateful to the Circle for allowing me this privilege. Actually the work took many hours to accomplish and at the time appeared to be disappointing in its results. However, since then I have often turned in its direction for some scrap of information and I sincerely hope that it may be of help to readers.

W. Duesbury in 1773 established a showroom in Bedford Street, Covent Garden, with W. Wood as his London Agent, who was succeeded by Joseph Lygo in 1777. The information in this chapter is derived solely from almost weekly letters written by Lygo to the Duesburys at Derby. Unfortunately I have not discovered any replies, so that as a rule one cannot know whether his requests or suggestions have been carried out at Derby, but occasionally Lygo refers to an item in a previous letter. This correspondence ceased in 1797, and from a mass of material I have tried to extract facts which may be relevant to fellow students of ceramics.

Joseph Lygo was devoted to the Duesburys and missed no opportunities of furthering their interests. In 1792 he was equally helpful to Richard Egan, who had married Miss Ann Duesbury and started as a china man (i.e. dealer) in Bath, 'where eight hundred houses are let before a brick is laid'. Wedgwood already had premises there and also a Mr Williams, a prolific buyer of figures of 'boys' from Derby. A great number of clients selected patterns[2] for services at Bedford Street and Lygo often had difficulties in procuring their orders from the factory, as transport was slow and business methods were primitive, many orders were lost. I have recorded the dates of some of the important orders in the hope that the services are still preserved in private houses. Names of dealers are given separately and also books or illustrations, which may have inspired figures or decorations, are similarly recorded; also the dates of issue of patterns in the list given on page 137.[3]

1784. Sales were being held in London and as the Irish dealers attended the India House sales, Lygo arranged his at the same time. The India House imported oriental china.

1786. There was still a great loss in firing the white, and Lygo suggested that faulty pieces should be finished like the Worcester – 'not anything like our patterns!' He also wanted more coloured patterns as many of the dealers were going to the Worcester and Salopian warehouses to buy unfinished goods which later they had gilded: 'the Trade almost every one of them are becoming manufacturers'; some of these goods were blue and white. Figures were declining in popularity, and Satyres and Neptune heads were underpriced; the latter may be drinking-cups with masks introduced in 1778. Lygo spent much time contacting merchants for good samples of blue which were mostly imported. Derby was using an overglaze, Smith's enamel blue, but had not mastered an underglaze of this colour and tried to find the cobalt glaze which had been supplied to Mr Turner of the Salopian Works and 'produces a strong colour under the glaze'. Apparently only in the last decade of the century was a reliable underglaze blue for services and ornamental pieces found.

Mr Vulliamy, the clockmaker, was an excellent but exacting patron. He decorated his clocks with biscuit figures, generally small ones of boys who had sometimes to appear leaning on one hand; they were sent in portions and the final work was done in London (Nos. 89, 90). From 1784–91 a great deal of correspondence was exchanged between the successive Duesburys and Vulliamy, and the clockmaker and Lygo were often in personal contact. The following facts have been elicited from this source and throw light on the figure-making business. J. Deare had made casts of figures for Duesbury (1786) and Vulliamy did not think that the modeller had been selling these himself. Jewitt (*Ceramic Art of Great Britain*, II, 109) states that Deare had modelled groups and figures for Duesbury in 1784 and was a modeller of considerable repute in London. 19 September 1784: 'I will wait on Mr. Deare in the morning.'

When one reads of other modellers working in the metropolis on their own, the opinion is formed that London was the birthplace of many new models needed by the large factories.

1787. Mr Catherine (*C.D.P.*, cf. p. 63) made moulds of boys and also busts from which W. Duesbury II was to make biscuit figures.

1787. Mr Vulliamy showed to Lygo a bill for thirty guineas to Mr Peart who had modelled and moulded the two new figures. Mr Catherine called about the same time on Lygo about the models of his two little boys done for him by Mr Peart and which failed to give satisfaction to Duesbury II.

Mr Vulliamy states that 'Mr. Banks is the modeller just in the same way as Mr. Bacon and does not think that he will do it for you – and he does not know of anyone so capable of doing your work in the modelling way as Mr. Peart and if you have any figures you would have done he will give them to him to do'. Mr Peart therefore appears as a person who would not design but would make moulds and figures.

1787. From Mr Vulliamy: 'Enclosed is a sketch of a figure[3] Mr. Horwell is going to model for you – he informs me that they stand in the clay 17½″ high. Zephanis and Flora are begun upon.' Later Mr Horwell was working in marble.

Turner and Abbott, Staffordshire potters, tried to see Vulliamy and to supersede Duesbury.

1788. The figure Mr Rossi is modelling is a female sacrifice figure (*C.D.P.*, Fig. 164) from a drawing Mr Vulliamy gave from one of his books and he suggests a male figure to match. Rossi made many figures for clocks. Rossi was also to make a female figure to match Aesculapius.

1790. Vulliamy sent modeller who could speak little English (Spengler).[4]

1791. Sitting figure for Mr Vulliamy was modelled by Spengler.

Spanish figures belonging to M. Daguesant were to be copied.

1790. Mr Catherine was in great need of his figures as they are for the same piece of work as the Lyons and Unicorns.

1793. Lygo: 'I could not get that beautiful figure of Rosina without buying it at the price of six shillings. Spengler is going to model it – have not found a male figure to match it and S wants to do one of his own idea. He is on his own making two female girls with a little poultry before them – for two guineas.' (Haslem No. 360.) 'Two pair female figures with dead bird Done Rosina, now a male figure.' Who is Rosina?

1793. Been with Vulliamy about the pair of figures modelled by Rossi. 'The drawing of the figure you have sent is done for Aesculapius and is meant to hold a serpent in the hand. The other female figure is an antique and out of one of Mr

Vulliamy's books [Thorpe's *Book of Ornaments*], and has not particular name than a sacrifice.[A] Mr. V. says there should be no fire represented; this pair of figures was meant for chimney ornaments – but Mr. V. wants to set them on marble and he will do a few marble stands if Mr. Duesbury wishes.'[5]

One must return to the weekly letters, and in 1786 memories of the past are resurrected when Lygo wishes Duesbury II to furnish him with the state of Giles' account, and Squibb's son, after his father's bankruptcy, is promising that Lygo will get a fair share of the assets. A. J. Toppin (English Ceramic Circle, *Trans.*, I, 33) showed how intimately connected were the affairs of Giles, the outside decorator who died in 1780, Squibb who sold him up and Duesbury who took to Giles's stock, according to Jewitt; Lygo's letters confirm this latter statement (No. 91).

W. Duesbury I died in November 1786, and early in 1787 his son, who had succeeded him at the factory, thought of opposing a proposed new treaty with France (in which only 10 per cent instead of, as formerly, 80 per cent duty was bilaterally imposed on porcelain and earthenware). Wedgwood canvassed the porcelain manufacturers to support the idea of the treaty and surprisingly Mr. Flight of Worcester and Mr. Turner, china manufacturer near Shifnal, who both 'manufactured a deal of common goods', did not disagree with him.

1787. The treaty passed and did a great deal of harm to the porcelain trade, but allowed us to export great quantities of earthenware and cheap porcelain services.

I have often tried to recognize pieces painted by amateurs on porcelain, a practice verified in the correspondence: 'plate done for Mrs. Hope to copy from, yellow enamel sent. Lady Fordyce some gold to gild a dejeune and have it fired at Derby.' Lady Plymouth is mentioned in the same connection.

At Kedleston Hall are three vases[6] painted with views of the house and grounds and figures and singularly marked with the crown, batons, and dots over 'D' in gold (*C.D.P.*, p. 83) which are referred to in the following: 'This morning took your letter to Lord Scarsdale. The vauses were delivered before agreeable to Mr. Clarke's instructions but no price put on them. His Lordship this morning [5 March 1787] sent Mr. Field with a message to inform me the Vauses were very much approved of and much admired by the Nobility that had seen them.' When I saw these vases I imagined the figure painting to be by Banford, but as the date of their origin is fixed this artist could not have been responsible, as it was before his second arrival at Derby. There was a potter at Derby named W. Clarke and a painter, J. Clarke, and the latter may have been concerned.

Dessert-pattern 65 caused Lygo a good deal of pleasure; gilt and pink border with a central group of pink roses, and was shown to Lord Aylesbury who bought pieces, and next we hear of the Prince of Wales, whose income had been raised by ten thousand pounds a year, also purchasing a service, but with dawn instead of pink on the border.[7] Miss Whitbread entertained the King and Queen at the Brewhouse and ingeniously set the tea-table with borrowed Derby China; three dejeuners were bought by the Queen. Lord Dunmore took leave of their Majesties on taking over a Governorship (?) and a good deal of Derby goods as well to sell on commission; the market was Spain. Plaques (instead of blue glass) were produced for girandoles to rest upon.

1788. Mr Flight of Worcester took two houses in Coventry Street (No. 1 as a showroom) and the sons have been over to France and brought a large quantity of French china'. Lygo sent green-and-gold plates made at Worcester to Derby. Soup-tureens and teapots caused great difficulty to the firm as they 'flew' when hot liquids were suddenly introduced, and the former were lined; the latter were not often sold with tea-sets as silver teapots were used. Asparagus servers enamelled with fine blue sprigs and blue edge, hot-water plates, cheese-plates and stands, thimbles, spoons, egg- and ice-cups and stands[8] were some of the stock sold, but rarely seen today.

1789. Brocklesby, a painter, was bought out of the Guards (who were never sent farther than to the Tower!) and Mr Complin had a trial on the white before going to Derby, and Withers, who was in London, said he was a better painter than Hilliard – another aspirant for the factory, who had worked with him on buttons at Chelsea but 'could make little of it'.

Royal patronage was obtained: '*Mr. Duesbury, Derby Porcelain Manufacturer to his Majesty and his Royal Highness the Prince of Wales*.' Lygo said: 'W. Duesbury I had the Royal Appointments first in 1775.'[9] As a result of the Treaty, Mr Flight imported French china cheaply and a sale of French china took place in a house in Albemarle Street at half the price of British. Lygo bought some for W. Duesbury II.

'In this box have sent you a specimen of flower painting done by one James Banford (recommended by Mr. Withers) he was apprentice at the Bristol Manufactory and has since been with one Brown an enameller here – he says he has been use to paint landscapes and figures as well as flowers – he says Mr. Boreman and Mr. Smith know him well. He had also enamelled for the jewellers.' Withers left Mr Harwood, his old employer, as he wished to return to Derby. John Smith, painter of tea-pattern 115, wants his cups and saucers. Tea-pattern 116 and dessert 87 just out – decorated with Greek honeysuckle border in blue and brown – Lygo thought too much in Wedgwood style to be approved of.

1790. 'Have sent the drawing book for which I have paid Mr. Bone 18/-.' Bone was the Bristol factory painter who achieved fame for his enamels on metal. Enough broken china (probably oriental) to warrant carriage by sea was sent to Derby.[B] Jars, two-handled cups of the India China to copy.

'Large sale of Save China – all the Nobility there. Mr. Catherine will copy some of the designs.'[10] No wonder Sèvres designs became common at Derby.

Duesbury sold his Chelsea wharf. Seals and trinkets still being sold (presumably from the Chelsea moulds).

Sertine is making a figure.

1791. Mr Vulliamy's order was so big that it held up figure production for a month. Mr Johnes wanted a saucer gilt all over to look like gold: this is interesting as Derby did use a gold ground for flower painting.[11] Mr Complin in Town – a very 'wavering' disposition. Bone ash had to be of good quality and not too contaminated with dirt and was not easy to procure and ship in quantity. (Pig's trotters sometimes used.)

1792. Wedgwood thought to have been behind a treaty with Saxony on the same lines as the French treaty. W. Duesbury II would not attend the Privy Council for Trade at Mr Cottrell's office at Whitehall as, like Mr Flight, he thought it would be useless. Mr Johnes had dinner with the Lord Chancellor and discussed the matter over the port and nuts.[12]

Tea-pattern 190. James Clarke returned to Derby. Plant dessert, with ice-pails, to Lord Wentworth – nineteen numbers of a botanical magazine[13] sent at the same time: this is before 'Quaker' Pegg's time. Sent four small comports of the Burton China painted with landscapes which are to be copied on a pair of ice-pails.

1793. Spengler trying to get to France was caught at Margate and delivered to the King's Bench:

'There has been part of some landscape dessert service made some time back, suppose waiting for Mr. Boreman to do, Nos. 116 and 134, and the things wanted for Lord Shaftesbury – a job for Boreman.' Mr Coffee, senior, wants the prints of the Elements done by his son returned.

1794. At this time it was proposed to model figures of Lord Howe and the Duke of York. Now there has been dispute about the identity of some of these statuettes, one of Marshal Conway being considered by Haslem as that of Lord Howe or Hood. The following information is amusing and throws light on how such mistakes might occur. It was difficult to get prints which would give a faithful likeness of Lord Howe. 'Mr. Latiefiere brought me a print of Lord Howe July 2 1794.' Lady Howe saw the print and said it was no likeness at all and the only good likeness was a 'picture painted by Coplin'. Lygo adds his version that 'Lord Howe is a strong young man, I think full six feet high, and carries very little flesh – bony and large featured'. 'There is a much better likeness of Lord Howe than Braithwaite being done at Braydons.' Duke of York, full length, being engraved by Dickinson. Eventually Mr Catherine gets a 'scratch' from a picture of the Duke of York which is going to be engraved. Tea-pattern 321 included.

August 1794. W. Duesbury II paid Wright (painter) and Coffee. Also Banford and Complin. Stevens given 15s to get to Derby.

The Prince of Wales getting married and orders a large service of eight dozen plates, but only two of one pattern. Mr Cosway, miniaturist, going to advise the Prince on his choice – suggests three Graces supporting the Prince's crest. No opportunity of seeing Mr Bartolozzi, engraver, who lives a few miles out at North.

December 1794. Mr Boreman back from Derby – 'behaved as cool as usual but would not discuss business'. Spengler in London signed on again. Coffee in London but difficult to get him. Trade very flat.

1795. Two sitting boys by Spengler not worth Duesbury's notice. Rossi said no chance of Coffee getting into employment here (from Jewitt we know that Coffee went to Church Gresley).

Spengler taken to Westminster Abbey to see the monuments there. Catherine will do a few sketches for W. Duesbury II who is badly in need of them – he wants six of his new boys No. 22, and some of his new-pattern botanic dessert plates are available.

Nelthorp asks after his 'hand and dagger' order. See article by Author, *Apollo*, February 1952 (No. 92). Mr Johnes gives an order for dejeune in figures, flowers and gold ground 321.[14] This pattern is not in the original pattern book.

1796. Business very poor. Formerille, a moulder, mentioned as having worked in Wardour Street. Mr Clunna has a figure business.

February 1796. Last letter W. Duesbury II; he dies without a will in 1796.

1797. Claret ground first mentioned. Tea-pattern No. 395 mentioned.

CHINA BUSINESSES IN LONDON

1784 Mr. Fogg – very safe people 'and now going into a finer way'.

1787 Neale & Co. dealers – china plaques for girandoles. Irish and Hichens for fine blue.

1793 Abbot and Newbury put crests on foreign china.

1789 Mr Purton – glass lamps.

1790 Turner and Abbots – dealers. Bradwell, dealer, lives at Sheffield, and a showroom at Nottingham.

1790 Baystock, the china man in St Paul's Churchyard, bankrupt. This was Mr Fiddler's shop and Simcock was in some way connected with it.
    Messrs Bailey and Clarkson are china men at York.
    James Bill or Bell, Oxford Street, bankrupt.
    The 'Great' Mr Horwood (china man) bankrupt. (Withers's employer.)

1793 Green and Ward[15] order vases with cyphers on them; also silver covers for china services.
    Neale & Bailey's order a large one. In 1794 sets with insects are done very bad compared with the French ones.

1796 Fogg, Connell, and Abbot – china men.

ORIGINAL ILLUSTRATIONS

1786 Mr Byrne. Six views all in Ireland.
Mr Byrne. Six views all in Cumberland.
1787 Mr Byrne. Six views all in Westmorland.
1790 Mr Eames has 'Harrington's Engravings of the Lakes', four numbers, twenty plates. 'Bill's "New Pantheon"' – too big to send by coach. Hookham's in Bond Street, 'Tour to the Isle of Wight', in two sizes – 3 gn. and 1 gn. – two vols., 15 plates in each vol. by Hazle. 'Gilpin's Northumberland' not in stock.
Took the letter from Withers to Simcock for prints of Baptiste.[C]
Simcock did not know about these prints. He, like Banford, had enamelled for jewellers and Flight's had wanted him. At this time he was painting a service with arms for Baystock in St Paul's Churchyard. Mr Eames found Baptiste's prints with large flowers but not all of them in baskets; also four other prints with horses, and a battle print with figures on horseback. (It was difficult to procure prints with horses for the workmen to copy.)[16]
1790 Mr Neale, engraver in the Strand, sent twenty impressions to Duesbury II. Cannot get a print of Callott's (for Mansion House dwarfs).
1792 Nineteen numbers of a Botanical magazine sent to Derby.
1793 Purchased twelve numbers of 'Sharpe's Crests'.
1794 'You will find a print of Soan (or Joan) Jennings in the end of the dictionary.' (S. Jennings, London, 1789–1834. Scriptural or Historical Shakespearian.) 'Cordell was very loth to let me have one.' Two prints sent up – one is of a boy lying on the ground and a girl tickling his ear; the other is a boy and girl playing with a dog.
1794 Mr de Boffe smuggled from France 19 'Volumes of the Arts', which include a treatise by Count de Milly on making porcelain. Mr Thorp's *Book of Ornaments*, possibly used by Vulliamy for inspiration for figures, e.g. Sacrifice figure.
1795 'Birds and Insects of Great Britain' coming out. Saw a very beautiful book of twenty-seven plates of birth of Cupid until he is drawn in the triumphal carriage – engraved from designs cut in paper by the Princess Elizabeth by the artist that did the plate for Thompson's Seasons, 'which you copied for the Prince's plate'. Mullins doing a copy.

ORDERS FOR DERBY PORCELAIN

1779 Lord Harcourt's order. Small stands for pint bottles and cream-bowls.
1784 Queen's order given by Sir Joshua Rake, one of 'The Gentlemen belonging to the Board of Green Cloth'.
Mr Jones orders figures for Dublin.
Mrs Pelham's order – (1) Six quart punch-bowls. (2) Punch Jugs with covers to hold three pints! (Mrs P. was expecting to be bedded and ordered these for the baby to be washed in!)
Mr Compton, the Queen's page – large ice-pails for the service to be 'vause' shape. Mr Williams in want of biscuit figures and orders for Holland.
1786 Lady Clive's Service. Earl of Exeter – Burghley, Nr. Stamford, Lincs – flower-pots. Lady Aylesford's dejeune. Mr. Ellior, tea-pattern 69; double shape tea-cup motif for Neale & Co. Derby lose order by Mr Williams selling to Lord Walsingham Turner's Prince of Wales pattern. Duke of Bedford admires floral decorations, not landscapes.
1787 Lord Aylesbury, same as Duke of Marlborough's, new pattern 52 or 53. Double shaped caudle cup with plain flowers or roses, with plain gold edge for Duke of Bedford, 'who is very difficult' to please. Lord Scarsdale's 'vauses' – much admired by the nobility.
1787 Prince of Wales muffin water plates. Lady Westmoreland – new embossed ware. 'Fawn' coloured tea-pattern No. 84 is a salmon colour in the pattern book. Mr. Dumbleton with crest in fawn colour and gold to match the border. Lady and Lord G. H. Cavendish, Brownlow's table set. Mr. Williams (china man) 145 of small and larger boys at 10d each: the order may be for 145 dozen. Blue and white tea-pattern No. 18, very similar to No. 16.
1788 Biscuit vases for Duchess of Northumberland and Lord Cremorne and asparagus servers with fine blue sprigs and blue edged. 'Mr. Johnes'[D] admired his dessert service; a present to the Chancellor.[17]
1789 Tea-pattern number 100. Dessert for Turner & Co. (Salopian warehouse). Cheese-stand for Mr Leigh. Mr Williams at Hammersmith wants another '100 dozen' of his small 4 in boys. Mr Fitzherbert and Mrs Lawes – No. 82 tea-pattern – 'Hamilton shaped' cups.[18] Cornflower decoration. 'Clarke' at Derby in 1779 may have done the pattern for the first set Mr Fitzherbert bought at Derby. Lady Spencer's – at Althorpe, Northants – tea-service with French-shaped cups and saucers. She bought a Wedgwood ewer and Derby copied the pattern. Green ground for cups with cypher 'L.S.' and garlands above, both in rose coloured flowers, as in Mr. Smith's cup; spoons, white and gold. Bust of a cock with well-done plumage for Mrs. Blackburne. Lady G. H. Cavendish, one biscuit group of four antique Seasons and a pair of 'vauses', No. 107.
1789 June. Mr. Fitzherbert wants cabinet cups, covers, and stands with best views in Dovedale, as this beauty spot belongs to his family. Lord Cremorne – toast mug and finger cups. Mr. Fogg – tea-pattern 106, Hamilton shape. Miss Whitbread – table service with flowers well painted. Lady Stamford's order – 'one of the best ladys in the world'.

Lygo does not admire the new tea-pattern 109 – looks best on plain Hamilton-shaped cups. Mr. Heathcote – 'crimson' pattern service; Lady Cremorne finger-bowls. Mr Fogg blue-and-white order. Figures for Mr Daguisant of Cadiz.[19] One hundred boys for Mr Williams for France and within a couple of months – 400 dozen more small boys. Dessert-pattern 84 sold. Mr Matthews's service with his crest. New pattern cup and saucer No. 117 – complete set should be forty-one pieces. Lord Cremorne's cypher 'B.O.' and a chaplet – Hamilton shape with handles.
1790 'I have this week sold the rich landscape Dessert Service to Lord Lonsdale – and his Lordship is having 24 more plates painted with landscapes in Cumberland from drawings of his own.'
Lady Neville wants her order off to the West Indies.[19]
Lord Maitland – yellow with fine blue edge. Tea-pattern very popular if on 'double shaped' ware.
Lord Dover – Cupid and dolphin jar. Blue chantilly pattern (No. 1 in Dessert pattern book) is small groups of blue flowers explained by Lygo to customer.
Cup in Etruscan style for Lady Albermarle to see.
Duke of Hamilton's order – three small oval comports and three larger – pattern (Dessert) 52 and 53.
Two dishes for Lord Scarsdale – for table service for second course. Lord Shaftesbury – 50 dozen small boys for Amsterdam[19] at 10s per dozen: standing sheep 3s a pair. Mr Cowper gives coffee-cups and cream-jugs to the King. Mr Williams of Bath has 100 dozen more boys. Mr Botham, dessert-pattern 82, blue ribbon to be done in dark puce on the brim and gold leafage in fine rose colour – not at all fitting in with the description in the pattern book. Figures and groups for Cadiz. £200 for Mr Martolini, who has considered dessert and table services. Mr Brander's tea-set with his crest. Duke of Beaufort's order. Duke of Hamilton's order: his first order was in 1779 – compoteers, fruit baskets – the present one for crested plates.
Rt. Hon. James Fitzgerald, the Prime Sergeant, Molesworth Street, Dublin, ordered frames and ornaments for a dressing-table.
Lady Shipworth's china.
1791 Mr Johnes wants saucers to be gilt all over the inside to look like gold and the same decoration for a small figure of Ariadne. New inkstands for Miss Vansittart and Mr Hardy. Five groups 257 in biscuit needed. Mr Daguesant wanting Spanish figures copied. Blue-and-white service for Mr Frankley. Not determined upon a border for the 'blue under the glaze' for Mr Digby's plate – in the meantime Taylor will be going on with the painting in the middle.
1792 Tea-pattern 190 mentioned. Lady Harrington wants two birds to put on ornaments for the Princess. Plant dessert service much admired 'before "Quaker" Pegg's time' to Lord Wentworth: nineteen numbers of a botanical magazine sent to Derby at this period. Mrs Hope's order for Amsterdam. Lord Macartney's order for the East Indies – vases with figures. Mr Jack services for America.
August: Warren Hastings, Park Lane, ordered pieces at Derby.[20] Mr Gunter's desserts are wanted for.
1793 Nankeen tea-cups and saucers sent to Derby, with landscapes. A most expensive service for the Margravene of Anspach. Ward and Silver are doing silver covers for the plates. Inkstands blue and gold. Lord Decie's china. Ashton Curzon – two mugs.
1794 February: Sir Francis Ford's arms on a service lost as an order because he got it cheaper on French china – the mantle round the crest must be like the Duke of Hamilton's, which is rose colour and ermine – 8 dozen plates of this needed (*C.D.P.*, Fig. 131).
Price of the Winchelsea cabinet cups and dejeune £9. Sets done for Neale and Bradley in insects. Order for Mr Pitt, the Prime Minister, tea-pattern No. 321 mentioned. Prince of Wales's service for wedding – 8 dozen plates but only two of the same pattern in flowers. Mr. Cosway suggests for the service three Graces supporting the Prince's crest. Inspiration for decoration of a plate for Prince of Wales from Thompson's Seasons illustrated by Stothard (?). Duchess of Marlborough, dessert-pattern 367 – 'worst pattern ever to come out of Derby!' (This may be a mistake and should read 'tea-pattern'.) The cheap patterns that are liked are 110, 129, 130, and 321. Mr Nelthorpe asks after Hand and Dagger order.[E] Five hundred tiles for the Duke of Bedford's dairy at Woburn. Mr Johnes gives an order for dejeune in figures, flowers, and gold ground, pattern number 321.[21] This number is missing in the patterns.
1795 Mr Johnes's address. Hafod, Cardigan.
1796 Claret colour is first mentioned in place of crimson. Blue and white basins. Tea-pattern No. 395 mentioned.

Notes and References

CHAPTER 1

1 The Mr Smith referred to in this letter was a member of the partnership of William and Richard Smith of Birmingham, who were mounters.
2 In 1967 St Alkmund's church was demolished to make way for a new road system
3 *E.E.C. Transactions*, Vol. 4, Part 5.
4 The *Derby Mercury*, according to Wallis, recorded Duesbury's death as Monday 30 October 1786. The *Leeds Mercury* notice of 7 November 1786 reads: '7th Nov. yesterday se'night [i.e. 30 October] died at Derby after a very long illness Mr William Duesbury, proprietor of the china manufactory in that town.'
5 Down to this line the names are in William Duesbury II's handwriting, and have been crossed through.
6 From here forward the names seem to have been the originally written ones of 1787.
7 According to Jewitt, written in the hand of William Duesbury II.
8 For a very early reference to apprentices, the following piece from the *Manchester Mercury* of 19 March 1765 is of interest: 'On Sunday the 10th of this instant March 1765 John Caulton and John Greenwood apprentices to Mr William Duesbury of the borough of Derby china and porcelain maker, absented themselves from their said master. Caulton about 19, Greenwood about 17. 2 gns reward for apprehension of each apprentice.'
9 Further sales were announced in similar terms for 12 and 31 October 1814.
10 Keys's story about Planché, and the reference to the pipe kiln, had doubtless been coloured by loyalty to the Duesburys.

CHAPTER 2

1 The famous stock-breeder: not to be confused with a Robert Bakewell, listed in the Derby poll lists in 1770s as a chinaman, i.e. a retailer of china.
2 A reverberating kiln is a kiln in which the porcelain is exposed to the action of flame and heat which are thrown back from a vaulted roof.
3 This translation was made from the Swedish edition, published in Stockholm in 1827 by Zacharias Häggström. Johanna Schopenhauer (1766–1838), the mother of the famous philosopher, was the author of a number of books. She visited England for the first time in 1787, and spent six months in England in 1803, during which time she could have made her visit to Derby. (Source Mrs R. Hoff.)

CHAPTER 4

1 See chapter 14.
2 See description of 278.

CHAPTER 5

1 1785 was the year of the visit to the factory of François de la Rochefoucauld, whose account is given in chapter 2.
2 Before 1800 Harlequin was dressed in a long, loose jacket and in trousers, as seen in the early statuettes. In this year, however, at Drury Lane in *Harlequin Amulet* James Byrne introduced the tight-fitting spangled 'shape' of the present British stage; the celebrated Grimaldi was Clown, and Miss Menage, afterwards the wife of Mr M. W. Sharp, the artist, Columbine in the pantomime. (Nightingale's note.)
3 A suite of five magnificent vases, with blue and gold borders, the bowls enamelled with flowers on a gold ground, and painted with subjects in oval medallions – the centre vase with Celadon and Amelia, the two smaller ones with subjects from Shakespeare, the remaining pair, which were ewers, with figures of Damon and Musidora, and all marked with the gold anchor, sold in 1872 for 600*l*. (Nightingale's note.)

CHAPTER 6

1 Blue John, a mineral from the Peak District.

CHAPTER 7

1 Still in current production at Osmaston Road.

CHAPTER 8

1 It seems likely that the first royal visit took place in 1775 (referred to in chapter 2), Lygo states, referring to the goods invoiced in June 1776, 'These was [*sic*] ordered by the Queen at the warehouse.'
2 The author assumes that Ward & Silver, and Green & Ward, are the same firm, since the date references, firstly in Lygo's letters of 1793 and secondly from the Duesbury manuscript papers in the Derby Public Library, also dated 1793, suggest.

CHAPTER 11

1 The Midland Counties' Fine Arts and Industrial Exhibition was held at Newland Street, Derby.
2 See Haslem, page 38.
3 Burgess Rolls, Bristol, 1780–86, Book 16.
4 Stated by Alfred Wallis to be Duesbury I's son, born in 1765.
5 The figure 7 used by Billingsley is known as the long-tailed 7, owing to the long vertical stroke used.
6 Now the cathedral.
7 See *Royal Crown Derby*, page 198.
8 Now in the British Museum.
9 According to Lygo's letters, Brocklesbury was found to have joined the Guards and in 1789 he was bought out in accordance with this warrant.
10 This William is allocated tea pattern 575 (*c.* 1805), described: 'Red Arrahbesk by Dodson & Talkington'.
11 Haslem, pages 34–5.
12 See *Royal Crown Derby*, page 16, for the Hancock family tree stemming from John Hancock.
13 Haslem, pages 128–9.
14 The row was caused by jealousy between John Haslem and Alfred Wallis over the production of *The Pottery and Porcelain of Derbyshire*, which was used as the official publication for the Midland Counties' Exhibition held in Derby in 1870.
15 The letter is in the Wedgwood Archives at Keele University.
16 It is not certain whether he is referring here to William Gadsby or James Goadsby, whose name, like that of James Rouse Senior, could have been mis-spelt (e.g. Rowse) by Haslem.
17 Now in the author's possession.
18 W. D. John, *William Billingsley*, page 32.
19 Mr W. H. Barron of Toronto, Canada, a descendant of Pegg the Younger, drew attention to and provided these two illustrations.
20 Nottingham County Asylum, Sneinton: Records.
21 Barrett and Thorpe, Appendix V, page 125.

22 *Zürcher Porzellan*, page 23.

23 *Zürcher Porzellan*, page 25.

24 It would appear that the sons of Thomas Steel, Edwin, Horatio and Thomas Junior, added a final 'e' to their surname.

25 *Royal Crown Derby*, page 218.

26 There is confusion from various sources regarding the initial of this painter.

27 This information is given in John Keys' *Old Derby and Neighbourhood*, 1895.

APPENDIX

(Note: Gilhespy's own notes, given first, are indicated by superscript letters in the Appendix, while the author's notes, given second, are indicated in the usual way by superscript numerals.)

A *Crown Derby Porcelain*, Fig. 154.

B Landed at Gainsborough in Lincolnshire.

C Baptiste (senior), seventeenth-century painter of flowers. Baptiste, Monnoyer, Lille 1636. Painted flowers and fruit; also decorated Montague House walls, Hampton Court, Kedleston Hall ceiling. Folio engravings. Son was Young Baptiste, 1704. Academy, Paris.

D Thomas Johnes of Hafod in Cardiganshire, where he arrived in 1784. He died *c.* 1816. See 'The Doom of Hafod' by Olive Cook in the magazine *Go*, April–May 1951. Also in this book, chapter XIII on Hafod.

E At some future date the dish with the Nelthorpe coat of arms will revert to a school which bears the family crest. (The service was used at Trinity College, Cambridge, where he became an undergraduate. It was painted by Askew (No. 92).)

1 *Crown Derby Porcelain* not only had the wrong title, but the jacket showed the Osmaston Road mark of the Derby Crown Porcelain Company, which was not founded until 1877. The term 'Crown Derby' was not used until the late nineteenth century.

2 An indication that sets of patterns were possibly available in London.

3 It is worth noting that most figures were modelled from prints or sketches. (See page 307.)

4 Confirmation of Vulliamy's introduction of Spängler.

5 This could refer to the group in the Royal Crown Derby Museum, which is incised with a script *V* and is obviously one fitted into a stand. This figure group, however, was made by Spängler.

6 There were two, not three, vases.

At this point Gilhespy got himself into some confusion by suggesting that the Mr Clarke mentioned was a potter named W. Clarke, or James Clarke the gilder may have been concerned. An obituary from the *Derby Mercury* of 10 July 1788 sheds some light: 'On Monday night died, after a lingering illness, Mr. Wm. Clarke, aged 44 – He was principal Clerk at the China Manufactory, which place he filled with great Reputation.' One week later, from the same paper: 'As Clerk and occasional Overlooker in a considerable Manufactory, a sober discreet person who can have an undeniable Character for his Honesty & Assiduity . . . .'

Gilhespy also here refers to his frontispiece in *Derby Porcelain*. The author visited Kedleston Hall and together with Ottilie, Lady Scarsdale, inspected the pair of vases, which regretfully no longer have their covers. They are of therm shape and have figure painting on one side – probably by Askew – and views of Kedleston and its grounds on the reverse – probably by Boreman. Gilhespy's frontispiece vase is colour plate 29 in this book, and is from an entirely different set of vases, of a later period.

7 Confusion should be avoided here: this pattern may be referred to as the 'Prince of Wales pattern [rather than 'service']'.

8 Illustrated in plate 212.

9 The date of the first royal appointment is often misquoted.

10 See colour plate 26 for an example.

11 See colour plate 34 for an example of gold ground.

12 Reference to friendship.

13 *Curtis's Botanical Magazine*.

14 The author believes this to refer to tea pattern 351, which, of course, is in the book.

15 Reference to retailers.

16 See colour plate 23.

17 The reference to 'Mr. Johnes' confirms the present to the then Chancellor, Edward Lord Thurlow. The views were of Hafod (summer house). The service was not, as stated by Barrett and Thorpe, for use at the estate.

18 Reference to 'Hamilton shape'.

19 This page alone makes reference to exports to Cadiz, the West Indies and Amsterdam. Another source, the *Montreal Gazette* of 20 September 1832, reported the landing of a shipment of '22 packages of China Tea, Coffee, Breakfast, Dessert, and Supper Setts [*sic*]', representing wares from 'the ROCKINGHAM, WORCESTER, AND DERBY Manufactories'.

20 A particularly interesting order.

21 Again a correction concerning pattern 321.

Glossary

BENDS   A slightly undulating line of uniform width round body of hollow-ware.

BLACKS   These look rather like forward-sloping fish-hooks and possibly owe their name to colour rather than to form.

BLOOM   Soft pink ground colour.

BRIM   Rim.

CELEST(E)   Clear sky-blue ground colour.

CHINTZ   Horizontal lines of prismatic colours.

FAWN   Pale apricot ground colour.

FEATHERS   These look like golden raindrops or teardrops. It is noted in the pattern books that a workman would receive for gilding '4½d. with feathers – without feathers 3¾d.'.

FLIES   Almost any type of insect from ladybird to butterfly.

LAURELLS (sic)   Tiny leaves of uniform size and shape in a continuous line.

ORANGE   Can vary from pale tangerine to deep orange-red.

PINK   Flower only; never used to describe colour at Derby.

RIBANDS   Bands in undulating form, usually narrowing and turning over at each bend.

STRAW   A very soft gold colour.

STRONG ROSE   Ground colour almost verging on claret.

VANDYKE   Shaped like the beards of the same name.

YELLOW   Can vary from light citrus yellow to a deep golden hue.

The most hazardous area of description concerns the gilding, particularly in regard to sizes. It is difficult to determine when a 'dot' becomes a 'spot' and a 'spot' is large enough to be termed a 'ball'. This also applies to 'lines' which are wide enough to be termed 'bands' and when 'bands' reach 'border' width. As a rough guide, a 'line' is the width produced by a felt-tip pen; a 'band' is at least double this width, and a 'border' is usually about three-tenths of an inch.

Bibliography

Place of publication is London, unless otherwise stated.

BARRETT F. A. and THORPE A. L.: *Derby Porcelain*, Faber & Faber 1971.

BEMROSE W.: *Bow, Chelsea and Derby Porcelain*, Bemrose 1898.

Bemrose Sale Catalogue, 1908. Neale's of Nottingham are currently reprinting this, with prices.

BRADLEY H. G. (ed.): *Ceramics of Derbyshire 1750–1975*, Bradley, 1978.

DUCRET S.: *Zürcher Porzellan*, Verlag Zürich 1944.

GILHESPY F. B.: *Crown Derby Porcelain*, Lewis 1951.

—— *Derby Porcelain*, Macgibbon & Kee 1961.

GODDEN G. FRSA: *Minton Pottery and Porcelain of the First Period*, Herbert Jenkins 1968.

—— *Coalport and Coalbrookdale Porcelains*, Herbert Jenkins 1970.

GRAVES A. FSA: *A Dictionary of Artists from 1760–1893*, Kingsmead Reprints (3rd Ed.) 1969.

HASLEM J.: *The Old Derby China Factory*, George Bell 1876.

—— *A Catalogue of China*, R. Keene, Derby 1879.

(The cornerstone of Derby research has always been regarded as John Haslem, but for the early history of the factory the author rates Llewellyn Jewitt second to none.)

HOYTE A. and PENDRED G.: Various articles on the Derby Porcelain Works in *Antique Dealer and Collector's Guide*, 1960–1978.

HURLBUTT F.: *Old Derby Porcelain*, T. Werner Laurie 1928.

JEWITT L. FSA: *Ceramic Art in Great Britain*, Virtue & Co. 1878.

JOHN W. D.: *Nantgarw Porcelain*, Ceramic Book Co., Newport Mon. 1948.

—— *Swansea Porcelain*, Ceramic Book Co., Newport Mon. 1958.

—— *William Billingsley*, Ceramic Book Co., Newport Mon. 1968.

NIGHTINGALE J. E.: *Contributions Towards the History of Early English Porcelain*, Salisbury 1881.

OWEN H.: *Ceramic Art in Bristol*, privately published 1873.

—— *William Duesbury's London Account Book 1751–1753*, English Porcelain Circle, Herbert Jenkins 1931.

RACKHAM B.: *The Schreiber Collection of English Porcelain*, Vol. I, His Majesty's Stationery Office 1915.

—— *Catalogue of the Herbert Allen Collection of English Porcelain*, His Majesty's Stationery Office 1923.

RICE D. G.: *Rockingham Pottery and Porcelain*, Barrie & Jenkins 1971.

TAPP W. H.: 'John and Robert Brewer, the Derby Painters', in *Transactions*, English Porcelain Circle, IV, 1932.

—— Various articles in *The Connoisseur* and *Apollo* during the 1930s.

TWITCHETT J. FRSA: *The Old Derby Pattern Books*, privately published 1971.

—— 'The Closing Years of the Old Derby Factory', in *Antique Dealer and Collector's Guide*, 1971.

—— 'The Old Derby Pattern Books', in *Antique Dealer and Collector's Guide*, 1971.

TWITCHETT J. and BAILEY B.: *Royal Crown Derby*, Barrie & Jenkins 1976.

WALLIS A. and BEMROSE W. Junior: *The Pottery and Porcelain of Derbyshire*, Bemrose 1870. (The author has Wallis's own copy of this title, together with the unpublished Wallis notes and press cuttings, which have been freely drawn upon in this book.)

Index